Stock Market Investing

Nancy B. King

Made E-Z

MADE E-Z PRODUCTS™ Inc.
Deerfield Beach, Florida / www.MadeE-Z.com

384 South Military Trail
Deerfield Beach, FL 33442

http://www.MadeE-Z.com

1 2 3 4 5 6 7 8 9 10

Stock Market Investing Made E-Z™
Nancy B. King

Grateful acknowledgment to the following for permission to use material as specified:

- Murray W. Teitelbaum, NYSE, for permission to use the trading post pictorial

- Securities Research Company, a division of Babson-United Investment Advisors, Inc., for permission to use financial charts

- Standard and Poor's, a division of the McGraw-Hill Companies, for permission to use stock reports

- Value Line Publishing, Inc., for permission to use industry and stock reports

Dedication

- To One whose project this has always been

- To friends and family who have been a sounding board and a quiet source of encouragement

- To readers whose lives this book will change

Acknowledgments

I wish to acknowledge the following people who have played a special part in the creation of *Stock Market Investing Made E-Z*:

Norma Fuller for saying, "Quit complaining that you can't find the information in a book; just write the book."; Kelly Fuller-Blue for obtaining editorial feedback on the first outline and for professionally editing the software help statements; Frank Enstice for verifying the validity of the stock analysis worksheet by immediately using it with his clients; Jane Evanson and LuAnne Dowling for sharing their expertise through *Breaking into Print* and Jane's writing for publication workshops; Marthy Johnson for editing my copy one chapter at a time and for always being kind, gracious, and exacting; Craig Mischenko for writing the stock analysis software program and for making something complicated seem simple; The Group for being there without exception; and my husband for quietly living through all the ups and downs.

About the author

Nancy B. King lives in Anchorage, Alaska, where she conducts workshops and seminars on investing in individual stocks. She developed her first course 14 years ago and has managed her own portfolio for 25 years. She understands firsthand the desire of new investors for easy-to-understand, usable information about buying stocks. She is an investment club member, director of the Alaska Chapter NAIC, executive board member of the Alaska Council on Economic Education, and a nonindustry NASD Regulation arbitrator.

For tech support of this product, email Ms. King at: **smartstocktech@gci.net**

Table of contents

Introduction 7

1 Stock ownership 9

2 Reading the stock quotations page 19

3 Stock market indices and averages 47

4 Stock exchanges 69

5 Story of a stock trade 93

6 Selecting a stockbroker 123

7 Working with a stockbroker 153

8 Picking a stock 181

9 Smart Stock Analysis Guide: Profitability 193

10 Smart Stock Analysis Guide: Financial condition and institutional ownership 211

11 Smart Stock Analysis Guide: Stock price evaluation.....221

12 Smart Stock Analysis Guide: Company background 229

13 Smart Stock Analysis Guide: The final analysis 233

14 Following a stock 237

15 Successful investing..247

Forms in this guide 255

Glossary of useful terms 269

Resources 289

Appendix A: McDonald's...295

Appendix B: Wendy's..309

Index 327

Introduction to Stock Market Investing Made E-Z™

Have you yearned to invest in stocks but are unsure where to begin or what to ask? Do you want to be self-reliant and take an active role in managing your investments? Are you looking for a concise approach to choosing quality stocks? *Stock Market Investing Made E-Z* is for you and for investors of all ages and financial means, and it will show you the way.

- Chapters 1 through 5 provide basic information about common stocks and how the market works. You will find visual aids and examples to aid your understanding.

- Chapters 6 and 7 help you set exciting and specific investment goals, determine your resources for investing in stocks, define your tolerance for risk, and help you select and work with a stockbroker.

- Chapters 8 through 13 present in-depth, guided instruction on choosing a stock. The guidelines are based on proven, fundamental principles that answer the questions, "Is the company profitable? Is it well managed? Is it financially sound? Is the stock overpriced?" This structured analysis provides an effective way to deal with the flood of financial information, advice, and opinions currently available. Analysis provides an alternative to chasing fads and hot tips.

- Chapter 14 discusses how to follow, update, and review company performance. It also supplies answers to the question, "When should I sell?"

- Chapter 15 reviews building a portfolio and concludes with rules for successful investing.

Stock Market Investing Made E-Z grew out of my 25 years of searching for concise information that would help me choose profitable stocks for my portfolio. The materials for this book have evolved over the past 14 years as I have developed and taught continuing education classes, seminars for new investment clubs, workshops in the private sector, and courses for teachers using the Securities Industry Association's Stock Market Game in their classrooms. In recent years, these settings have been an excellent proving ground for *Stock Market Investing Made E-Z*.

Participants begin the sessions feeling timid and confused. By the end they are enthusiastic and self-confident. They have a tool for selecting their own stocks and sufficient information to work comfortably with a stockbroker. *Stock Market Investing Made E-Z* will give you the same knowledge to make your own independent, well-thought-out decisions about buying individual stocks. It equips you to sort through a bewildering maze of information and gain a sense of control about investing. Begin reading, and you are on your way to becoming a confident, successful, self-reliant investor.

Chapter 1

Stock ownership

What you'll find in this chapter:

➠ Why you should own stock

➠ Types of investors

➠ Types of stock ownership

➠ What is a stock certificate

➠ Stockholders' rights

You have what it takes to be a successful stock investor. You are interested in stocks. You recognize when you need more information. You can find that information on your own. You proved it by picking up this book. In *Stock Market Investing Made E-Z*, you will explore the world of stocks and the stock market. You will learn how to read the stock pages in the newspaper, what it means to own a stock, how to choose a stockbroker, and how to open an account. You will be guided step-by-step in using specific criteria to determine if a company is profitable, financially sound, and fairly priced. This analysis tool will help you find quality companies and give you the knowledge you need to wisely invest in stocks.

Growth of stock ownership

As an investor you have joined an important and exciting part of the population. The percentage of Americans who own stock has grown from 10 percent in 1965, to 21 percent in 1990, and to 43 percent in 1997 (*Peter D. Hart Research Associates 1997*). The next time you are in a group, look at those around you: nearly one person out of two owns stock directly or through a corporate pension plan or indirectly through a mutual fund.

In the United States on an average day people like you buy and sell 526 million shares of stock on the New York Stock Exchange (NYSE) (*New York Stock Exchange Fact Book 1997*). If it is a slow day, they may buy and sell as few as 150 million shares. However, on busy days one billion or more shares may be traded.

Why own stock?

Why invest in stocks? If in 1925 you had invested $100 in a savings account, long-term government bonds, or large company stocks, and the money had compounded tax-free, at the end of 1998 you would have had the following amounts, unadjusted for inflation:

Savings account	$ 2,327	
Long-term government bonds	4,400	(Ibbotson Associates 1998)
Large company stocks	235,100	(Ibbotson Associates 1998)

Despite stock market crashes, recessions, depressions, civil unrest, wars, seven Republican presidents and six Democratic presidents, stock would have made 31 times more money than government bonds.

> **E-Z TIP**
> Over the long term, money grows faster invested in stocks than in other liquid assets such as bonds or savings accounts.

Also, investing in stock is a way to participate in a growing economy. When the economy grows, the corporation grows. You might buy stock to share in the growth and profits of a particular company that interests you. You are not limited to the success of the company that employs you. Also, you, like other knowledgeable investors, may wish to manage your Keogh, 401(k) plan, or Individual Retirement Account (IRA). You want to make your own decisions and manage your own investments. Stocks add growth and diversification to a financial plan—one that includes a retirement plan, insurance (home, car, health, and life) policies, money in a savings account, and perhaps equity in a home. Finally, you want to share in the American free enterprise system. *The New York Stock Exchange Fact Book 1991* says, "In no other country does the general public involve itself so extensively and so directly in the ownership of business." In the United States, investors can own parts or shares of more than 12,000 companies; in other words, there are 12,000 companies to choose from when you are ready to buy a stock.

> **note**
> As part owner of the corporation, you benefit from its growth through increased dividends and appreciated stock prices.

Be an investor at any age

You are never too young or too old to purchase a stock. You do not have to wait until you are middle-aged. Nor is it something that only people in their 20s and 30s do. Buying stock is a good way for children to learn about the free

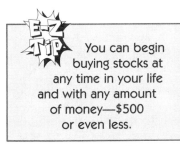

You can begin buying stocks at any time in your life and with any amount of money—$500 or even less.

enterprise system, economics, companies, profit, and loss. For teenagers, investing in stock can be an exciting alternative to consumerism. During retirement years, people enjoy spending time investigating companies, buying stock, following the stock market, and fine-tuning their stock purchases.

Indirect investor

DEFINITION

You probably own stock, and do not realize it. You and millions of people like you own stock indirectly through institutions. What does that mean? An *institution* is an established organization such as a bank, insurance company, mutual fund, or a pension fund. If you buy a house, car, health, or life insurance, you invest indirectly in stock. The insurance company invests some of the money from your premiums in stocks to make additional money to pay claims. If you have money in a pension fund or in a mutual fund, the institutional fund manager invests your money in stock. Because you have no say about the choice of stocks, you are an indirect investor. That is all well and good, but wouldn't you prefer to take an active part in choosing stocks and deciding when to buy and sell them? If so, you are ready to become an involved individual investor.

Individual investor

When you are an active individual investor, you participate directly in the stock market. You choose the stocks to buy. You decide when to buy them. You place the order. You pay for them directly. If you are an individual investor, you are where the action is. You *are* the action.

Certain limitations are placed upon institutional investors; they must follow rules and regulations for their funds that do not apply to individual investors. One common rule states that fund managers may not invest more than 5 percent of their money in one company. Nor may they invest more than 25 percent in a single industry. Often fund managers are not allowed to invest in newer and smaller companies which tend to be risky. Frequently, however, the newer and smaller companies have the highest growth rates. We, as individual investors, are not held back by these and other rules and regulations. We are free to invest in companies of any size. We may buy as much of a company's stock as we can afford. We may invest all our money in one industry if that is a risk we want to take.

HOT spot Individual investors do well in the stock market. They regularly outperform institutional investors and money managers.

note We, as individual investors, can pursue our own goals, interests, and expertise. Each of us is unique, using unique approaches to picking stocks. We are accountable only to ourselves.

Institutional investors tend to follow one another. They listen to the same analysts and read the same reports. They hesitate to deviate from the crowd for fear of being wrong. If their stocks decline in value and those of other money managers decline also, it seems to be okay. There is no question of poor judgment. If, however, their stocks are the only ones that decline, judgments are questioned and jobs are at stake. There is more risk in being the only one wrong than there is reward in being the only one correct.

In this information age, we have the same access to company financial data as institutional money managers. We can obtain similar analysts' reports from our stockbrokers. We can read the same newspapers and magazine articles. We can receive the same fast-breaking news via computers. The information is there for us to use to make money investing in stock.

Share ownership

DEFINITION

When you own a share of stock, you own a share, or unit, of the company. A share of stock represents part ownership in the company. You own part of everything the company owns: part of every building, plot of land, and piece of machinery, and of any natural resources they might have. Anyone who owns one or more shares of stock is a *shareholder* or *stockholder*. These two terms—shareholder and stockholder—are used interchangeably.

When you are a stockholder, you share in the success of the company. As the company's profits (income after expenses and taxes) increase, its stock price rises. If the company pays a dividend from its profits, you receive a portion of that dividend. Thus, you participate directly in the company's earnings.

Ownership also involves risk. You risk the money you invested in the company—the price you paid for the stock. There are no guarantees that the fortunes of the company will increase and the price of the stock will rise. If the company does not do well, its' stock price will decline. The stock price might continue to fall. In fact, it could drop to zero—or nearly to zero. If you still owned the stock, you would lose all the money you had invested in the company—the amount you paid for the stock. This does not need to happen to you. The remedy is simple. Sell the stock when the company is no longer doing well, and the stock price begins to decline. Find another company that is growing, and buy shares. Take part in its growth as long as the growth continues. Recognizing when to sell is as important as knowing what to buy.

Proportional ownership

When you buy a company's shares, you buy a specific proportion of the company. What part of the company do you own if you own 50 shares, 100 shares, or even 1,000 shares? It depends on the total number of shares the company has sold. If you own 100 shares of McDonald's, a large corporation whose ownership totals 1,358,000,000 shares, you own 0.00001 percent of the company. If you own 100 shares of NCH Corporation, which has only 5,604,689 shares, you own 0.002 percent of the company. Proportional ownership is the percentage of the whole company your shares represent. If you are interested in calculating proportional ownership, the equation is: (number of shares you own ÷ number of company shares outstanding) x 100 = percent of corporation you own.

Definition:

Proportional ownership is the percentage of the company you own as a shareholder.

Forms of company ownership

note

Whether you can buy stock in a company depends on how its ownership is organized. A proprietorship is owned by one person—the sole owner. He or she makes all the decisions and runs the company. The sole proprietor reaps all the rewards and personally assumes all business risks, including all debts.

If a company is organized as a partnership, two or more people own the company. They own and operate the company together. Each partner is personally responsible for the company's debts and shares the benefits and successes of the company.

A company organized as a corporation is owned by its shareholders and run by an elected board of directors that makes company policy and hires key management personnel. A corporation is a separate legal entity and can be thought of as an individual. It can sell goods and services, it must pay income tax (corporate tax), and it can sue and be sued. Yet because it is a corporation and not an individual, its owners' (the shareholders') personal assets are protected from the company's debts and lawsuits. If a corporation is in financial trouble, the maximum its shareholders can lose is the amount they paid for their stock. They have no liability for the

A public corporation's shares may be purchased by anyone. A public corporation is owned by its public shareholders.

corporation's debts and misdeeds. On the other hand, their profit depends on a rise in the stock price and on dividends the corporation declares.

A corporation can be either private or public. A private corporation's shares are owned by a small group of people—four or five family members or close business associates. By law they must hold their shares for investment purposes and may not sell them to the public. Therefore, public investors cannot buy shares of private corporations. Most small corporations are privately held.

Forms of company ownership

Ownership	Definition	Advantage	Disadvantage
Proprietorship	Owned by one person	Total control	Success and continuity depends upon one person
		Small initial investment	New money difficult to raise
		Individual receives all the rewards	Personal liability for all company debts
Partnership	Owned by two or more people	Shared management responsibility	Division of authority
		More money to invest in business	New money still difficult to raise
		Losses shared personally by partners	Rewards shared with partners
Corporation	Owned by shareholders: A separate legal entity	Owned by many institutions and individuals	Most expensive to start
		Management easy to change	Owners (shareholders) have little direct control
		Continuous life span	
		Additional capital easy to raise	
		Limited liability: owners not personally responsible for company debts	

McDonald's Corporation is owned by 925,000 stockholders. Institutions such as retirement funds, insurance companies, and mutual funds own 63 percent of McDonald's (*Standard & Poor's Stock Reports 1998*). Individuals—men, women, grandmothers, grandfathers, aunts, uncles, and children—own the remainder. In the United States more than 86 million people own shares of public corporations.

The stock certificate

DEFINITION

A *stock certificate* is a document which proves you own shares in a particular corporation.

It is printed on heavy paper that contains planchettes, small chemically treated colored disks. Planchettes are among several design features which identify the stock certificate as authentic and make it difficult to counterfeit. Geometric designs decorate the border of the certificate. These intricate designs—at least 20 square inches—can be duplicated only if one knows the exact machine settings used to produce them.

> **E-Z TIP**
> As an added deterrent to unauthorized duplication, companies whose stock is traded on the New York Stock Exchange must include a three-quarter view of a human being on their stock certificates.

Each stock certificate has an identification number assigned by the Securities Exchange Commission (SEC). This number is found in the upper left hand corner. In the center of the certificate below the design of the human figure, you will find the name of the issuer of the shares—the corporation. Below the corporation's name, you will find your name—the owner of these shares. Below your name, the number of shares you purchased is written in words. The number is written in numerals in the top right hand corner.

If you purchase the stock only once, regardless of the number of shares, you will receive one certificate. If you buy stock in that corporation several times, you will receive a certificate each time you purchase the stock.

> *note*
> The stock certificate can be issued for any number of shares. The certificate represents the number of shares you purchased at that time.

The Committee on Uniform Securities Identification Procedures (CUSIP) assigns a different number to each publicly traded corporation. The CUSIP number, which is found in the center of the certificate, is used when recording stock purchases and sales. In the lower center section, the script writing states that you, the shareholder, are under no legal financial obligation to the corporation. In the lower left hand corner of the certificate, you will find the seal of the corporation and the date of your purchase.

When you buy a stock, you own it immediately. However, it might be several weeks before you receive the certificate from the corporation.

HOT spot You are not personally liable for any debts the corporation might have.

Rights of ownership

First, as a shareholder and part owner, you may receive a portion of the corporation's profits in the form of dividends. You receive a portion of any dividend the corporation declares.

Second, as a shareholder you have the right to information about the corporation's financial condition. Each shareholder receives an annual report. The annual report discusses how the company progressed financially during the fiscal year—business year—that just ended. The company's fiscal year does not always match the calendar year. The Christmas season and the end of the year are busy enough for companies without the added work of closing their fiscal year. Also, companies have natural cycles of activity which end at times other than December 31. Several weeks after the close of the fiscal year, you will receive your copy of the corporation's annual report. This attractive, glossy report reviews the company's business for the past year, including its various products and divisions. It presents the corporation's financial data and compares its performance this year with that of the two preceding years. In the section Letter to Stockholders, the chairman of the board summarizes the operations for the year and discusses plans for the next year. Read and refer to this section from one annual report to another. Has the board of directors been successful in carrying out its plans? It should have been.

CAUTION The stock certificate is as negotiable as a signed check. Someone could endorse the back of your stock certificate and sell the stock so keep it in a safe place, such as a safe deposit box.

In addition to the annual report, you will receive four interim or quarterly reports during the year. The quarterly report, an abbreviated annual report, gives income and expense figures for the quarter just completed and for the corresponding quarter a year ago. Therefore, you can easily make comparisons. Is the company losing money, making more money, or doing about the same? If you read the quarterly report that arrives every three months, you should find few surprises in the annual report.

Third, you have the right to attend the corporation's annual meeting and to vote on certain matters. The annual meeting is held to inform stockholders about the progress of the company. After the company report, shareholders elect the directors who will guide the corporation during the next year. If there are issues to come before the stockholders for a vote, they are presented at this time. The corporation encourages all its shareholders to attend the annual meeting and to vote.

Your right to vote is a basic shareholder right. Shareholders exercise control in the corporation by electing the board of directors. The board establishes the basic policies of the corporation but does not run its daily operations. Instead, the board hires top management personnel who are responsible for the company's day-to-day activities. The board of directors reports and answers to the stockholders.

DEFINITION

When you elect the board of directors, you use either *statutory voting rights* or *cumulative voting rights*. The corporate charter and state statutes determine whether stockholders have statutory or cumulative voting rights. With statutory voting rights one share of stock equals one vote for each director. For example, if you have 50 shares and there are three directors to be elected, you cast 50 votes for each director. Statutory rights require a majority vote, 51 percent, to elect a director. With cumulative voting rights, your votes equal the number of shares you own times the number of directors to be elected. If you own 50 shares and three directors are to be elected, you have 150 votes. You may cast all 150 votes for one director and zero votes for the other two directors. Or you may cast your votes in any proportion. You might cast 75 votes for one director, 20 for the second, and 55 for the third. Cumulative voting rights require only a plurality—a greater number—of votes to elect a director. Cumulative voting rights give minority stockholders more voting power.

> *note* Companies prefer to end their fiscal year when they have the least inventory and the most cash.

Besides electing the board of directors, shareholders vote for or against mergers, reorganization, and stock splits. What happens if you cannot attend the annual meeting? Do you lose your opportunity to vote? No. Each shareholder receives a proxy.

DEFINITION

A *proxy* is written authorization from you, the shareholder, to someone else who will vote your shares in a specific way at the annual meeting. Before the annual meeting, you will receive official notice of the meeting, the proxy card, and material explaining the matters to be voted on. This material includes short biographical notes on each potential board member. It also includes facts and opinions—pros, cons, and the board's position—on the issues which require a shareholder's vote. First, read the background information. Then, indicate your choices—for, against, abstain—on the proxy card, sign it, and mail it. At the meeting, your vote will be cast as you indicated on the proxy card. If you decide to go to the meeting, you can cancel your proxy. The proxy can also be canceled if you request, sign, and return a later authorized proxy. These proxies are short-term and issued for a specific meeting.

Your fourth shareholder right is the right to transfer the ownership of your shares.

Fifth, as a shareholder, you have the right to residual claims on the corporation's assets at the time of dissolution. If a company fails and is dissolved, after all its debts have been paid or satisfied you may make a claim on its assets. Because you receive what is left, it is called a residual right. Usually there is little or nothing left for shareholders.

> *note* Shareholders cannot vote to declare a dividend. Only the board of directors has the right to declare a dividend.

Finally, the most important right you have as a shareholder is the right of limited liability. You, as an individual, are not financially responsible for any of the corporation's debts. The liability for the corporation's debts is limited to the assets of the corporation. You cannot lose more than the amount you paid for the stock.

Conclusion

As an individual investor, you become involved in the world of business. You, the shareholder, vote for the company's board of directors and watch how the company grows under the board's guidance. You share in the company's profits through dividends. When you receive its dividends, you think of the goods and services it has sold around the world. As the company grows and prospers, the price of its stock increases. You pay attention not only to the price of its stock, but also to the quality of its products and services. You are interested in its research and development as well as in its marketing of new products. As you read the newspaper and watch the evening news, you notice and look for the company's name. You are no longer limited to buying a McDonald's hamburger and fries or one of Pfizer's prescription drugs—you can buy part of the whole company.

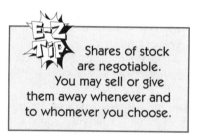
> **E-Z TIP** Shares of stock are negotiable. You may sell or give them away whenever and to whomever you choose.

Chapter 2

Reading the stock quotations page

What you'll find in this chapter:

➡ How to read a stock table

➡ What the footnotes mean

➡ Dividends and yields

➡ The price-earnings ratio

➡ The importance of volume

In this chapter you will learn the meaning of each column of figures in the stock table and the importance of those figures in relation to your stock.

note The stock table summarizes the price activity of the previous day, gives the high and low prices for the year, and tells you how many cents per share the company is paying in dividends this year.

Stock quotations keep you informed about the present price of individual stocks of publicly owned corporations. Do you want to know how your stock is progressing, whether its price is moving up or down? Check the stock table in your daily paper.

You can find the stock tables in the business section of your newspaper. There are separate tables for the stocks traded on the New York Stock Exchange, the American Stock Exchange, and the Nasdaq (pronounced "naz dak") Stock Market. Your newspaper also may publish stock tables from the smaller regional exchanges such as the Boston, Chicago, and Pacific Exchanges. In addition to the stock tables in the business section, you may find quotation tables for mutual funds, bonds, foreign currencies, and quotation tables from foreign stock markets such as London, Paris, Tokyo, and Hong Kong.

The first stock quotations were published in 1884 in *The Customer's Afternoon Letter*, a handwritten bulletin by Charles H. Dow and Edward D. Jones of Dow Jones and Company. In 1889 their paper became the *Wall Street Journal*, which is the leading business newspaper in the United States today. The *Wall Street Journal* sets the standard for reporting business and financial news, including stock market quotations.

You can find the stock quotation tables in the third section of The *Wall Street Journal*. Begin by looking at the NYSE table. Its title is New York Stock Exchange Composite Transactions. The word composite means that some stocks are traded both on the NYSE and on a regional exchange. A composite figure is the total of the trading on the regional exchanges and on the NYSE exchange. You can also find stock quotation tables in the business section of your local newspaper. Local newspapers may list the NYSE stock quotations as New York Stock Exchange Issues, NYSE-Composite Transactions, Combined New York Stock Exchange Trading, or New York Stocks. The newspaper chooses the title—whatever the title, the tables give the same basic information.

The following stock quotations from the New York Stock Exchange Composite Transactions were listed in the *Wall Street Journal*.

| 52 Weeks | | | | Yld | Vol | | | | Net |
Hi	Lo	Stock	Sym	Div	%	PE	100s	Hi	Lo	Close	Chg
16¾	8⅛	Huffy	HUF	.34	3.3	33	415	10⁷⁄₁₆	10⅛	10³⁄₁₆	− ⅛
30	17⅞	HughsSply	HUG	.34	1.5	9	108	23⅛	22⅞	22⅞	− ¼
n 10⅞	9½	HugotonRylty	HGT	.50e	5.0	...	206	10	9¹⁵⁄₁₆	10	...
22⅛	6⁵⁄₁₆	Humana	HUM		...	29	9897	6⅞	6⁷⁄₁₆	6⅝	− ⅛
15⅜	7¹⁵⁄₁₆	HuntCp	HUN	.41	5.0	11	86	8⅛	8	8⅛	+ ⅛
6⅛	2⅜	Huntco A	HCO	.11j	...	dd	36	2¹⁵⁄₁₆	2⅞	2¹⁵⁄₁₆	+ ¹⁄₁₆

The above columns of figures are grouped in the following way:

| 52 Weeks | | | | | Yld | | Vol | | | Net |
Hi	Lo	Stock	Sym	Div	%	PE	100s	Hi	Lo	Close Chg
16³/₄	8¹/₈	Huffy	HUF	.34	3.3	33	415	10⁷/₁₆	10¹/₈	10³/₁₆ −¹/₈

1   2   3   4   5   6

1—Price range of the stock during this past year
2—Abbreviated name of the company and the company's trading symbol
3—Dividend amount per share and the percent of return
4—Price- earnings ratio
5—Number of shares that changed hands yesterday
6—The stock's price range during yesterday's trading

52-Week high and low

The first and second columns of the stock quotation table list the **highest and the lowest price** paid per share for the stock during the past 52 weeks.

52 Weeks					Yld		Vol				Net
Hi	Lo	Stock	Sym	Div	%	PE	100s	Hi	Lo	Close	Chg
$16^3/_4$	$8^1/_8$	Huffy	HUF	.34	3.3	33	415	$107^7/_{16}$	$101^1/_8$	$103^3/_{16}$	$-^1/_8$

The figures for the 52 Weeks column will move along by picking up any new high and low figures next week and by dropping those that occurred a year ago this week. The 52 Weeks Hi and Lo column does not include any new highs and lows that were reached during the day's trading. Instead, the new high or low will be indicated by an arrow in the left margin of this column and will be recorded in the Hi, Lo, Close, Net Chg sections of the table. Tomorrow this new high or low figure will be shown in the 52 Weeks Hi and Lo column.

52 Weeks					Yld		Vol				Net
Hi	Lo	Stock	Sym	Div	%	PE	100s	Hi	Lo	Close	Chg
▲ 74	$15^3/_8$	LandsEnd	LE			61	1700	$74^3/_{16}$	$71^{15}/_{16}$	$73^5/_8$	$+1^3/_8$

Prices quoted in points

Prices are quoted in points and fractions of points—halves, fourths, eighths, sixteenths, and thirty-seconds. The points represent dollars, one point equals $1.00. A fraction of a point equals a fraction of a dollar.

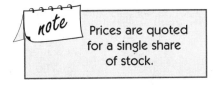

note Prices are quoted for a single share of stock.

The following table of sixteenths, eighths, and fourths of a dollar will help you convert fractions of points into cents.

Sixteenths of a Dollar				Eighths of a Dollar				Fourths of a Dollar			
1/16	=	$.0625	6 1/4¢	1/8	=	$.125	12 1/2¢	1/4	=	$.25	25¢
3/16	=	.1875	18 3/4¢	3/8	=	.375	37 1/2¢	3/4	=	.75	75¢
5/16	=	.3125	31 1/4¢	5/8	=	.625	62 1/2¢				
7/16	=	.4375	43 3/4¢	7/8	=	.875	87 1/2¢				
9/16	=	.5625	56 1/4¢								
11/16	=	.6875	68 3/4¢								
13/16	=	.8125	81 1/4¢								
15/16	=	.9375	93 3/4¢								

When the purchase price has been figured and fractions of cents remain, they are rounded to the nearest cent. A 1/2 cent is rounded to the next highest cent.

The quoted 52-week high for Huffy is $16^3/_4$ points. The figure $16^3/_4$ tells you that the highest price paid for a share of Huffy during the past year was $16^3/_4$ dollars or $16.75. The lowest price for Huffy this year was $8.12 a share. If you had purchased 100 shares at $8.12 per share, you would have paid $812 for the stock ($8.12 x 100 shares = $812). The quoted price does not include the stockbroker's fee. Therefore, your total purchase price would have been $812 plus the broker's commission.

When a stock trades below a dollar such as 7/16 and the paper does not use reduced type for fractions, it looks strange to the untrained eye and can be confusing. Look at the example below, note the 52 Weeks Lo and the Lo and Close figures.

52 Weeks					Yld		Vol				Net
Hi	Lo	Stock	Sym	Div	%	PE	100s	Hi	Lo	Close	Chg
$2^7/_8$	$^7/_{16}$	LomNM					393	$^7/_{16}$	$15/_{32}$	$10^3/_{16}$	

Footnote letters and symbols.

Throughout the stock tables small letters and symbols indicate additional information. The following letters and symbols are found in the left margin of the 52 Weeks Hi and Lo column:

▲ or ▼: The stock hit a new high or low during the day's trading. The new high or low figure will be included in the **52 Weeks Hi and Lo** column in tomorrow's paper.

n: A new stock has been issued within the last 52 weeks. The new stock issue may be a company that has just begun trading on the NYSE. Or the **n** may indicate that a company which has been trading on the NYSE for some time has issued new stock. The high and low figures are from the date the stock began trading to the present date. The **n** is carried until the full 52-week period has been covered.

s: The stock has split within the past 52 weeks. Often, when a stock's price moves above $90 a share, the company splits the stock so it becomes more affordable for individual investors. If a corporation decides to split its stock, it is usually a 2-for-1 split. However, it can be a 3-for-1 or perhaps even a 4-for-1 split. If it is a 2-for-1 split, for every share of stock you own, you automatically own two shares. If you own 100 shares, after the split you would have 200 shares. Because everyone's shares split in the same proportion, your shares still represent the same proportion of company ownership. As a result of the 2-for-1 split, the price per share is cut in half. You have twice the number of shares at half the price per share. Also, the dividend per share drops proportionately. Because of the impact of the stock split on the price per share and on the dividend per share, the **s** remains in the margin for the full 52 weeks. This is to let investors know that the old price and the dividend did not drop by 50 percent but instead have been adjusted for the stock split.

Stock table variations

Not all newspapers include the 52 Weeks Hi and Lo column each day. Often local newspapers want to conserve space so they print the 52-week information only in the Saturday or Sunday edition.

Ex.		Tick	Last	Chg
Closing stock prices of 2,000 of the largest companies on the New York and American stock exchanges, NASDAQ and stocks of particular interest to our readers. EXCHANGE KEY: (n) NYSE; (a) American; (o) Over the counter.				
- A -				
n	ABN Amro	ABN	25 9/16	-3/16
n	ABN pfA	ABNpA	22 7/16	-3/16
n	ABN pfB	ABNpB	21 13/32	-13/32
n	ACE Ltd	ACL	19	+1/4
n	ACNiels	ART	24 11/16	-3/16
o	**ACTV**	**IATV**	**25 5/8**	**+1 7/8**
n	BJs Whls s	BJ	34 1/2	+1/16
o	BMC Sft	BMCS	77 7/16	+5/16
n	BOC ADS	BOX	42 9/16	+1/16
o	BOK s	BOKF	21 5/16	-3/16
n	BPAmoc s	BPA	59 7/16	-1
n	BRE	BRE	22 1/2	-5/16
o	Baan Co	BAANF	13 3/8	-5/16
o	BackWb n	BWEB	43 1/4	-3/4
n	BakerF s	BKF	13 13/16	
n	BakrHu	BHI	26 15/16	-3/16
n	Ball	BLL	38 1/8	-3/4
o	BallardPw	BLDP	23 7/8	-1/2
o	**Baltek**	**BTEK**	**8**	**+1/2**
n	BcoBilV	BBV	13 1/2	-1/8
n	BnCPort	BPC	29 3/8	+1/8
n	BncoFrn	BFR	23 1/2	+5/8
n	**BGndo pr**	**BGAp**	**6 15/16**	**+7/16**
n	BcoRioP	BRS	12 5/8	+3/16
n	**BcoSnCH**	**STD**	**10 7/8**	**-3/8**
n	BcoSanti	SAN	20	-1/8
o	**BncGalic**	**BGALY**	**20**	**+7/8**

- Anchorage Daily News

Check the time of the quotations. The time is found at the top of the **A's** column. The newspaper may have received quotes from the exchange in the morning, at noon, or in the afternoon. Important changes in a stock's price may occur after press time and before the closing of the exchange at 4:00 p.m.

Quotations as of 5 p.m. Eastern Time
Thursday, October 14, 1999

52 Weeks Hi	52 Weeks Lo	Stock	Sym	Div	Yld %	PE	Vol 100s	Hi	Lo	Close	Net Chg
		-A-A-A-									
25 7/8	14 5/8	AAR	AIR	.34	1.9	12	1132	18 1/16	17 3/4	17 3/4	...
35 1/16	21 7/8	ABM Indus	ABM	.56	2.3	16	159	24 15/16	24 7/8	24 7/8	...
25 1/2	21 11/16	ABN Amro pfB		.40	1.8	...	1309	22	21 1/2	21 11/16	– 1/4
25	17 1/2	ABN Am ADR	ABN	.65e	2.8	...	124	23 3/4	23 1/2	23 9/16	...
26 5/8	22 5/8	ABN Am pfA		1.88	8.1	...	360	23 9/16	23 1/4	23 1/4	– 1/4
35 13/16	15 1/2	♣ ACE Ltd	ACL	.44	2.7	7	5643	16 9/16	16 1/8	16 3/8	...

- Wall Street Journal

Significance for the investor

The 52-week high and low prices give investors valuable information. The figures may reveal a current trend in the stock price—whether the price is moving up or down. The figures also give investors an idea of how much the stock price increases and decreases during a year. Investors often use these figures when making their decisions to buy or sell.

Indication of price trend

Is the price of the stock moving generally up or down? Compare the stock's 52-week high and low prices with its current closing price. You will find the closing price in the next to the last column. This comparison, between the present closing price and the 52-week high and low, may indicate a price trend for the stock—either an uptrend or a downtrend. If the present price is near its yearly high, the stock is likely to be in an uptrend. On the other hand, if the present price is near its yearly low, the stock is likely to be in a downtrend. The closing price for Huffy was $10^3/_{16}$ which is near the middle of its 52-week high and low of $16^3/_4$ and $8^1/_8$. Therefore, the stock may be in a downtrend.

Implication for buying and selling

You are ready to buy a stock, and its price is at or very near its 52-week high. What do you do? If the price is at its high, the risk of a decline is greater than when it is nearer the middle or lower end of the 52-week range. Therefore, you might wait to buy until the price drops a little. On the other hand, you might decide to buy at the current high price. If you believe the stock is a good buy at this price—it may well be—and if you believe the price will continue to rise, go ahead and buy. Either approach can work.

If the stock's price is at or near its 52-week high and you are thinking of selling, what do you do? It might be a good time to sell and take your profits unless you feel the price will go higher. If you are a long-term investor, the company is profitable and in good financial condition, and you can handle short-term declines in price, consider keeping the stock.

When the price of the stock is near its 52-week low, do you immediately buy? The stock might be a real bargain. But beware! Is this a temporary downturn in price—a time for bargain buying—or is there a significant reason the price has dropped to its low for the year? What looks like a bargain may not be one. Has the company's growth slowed? Is the company having problems with its products or services? Is the company having financial difficulties? If so, the stock price may continue to decline for some time.

Indication of price volatility

The figures for the 52-week highs and lows may indicate price volatility—frequent and substantial percentage increases and decreases in price. The percentage change between the high and low prices for the year may be more significant than the dollar amount suggests. For example, for a stock that has a high of $20 and a low of $15, the five-dollar move represents a 33 percent change in price. (To figure percent of change: [(high price - low price) ÷ low price] x 100 = percent change. For example: [(20-15) ÷ 15] x 100 = 33 percent) But if a stock has a high of $50 and a low of $45, the five dollars represent only an 11 percent move. The greater the percentage move, the more volatile the stock price. Huffy has a 106 percent difference between its 52-week high of $16^3/_4$ and low of $8^1/_8$. ICICI has a 21 percent difference between its 52-week high and low. Huffy's higher percentage move indicates that its price has been more volatile than ICICI's during the past year.

> **HOT** spot The more volatile the stock price, the greater the risk the price will drop suddenly. On the other hand, the more volatile the stock price, the greater the possibility the price will rise quickly as the stock market rises.

Stock Name

The third column of the stock table lists the name of the company.

52 Weeks						Yld		Vol			Net
Hi	Lo	Stock	Sym	Div	%	PE	100s	Hi	Lo	Close	Chg
$16^3/_4$	$8^1/_8$	Huffy	HUF	.34	3.3	33	415	$107/_16$	$101/_8$	$103/_16$	$-1/_8$

If there is room in the column, the stock table lists the full company name, except for the words company and corporation. Otherwise the name is abbreviated. The abbreviation resembles the company name as closely as possible.

HughsSply	Hughes Supply
HugotonRylty	Hugoton Royalty Trust
LaZ Boy	La-Z Boy

HOT spot As a rule, the abbreviated company name is not the same as the stock symbol. However, they may resemble each other.

Huffy	HUF
IBP Inc.	IBP

Some company names are difficult to abbreviate. In that case, the shortened form may not parallel the company name, and the abbreviation may be harder to figure out.

LabCpAm	Laboratory Corporation American Holdings
LandAmFnl	Landamerica Financial Group

In addition, the Associated Press (AP) and the United Press International (UPI) news services may use different abbreviations for company names. Therefore, the abbreviations may differ from newspaper to newspaper depending on whether the paper obtains its quotes from the AP or the UPI. Most newspapers use quotes from the AP so the problem is not as serious as it could be, but remember, the difference does exist.

Finding your stock

How can you find your stock in the stock tables? First, is the name you are looking for a corporation name, or is it a brand name? Perhaps you love chocolate and wherever you go you find yourself in a Godiva Chocolatier. Since Godiva chocolates are your favorite, you would like to buy stock in the company or at least would like to know whether the price of the stock is going up or down. If you look in the stock tables for the name Godiva, you will not find it because it is a brand name. Godiva Chocolatier, Inc. is owned by Campbell Soup Company. In order to own stock in Godiva chocolates, you will need to buy stock in the parent company, Campbell Soup Company. Then you will own Godiva Chocolatier indirectly, along with SpaghettiOs and Pepperidge Farm. Three good sources for brand names and their parent companies are *Trade Names Dictionary* published by Gale Research, Inc. of Detroit, Michigan, *Directory of Corporate Affiliations* published by National Register Publishing Company, and *America's Corporate Families and International Affiliates* published by Dun & Bradstreet.

Next, it is necessary to know on which exchange the stock is traded. You can find out by asking a broker, or you can look up the stock in *Value Line Investment Survey* (*Value Line*) or *Standard & Poor's* (S&P) *Stock Guide* at your library. However, if you prefer, check the stock tables for your company's name. The company will be listed on only one of the three major exchanges. The NYSE stock table is a good place to begin—the largest and best-known companies trade on the NYSE. Then look for the company name in The Nasdaq Stock Market (Nasdaq) table and finally in the American Stock Exchange (AMEX) table. Company names are listed alphabetically by the full company name rather than by the abbreviated form. Company names made up of all capital letters are listed first under a particular letter and are followed by company names made up of full words.

LASMO   LG&E Engy   LaZ Boy   Labor Roly

Watch closely not only for similar names and abbreviations listed on the same exchange, but for similar names and abbreviations listed on the different exchanges. A company listed on the NYSE might have an abbreviated name much like that of a different company listed on the AMEX or the Nasdaq.

If you cannot find your stock listed in any of the tables, perhaps it did not trade that day. Unless the stock tables are for all stocks, a stock that was not traded may not be included in the day's newspaper. In that case, check the tables from preceding days.

Finally, if you are unsuccessful, look in the Yellow Pages under Stock and Bond Brokers, and choose a firm. Call, ask to speak to the broker-of-the-day, then inquire on which exchange the company is traded.

Footnote letters

The following are some of the more common footnote letters:

pf: **A preferred stock**—A company issues preferred stock only after it has issued common stock.

FordMotor FordMotor pf

The preferred stockholder receives preferential treatment. A preferred stock pays a fixed annual dividend. Usually, the dividend is higher than the common stock dividend. A corporation pays a dividend on its preferred stock whether it pays a dividend on its common stock or not. If a company fails and is dissolved, a preferred stockholder's claims on the company's assets have priority over those of a common stockholder. However, preferred stock ownership does have limitations. The fixed dividend limits a preferred stockholder's opportunities to share in the company's increased dividends. The price of a preferred stock does not appreciate like that of a common stock. Even though preferred stock represents ownership in the company, the shareholder's ownership is restricted. In most cases it means ownership without voting rights.

A or B: **A different issue**—a different class of common stock or preferred stock. The two stock issues—ReadersDigest and ReadersDigest B—have different voting rights and dividend priorities. They may differ in other ways as well.

ReadersDigest LTC Prop

ReadersDigest B LTC Prop pfA

LTC Prop pfB

DEFINITION

wt: **Warrant**—A warrant is not a stock, but investors trade it like a stock. A *warrant* is the right to buy a limited number of shares directly from the company. These shares are bought for a certain price during a specific time. Warrants do not give you ownership in the company as shares of stock do. Usually, warrants are valid from two to five years, but may be good for ten years or more. It depends on the particular warrants.

DEFINITION

rt: **Right**—A *right* allows the stockholder to buy newly issued shares of stock directly from the company before the company offers the shares to the public. The company offers these shares to existing stockholders at a lower price. The company decides how many rights are required to buy one share of new stock. In most cases the stockholder receives one right for each share of stock owned. A right is valid from two to four weeks and can be traded until it expires.

vj: **Bankruptcy**—The company is in bankruptcy or is being reorganized under Chapter 11 of the Bankruptcy Code. The **vj** is listed in front of the company name.

s: **Stock split**—In some newspapers the **s**, which denotes a stock split, is found at the end of the company name rather than in front of the 52-week high column.

n: **New issue**—In some newspapers the n, which denotes a new stock issue, is found at the end of the company name rather than in front of the 52-week high column.

Others: Additional explanation of these footnote letters and others can be found near the stock tables under **Explanatory Notes**, or How to Read a Stock Chart.

Stock symbol

The fourth column of the stock table lists the company's trading symbol.

52 Weeks					Yld		Vol				Net
Hi	Lo	Stock	Sym	Div	%	PE	100s	Hi	Lo	Close	Chg
$16^3/_4$	$8^1/_8$	Huffy	HUF	.34	3.3	33	415	$107^7/_{16}$	$10^1/_8$	$10^3/_{16}$	$-^1/_8$

Each stock has its own trading symbol—one, two, or three letters that stand for that particular stock. This official symbol is used not only in the stock tables, but also on the quote machines and on the stock exchange ticker tapes. Stockbrokers use the trading symbol when they place an order to buy or sell. Because of the high volume of trading on the stock exchanges, this symbol is much easier and faster to use than the full name of the company and more accurate than an abbreviation of the company name.

Often the symbols are closely related to the company name.

General Electric	GE
Reebok	RBK
McDonald's	MCD

Other times the symbols seem to be unrelated to the company name.

Goldfield Corporation	GV
Milacron, Inc.	MZ
Starrett	SCX

note

Each stock has three different labels: first, the full company name, second, the abbreviated form of the company name used in the stock tables, and third, the trading symbol.

Huffy Corporation	Huffy	HUF
HEALTHSOUTH Corporation	Hlthsouth	HRC
Merrill Lynch	MerLynch	MER

Dividends

The fifth column of the stock table lists the annual **dividend** per share.

52 Weeks					Yld		Vol				Net
Hi	Lo	Stock	Sym	Div	%	PE	100s	Hi	Lo	Close	Chg
$16^3/_4$	$8^1/_8$	Huffy	HUF	.34	3.3	33	415	$107^7/_{16}$	$10^1/_8$	$10^3/_{16}$	$-^1/_8$

Dividends allow the stockholder—part owners of the company to share directly in the firm's profits. Each stockholder receives an equal amount per share of stock owned. The more shares you own, the larger your dividend check. In most cases, the dividend is paid in cash, but it may be paid in additional shares of stock or in a combination of cash and stock. Dividends are paid on a regular basis, usually quarterly, but may be paid monthly, semiannually or annually. Some companies pay only irregularly, and others do not pay dividends at all.

Definition:

A *dividend* is the share of the company's profits the corporation pays its shareholders.

In the stock table, dividends are expressed as dollars and cents per share of stock. The figure, an annual amount, is paid quarterly. Consequently, every three months the stockholder receives one-fourth of the amount listed in the dividend column. Huffy will pay $.34 per share in dividends this year so the stockholder will receive $.085 per share each quarter. If you own 100 shares, you will receive $8.50 every quarter (100 shares x $0.085) for a total of $34 by the end of the year. If the dividend column is blank, the company does not pay a dividend.

The amount listed as the annual dividend is an estimate. It is necessary to estimate annual dividends because the company's fiscal year is in progress and the dividend amount is decided quarter-by-quarter. The estimate, however, is close because it is based on the last quarterly dividend the company paid and dividends change little.

Directors declare dividends

The board of directors at its quarterly meeting decides whether to pay a dividend. However, once the company begins paying common stock dividends, it is important that it continue doing so at the current rate or at a higher one. Stockholders do not vote on this issue. It is the board's responsibility to decide how to best use the company's profits. The board considers the following: how much profit the company is making, how fast profits are growing, how much cash the company needs for business operations next quarter, and how much money is required to carry out long-term plans.

> **HOT spot** The board of directors is not obligated to pay a dividend on the company's common stock—only on the preferred stock.

If a company has had a profitable quarter and is in good financial condition, the board of directors declares a dividend. The board decides the amount—the same as the previous quarter or an increase of one or two cents per share—and the date to pay it. The dividend is stated as a specific dollar amount per share of stock and is paid to all shareholders who own the stock as of a specific date.

If a company's profits have been higher than usual for several quarters, the board of directors may vote to declare an extra dividend and share the additional profit with the stockholders.

On the other hand, if the corporation has had a serious decline in profits, the board may decide that it is in the best interest of the company to cut the dividend, which means to decrease it. The board may decide not to pay a dividend at all this quarter or to eliminate it completely. However, companies try to avoid doing this. Stockholders sell their shares, and the price of the stock drops suddenly and remains depressed for some time.

> **CAUTION** If a company cuts, skips, or eliminates its dividend, it signals the company is in serious financial trouble.

Sometimes a company pays its dividend in the form of additional shares of stock rather than cash. By doing this, the company conserves its cash. For example, the company might declare a 5 percent stock dividend. In other words, you, as a stockholder, would receive five additional shares for every 100 shares of stock you own. Your total number of shares increases as does the total number of shares the company has in circulation. Therefore, your proportional ownership remains the same, and the stock price drops proportionately. If the company also decreases its future cash dividends proportionately, you have gained nothing. At least with a cash dividend you have an additional check to put in the bank. On the other hand, because you own the additional shares of stock, you will be ahead later if the stock price rises more than it dropped at the time of the stock dividend.

Dividend dates

The process of declaring and paying a dividend involves four dates. The first, the declaration date, is the date the board of directors votes for and announces the dividend—declares the dividend. On the declaration date the board announces how much the dividend will be per share and sets the record date and the payment date.

HOT spot When a stock splits, your total shares are worth the same as before the stock split. Your investment has the same value because the stock price and cash dividend dropped in the same proportion as the number of shares increased.

The second date, the record date, establishes eligibility for the dividend. All stockholders who are on record as owning the stock on that day—the date of record—will receive the dividend.

The third date, the ex-dividend date, is the first day the stock will trade without the dividend—ex-dividend. If you buy the stock on that or a later date you will not be eligible for this dividend. The ex-dividend date, which is necessary for bookkeeping purposes, is two working days before the record date. When you buy a stock, you have three working days in which to pay for it. On the third day ownership is transferred from the seller to the buyer when the transaction is recorded in the corporation's books. If you buy on the ex-dividend date or on the days between the ex-dividend date and the record date, there will not be time for the transaction to be completed by the date of record. The ex-dividend date informs you of this and lets you know that you will be buying the stock without receiving the dividend. On the ex-dividend date the price per share drops by an amount equal to the dividend per share because people who buy on this date will not receive the dividend. Since they will not receive the dividend, they are unwilling to pay the full price for the stock. In contrast, if you sell your stock between the ex-dividend date and the record date, you, the seller, will receive the dividend. This is because there is not enough time—the required three days—between the date of sale and the record date for the transaction to be completed, recorded, and for your name to be deleted from the ownership records. However, what you gain through retaining the dividend is lost through a proportionately lower stock price at the time of sale on the ex-dividend date. It all balances out.

The fourth date of importance to investors is the payment date. It is the date the dividend is actually paid. The payment date is not listed in the stock tables, but it can be found in the dividend announcements in *Barron's*, a weekly financial newspaper, and in the *Wall Street Journal*.

Dividend dates

S	M	T	W	T	F	S
	1	2^1	3	4	5	6
7	8	9	10	11	12	13
14	15	16	17^3	18	19^2	20
21	22	23	24	25	26	27
28	29	30^4				

1- Declaration Date
2- Record Date
3- Ex-dividend Date
4- Payment Date

Footnote letters

The following are some of the more common footnote letters found in the dividend column. You can find further explanations of these and other footnotes in the Explanatory Notes located near the stock tables.

a: an extra dividend paid

b: the annual cash dividend rate (A stock dividend has also been paid.)

e: the amount declared or paid within the last 12 months (The company doesn't have a regular dividend rate.)

j: the dividend amount paid this year (At the last meeting the board either omitted or postponed a dividend.)

m: the annual dividend rate (The last dividend was reduced.)

p: an initial dividend (Because this is the first dividend, the yield is not yet calculated.)

stk: the estimated value of a dividend paid in stock (The company does not pay a cash dividend.)

x: ex-dividend (The stock trades without the current declared dividend. The **x** is found to the left of the 52-week high column.)

Significance for the investor

Companies are conscientious about paying and increasing their dividends. It helps to maintain stockholder interest and demand for their stock. Some investors buy specific stocks because of the dividend the company pays.

> As an investor, pay close attention to the actions the boards of directors take. They are sending quiet messages about the condition of their companies.

Stability

Regular dividend increases show that a company is doing well and is growing steadily. It is a sign of a company's stability. Some companies have a long history of paying and increasing their dividends each year. For example, Bristol-Myers Squibb has been paying dividends since 1900. It has never missed nor cut a dividend. In fact, for more than 40 years it has annually increased its dividend.

Short-term financial problems

A company that increases its dividend even though its earnings have decreased tells investors that it expects the decline in earnings to be temporary. This may or may not be correct.

Long-term financial difficulties

CAUTION

If a company runs into serious business problems, it may have to decrease its dividend or even eliminate it. Decreasing, skipping, or eliminating its dividend indicates the company is in serious financial trouble that will require some time to correct.

Continued expansion

Generally, small, rapid-growth companies do not pay dividends. The company uses all profits for further expansion, so it will continue to grow and increase in value to its shareholders. Thus, at this stage in the company's life its shareholders benefit from the company's increased growth and profits through a rising stock price.

Yield

The sixth column of the stock quotation table lists the **yield** for each stock that pays a dividend.

52 Weeks					Yld		Vol				Net
Hi	Lo	Stock	Sym	Div	%	PE	100s	Hi	Lo	Close	Chg
$16^3/_4$	$8^1/_8$	Huffy	HUF	.34	3.3	33	415	$107/_{16}$	$10^1/_8$	$10^3/_{16}$	$-^1/_8$

DEFINITION

Yield is the percentage of profit earned on a stock investment through its dividend payments. It is figured and quoted on a per-year basis. If the company does not pay a dividend, there is no dividend yield. The yield column will be blank. Additional terms for yield are *dividend yield, current yield,* and *rate of return*.

Yield calculation

If you put $200 in a savings account and receive $8 in interest by the end of a year, the yield on that money is 4 percent. Figure the yield by dividing the income from the investment ($8) by the amount of the investment ($200) and multiplying by 100 to give the percentage. The calculation is $8 ÷ $200 = .04 x 100 = 4%. Four percent is the interest rate on the savings account. If you bought Huffy ($10.18 a share), you would receive $0.34 a share in dividends by the end of the year. The yield on the money used to purchase Huffy would be 3.3 percent. Again, you can figure the yield by dividing the income from the annual dividend ($0.34 per share) by the amount of the investment—the purchase price of the stock ($10.18 per share)—and multiplying the resulting figure by 100 to give the percentage. It works as follows: $0.34 ÷ $10.18 = .033 x 100 = 3.3%. Use the same formula to find the dividend yield or the rate of return for any investment where income is involved.

Effects of a price change

In the following examples the price of the stock changes, but the dividend remains the same. If you buy Huffy at $8 a share, instead of $10.18 a share, and the annual dividend remains at $0.34 a share, the yield will be 4.25 percent instead of the 3.3 percent in the above example. The calculation is $0.34 ÷ 8 = .0425 x 100 = 4.25 percent. Therefore, if you buy the stock at a lower price per share and the dividend remains the same, the yield goes up. But if you purchase the stock at a higher price per share and the dividend remains the same, the yield goes down. For example, purchase

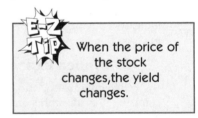

When the price of the stock changes, the yield changes.

Huffy at $12 a share with the dividend still at $0.34 a share, and the yield drops to 2.8 percent. When the dividend is constant, the price per share and the yield move in opposite directions.

The yield listed in the stock table changes every day because the price per share changes. The stock's yield is figured at the end of each day using the stock's closing price.

Yield on stocks owned

When calculating yield on a stock you own, use the price per share you paid for the stock and the amount of dividend you received during the past four quarters. The price you paid for your stock—that part of the yield formula—does not change during the time you own the stock. Consequently, your yield on the stock changes only if the dividend changes. If the dividend goes down, the yield goes down. If you paid $10.18 a share for Huffy and its annual dividend declined to $0.30 a share, the yield would drop to 2.9 percent. In contrast, if the dividend goes up, the yield goes up. If you paid $10.18 a share and the annual dividend increased to $0.40 a share, the yield would rise to 3.9 percent. When the price per share is constant, the dividend and the yield move in the same direction. Dividend rates seldom change more than once a year.

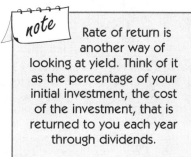

note Rate of return is another way of looking at yield. Think of it as the percentage of your initial investment, the cost of the investment, that is returned to you each year through dividends.

Rate of return

In the example of Huffy, you paid $10.18 per share with an annual dividend of $0.34 per share. By the end of a year 3.3 percent of the cost of your investment has been returned to you through dividends—that is a 3.3 percent rate of return.

Significance for the investor

Investors buy stocks not only for the price appreciation but also for the dividend income. People, particularly in their retirement years, may depend on the income to help cover their expenses. These investors look for stocks that have a high dividend yield, one that is high in relation to the price of the stock.

When investing in a stock because of its high yield, consider the following: Is the company financially sound so it will be able to continue paying dividends year after year? Are the company's profits growing sufficiently so it can afford to raise its dividends? Is the dividend growth rate greater than the inflation rate? If there is a recession, will the company be able to make enough profit to maintain its level of dividend payments throughout the downturn?

In conclusion, if a company's dividends do not continue to grow or if dividends are cut, the dividend income declines and the price of the stock drops because investors feel it is less valuable. Stocks that pay high dividends can be good investments, so keep the above questions in mind.

Price-earnings ratio

The seventh column of the stock table lists the **price-earnings ratio**.

52 Weeks					Yld		Vol				Net
Hi	Lo	Stock	Sym	Div	%	PE	100s	Hi	Lo	Close	Chg
$16^3/_4$	$8^1/_8$	Huffy	HUF	.34	3.3	33	415	$10^7/_{16}$	$10^1/_8$	$10^3/_{16}$	$-^1/_8$

DEFINITION

The *price-earnings (PE) ratio* is the relationship between the price of the stock and the earnings of the company. It compares the stock's price per share to the company's *earnings per share* (EPS). The price-earnings ratio is a measurement, an evaluation tool investors use to determine whether a stock is fairly priced. Each industry has its own PE range, so it is important to compare companies within the same industry. Otherwise, it would be like comparing apples and oranges. Two other terms for price-earnings ratio are *price-earnings multiple*, and *multiple*. Generally, people use the term *PE*.

The *earnings* in the price-earnings ratio refers to the company's net profit— the money that is left after all expenses, including taxes, have been paid. Earnings, in this instance, means the money the company has made from doing business rather than the earnings the stockholder has made from dividends. Dividends and dividend yield are concepts that are different from the earnings in the price-earnings ratio. If a

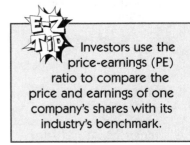

Investors use the price-earnings (PE) ratio to compare the price and earnings of one company's shares with its industry's benchmark.

company has lost money, it has a deficit—it has no earnings. These stocks will have a *dd* in the PE column. Also, price-earnings ratios are calculated only for common stocks—therefore, the PE column is blank for all other types of securities.

PE calculation

DEFINITION

The *price-earnings ratio* is determined by dividing the stock's price per share by the company's earnings per share. The PE ratio is figured using the stock's closing price. Because the closing price changes every day, the PE changes daily. On the other hand, the earnings figure changes only once every three months. It changes when the company announces its new earnings per share (profit per share) at the end of each quarter. The stock tables do not list the company's EPS. Instead, the PE is figured daily for investors and is listed in the stock tables.

The PE can be calculated using the closing price and different time spans for the earnings as given below.

- **Trailing PE**: Current closing price divided by the earnings per share for the past four quarters

- **Current PE**: Current closing price divided by the earnings per share for the past six months and an estimate of the earnings for the next six months

- **Forward PE**: Current closing price divided by an estimate of the earnings per share for the next twelve months

- **Average**
  Annual PE: Average closing price of the stock for the year divided by the earnings per share for the year

Stock tables use the trailing price earnings ratio. When P/E is used in a general way, it simply means trailing P/E. If another P/E is used, it is referred to specifically.

Meaning of PE

What does PE mean? One way to look at PE is to ask yourself how much you, the investor, are willing to pay for a **company's earning power.** You are buying the company's potential to grow and to increase its earnings. For example, in the auto manufacturing industry General Motors has a PE of 7, so you would pay $7 for each dollar of prospective earnings. Honda has a PE of 13, so you would pay $13 for each dollar of future earnings. On the other hand, Toyota has a PE of 36, so you would pay $36 for each dollar of Toyota's ability to grow.

Looking at PE differently—if you invest $1.^{00} in a company, how much earning power will it buy? With General Motors PE at 7 your $1.^{00} would buy $0.14 of company earnings. To calculate it, divide $1.^{00} by the PE, $1.^{00} ÷ 7 = $0.14. With Honda your $1.^{00} would buy $0.07 of the company's earnings; with Toyota, $1.^{00} would buy $0.02 of earnings. Again, you are not actually buying $0.02 of Toyota's profits. Instead, how much potential earning power is your dollar buying?

There is yet another way to look at the price-earnings ratio. How much greater is the stock price than the company's earnings? General Motors' PE of 7 states that its price is 7 times greater than its earnings. Its multiple is 7. Honda's price is 13 times its earnings, and Toyota's price is 36 times its earnings.

Significance for the investor

Why do PE's rise? Why do they fall? What do high PE's indicate? What do low ones mean? How high is a high PE? Are all high PE stocks overpriced? Are all low PE stocks bargains?

PE increases

A price-earnings ratio rises due to an increase in the price compared with the earnings. If the price per share increases and the earnings remain constant, the PE increases. If the price increases by a greater percentage than the earnings increase, the PE increases. If the price remains constant and the earnings drop, the PE increases.

Price Up	Earnings per Share Constant	PE
$30.00	$2.00	15
$34.00	$2.00	17

Price Up	Earnings per Share Up	PE
$30.00	$2.00	15
$36.00	$2.25	16

Price Constant	Earnings per Share Down	PE
$30.00	$2.00	15
$30.00	$1.75	17

High PEs

Currently, a high PE is one that is above 20. The higher the PE, the more growth investors expect from the company. The higher the PE, the more difficult it is for the company to sustain its level of growth. Investors should be sure the company can deliver the growth. Their optimism may or may not be realized.

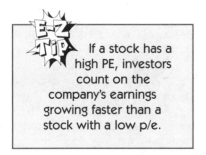

If a stock has a high PE, investors count on the company's earnings growing faster than a stock with a low p/e.

As a PE moves above 20, the stock price becomes more vulnerable to sudden price drops from negative news or rumors—company, industry, market, or economic. Some investors enjoy the risk and feel it is worth the potential reward. The compensation for owning high PE stocks is their price, during a bull market, tends to climb faster than those of low PE stocks. These stocks can be profitable additions to a portfolio while the market is expanding.

PE decreases

A price-earnings ratio falls if the price declines and the earnings remain constant. It also decreases if the price remains constant and the earnings increase.

Price Down	Earnings per Share Constant	PE
$30.00	$2.00	15
$28.00	$2.00	14

Price Constant	Earnings per Share Up	PE
$30.00	$2.00	15
$30.00	$2.25	13

Low PE'S

An entire industry may have a low PE. The whole industry may be in trouble. It may have stopped growing. Or, it may simply be out of favor with investors because they no longer see it as an expanding industry. Their perception may or may not be correct. If a company has a low PE, is the company in trouble? Has it stopped prospering? If investors see little possibility for growth, they are unwilling to pay for it.

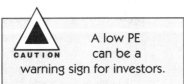 The higher the PE, the greater the risk and the greater the rewards.

On the other hand, a low PE may indicate a bargain for investors. Is the company beginning to move ahead? It may be recovering from a difficult period; its earnings may be starting to improve. Did the PE drop because of increased earnings per share? A good company may have just gotten better. Is the company waiting to be discovered? The company may be thriving, financially sound, yet underpriced—currently, the market has not recognized its value. Is it a strong, low-growth company that pays good dividends? Investors buy these mature, financially secure companies with low PE's and hold them long term for the generous dividends.

 Generally, investors prefer stocks with low PE's. First, they pay less for each dollar of potential earnings. In the previous example, investors who buy General Motors and Toyota pay $7 and $36 respectively for the company's earning power. Will Toyota's earnings grow that much faster than General Motors'? Maybe, maybe not. Second, investors like low PE stocks because of the price stability. If there is negative news, the price of a low PE stock does not drop as abruptly nor as far as that of a high PE stock. Third, a low PE stock has more room for earnings growth. It may grow for a longer period, and its price may rise by a greater percentage than a stock whose PE is already high. If buying a low PE stock, be sure the company is well managed and financially sound with an earnings growth rate and earnings potential that matches or surpasses its competition. Otherwise, the bargain may not be a bargain. You may discover the company has problems and deserves its low PE; it could be out of favor for a reason.

A low PE can be a warning sign for investors.

PE comparisons

The price-earnings ratio is a tool for evaluating the price of a stock. Is the stock fairly priced, overpriced, or underpriced? To evaluate the price of a stock, compare the stock's PE with the PE of the market as a whole, the PE of the industry, the PE's of other companies in the industry, the company's own historical

PE, and the company's earnings growth rate. How these comparisons are made is the subject of a later chapter.

In conclusion, the price-earnings ratio can be a difficult concept to understand. The term PE is often tossed about and at times seems to take on more importance than it merits. It is only one tool for evaluating a stock and says little about the financial condition of the company and the actual potential of the company. The price-earnings ratio is one piece of the picture.

Volume

The eighth column of the stock table lists the **volume**.

52 Weeks					Yld			Vol				Net
Hi	**Lo**	**Stock**	**Sym**	**Div**	**%**	**PE**	**100s**	**Hi**	**Lo**	**Close**	**Chg**
$16^3/_4$	$8^1/_8$	Huffy	HUF	.34	3.3	33	415	$10^7/_{16}$	$10^1/_8$	$10^3/_{16}$	$-^1/_8$

DEFINITION

The *volume* figure tells how many shares investors traded that day. The number of shares traded is given in hundreds. Therefore, a volume figure of 125 means 12,500 shares. For example, the stock table shows the volume for Huffy as 415 which means investors traded 41,500 shares (415 x 100). Add two zeros to each number in the volume column. The stock table lists the volume figure in hundreds because, generally, a trade is made in what is called a round lot. A round lot is a bundle of 100 shares of one stock. If an investor trades less than a hundred shares at one time, it is called an odd lot. A trade of 75 shares would be an odd lot trade and would not be included in the volume figures for the day. The volume figure reports only round lot trades. If an investor trades 350 shares, the trade would consist of three round lots and an odd lot of 50 shares. The three round lots would be included in the volume figure but the odd lot of 50 shares would not.

> **note**
> A single trade involves both a buyer and a seller. Without one or the other, nothing happens—a trade does not take place.

HINT

A trade is like one round trip. The buy and the sell orders are counted as one complete trade. Therefore, the volume data refer to the number of completed trades.

This column may vary slightly from one newspaper to another. For example, it may be labeled **Volume 100s, Sales,** or **Sales Hds.** Some newspapers report composite figures, such as the New York Stock Exchange Composite Transactions in the *Wall Street Journal*. In that case, the volume figure includes the number of shares—round lots—traded on the NYSE plus the round lots traded on the regional exchanges. In addition, Saturday and Sunday papers report the volume figure for each stock as the total volume for the week—the total number of shares (round lots) that were traded during the week.

DEFINITION

Footnote letters

Further explanation of the following and other footnote letters found in the volume column is located in the Explanatory Notes near the stock tables.

z: The exact number of shares traded. Therefore, z375 means that 375 shares were traded, not 37,500. The actual number, rather than the round lot number, is used for stocks that trade a small number of shares per day.

An Underlined Stock: Stocks with largest daily increase. Each day the *Wall Street Journal* underlines the 40 stocks that have had the greatest increase in volume. This underlining alerts investors to the added interest in these stocks.

Significance for the investor

Additional buying and selling may be caused by good news, bad news, or merely rumors about the company. Increased volume may also result from recommendations by well-known stock analysts. Investors read the comments and buy and sell according to the advice.

News or rumors about the company can trigger a sudden spurt in volume.

Because each trade involves both a buyer and a seller, there is no way to tell from the volume figure whether more people wanted to buy or to sell the stock. However, the closing price of the stock indicates whether there was greater interest in buying or in selling. If the closing price is up, more people wanted to buy than to sell. If the closing price is down, more people were interested in selling than in buying, to find buyers, the sellers settled for a lower price.

High, low, close and net change

The last four columns of the stock table give the stock's **price range** for the day.

52 Weeks					Yld		Vol				Net
Hi	Lo	Stock	Sym	Div	%	PE	100s	Hi	Lo	Close	Chg
$16^3/_4$	$8^1/_8$	Huffy	HUF	.34	3.3	33	415	$107/_{16}$	$10^1/_8$	$10^3/_{16}$	$-^1/_8$

DEFINITION

High is the highest price paid for the stock during the day. *Low* is the lowest price paid for the stock. *Close* is the price an investor paid for the stock at the stock's last trade of the day. *Net Change* is the difference between the previous day's closing price and the current closing price.

For each stock, the Hi and Lo columns indicate the extent to which the price varied during the day—this one day. Generally, the price of a stock changes little, perhaps 1/2 or 3/4 point—$0.50 or $0.75 a share. For example, Huffy had a high of $10^7/_{16}$ points ($10.4375 a share) and a low of $10^1/_8$ points ($10.125). The difference between its high and low for the day was 5/16 point or $0.3125. Other times, however, the spread between the high and low may be larger. If news or rumors about the company attract investors' attention, the stock's price may fluctuate two, three, or more points in one day.

Definition:

Although the stock price rises and falls, the *closing price* is the price of the stock's last trade.

The last trade may take place early in the morning or just before the final gong and closing of the exchange. The closing price for Huffy was $10^3/_{16}$ or $10.18 a share.

A misconception exists that the opening price of a stock is always the same as its closing price from the previous day. The stock may open at a higher or lower price due to news or rumors about the company that became public after the exchange closed. In another situation, if a stock begins trading ex-dividend, it opens lower. The buyers will not receive the declared dividend, so the opening price will be proportionately lower.

note

The net change figure represents the difference between the previous closing price and the current closing price.

Some stocks with low volume (**z** in front of the volume figure) do not trade every day. Therefore, the previous closing price comes from the last time the stock traded. The previous trade may have taken place two days, several days, or a week ago. Investors are unable to tell from the stock quotation tables when the last trade occurred.

The net change, like the price, is quoted in points and fractions of points. For example, the net change for Huffy was -1/8. You would read it as "Huffy closed down an eighth" or "Huffy lost an eighth today." The -1/8 means that the last trade for the day was an eighth point lower, $0.125 a share lower, than the last trade on the previous day. Yesterday, Huffy closed at $10^5/_{16}$ or $10.3125 a share, today it closed at $10^3/_{16}$ or $10.1875 for a loss of $0.125 a share—down 1/8. If you owned 100 shares, yesterday they would have been worth $1,031.25, and today they would be worth $1,018.75. Your stock investment would have lost $12.50 in value. On the other hand, if a plus sign precedes the net change figure (+1/8), it means the stock closed higher. You would read the quote as "Huffy closed up an eighth" or "Huffy was up an eighth." The value of your 100 shares would have increased $12.50.

Finally, if the **Net Chg** column for a stock is blank or has a series of dots in it (. . .), the closing price for the two days is the same. The previous closing price is exactly the same as the current closing price—the net change is zero.

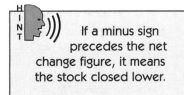

If a minus sign precedes the net change figure, it means the stock closed lower.

If the paper is a Saturday or Sunday paper that gives quotes for the week, the figures in the **Hi and Lo** column will be the high and low prices for the week. The figure in the **Close** column will be the stock's closing price on the last day of the week. Weekly quotes for the **Net Chg** column represent the difference between the stock's closing price on the last day of the previous week and the stock's closing price on the last day of this week.

Footnote letters

The following footnote is a result of the information in the **Net Chg** column of the stock quotation table.

Bold Type: In the *Wall Street Journal* a stock printed in bold type indicates a 5 percent change in its closing price. The bold type alerts investors to a significant price change.

Significance for the investor

Check the stock's high and low price for the day. Is the price spread greater than normal? Perhaps important company news or rumors are attracting the attention of investors. Search the business news to learn what is happening.

When you are ready to buy or sell, compare the stock's closing price with its 52-week high and low. The comparison may indicate a price uptrend or downtrend.

Follow the stock's closing price from day to day or week to week. Is the price advancing or declining? Price differences, even a quarter or a half point per share, make a difference when you are buying and selling stock. Whether you are dealing in 50 or 500 shares, any price difference is important.

American Stock Exchange quotation tables

The American Stock Exchange stock quotation tables are like those of the NYSE. You can find them in the business section of your local newspaper and in the third section of the *Wall Street Journal*. They may have the title American Stock Exchange Composite Transactions, Amex-Composite Transactions, American Stock Exchange, or American Exchange Prices.

Nasdaq Stock Market quotation tables

The Nasdaq Stock Market divides its stocks into two groups. Tables for both are in the third section of the *Wall Street Journal.* You will find quotes for the larger, more actively traded stocks in the Nasdaq National Market Issues tables. Their format follows that of the NYSE. Local newspapers may use the title Nasdaq National Market, Nasdaq National Market Prices, or NASDAQ. To conserve space, some papers do not list all columns.

The Nasdaq lists its second tier of stocks, the small companies, in the Nasdaq Small-Cap Issues tables. Small-cap refers to the market capitalization or the market value (the number of shares outstanding multiplied by the price per share) of the company. It is a way to describe the size of a company. Many of these small-cap stocks sell for less than $10 and most for less than $5 a share. Because these stocks are less actively traded, the stock table includes fewer data—company name, dividend amount, volume, closing price, net change.

NASDAQ SMALL-CAP ISSUES

Issue	Div	Vol 100s	Last	Chg
DelpInf		543	7 1/4	– 1/16
DltaPtr		30	2 5/8	+ 1/8
DntlMed		38	4 1/4	– 1/8
DntlMd wt		34	1 25/32	+ 1/32
DrmSci		45	1	– 1/32
♣ DstFear		302	2 1/16	– 3/32
DexterityS		158	1	– 1/8
DiaSys		282	9 3/16	+ 3/16
DialCpA		20	2 1/8	...
DiehlG		332	5 1/2	+ 9/16
DigtlOrgn		160	6 11/16	– 3/16
DigitRec		5	1 13/16	– 1/32
DigVd wtA		50	1/16	...
DigVid h		31	3 1/2	– 1/4
DiscGph n		24	3 3/4	...
DscGph wt		600	1/32	– 1/32
♣ DiscvLabs		279	1 5/8	+ 1/16

Issue	Div	Vol 100s	Last	Chg
Geores		18	1 1/4	...
GibbsCn		32	1 7/16	– 1/16
♣ GlobalPh		16	3 5/8	– 1/4
♣ GoldRs		615	1 3/8	– 1/32
GoldStd		29	2 1/4	– 3/8
GoldIsl		9	7 3/4	...
GoldSt wt		200	6 3/4	...
GoldTri		31	3 11/16	– 7/16
GolfEnt		80	23/32	+ 1/8
GlfEnt pf	1.00	1	3/8	– 1/16
GoodTm		28	2 3/4	– 1/8
GrndAdv		190	2 3/4	– 1/8
GrndToy		6944	13 9/16	– 1 1/16
GraphOn n		276	7 1/8	+ 5/16
GrOn wtB		67	2 3/8	+ 1/8
GrnDan		4	3 13/16	+ 5/32
GrekaEgy		24	9 1/2	...

Issue	Div	Vol 100s	Last	Chg
IntSmrt wt		142	7/8	– 1/16
IntlSprts	.06	2161	3/4	+ 1/16
ItrnetCm		261	12	+ 1/8
Internt		24	2 1/4	– 1/8
IntrstHot n		22	3	+ 1/16
♣ IntwstHM		120	3 7/16	+ 1/4
IonNet n		575	6 17/32	– 1/32
Irvine		490	1 17/32	...
Isomet		143	2	...
Isramc		23	3 5/16	– 1/16
IxysCp		10	4 7/8	...
JB Oxfrd		1205	7 15/16	+ 1/16
JLM Ctre		1	2 5/32	...
J2 Com		145	18 1/4	...
JadeFncl n		44	8 1/16	– 1/16
JenkonI		628	1 5/8	– 1/8
♣ Jmar wt		48	7/32	+ 1/16

Issue	Div	Vol 100s	Last
Navidec		53	11 7/8
NeoMdia		345	5 3/16
NetLojix		518	2
Netplex		800	1 25/32
Netsmrt		1175	6 9/16
NetterD		141	1 1/8
NtwkCn		230	1 21/32
NtwkSix		49	3 3/4
NetwSys n		646	6 7/8
♣ Network1 n		64	1 3/4
NetwNrth		51	2
NtrlPst n		4	1 11/16
NevStar		6	13/16
NewFrnt		57	5 11/16
NHKidQ n		31	1 1/16
NYHlthC		85	1/2
NewStar		90	19/32

- The Wall Street Journal

Footnote letters and symbols

The Nasdaq National Market Issues use the same footnote letters and symbols as the NYSE tables except for the trading symbol. All Nasdaq stocks have four-letter symbols and many have five. The fifth letter stands for additional information. For example, **A** for *class A stock*, **F** for a *foreign stock*, **K** if the stock *does not have voting rights*, and **Q** for companies in *bankruptcy*. You can find a complete list and explanation of these letters near the Nasdaq stock tables.

The Nasdaq Small-Cap Issues tables use a minimum of footnote letters—**s, n, wt, pf**. The letters are listed after the company name.

Now try this

In a newspaper locate the Nasdaq National Market Issues and the Nasdaq Small-Cap Issues quotation tables. Browse through them, look for familiar names such as Microsoft and Intel. Scan the dividend column. Notice how few companies pay a dividend. These companies are the smaller, new companies that reinvest all profits for future growth. Glance at the volume figures. Some stocks have few shares traded while others have many. Survey the closing prices. Observe the number of low-priced stocks. Later in this book—after you have learned to analyze a company—you may find companies here that are good, affordable stocks to buy.

Conclusion

The following is a brief summary of the information given in the stock tables.

52 Weeks					Yld		Vol				Net
Hi	Lo	Stock	Sym	Div	%	PE	100s	Hi	Lo	Close	Chg
$16^3/_4$	$8^1/_8$	Huffy	HUF	.34	3.3	33	415	$10^7/_{16}$	$10^1/_8$	$10^3/_{16}$	$-^1/_8$

- **52 Weeks Hi and Lo:**—The high and low price for the stock during the past 52 weeks
- **Stock:**—The company name, often in abbreviated form
- **Symbol:**—The stock's trading symbol
- **Dividend:**—The dollar amount the company pays annually in dividends
- **Yield:**—The percentage an investor would earn from the dividends if the stock were purchased at the current closing price
- **PE:**—The price-earnings ratio. The relationship between the price of the stock and the earnings of the company
- **Volume:**—The number of shares traded, quoted in 100s. Add two zeros to each figure.
- **High:**—The highest price paid for the stock on this day
- **Low:**—The lowest price paid for the stock on this day
- **Close:**—The price of the last trade for the day
- **Net Change:**—The difference between the previous day's closing price and the current day's closing price

Looking ahead

In the next chapter, *Stock Market Indices and Averages*, you will become familiar with stock market indexes, such as the Dow Jones Industrial Average, the S&P 500, and the Russell 2000. Market indexes keep you informed about the stock market as a whole.

While reading about the market indexes, you can use the stock tables we have discussed in this chapter and the forms on the following page to track four individual stocks. Below is an example of the form.

Company Name **Quaker State**   Exchange **NYSE**

Date	P/E	Volume	Close
8/19	25	674	13 5/8
8/28	26	272	14 1/2
9/4	25	481	14

Look through the quotation tables and choose three or four stocks to follow. You might choose one stock each from the NYSE, the AMEX and the Nasdaq stock tables. Check them daily, three times a week, or weekly—whatever fits your schedule. Have fun using your knowledge. In the meantime, begin reading the next chapter, *Stock Market Indices and Averages.*

Stock tracking chart

Company Name   Exchange

Date	P/E	Volume	Close

Company Name   Exchange

Date	P/E	Volume	Close

Company Name   Exchange

Date	P/E	Volume	Close

Chapter 3

Stock market indices and averages

What you'll find in this chapter:

➡ How the Dow Jones Industrial Averages began

➡ Most frequently followed indices and averages

➡ Where to find daily closing figures

➡ How indices and averages are used

➡ Understanding "bull" and "bear" markets

As you listen to the news on radio or television and to people's conversations in the elevator and at the bus stop, you hear, "What did the market do today?" "The market is up ten points." "The market is down six points." What does that mean? People are quoting the change in an index or an average. In this chapter you will learn about stock market indices and averages and how they are used to measure stock market performance.

You, the investor, not only want to know how your stock is doing, but you also want to know how the stock market as a whole is performing. Is the market moving up, down, or sideways? Is the market trend—the long-term direction of stock prices—up or down? Because stock prices, as a group, tend to move in the same direction, representative stocks are combined to form a market index or average. Index and average movements are quoted in points. However, the points are simply a unit of measure, they do not equal dollars and cents.

> **note**
>
> Stock market indices and averages are a way for investors to measure what the stock market did during a period of time: an hour, a day, a year, or a decade.

Stock market indices and averages are either broad-based or narrow-based. A broad-based index or average contains stocks from a wide range of industries and represents the overall market. The broad-based indices are the S&P 500 Composite Index, the NYSE Composite Index, the Nasdaq Composite Index, and the Value Line Composite Index. A narrow-based index or average represents a particular segment of the market or a specific industry such as utilities or transportation. It is composed of a variety of stocks from that industry or market segment. The narrow-based indices and averages are the Dow Jones Industrial Average, the Dow Jones Transportation Average, the Dow Jones Utility Average, the Dow Jones Composite Stock Index, the NYSE Industrial Index, the NYSE Transportation Index, the NYSE Utility Index, and the NYSE Financial Index.

Dow Jones Industrial Average

DEFINITION

The Dow Jones Industrial Average, the grandfather of all indices and averages, is known as the Dow, the 30 Industrials, the Industrial Average, and the DJIA. It is the oldest, best known, and the most often quoted measure of stock market performance—it is the most popular indicator of market trends. When you hear, "the market is up ten points," people are talking about the Dow Jones Industrial Average.

History

In the 1880s Charles H. Dow wanted a figure that expressed the level of the overall market and tracked market variations. From the stocks that were traded on the New York Stock Exchange in 1884, Dow chose 11 major stocks—9 railroads and 2 business firms. Each day he totaled their closing prices and divided the total by 11, thereby creating an average that represented the market as a whole. The 11 companies in this first market average were:

Chicago & North Western	Union Pacific
Delaware Lackawanna & Western	Missouri Pacific
Lake Shore Line	Louisville & Nashville
New York Central	Pacific Mail
St. Paul	Western Union
Northern Pacific	

Dow published his average for the first time on July 3, 1884. Thereafter, he included it in his daily bulletin, *The Customer's Afternoon Letter.*

By 1896 Dow had reorganized his average to create two averages: the Dow Jones Railroad Average and the Dow Jones Industrial Average. The railroad average consisted of 20 railroad stocks, and the new Dow Jones Industrial Average was composed of 12 manufacturing companies. By 1896 manufacturing had become an important part of the American business scene. The 12 industrial firms that constituted the average in 1896 were:

American Cotton	Laclede Gas
American Sugar	National Lead
American Tobacco	North American
Chicago Gas	Tennessee Coal & Iron
Oil Distilling & Cattle Feeding	US Leather
General Electric	US Rubber

The Dow Jones Industrial Average continued to grow. In 1916 another 8 companies were added for a total of 20. In 1928 an additional 10 companies were included for the present total of 30. This list of the 30 manufacturing and service companies which currently make up the Dow Jones Industrial Average can be found each day in the *Wall Street Journal*. These 30 companies, which trade on the NYSE, were chosen to compose the DJIA because they represent major industries in America—each company is a leader in its industry. These large, high-quality corporations are mature, reliable firms with long histories of earnings and dividend growth. The stocks of companies with these characteristics

DEFINITION

are known as *blue chip* stocks.

Stocks that constitute the Dow Jones Industrial Average are rarely changed. However, changes are made when a company merges with another company or when a company is no longer representative of its industry or of the overall market. In the latter case, when trading in the stock has diminished to the point that the stock's price movements have little effect on the average, the company is removed and a more representative company is added. These infrequent changes are made by the editors of the *Wall Street Journal*. When making changes to the Dow, the editors do not confer with the companies involved, nor do they confer with any government body.

> *note*
>
> General Electric, one of the original 12 industrial companies, is currently part of the Dow Jones Industrial Average and has been part of the Dow, off and on, for the past 103 years.

Calculations

The 30 individual stock prices are added, and the resulting total is divided. The divisor is no longer 30, the number of stocks being averaged, but 0.24275214. The current divisor is listed in the *Wall Street Journal*. Whenever one of the 30 companies splits its stock or pays a dividend in stock, the divisor is decreased. The decrease in the divisor ensures that the value of the average is the same as it would have been without the stock split or stock dividend. Therefore, comparisons of the level of the average can be made from year to year and from decade to decade—after 1928. Currently, the DJIA is at 9,363, which means if there had been no stock splits nor dividends paid in stock, theoretically, the average price per share of these 30 stocks would be $9,363.

> **note**
>
> The Dow Jones Industrial Average is calculated continuously throughout the day by Dow Jones & Company. The DJIA, like all stock market averages, is a price-weighted, arithmetic average.

Increases and decreases

Each day the *Wall Street Journal* publishes graphs and tables in its newspaper that show the yearly, monthly, daily, and hourly movement of the Dow Jones Industrial Average. You can find these graphs and tables in the third section—Money & Investing—under the heading Markets Diary. The first graph shows the movement of the DJIA during the previous 18 months. The second shows the movement of the DJIA during the past five market days. Following these two graphs, a table lists the Dow's close, net change, and percentage change for the current day. The table also lists the 12-month high and low for the average, the 12-month point and percentage change and the point and percentage change since 12/31. Included in the table is similar information about the Dow Jones Global, the S&P 500, the Nasdaq Composite, and the Russell 2000 averages.

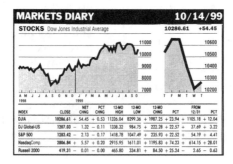

- Wall Street Journal

In the column by the New York Stock Exchange stock tables, the *Wall Street Journal* publishes a detailed graph showing the daily high, low, and close for the Dow Jones Industrial Average during the previous 26 weeks. Here you can also find a list of the 30 stocks that make up the Dow Jones Industrial Average.

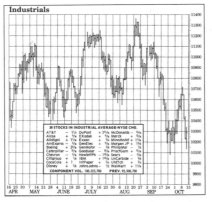

- Wall Street Journal

Near the graph showing the daily action of the DJIA, the *Wall Street Journal* publishes a table that shows the hourly average of the 30 Industrials during the previous five days. Here you can find the divisor used in calculating the average. Also included in this table are the hourly prices for the 20 Transportation Companies, the 15 Utilities, and the 65 Stocks Composite Average.

THE DOW JONES AVERAGES HOUR BY HOUR

DATE	OPEN	10 AM	11 AM	12 NOON	1 PM	2 PM	3 PM	CLOSE	CHG	% CHG	HIGH	LOW	HIGH	LOW
30 INDUSTRIALS: (divisor: 0.19740463)											(THEORETICAL)		(ACTUAL)	
Oct 14	10230.89	10226.46	10218.54	10189.10	10266.35	10277.75	10254.32	10286.61	+ 54.45	+ 0.53	10416.74	10071.64	10342.97	10133.69
Oct 13	10412.31	10440.48	10349.30	10335.69	10301.18	10322.39	10310.99	10232.16	− 184.90	− 1.77	10495.89	10173.58	10443.02	10226.46
Oct 12	10648.81	10556.05	10527.55	10525.34	10506.97	10522.17	10466.76	10417.06	− 231.12	− 2.17	10659.58	10366.08	10648.81	10417.06
Oct 11	10649.76	10669.71	10680.79	10695.67	10670.97	10645.01	10653.88	10648.18	− 1.58	− 0.01	10781.16	10545.60	10719.10	10634.88
Oct 8	10534.52	10533.57	10572.19	10602.27	10645.65	10612.40	10636.15	10649.76	+ 112.71	+ 1.07	10743.48	10423.70	10655.78	10506.34

- Wall Street Journal

When tracking the Dow Jones Industrial Average, you as an investor will want to weigh these facts. First, even though no special consideration is given to any of the 30 companies because of size or number of outstanding shares—equal weight is given to each company—a high-priced stock affects the average more than a low-priced stock. A 5 percent movement of a high-priced stock causes the Dow to move more than a 5 percent movement of a low-priced stock. For instance, if International Business Machines (IBM) at $178.50 increased by 5 percent ($8.93) to $187.43 per share, the DJIA would move from 9356.62 to 9393.40, an increase of 36.78 points. On the other hand, if Walt Disney at $35.18 increased by 5 percent ($1.76) to $36.94, the Dow would move to 9363.87, an increase of only 7.25 points. When the Dow moves, find out which stock or stocks caused the movement. The message about what is happening in the market is different if it is one high-priced stock or several low-priced stocks. You can find the net change for each of the 30 industrial stocks as part of the graph that shows the daily high, low, and close for the Industrials.

A second factor to bear in mind as you track the DJIA is the effect of the divisor as it decreases due to stock splits. The smaller the divisor becomes, the greater the impact on the average. When the divisor was at 1.0, a $1 change in the price of any stock in the average would move the average one point. When the divisor fell below 1.0, it became a multiplier. With the divisor-multiplier now at 0.24275214, a $1 change in the price of any stock in the average will move the average more than four points. The multiplier effect is steadily increasing as stock splits become more common. When the present 30 Industrials began on October 1, 1928, the divisor was 16.67; in 1950 it was 8.57. By 1986 it had decreased to 0.956. Because the divisor was less than one, in effect it became a multiplier. In 1992 it had shrunk to 0.46268499 and by 1999 it had been reduced to 0.24245214. How much smaller has it gotten since 1999? The smaller the divisor, the more volatile the market appears to be.

The third factor to keep in mind when tracking the DJIA is to think beyond the number of points the average moves—and focus on the percentage change the move represents. The percentage change indicates the importance of the 25-, 50-, or 100-point move. When the market was at 2000, a 100-point move represented a 5.0 percent change; at 4000 this same move represented a 2.5 percent change, and at 9000 it represents only a 1.1 percent change. The percentage change gives a more accurate picture of what is happening in the market than the point change. By using the percentage change you can compare the point movement of one period with that of another. The following table lists some of the large point and percentage changes for the industrial average:

Dow Jones Industrial Average
Major Point and Percentage Changes

Date	Point Change	Percentage Change	Closing
December 18, 1899	– 5.57	– 8.72	58.27
November 6, 1929	- 25.48	– 9.92	232.13
October 28, 1929	– 38.33	– 12.82	260.64
October 29, 1929	– 30.57	– 11.73	230.07
October 30, 1929	+ 28.40	+ 12.34	258.47
October 6, 1931	+ 12.86	+ 14.87	99.34
August 3, 1932	+ 5.06	+ 9.52	58.22
September 21, 1932	+ 7.67	+ 11.36	75.16
October 19, 1987	– 508.00	– 22.61	1738.74
October 21, 1987	+ 186.84	+ 10.15	2027.85
October 27, 1997	- 554.26	- 7.18	7161.15
October 28, 1997	+ 337.17	+ 4.71	7498.32

note

The percentage change also allows you to compare the movements of the Dow Jones Industrial Average with the movements of other indices, both foreign and domestic.

Look in the *Wall Street Journal* under the heading Markets Diary and compare the point movement of the DJIA with the S&P 500, Nasdaq Composite, and Russell 2000. Then, under the heading Stock Market Data Bank, find the table that lists the major domestic indices and averages and compare the percentage change for each indicator.

From time to time as the Dow Jones Industrial Average moves up and down, it sets new records. The record may be a new high, a major decline, or the first time the average crosses a new hundred mark. Radio, television, and newspapers note these significant events.

The following are some milestones in the history of the Dow Jones Industrial Average:

July 3, 1884	Charles H. Dow published his average for the first time.
May 26, 1896	Dow published his newly created Dow Jones Industrial Average. The average closed at 40.94.
August 8, 1896	The Industrial Average declined to its all-time low of 28.48.
October 7, 1896	Dow began publishing the Industrial Average each day.
January 15, 1906	The Industrial Average closed at 100.80, exceeding 100 for the first time.
October 4, 1916	The number of companies that composed the Industrial Average was increased from 12 to 20.
December 19, 1927	The Industrial Average closed at 200.93, topping 200 for the first time.
October 1, 1928	Ten companies were added to the Dow Jones Industrial Average for a total of 30. This was the beginning of our present 30 Industrials. The average closed at 240.01.
December 31, 1928	The Dow closed at 300, for a new high.
September 3, 1929	The DJIA closed at 381.17, the high before the Crash of 1929.
October 29, 1929	The market crashed, the Dow closed at 230.07 a 11.73 percent decline from the previous day.
July 8, 1932	The DJIA closed at 41.22. This was its lowest closing since August 8, 1896.
March 11, 1954	The DJIA closed at 300.83, exceeding 300 for the first time since 1929.

February 20, 1959   The Dow closed at 602.21, breaking 600 for the first time.

November 14, 1972   The Dow closed at 1003.16, setting a new record above 1000.

December 16, 1982   The Dow closed at 990.25, this is the last time the Dow closed below 1000.

January 8, 1987   The Dow closed at 2002.25, for a new high above 2000.

August 25, 1987   The Dow closed at 2722.42, the high before the sudden drop in October 1987.

October 19, 1987   Stock prices collapsed, the Dow fell from its previous closing of 2246.74 to 1738.74 for a 22.61 percent drop.

August 23, 1988   The Dow closed at 1989.33, the last time the Dow closed below 2,000.

April 17, 1991   The Dow closed at 3004.46 for a new record high above 3000.

October 14, 1996   The Dow closed above 6000 for the first time.

April 6, 1998   The Dow closed at 9033.23 for a new high above 9000

Throughout the market day, computers continuously calculate the Industrial Average for Dow Jones & Company. The Dow Jones News Service immediately distributes the information around the world. The Dow is published not only in the *Wall Street Journal* and *Barron's*, but also in foreign papers and in your local newspaper. It is also quoted on radio and television newscasts. Investors can track the Dow by calling their brokers—by using brokerage firms and local newspapers' recorded message or touch-tone phone lines, or by accessing financial Internet Web sites, and by watching the ticker tape during market hours on Cable News Network (**CNN**) broadcasts.

Significance for the investor

Even though the Dow Jones Industrial Average is the most often quoted market indicator, some investors feel that the Industrial Average is too narrow to measure the market as a whole—only 30 stocks out of more than 12,000. Others feel the Dow is a better measure of blue chip stocks than of the whole market. Yet, over a long period the percentage moves in the Dow Jones Industrial Average closely match the percentage moves in the broader market indices and averages.

The 30 companies which constitute the Dow Jones Industrial Average represent the backbone of American industry. Historically, the rise and fall of the DJIA has reflected the expansion and the contraction of industry in response to the increased or decreased growth of the economy.

Dow Jones Transportation Average

The Dow Jones Transportation Average, also known as the DJTA and the 20 Transportation, consists of the stocks of 20 transportation companies.

History

The transportation average began at the same time as the industrial average. Both were part of the first average Charles Dow published in 1884. On May 26, 1896, Dow split his stock average and created two new averages—the Dow Jones Railroad Average and the Dow Jones Industrial Average. Eighteen railroad companies and two non-railroad companies—Pacific Mail, a steamship company, and Western Union, the telegraph company—formed the railroad average. This new Dow Jones Railroad Average was the beginning of our current Dow Jones Transportation Average.

On October 26, 1896, Manhattan Elevated and Wabash pfd. replaced Pacific Mail and Western Union—for the first time the railroad average included only railroad stocks. The companies were as follows:

Atchinson	Missouri Pacific
Burlington	New York Central
CCC & St. Louis	Northern Pacific pfd.
Chesapeake & Ohio	Northwest
Erie	Philadelphia & Reading
Jersey Central	Rock Island
Kansas & Texas pfd.	Southern Railway pfd.
Lake Shore	Susquehanna & Western pfd.
Louisville & Nashville	St. Paul
Manhattan Elevated	Wabash pfd.

On October 26, 1896, this all-railroad average closed at 51.72. By this time, Charles Dow was including the railroad average each day in his *Customer's Afternoon Letter.*

Through a series of substitutions, which began in 1898, the preferred stocks were replaced with common stocks. By 1905 the Railroad Average was composed of all common stocks.

Except for the usual substitutions of companies to maintain market representation, no further changes were made in the railroad average until January 2, 1970, when the editors of the

> **note** A continued rise in the Dow is a sign of United States economic strength. Likewise, an extended decline in the Dow is a signal the economy is weak or in a recession.

Wall Street Journal introduced the Dow Jones Transportation Average. Over the years the transportation business had changed significantly. Railroads no longer dominated the industry—they no longer represented the transportation market. The following explanation was written by a staff reporter for the *Wall Street Journal* and published in paper on January 5, 1970:

> *Dictating the change in the average is the drastically altered pattern of commercial transportation itself. When the railroad average was begun toward the end of the 19th century, the rails were the giant movers of both freight and people. Automobiles, trucks, buses and airplanes hadn't even arrived on the scene.*
>
> *As recently as 20 years ago, the rails still carried 62% of all intercity freight on a ton-mileage basis. By 1969, though, that share had shrunk to 41%. And, over the same 20 years, the share carried by commercial truckers nearly doubled, rising from 11% to 21%. The rest of the load is moved by pipelines, water transport and airplanes.*
>
> *By 1969 the railroad movement of intercity passengers had shrunk to a thin 1.2% of the total, on a passenger-mile basis, from nearly 10% two decades earlier. Private autos carried a huge 86% of the intercity passenger load last year, airlines had 9.4% of the traffic and buses 2.5%.*
>
> *Also considered in revision of the average was the contraction through merger of the number of leading railroads and the diversification of some railroad companies into non-transportation business.*

note

To reflect the changes that had taken place in transportation, the editors of the *Wall Street Journal* deleted nine railroads from the Dow Jones Railroad Average and added nine companies that represented the airline and trucking industries. Thus, the railroad average became a broader transportation average and was named the Dow Jones Transportation Average. The following 20 companies composed the new DJTA:

Canadian Pacific Railway	American Airlines
Great Northern Railway	Eastern Airlines
Louisville & Nashville Railroad	Northwest Airlines
Norfolk & Western Railway	Pan American World Airways
Penn–Central	Trans World Airlines
St. Louis–San Francisco Railway	UAL
Santa Fe Industries	Seaboard Coast Line Industries
Southern Pacific Company	Consolidated Freightways
Southern Railway	Pacific Intermountain Express
Union Pacific Corporation	U. S. Freight Company

In 1991 Roadway Services, Inc. replaced Pan Am Corporation. For the first time in history, a stock not listed on the NYSE was included in a Dow Jones average.

On its first day, January 2, 1970, the Dow Jones Transportation Average closed at 181.07. By 1999 the DJTA had climbed to 3161.76. You can find the current closing figure for the average in the business section of your local newspaper or in the third section of the

> **note** A current list of companies that compose the Dow Jones Transportation Average can be found in the third section of the *Wall Street Journal* under the heading "The Dow Jones Averages."

Wall Street Journal under the heading Stock Market Data Bank. There, you will find a table that lists the day's closing, net change, and percentage change for the 20 transportation stocks.

THE DOW JONES AVERAGES HOUR BY HOUR

DATE	OPEN	10 AM	11 AM	12 NOON	1 PM	2 PM	3 PM	CLOSE	CHG		% CHG	HIGH (THEORETICAL)	LOW	HIGH (ACTUAL)	LOW
	20 TRANSPORTATION COS.: (divisor: 0.22276590)														
Oct 14	2920.95	2925.16	2922.07	2901.03	2904.11	2911.13	2917.02	2914.49	−	7.02	− 0.24	2963.59	2871.15	2934.55	2894.01
Oct 13	2960.51	2948.16	2942.83	2945.64	2941.99	2944.23	2944.23	2921.51	−	39.98	− 1.35	2988.26	2893.17	2960.51	2916.46
Oct 12	3026.58	2995.58	2973.41	2971.45	2979.45	2985.34	2986.46	2961.49	−	64.53	− 2.13	3031.21	2927.68	3026.58	2959.38
Oct 11	3080.87	3058.14	3049.16	3036.82	3030.37	3025.88	3026.44	3026.02	−	55.69	− 1.81	3102.75	2991.93	3081.85	3019.43
Oct 8	3046.64	3100.93	3086.83	3082.55	3085.78	3084.52	3082.55	3081.71	+	34.79	+ 1.14	3138.38	3041.59	3102.89	3046.64

For a picture of the DJTA activity for the previous 26 weeks, check the Transportation graph which shows the daily high, low, and close. This graph is under the heading, "The Dow Jones Averages."

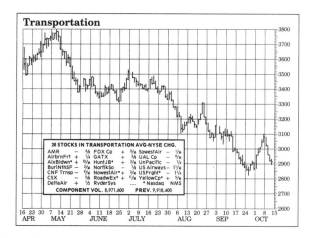

Also, hourly figures for the DJTA are published. You will find them listed in a table near the above graph.

Calculations

To calculate the average, the prices of the individual stocks are added, and the resulting total is divided. The divisor used in the calculation is adjusted for stock splits, stock dividends of 10 percent or more, and changes in companies that constitute the average. The transportation divisor, like the industrial divisor, has decreased to less than 1.0 and now has the effect of a multiplier. The *Wall Street Journal* prints the current divisor in the table that lists the hourly figures for the DJTA.

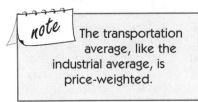

note The transportation average, like the industrial average, is price-weighted.

Significance for the investor

The Dow Jones Transportation Average is used to confirm stock market trends. The Dow Theory states that a major market trend must be confirmed by similar movements in the Dow Jones Industrial Average and the Dow Jones Transportation Average. If both the Industrial Average and the Transportation Average reach a new high or a new low, the market trend is thought to be confirmed and it is assumed the trend will continue. Even though this theory has not always proven to be accurate, it is an important market indicator that has been used for many years.

Other Dow Jones averages

The Dow Jones & Company also owns and publishes a utility average, a composite average, and a group of world stock indices.

Dow Jones Utility Average

DEFINITION

The *Dow Jones Utility Average,* also known as the DJUA, the 15 Utilities, and the Utility Average, is currently composed of 15 gas and electric companies. These companies are representative of utility companies in different parts of the United States. For instance, Pacific Gas & Electric operates in California; Texas Utilities produces electricity for the Texas area, and Consolidated Edison supplies electricity, gas, and steam to New York City.

When the Dow Jones Utility Average began in 1929 it included 20 utility companies as well as Western Union, International Telephone, and American Telephone & Telegraph. The first closing figure for the average was 80.70 on December 24 of that year.

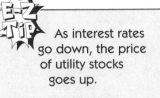

As interest rates go down, the price of utility stocks goes up.

The current closing figures for the Utility Average are listed in the business section of your local newspaper. Also, the third section of the *Wall Street Journal* contains a graph and two tables which list the closing figures.

The movement of the 15 Utilities indicates what is happening to the price of utility stocks. Because utility companies depend heavily on borrowed money, the price of utility stocks and interest rates tends to move in opposite directions. By tracking the interest rate changes and the movement of the Utility Average, an investor is able to determine trends in the price of utility stocks. When an investor is deciding whether to buy or sell utility stocks, this market trend information is helpful.

Dow Jones Composite Average

DEFINITION

In 1933 the editors of the *Wall Street Journal* created a composite average, the *Dow Jones Composite Stock Index*. It is also called the 65 Stocks Composite Average, the 65 Stock Average, and the 65 Stocks. This average is composed of the 30 industrial companies in the DJIA, the 20 transportation companies in the DJTA, and the 15 utilities in the DJUA. The 65 Stock Average is a price-weighted average and is calculated like other Dow Jones averages. A table that lists the divisor, the previous five days' high, low, and close figures, and the percentage change can be found in the *Wall Street Journal*.

> *note* The 65 Composite Stock Average indicates what is happening to the prices of a broad group of blue chip stocks.

Dow Jones Global Stock Index

DEFINITION

In response to investor interest in world markets, Dow Jones & Company created the *Dow Jones Global Stock Index*. Stocks of approximately 2,800 companies from 29 countries form the index. These companies are located in North America, South America, Latin America, Europe, Asia/Pacific, and Africa. The stocks must be actively traded common shares. Each issue must have at least 25 percent of its shares available for foreign ownership.

The index is subdivided into region and country indices. Closing and percentage change figures are given for each region index, each country index within a region, and the world index with and without the United States. To furnish more in-depth information, the stocks are divided into nine economic sector indices such as consumer cyclical, consumer non-cyclical, energy, and financial. These are further subdivided into 124 industry indices— airlines, medical supplies, building materials, office equipment, etc. Closing

> EZ TIP The Dow Jones Global Stock Index and its sub-indices provide a comprehensive look at worldwide stock performance.

prices are given for each sector and industry group by region—United States, Americas, Europe, Asia/Pacific. These indices allow investors to look at a sector's or an industry's performance throughout the world. How is the automobile industry doing in the Pacific Rim, in Europe, and in the Americas? In which region are automobile stocks rising? How is the automobile industry doing in the world as a whole?

Standard & Poor's 500 Composite Stock Index

DEFINITION

The *Standard & Poor's 500 Composite Stock Index* is the official name of the S&P 500. It is the most closely followed index after the Dow Jones Industrial Average. The S&P 500 is a broad-based index composed of widely held and actively traded stocks of blue chip companies (leading companies in leading industries) that trade on the New York Stock Exchange, the American Stock Exchange, and the Nasdaq Stock Market. The S&P 500 consists of stocks from approximately 400 industrial companies, 20 transportation companies, 40 public utilities, and 40 financial firms. Because small companies compose some of the industries represented in the S&P 500, the companies in the index are not necessarily the 500 largest companies in America. The breadth of the S&P 500 index gives investors a good picture of what is happening in the stock market.

The *Standard & Poor's 500 Composite Stock Index* is published by the Standard & Poor's Corporation, which gathers and interprets business and financial information. The Corporation's S&P 500 Committee makes all decisions concerning the index and its contents. Each stock included in the index must be representative of its industry. Also, each stock's price must reflect changes that occur in its industry. The committee does not include a stock in the index merely because the stock is popular with investors.

History

In 1928 the Standard & Poor's Corporation began publishing a daily stock index that included 90 stocks. As the years passed the number of stocks in the index increased. Finally, in 1957 the Committee set the number at 500. It included 425 industrial, 60 utility, and 15 rail stocks. This index is considered the beginning of the S&P 500.

In 1976 the S&P 500 Committee added a new category of stocks, the financial industry stocks. The distribution of stocks in the index then became 400 industrial companies, 20 transportation companies, 40 utilities, and 40 financial companies. Because most of the banks and insurance companies in the financial industry trade on the Nasdaq Stock Market, the Committee broke a tradition for all indices and averages by including stocks in the index that traded on an exchange other than the NYSE.

The most recent change in the S&P 500 occurred in 1988 when the Committee adopted a flexible structure for the index. The total number of stocks remains at 500 but the number within each category now varies. Therefore, at any one time the distribution of stocks in each sector may not be 400 industrial stocks, 20 transportation stocks, 40 utility stocks, and 40 financial stocks. This new structure allows the Committee more flexibility in choosing a replacement company for a company that has been removed from the index. A list of the companies that currently compose the index can be found in each month's issue of the *S&P 500 Information Bulletin.*

Calculations

The *S&P 500* is a market-value-weighted index as are nearly all indices. It is based on the market value—the number of shares outstanding multiplied by the price per share—of its component stocks. The index is calculated by adding the market values of all 500 stocks, dividing the total by the current baseline market value figure published in the *S&P 500 Information Bulletin*, and multiplying the quotient by the baseline value figure of 10. Automatic Data Processing (ADP) calculates the index each second the exchanges are open and sends the figures to Standard & Poor's every 15 seconds. The Standard & Poor's Corporation then sells the index figures to the quote providers such as Reuters and Bloomberg. Also, throughout the day Standard & Poor's Corporation sends the index data to newswire services—Associated Press and United Press International. Newspaper, radio, and television news rooms pick up the material from the wire services and report it in their newspapers and in their broadcasts.

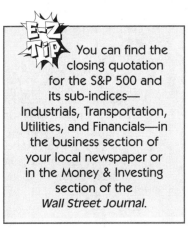

You can find the closing quotation for the S&P 500 and its sub-indices—Industrials, Transportation, Utilities, and Financials—in the business section of your local newspaper or in the Money & Investing section of the *Wall Street Journal.*

Significance for the investor

The *Standard & Poor's 500 Composite Index* is used as a performance gauge for institutional investors and mutual fund managers. Is the money manager's stock portfolio doing as well or better than the S&P 500, or is it lagging behind the index? If the money manager's portfolio of stocks has risen more than the S&P 500 or has declined less, the money manager has been successful. Some mutual funds and institutions restrict their stock purchases to companies in the S&P 500. This guarantees a performance at least equal to the index. However, this practice eliminates the opportunity to outperform the S&P 500. You, too, can compare the performance of your portfolio with that of the S&P 500. Are your stocks keeping up with the S&P 500, falling behind, or outperforming it?

Because the S&P 500 contains a diverse group of stocks that indicates what is happening in American industry, the U. S. Department of Commerce includes the Standard & Poor's 500 Composite Index in its monthly Index of Leading Indicators, which is used in forecasting the direction of the economy.

The New York Stock Exchange Index

DEFINITION

The *New York Stock Exchange Composite Index* contains all common stocks—approximately 3,000—listed on the NYSE. Thus, this market-value-weighted index represents a wide cross section of publicly traded companies. The Exchange introduced the index in 1966 because investors wanted a broader view of the New York Stock Exchange market than that given by the Dow Jones Industrial Average.

The NYSE has calculated the index weekly since January 1939. Daily closing figures are available from May 1964 to the present. The index is computed continuously after each transaction and the point changes, expressed in dollars and cents, are transmitted electronically minute by minute. The figures for the New York Stock Exchange Composite Index are available through commercial

> **E-Z TIP**
>
> Each day the *Wall Street Journal* lists the closing price for the NYSE Composite Index and its four sub-indices—Industrials, Utilities, Transportation, Finance—in the column Stock Market Data Bank.

quote services, Internet web sites, and newspapers. Check today's closing price. How much has the index appreciated since the end of its first year when it stood at 43.72?

Nasdaq Composite Index

The Nasdaq Composite Index is composed of approximately 5,500 stocks listed on the Nasdaq Stock Market. It is a market-value weighted index that measures the performance of the Nasdaq Stock Market. It was created in 1971 by The National Association of Securities Dealers. Many of the stocks that trade on the Nasdaq and make up the Composite Index are stocks of smaller, lesser-known companies. They often have lower prices, higher risk factors, and greater volatility than stocks listed on the NYSE and the AMEX. The movement of the Nasdaq Composite Index is a gauge of investor interest in the smaller, more speculative stocks. When the economy is booming and the market is surging ahead, investors are inclined to take more chances and buy these riskier stocks. Consequently, the Nasdaq Composite Index will rise dramatically. On the other hand, when the economy begins to slump and investors leave the small, speculative companies to invest in the large, long established companies, the index may fall just as dramatically.

Other indices

Other often quoted stock market indices are the American Stock Exchange Composite Index, the Russell 2000 Index, and the Value Line Composite Index. Their closing prices and percentage change can be found in the Market & Investing section of the *Wall Street Journal* under the heading Stock Market Data Bank.

> You can find closing prices for the Nasdaq Composite Index and its sub-indices such as Industrials, Banks, Computer, and Telecommunications in your local newspaper and in the *Wall Street Journal* under the heading Stock Market Data Bank in the Money & Investing section.

American Stock Exchange Composite Index

The AMEX Composite Index, a market-value-weighted index, is published by the American Stock Exchange. It measures the performance of issues traded on the AMEX. The Index includes all common stocks or American depository receipts (ADRs) of listed companies as well as Real Estate Investment Trusts (REITs), master limited partnerships and closed-end mutual funds. The index is divided into five sub-indices: Healthcare, Financial, Industrials, Natural Resources, and Information Technologies.

Russell 2000 Index

The Russell 2000 Index, a market-value-weighted index, measures the performance of small-company stocks. Small companies respond differently to economic conditions than large companies. Stocks are chosen for the Russell 2000 by taking the 3000 largest common stocks trading on the NYSE, AMEX and Nasdaq and eliminating the top 1000. The remaining 2000 stocks compose the Index. The index is owned by the Frank Russell Company.

> *note* Mutual funds specializing in small stocks use the Russell 2000 as a performance gauge to measure their success.

Value Line Composite Index

DEFINITION

The *Value Line Composite Index* is published by the Value Line Investment Survey. It includes all stocks reviewed by the investment survey—approximately 1,500 industrial companies, 160 utilities, and 11 rails. The *Value Line Composite Index* is one of the broader-based indices because it covers both large industrial companies and small-growth companies. About 80 percent of the stocks are traded on the NYSE, and the remainder are traded on the AMEX and the Nasdaq Stock Market. The index is calculated as a geometric average of the percentage change in each stock's price from the previous day. High-priced stocks have the same impact as low-priced stocks. Companies with a large number of outstanding shares have the same impact as companies with a small number of outstanding shares.

> HINT
>
> The Value Line Composite Index is neither price weighted nor market value weighted. It is an unweighted index; each company is treated equally.

Market trends

Stock market trends are long-term, repetitive patterns of stock price movements—movements that continue for two or three years in an upward, downward, or sideways direction. Because trends vary in length and magnitude, analysts and institutional money managers have difficulty determining and agreeing on when a trend is changing. Much speculation and discussion takes place about what the stock market is going to do. Will the market continue to advance? Is the market going to drop? How long will the market trade within this narrow range? Is the trend going to change? Such factors as economic growth, high employment, and low interest rates, as well as recessions, high unemployment, and high interest rates influence the feelings and actions of investors. These actions are translated into market trends which develop into bull and bear markets.

> **HOT spot** Professional market analysts track the movement of indices and averages—market indicators—to determine the trend of stock prices. Trends provide a general view of what the market is doing. Institutional investors use this information to help them manage their portfolios.

Bull markets

If the trend is up, the market is called a bull market. The indices and averages regularly hit new highs. The volume of trading increases as these new highs are reached. When people are feeling prosperous and optimistic about the economy, they buy stocks. Stock prices go up, the market indicators rise. The market trend is up. Businesses are growing and profits are increasing. Everyone is talking about the booming economy and the stock market. More people buy stocks, which drives the market up further. In a bull market, despite brief declines and sideways movements, the overall direction of stock prices is up. Bull markets may last for several months or for several years.

Definition:

A *bull market* is defined as a period of generally rising stock prices.

Since the early 1920s, there have been at least 12 bull markets. The most publicized bull market began in the mid-1920s and ended on October 29, 1929, with the Crash of 1929. More recently, stocks have been in a bull market from 1970 to 1973, 1974 to 1976, and 1982 to 1999 with a brief down period in 1987 and in 1990. Market analysts do not always agree whether a specific movement in stock prices should be classified as a bull market. Nor do they always agree on the date a particular bull market began.

Bear markets

If the market is in a prolonged down trend, it is called a bear market. When investors feel pessimistic about the economy and believe that a recession is coming or has already arrived, many sell their stocks. When stock prices decline, market indicators fall. In addition, when sales of products and services are down, profits are down. As company profits decline, fewer people buy stocks, more people sell their stock, and stock prices decline further. Even though stock prices will rise for brief periods, the down trend and the bear market will continue until the economy and company profits begin to improve.

Since the 1920s, there have been 11 bear markets. The most famous bear market began in October 1929 with the Crash and lasted until mid-1932. The three most recent bear markets have been from 1981 to 1982, from October 19, 1987 to the end of 1987, and from July to October 1990. As with bull markets, market trend analysts do not always agree that the trend is actually a bear market. Neither do they agree when a particular bear market began and when it ended. Some market analysts feel the October 1987 drop was just a correction while others feel it was a brief bear market.

Definition:

A *bear market* is defined as a period of generally falling stock prices— a decline of 15 percent or more.

Significance for the investor

How can one remember in which direction a bull and a bear market move? Think of how each animal attacks. When a bull attacks, it thrusts upward with its horns. In a bull market stock prices rise. When a bear attacks, it rakes downward with its claws. In a bear market prices fall.

In a bear market stock prices may decline slowly, which is difficult to discern, or they may drop sharply. Generally, during a bull market stock prices rise slowly. Bull markets last nearly twice as long as bear markets. Stocks gain more in bull markets than they lose in bear markets. Therefore, the stock market, since its inception, has been in a long, overall upward trend.

As an investor, you need only to be aware of the current trend and the conversations about it; you do not need to be an expert on trends. By investing in quality stocks and holding them long term, you will be able to take advantage of the up trends and to weather the down trends.

Conclusion

When you hear "The market is moving up," or "The market is moving down," it sounds as if the prices of all publicly traded stocks are moving in the same direction at the same time. Yet, not all indices and averages move in step with one another. They are composed of different types of stocks whose prices move at different times. Blue chip stocks make up the DJIA. Smaller companies with a higher growth rate form the Nasdaq Composite Index. Therefore, in the short run these indices and averages may perform differently, yet in the long run they tend to move in the same direction.

To compare the performance of a stock you own to the performance of an index, choose an index or average that reflects the type of stock. For instance, if it is a small, high-growth stock, compare its performance with that of the Nasdaq Composite Index. If your stock is an airline stock, use the Dow Jones Transportation Average or the NYSE Transportation Index. If the index is advancing and your stock is not, find out why the stock is lagging. There may be good reasons to sell the stock or to keep it. Be informed.

As you follow the movements of stock market averages, you develop a better understanding of the action of your own portfolio. If your stocks are down, perhaps the entire market is down. Watching the whole market helps you keep things in perspective.

Summary

The following table summarizes the major indices and averages used to measure stock market movements.

	Indices and Averages	
Name	**Composition**	**Sub-indices**
Dow Jones Industrial Average	30 blue chip industrial stocks traded on the NYSE	
Dow Jones Transportation Average	20 transportation stocks traded on the NYSE	
Dow Jones Utility Average	15 utility stocks traded on the NYSE	
Dow Jones Composite Average	65 stocks—30 industrial, 20 transportation, 15 utility stocks—traded on the NYSE	
Dow Jones Global Stock Index	Approximately 2,800 actively traded, common stocks available for foreign ownership from 29 countries.	a. 8 regional indices b. 33 country indices c. 9 economic sector indices d. 124 industry indices
Standard & Poor's 500 Composite Stock Index	400 industrial, 20 transportation, 40 utility, and 40 financial stocks traded on the NYSE, the AMEX, and the Nasdaq	a. Industrial b. Transportation c. Utilities d. Financial
New York Stock Exchange Composite Index	All stocks— nearly 3,000— traded on the NYSE	a. Industrials b. Utilities c. Transportation d. Finance
Nasdaq Composite Index	The nearly 5,500 stocks traded on the Nasdaq Stock Market	a. Industrials b. Insurance c. Banks d. Computer e. Telecommunications
American Stock Exchange Market Value Index	The nearly 900 issues traded on the AMEX	a. Healthcare b. Financial c. Industrials d. Natural Resources e. Information Technologies
Russell 2000	2,000 smaller companies	
Value Line Composite Index	The nearly 1,700 stocks reviewed by the Value Line Investment Survey	a. Industrial b. Railroad c. Utility

Looking ahead

In the next chapter, *Stock Exchanges*, you will become acquainted with the two major exchanges, the NYSE and the AMEX. In addition, you will learn about a fast-growing, action-filled market—the Nasdaq Stock Market. While you are reading the next chapter, take a few minutes once or twice a week—more often if you wish—to track two or three of the indices or averages we have discussed. Use those in the following example or choose indices and averages to match the stocks you are following from Chapter 2.

Index Tracking Chart

Index:	DJIA			Index:	S&P	500	Index:	Nasdaq	Comp
Date	Close	Net change	% change	Close	Net change	% change	Close	Net change	% change
6/30	3516.08	– 2.77	– 0.08	450.53	– 0.16	– 0.04	703.95	+ 2.88	+ 0.41
7/1	3510.54	– 5.54	– 0.16	449.02	– 1.51	– 0.34	703.59	– 0.36	– 0.05
7/6	3449.93	– 34.04	– 0.98	441.43	– 4.41	– 0.99	702.22	– 2.27	– 0.32
7/7	3475.67	+ 25.74	+ 0.75	442.83	+ 1.40	+ 0.32	698.78	– 3.43	– 0.49

Index Tracking Chart

	Index: DJIA			Index: S&P 500			Index: Nasdaq Comp		
Date	Close	Net change	% change	Close	Net change	% change	Close	Net change	% change

Chapter 4

Stock exchanges

What you'll find in this chapter:

- ▸ The background of each exchange
- ▸ How Nasdaq differs from NYSE and AMEX
- ▸ Are stockbrokers necessary?
- ▸ How stock prices are determined
- ▸ ADRS—investing in foreign stocks

"What do you mean I can't just call up the exchange and buy 50 shares of Reebok! That I have to go through a stockbroker! Where did that practice come from?" In this chapter, Stock Exchanges, you will learn why you have to use a stockbroker and how the practice began. You will also learn how the New York Stock Exchange has become one of the dominant stock exchanges in the world. Furthermore, you will become acquainted with the exciting, fast-growing electronic market for trading stocks, the Nasdaq Stock Market.

DEFINITION

A *stock exchange* is a marketplace where members of the exchange buy and sell shares of stock for their customers—institutional investors and individual investors, like you. Because of the large number of people wanting to buy and sell shares of stock, the actual trading is done at the exchange by a limited number of individuals and firms who have paid for the right to trade stocks—they have bought a "seat" on the exchange.

When you are ready to buy a stock, a stockbroker in the brokerage office where you have an account, electronically transmits your order to the exchange that trades the stock. A member of the exchange immediately fills your order by purchasing the shares of stock you requested.

The stock exchange does not own the stocks that are traded on the exchange nor do the members of the exchange nor the brokers. Stocks are traded between investors—rather than between an investor and the exchange, an investor and the broker, or an investor and the company. The shares traded on an exchange are owned by investors and are bought and sold by members of the exchange for investors.

No one, including the exchange and the corporation, predetermines or sets the price for a stock. Members of the exchange, representing the buyers and the sellers, bid for the best price—the highest possible price for the seller and the lowest price for the buyer. Because several thousands of shares of each stock are traded daily, there are buyers competing for the lowest price and sellers competing for the highest price. Often, only an eighth or a sixteenth of a point separates the buy (bid) and the sell (asking) prices. This small difference becomes important when an investor is buying or selling several hundreds or thousands of shares.

> **HOT** spot All stocks are sold by auction on the floor of the exchange.

Organized exchanges, whether national or regional, function in much the same way. They merely differ in size and geographic emphasis. In the United States we have three national markets: the New York Stock Exchange, the American Stock Exchange, and the Nasdaq Stock Market. Other countries have their national exchanges, such as the Tokyo Stock Exchange, the Paris Bourse, and the London Exchange.

A regional exchange is much smaller than a national exchange and lists stocks of local or regional companies. A regional exchange also trades a limited number of stocks that are listed on the NYSE, the AMEX, and the Nasdaq—those that have a strong local following. The regional exchanges are the Pacific Stock Exchange (San Francisco and Los Angeles), the Chicago Stock Exchange, the Cincinnati Stock Exchange, the Philadelphia Stock Exchange, and the Boston Stock Exchange. Computers and telephones allow investors across the United States—from the most remote to the most populous places—to buy and sell stocks on any of the five regional exchanges or on either of the three national markets.

 Definition:

An *exchange* is considered a national exchange if it trades a large number of stocks and if its clients and its listed companies are representative of all parts of the country.

The New York Stock Exchange

 Located at 11 Wall Street, the New York Stock Exchange is the best-known and the most often quoted exchange in the United States. The NYSE, a national exchange, is known as the *Big Board* and *The Exchange*. How did it all start?

History

In 1790 Alexander Hamilton, secretary of the treasury, suggested the new federal government issue bonds to replace a group of old bonds that had been issued by the Continental Congress and by the thirteen colonies to pay for the Revolutionary War. Anyone who owned these Revolutionary War bonds, which by 1790 were of little value, would be able to exchange them for the new, higher-value bonds backed by the federal government. Bankers, congressmen, and speculators raced to buy up these old issues. Prior to this time, stocks and bonds were sold either by merchants in their stores or by auctioneers at street auctions where commodities—bundles of furs, bales of cotton and casks of sugar—were exchanged. With this surge in bond activity, brokers and auctioneers began to specialize in trading securities. They started public markets where only stocks and bonds were sold. People who wanted to speculate in these securities hired brokers to go to the auctions to buy and sell for them.

The next year, 1791, Hamilton gave the securities business another boost when he established the first national bank and issued stock for $100 a share. Financiers, brokers, and politicians rushed to buy and sell shares of the First Bank of United States. During the year the price rose to $195 a share. Later, when speculators sold their stock to take their profits, the stock fell to $108 in one month. The public created an uproar. They called the speculators' and politicians' profits scandalous.

As trading increased, the brokers became concerned that the auctioneers were taking over the securities market. By 1792 a group of brokers who met regularly at an auction held under the buttonwood tree at 68 Wall Street decided to bypass their competitors—the auctioneers. On May 7, 1792, after secret meetings and discussions, 24 brokers signed the Buttonwood Agreement which eventually put the auctioneers out of business. The brokers agreed to trade only among themselves, to forgo trading at other auctions, and to charge a minimum commission of one quarter of one percent on all sales of securities. The Buttonwood Agreement and the 24 brokers who signed the pact were the predecessors of the New York Stock Exchange. Still the case today, only members of the NYSE have the right to buy and sell securities on the floor of the Exchange. If non-members want to buy or sell a stock listed on the Exchange, they must engage a member to execute the trade for them. Members charge a fee—a commission—for their service. They charge for each buy and each sell.

The Buttonwood brokers continued trading outdoors under the tree until 1793. As soon as the Tontine Coffee House opened on the corner of Wall and Water Streets, they moved indoors and conducted their trading in an upstairs room. Although trading was active, the low volume did not provide enough income to support a broker. Thus, trading stocks and bonds was a part-time job—yet, it had become an organized activity.

In 1817 this same group of brokers adopted a constitution and created the New York Stock & Exchange Board (NYS&EB). Trading was conducted in a rented room at 40 Wall Street. During the trading day, from 11:00 a.m. to 1:00 p.m., the president of the Exchange called out each of the stocks on the list—approximately 30. Members shouted bids and offers from their assigned wooden arm chairs. The term "seat" on the exchange originated with these assigned seats.

Although the number of members of the NYS&EB increased from the original 24, the group continued to be an exclusive organization. An initial step toward membership was to gain experience as a broker or as a broker's clerk. The final step was to be voted in by the membership. Three votes against a prospective member would prevent his joining the Exchange. After all other requirements had been met, the initiation fee or the price for a seat on the Exchange was insignificant, only $25. However, by 1827 the price had risen to $100. By the late 1850s when many young men were wanting to become members of the Exchange, the membership fee was raised to $1,000. This effectively kept most of the younger generation from seeking membership on the exchange.

As new securities were added to the trading list, the volume steadily increased. The first railroad stock, the Mohawk and Hudson Railroad, began trading in August 1830. As the country expanded, other important stock and bond issues followed—millions of dollars' worth. Cities and towns issued municipal bonds to finance water, sewer, and lighting systems. Companies, as well as states, issued bonds to finance the building of roads, bridges, canals, and railroads. Banks and fire and marine insurance companies issued stock to finance their businesses. The average daily trading on the NYS&EB had increased from 100 shares in 1827 to 5,000 shares in 1834. By 1848 both a morning and an afternoon trading session were held.

In 1863 the Exchange changed its name from the New York Stock & Bond Exchange to the New York Stock Exchange. That same year it built its own building, its first permanent home, at 10 Broad Street just south of Wall Street. Its' new trading room was a small amphitheater where members, from their assigned seats, could easily see and hear the vice president call the stocks. By this time the stock call was held three times a day, and the membership initiation fee had risen to $3,000.

After the Civil War, stock and bond trading continued to prosper due to the westward expansion and the growth of railroad and manufacturing corporations. New exchanges sprang up; two of these, the Open Board of Brokers and the Government Bond Department were the most successful. They began to rival the NYSE. The Government Bond Department traded bonds that had been issued to pay for the defense of the Union. The Open Board of Brokers, the more serious challenger, rented a trading room next door to the NYSE. Again, the New York Stock Exchange was threatened by significant competition as it had been by the auctioneers in 1792. This time members of the NYSE decided to absorb their foes rather than eliminate them. In May 1869, the 354 members of the Open Board of Brokers and the 173 members of the Government Bond Department joined the 533 members of the New York Stock Exchange. The NYSE's position was once more secure.

The merger resulted in changes at the NYSE that continue today. First, the exchange tightened its rules for listing a security. It now required a company to have two separate entities to keep track of the shares that were bought and sold—a transfer agent and a registrar. This provides a system of checks and balances. The transfer agent records the trade, cancels the sold certificates, and reissues new certificates to the buyers. The registrar maintains a list of current stockholders and makes certain the number of shares bought equals the number of shares sold. Also, the registrar ensures that the total number of shares owned by investors does not exceed the number of shares issued by the company (overissue). Today, a commercial bank acts as the registrar and the company acts as the transfer agent.

Second, the New York Stock Exchange fixed the number of memberships or seats at 1,060 (currently 1,366) and established that seats on the Exchange were personal property. Members now owned their seats and could either bequeath them or sell them to approved individuals. Through the years, seats have sold for as little as $4,000 in 1876 and for as much as $1,750,000. The price individuals are willing to pay for a seat on the Exchange depends on the activity of the stock market—how much income the seat will generate. Prospective members carefully consider the market. Is it a bull or a bear market? Is the trading volume increasing or decreasing? How much money can be made from commissions, and how much can be made from buying and selling stocks for their own portfolios?

note Prior to 1869 companies had been known to sell shares that had not been issued—that didn't actually exist.

Third, the call-out method of trading ceased to work efficiently because of the large number of members and the increased number of listed stocks. By 1871 the NYSE began floor trading in a remodeled open room. Members dealing in a specific stock or type of stock stood in one place on the floor next to a pole. A sign on the pole indicated which stocks were traded by the dealer at that post. To fill a customer's order, members of the Exchange went to the appropriate post and made their bids and offers. It is done the same way today. The continuous trading of securities had begun.

Activity on the New York Stock Exchange continued to expand. In 1865, 500 stocks were listed on the Exchange and by 1900 there were 1,000. In 1867 there were 15 listed manufacturing stocks and by 1913 there were 191. In addition, the annual trading volume had increased from approximately 51 million shares in 1879 to nearly 104 million shares in 1885. After some ups and downs, the annual trading volume reached 265 million shares in 1901. Speculators, rather than long-term investors, continued to account for most of the trading.

note By 1901, the Exchange had once again outgrown its facilities. It purchased adjoining land, moved into temporary quarters, tore down the old exchange building, and built the current building located at 11 Wall Street.

As the volume on the NYSE increased, the Exchange became more sophisticated and self-regulated. For example, listed companies could no longer speculate in their own stock or in the stock of any of their subsidiaries. The Exchange insisted that listed companies give investors additional information. Thus, companies were requested to publish annual and quarterly income statements and to notify shareholders when new shares were being issued.

> **note** One of the most famous bull markets of all times started in 1922 and lasted until the Crash of 1929.

By 1921 the New York Stock Exchange had weathered World War I and the economic downturn that followed as production changed from war material to consumer goods. By 1922 the nation was ready for expansion and prosperity. Buying stocks became the popular thing to do. Brokerage offices opened in large cities and small towns across the country. More and more people entered the market and purchased stocks both for investment and for speculation. Before the war, an estimated one to two million people were stockholders; by 1929 between 10- and 20-million Americans owned stock. Speculators borrowed vast amounts of money to buy stocks; they assumed that stock prices would only go up—that the bull market was the wave of the future. In 1921 the annual volume on the NYSE was 171 million shares; by 1925 it had increased to 450 million shares, and by 1928 it had reached 920 million shares. The average price for a share of stock had risen 40 percent. The exchange added 275 new members to its roster and built new trading posts to handle the large volume of trading.

The crash began on October 23, 1929; the Dow Jones Industrial Average dropped 20.66 points as 6,000,000 shares were traded. Thursday, October 24th, the market fell 6.38 points as a record 12,894,650 shares were traded. Monday, October 28th, the Dow Jones Industrial Average fell 38.33 points (12.82%) on a volume of 9,500,000 shares. The DJIA fell farther on Monday than it had fallen the entire preceding week. Finally, on Tuesday, October 29th, the market plunged an additional 30.57 points (11.73%) on a new record volume of 16,410,030 shares. October 29, 1929, has become known as Black Tuesday, the day the stock market crashed. Extensive studies have been conducted and whole books have been written about the Crash of 1929, its causes, the Great Depression that followed, and the eventual long, slow recovery. If this subject interests you, your public library will have a number of good sources from which to choose.

> **HOT spot** On October 29, 1929, the "wave of the future" came to an abrupt end—the bubble burst. The stock market crashed.

During 1933 and 1934, following the stock market crash, the United States Senate conducted an in-depth investigation of the securities markets and the New York Stock Exchange. As a result of their findings, Congress enacted several new laws. For the first time, stock exchanges were subject to federal control. The Securities and Exchange Commission, a federal agency, was created to enforce the new federal securities laws. The SEC was charged with ensuring that securities markets were free of price manipulation and unfair practices. The SEC continues to play an important role in today's securities business.

Beginning in 1949, the economic expansion that followed World War II started one of the longest bull markets on record. During the 1950s, the New York Stock Exchange worked to bring investors back into the market. They stiffened the listing requirements for stocks and continued careful regulation of trading practices. To encourage individual investor participation, the Exchange ran advertisements in newspapers and magazines selling the financial merits of informed, long-term investing in stocks. To increase institutional participation, The Exchange successfully lobbied Congress to pass a bill that allowed money managers to invest a greater percentage of their portfolios in common stocks. This legislation led to a significant rise in trading volume. Yet, it was not until April 1968 that volume on the NYSE surpassed the previous record set on October 29, 1929.

During the 1970s and 1980s other changes took place. Congress created the Securities Investor Protection Corporation (SIPC). The SIPC, a nonprofit corporation, insures each investor's cash and securities that are deposited with a brokerage firm. They are insured against loss should the firm go bankrupt (not against market loss). The SIPC works much the same as the FDIC, which insures bank accounts against a bank's failure. An investor's account is insured up to $500,000. All brokerage firms registered with the Securities Exchange Commission, the NYSE and the AMEX must be members of the SIPC.

In 1975 the SEC required exchanges and brokers to abolish the system of fixed commission rates, the system that had existed since the Buttonwood Agreement of 1792. The competition in commission rates has given rise to discount brokers.

In 1978 the New York Stock Exchange passed a ruling that allowed members to lease their seats to non-members, who must meet the regular qualifications for membership. Leasing allows owners an opportunity to rent their seats and obtain income until they are ready to sell. On the other hand, leasing allows non-members access to floor trading without tying up their capital. Leasing allows others to acquire a seat on the Exchange for investment or speculative purposes. They buy the seat, lease it for income, and sell it when the price goes up. In 1997, 831 were members leasing their seats (*NYSE Fact Book*).

In the late 1970s, foreign brokers for the first time were allowed to become members of the NYSE. During the same period the Exchange began listing the stock of qualified foreign corporations.

In 1980 the New York Stock Exchange renovated its trading facilities at a cost of $24.5 million. They replaced the trading posts that had been used for 50 years with 14 up-to-date posts that could accommodate new computer, data processing, and high-tech communications equipment. Each post could now handle a greater load more efficiently—approximately 100 specific stocks are traded at each post.

The history of the New York Stock Exchange is to a large degree the history of stock trading in the United States. The NYSE, because of its preeminent position, will continue to mirror the growth and the changes that occur as investors buy and sell stocks in the years to come.

Board of directors

note

The New York Stock Exchange is governed by a 26-member board—a chairman, a president, and 24 directors. Members of the Exchange elect 12 directors from their membership and 12 directors from outside the Exchange who are not affiliated with brokers or dealers. Those elected to represent the public interest might be lawyers, officers of financial institutions, corporate officers and executives of traded and non-traded companies, and representatives from other public sectors. When electing directors, members of the Exchange must follow specific guidelines to ensure that various segments of the industry are represented and that no single segment dominates. The chairman of the board is chosen by the members of the board. To avoid conflict of interest while serving, the chairman may not belong to the Exchange nor be affiliated with a brokerage firm. The names of the current members of the board are listed in the annual fact book published by the NYSE.

Exchange membership

The New York Stock Exchange has 1,366 members, individuals who own seats on the Exchange. A firm's seat must be purchased in the name of an individual. To qualify for membership on the New York Stock Exchange the potential member must be sponsored by two current members and be able to meet significant financial criteria. In 1997 seats on the Exchange sold for a low of $1,175,000 and a high of $1,750,000 (*1997 NYSE Fact Book*). Some years as many as 28 seats have been sold and other years as few as 7.

Listing requirements

Before a stock can be listed on the New York Stock Exchange, the company must apply to The Exchange, meet the criteria for listing, and be accepted for trading. Each applicant is considered carefully and individually according to its own merits. Some of the factors the Exchange considers are:

✦ **Prominence**

- There is broad national interest in the company.
- The company is a member of an expanding or a stable industry.
- The company has a solid position within its industry.

+ **Earning power**

  • The company should have earned $2.5 million before taxes in the most recent year and at least $2 million in each of the previous two years.

+ **Market value**

  • The company's market value should be $40 million.

+ **Number of shares and shareholders**

  • The company should have at least 1,100,000 publicly traded shares and 2,000 stockholders who each own at least 100 shares.

For more detailed listing requirements refer to the annual *NYSE Fact Book*.

When a company is listed on the New York Stock Exchange, it gains prestige, publicity, and investor visibility. Some companies feel that a NYSE listing provides greater access to investors; more shareholders means additional customers for their products and a greater diversity in their company ownership.

Yet, some large companies, such as Intel and Microsoft, which qualify for listing on the NYSE, choose not to do so—they are happy to continue trading where they are. They feel that the additional expense, rules, regulations, and paperwork of an NYSE listing outweigh the benefits.

At the end of 1997, a total of 3,047 companies was listed on the New York Stock Exchange—1,628 industrial and service companies, 54 transportations, 278 utilities, and 1,087 finance and real estate companies. The five largest domestic companies were General Electric, Coca-Cola, Exxon, Merck, and Philip Morris. Of the listed companies, 356 (nearly 12 percent) were foreign corporations. More companies were from Europe (131) than from any geographic region outside the United States *(1997 NYSE Fact Book)*. Some of the well-known foreign corporations were Barclays, a British bank; British Airways; Smith-Kline Beecham, a British drug company; Schlumberger Limited, a Netherlands Antilles oil field service company; KLM Royal Dutch Airlines; Sony Corporation; Honda Motor Company; Moore Corporation, a Canadian business forms company; and Benetton Group, an Italian company that makes casual clothes.

Stock delistings

The New York Stock Exchange reserves the right to decide at any time whether a company will be permitted to continue trading on the exchange. However, removal is not an automatic process. Instead, the Exchange sends written notice to the corporation that a hearing will be held to discuss the matter. If it is determined, through evidence presented at the hearing, that

> **HOT spot** If a company violates the listing agreement or if the Exchange feels that continued trading of a particular stock is no longer in the public's best interest, the company is delisted.

the stock no longer qualifies for listing, written notice is sent to the corporation and to the SEC, and the stock is dropped. Generally, removal occurs because there is insufficient activity in the stock to merit continued trading on the NYSE. In 1997, the Exchange removed 183 companies and accepted 221 new listings (*NYSE Fact Book*).

Conclusion

The New York Stock Exchange is not only the largest United States exchange, but also one of the largest in the world. Its listing requirements are the most stringent. Of the more than 12,000 publicly traded domestic companies, the NYSE lists only 3,047. In addition to stocks, the NYSE lists bonds, warrants, rights, and options. Trading on the NYSE must follow all SEC rules and regulations, as well as federal and state laws that pertain to the securities industry. The New York Stock Exchange is open for trading from 9:30 a.m. to 4:00 p.m. (EST) five days a week excluding legal holidays.

The American Stock Exchange

The American Stock Exchange at 86 Trinity Place, three blocks from the New York Stock Exchange, specializes in listing mid-sized, growth companies and in trading derivative products (options, warrants). The AMEX is the second most important floor-trading exchange in the United States. However, it is significantly smaller than the NYSE.

History

The American Stock Exchange developed during the 1840s as a curbside market. The corner of Wall and Hanover Streets teemed with activity and eventually became clogged as the "curbstone brokers" congregated every day regardless of the weather to buy and sell stocks. Known as the Outdoor Curb Market or the Curb, it traded the stocks the NYSE considered too risky to list. Railroad and mining stocks were among the favorites.

During the 1870s, when the trading area became too congested at Wall and Hanover streets, the Outdoor Curb Market moved to the corner of William and Beaver Streets. By the 1890s it had moved to the corner of Wall and Broad Streets. It kept outgrowing its space on street corners, so it finally moved down Broad Street. Because Broad Street was wider than the surrounding streets, the curbstone brokers now had room to expand.

When the "Curb" moved down Broad Street many of the brokers rented office space in the Mills Building that overlooked the outdoor trading. In the offices, clerks took customers' orders by phone, then stood on the window sills or leaned out of the windows as far as they dared and shouted the orders to the firm's brokers in the street. The brokers wore distinctive colored derbies or jackets so they could be easily identified. On the street the brokers knew exactly where to go to trade a particular stock. Each stock or type of stock was traded under a specific lamp post. Pandemonium seemed to reign in the street with clerks shouting orders and brokers yelling out their bids and offers. As it became more and more difficult to hear and be heard, a system of hand signals evolved to indicate the number of shares and the price per share.

In 1908 Emanuel S. Mendels, one of the leading curbstone brokers, attempted to formally organize the curb trading. He founded the New York Curb Agency. The Agency, however, had no powers of enforcement so brokers paid little attention to its rules and regulations. Mendels' efforts to create a more orderly market were virtually unheeded. Yet, the idea had been planted, and the New York Curb Agency is considered a forerunner of the American Stock Exchange.

In 1911 Mendels once again tried to organize his fellow curbstone brokers—this time he succeeded. Mendels and a group of associates drew up a constitution, including formal trading rules, and established the New York Curb Market Association.

note Variations of the hand signals used by the Outdoor Curb Market—the forerunner to the American Stock Exchange— are still used today.

On June 27, 1921, the curbstone brokers finally moved indoors into their own building at 86 Trinity Place behind the Trinity Church, which is at the end of Wall Street. Their new trading floor retained some of the flavor of the outdoor market—the trading posts looked like the lamp posts on Broad Street. In addition to moving, the Association shortened its name to the New York Curb Market.

The New York Curb Market flourished throughout the boom of the 1920s. Its annual volume increased from 15.5 million shares in 1921 to 476 million shares in 1929. Likewise the demand for a seat on the exchange grew. In 1921 seats sold for $3,750 and by 1929 (before the crash) they were selling for $254,000. The exchange also updated its name in 1929—it became the New York Curb Exchange.

For 20 years after the Crash of 1929, the New York Curb Exchange felt the effects of the disaster. By 1942 the annual volume had fallen to 22.5 million shares and a seat on the exchange sold for a mere $650. During the bull market that followed the end of World War II, the New York Curb Exchange grew in importance and stature. In 1953, to reflect this wider recognition, the membership of the New York Curb Exchange voted to change its name to the American Stock Exchange.

By the late 1960s the bull market was coming to an end with the usual surge of speculation in smaller companies—the type listed on the American Stock Exchange. In 1968 nearly 1.5 billion shares were traded on the AMEX. This increase in volume represented a gain in market share from 12 percent of NYSE volume in the early 1940s to 47 percent in 1968.

The 1970s brought unwelcome changes for the American Stock Exchange. The ensuing bear market and the competition from the growing National Association of Securities Dealers Automated Quotations (NASDAQ) system—the forerunner of the Nasdaq Stock Market—wiped out the AMEX's gains in market share. To find a new niche in the securities industry, the American Stock Exchange began experimenting with trading stock options and other derivative products. Generally, stock options are bought and sold by speculators rather than by investors. Since 1975 the American Stock Exchange has been one of the leaders in listing and trading stock options.

Definition:

An *option* is the right to buy or sell a stock at a specified price within a stated time period.

During the 1980s and 1990s the American Stock Exchange faced increased competition from both the Nasdaq Stock Market and the NYSE. In the past, companies began public trading on the NASDAQ over-the-counter market. When companies had grown enough to qualify for listing on the AMEX, they moved to the exchange. The American Stock Exchange gave them access to floor trading, full price quotations in the newspaper, and increased corporate visibility. For many years the AMEX was a way station between the over-the-counter market and the New York Stock Exchange. In the 1990s, because of the Nasdaq Stock Market's efficient, computerized trading system and its fully detailed stock quotations, many companies remained with the Nasdaq Stock Market rather than moving to the AMEX. At the other end, the New York Stock Exchange lowered its listing requirements. Smaller companies, which would have previously listed on the AMEX, went to the NYSE instead. To meet this competition the AMEX increased the number and variety of derivative products, such as index and currency options and warrants, available for investors' trading.

 note Companies traded on the AMEX until they could fulfill the listing requirements for the New York Stock Exchange.

At the end of 1998, to alleviate its competitive struggle, the AMEX merged with the Nasdaq Stock Market. The Amex offers floor trading and the Nasdaq furnishes dealer-electronic trading as the new entity heads towards its goal of becoming a global Market of Markets.

Board of directors

The American Stock Exchange is governed by a 25-member board of directors. The board consists of the chairman, 12 members who represent the securities market industry, and 12 members who represent the public sector.

Exchange membership

The American Stock Exchange has 661 members. The record price paid for a membership or seat on the exchange was $420,000 in 1987. In 1996 seats sold for a low of $150,000 and a high of $210,000 (*1997 AMEX Fact Book*). Like seats on the NYSE, some AMEX seats are purchased for investment purposes and are leased to individuals or to brokerage firms. Most large brokerage firms are members of both the American Stock Exchange and the New York Stock Exchange.

Listing requirements

The American Stock Exchange specializes in listing small to mid-sized companies. The requirements for trading on the American Stock Exchange are less stringent than those for the New York Stock Exchange. For example, a company may have a pre-tax income of $750,000 during the two most recent years; a total of 500,000 publicly owned shares; 800 shareholders; and a share price of at least $3 (*1997 AMEX Fact Book*). In addition to these requirements, the exchange considers other relevant information about the company such as the company's past growth, its potential for future growth, and the quality and integrity of its management. If a company has demonstrated the ability to expand its sales and earnings and its future looks bright, it may be approved for trading even though it does not meet the numerical guidelines. On the other hand, even though a company satisfies all the quantitative criteria, it may not be accepted for listing. The exchange reserves the right to accept or reject any applicant.

> **note** Many companies listed on the American Stock Exchange are involved in banking, electronics, drug manufacturing, and oil and gas production.

Approximately 750 companies are listed on the American Stock Exchange. Nearly 8 percent are foreign corporations with Canada having the highest number (more than half). Some familiar domestic companies that trade on the AMEX are Viacom, Forest Laboratories, and Trans World Airlines.

Conclusion

The American Stock Exchange gives small, growing companies access to regular auction trading on the floor of an exchange. In addition to common stocks, the exchange lists corporate and government bonds, stock rights and options, commodity trust units, Super Units based on the S&P 500, and warrants on stocks, currencies, and foreign stock indices. The AMEX must follow all SEC rules and regulations as well as federal and state securities laws. The American Stock Exchange is open for trading Monday through Friday, excluding legal holidays, from 9:30 a.m. to 4:00 p.m. (EST).

The Nasdaq Stock Market

The Nasdaq Stock Market is an electronic marketplace. The "floor of the exchange" consists of more than 335,000 display terminals and 6,000 trading computer terminals located in the offices of securities firms across the United States and around the world. Stocks are bought and sold via computer screens rather than face-to-face on the floor of an exchange.

> **note**
>
> The Nasdaq Stock Market is the fastest-growing equities market.

Approximately 5,500 companies are listed—more companies than are listed on the New York Stock Exchange, the American Stock Exchange, and the regional exchanges combined. The dollar trading volume of the Nasdaq Stock Market ranks second in the world after the NYSE.

History

DEFINITION

The *Nasdaq Stock Market* is an outgrowth of the over-the-counter (OTC) market. An over-the-counter market is a securities market that trades those stocks not listed and traded on an exchange. The term "over-the-counter" seems to have originated during the 1800s when many companies whose stock was unlisted established their corporate offices or their treasurer's offices near the brokerage firms and the New York Stock Exchange on Wall Street. This site made it convenient for investors and speculators who wanted to buy these unlisted stocks to go to the company's office, walk up to a counter much like an old-fashioned bank teller's window, pay for the stocks, and receive the certificates over the counter.

The over-the-counter market later evolved into a market in which dealers bought and sold unlisted stocks for their own inventory. They made their living by continually trading—dealing in—the same stocks over an extended period of time. Some dealers operated from store-like offices in the exchange district and traded stocks over their front counters, which offers another possible explanation for the term "over-the-counter."

When the telephone came into use, the over-the-counter dealers discovered they could operate from offices located anyplace in the United States. Thus, the over-the-counter market developed into a nationwide network of competitive dealers making a market in unlisted stocks via telephone. Several dealers would *make a market* for the same stock by being willing to always buy and sell from their inventory. The transactions took place between the dealer and either a broker trading for a customer or another dealer buying for his own inventory. The price of the stock was determined by negotiation between the two individuals rather than by auction among many buyers and sellers on the floor of an exchange. The terms dealer and market maker are synonymous.

Buying and selling over-the-counter stocks was a time-consuming process for a broker. The OTC did not have a system for reporting the price of each trade; it did not have a ticker tape system like the New York Stock Exchange. The National Quotations Bureau, a private company, collected sales information and tentative bid and ask prices from market makers and mailed this information daily to stockbrokers on a sheet of thin, pink paper—hence the term pink sheets. When a customer wanted to buy a stock that was traded over the counter, the broker checked his pink sheet for the list of market makers and their telephone numbers. He then called four or five dealers to obtain their asking price. The broker reported this information to his client—the client then made his final decision regarding the purchase. To complete the trade the broker phoned the market maker with the best price, verified the current price, and made the trade. Often, while the broker was checking with the various dealers and with his customer, the stock price would change, which necessitated further price checking or canceling the trade altogether.

Because these stocks were speculative in nature, they afforded the stockholder an opportunity to make a great deal of money in a short time. Consequently, the popularity of the over-the-counter market grew despite the limited availability of price data and the time and effort needed to complete a trade. Eventually newspapers printed the stock prices in over-the-counter stock tables, but the information was minimal—the company name and the last trade price for only the most actively traded stocks.

In 1938 Congress passed a law that required the securities industry to self-regulate the activities of the over-the-counter market. Under the guidance of the Securities Exchange Commission, the industry created the National Association of Security Dealers (NASD).

In 1971 the National Association of Securities Dealers introduced a computerized trading system called the National Association of Securities Dealers Automated Quotation system. This electronic securities trading system transformed the over-the-counter market. The central computer system located in Trumbull, CT, uses interactive screens to connect investment bankers, securities firms, market makers, and brokerage offices around the world.

note The NASD has the power to make and enforce regulations that help to protect public and investor interests.

When a customer wants to trade an over-the-counter stock, the broker types in the ticker symbol and the computer screen instantly displays a list of the market makers with their firm bid and ask prices. The broker no longer has to price-shop by telephone. Instead, he simply chooses the best price, immediately communicates with the market maker via computer, and buys or sells the stock.

The NASD did not include all over-the-counter stocks on the NASDAQ system. Some remained as pink sheet stocks covered by the National Quotation

Bureau. These stocks tended to be the ones that traded for an unusually low price (as little as a fraction of a cent per share), traded only a few shares per day (100 shares or less), or traded infrequently (once a week or so), as well as quality companies whose stock traded on an irregular basis. Brokers still had to telephone market makers for firm bid and ask prices for these stocks.

Market makers deal in a stock at their own risk. Some dealers have made a market in the same stocks for years. They make their money on the difference between the bid and ask price—the spread. For example a stock may have a bid price of 40 and an ask price at 40-1/4; the spread would be 1/4 or $.25. Dealers buy at the bid price—the lower price—and sell at the ask price—the higher price. Consequently, investors buy at the ask price (the higher price) and sell at the bid price (the lower price).

| Bid 40 | Dealer's buying price | Investor's selling price |
| Ask 40-1/4 | Dealer's selling price | Investor's buying price |

Market makers constantly monitor each other's prices. For example, if a dealer's bid is lower than his competitors' bids, investors will not sell their stock at the lower price and the dealer will be unable to purchase any stock at that price. If a dealer's bid is higher than his rivals' bids, the dealer will be flooded with business. However, the business will be unwanted because the dealer will have to buy investors' shares at a higher price than his competition is paying.

> **HOT spot** Market makers vie with one another to offer the best bid and ask prices.

A market maker may be any securities firm that meets certain capital requirements and registers with the National Association of Securities Dealers. Dealers may discontinue trading a stock whenever they choose as long as they observe the notification regulations. Dealers are subject to rules and regulations made by the NASD and the SEC. Market makers include large retail brokerage firms such as Merrill Lynch and Prudential, institutional firms, and small regional and local firms. Making a market in an over-the-counter stock is one way in which a brokerage firm is able to increase its income.

In 1990, a major change took place in the securities industry when the National Association of Securities Dealers registered the name Nasdaq Stock Market as a service mark and created a new stock market from the over-the-counter stocks traded on the NASDAQ system. Stocks traded on the Nasdaq Stock Market are no longer considered over-the-counter because they are now listed on an "exchange." The Nasdaq Stock Market is a full-fledged, electronic stock exchange—a stock market where stocks are traded via computer and prices are determined through the competition of market makers. It is composed of two segments—the Nasdaq National Market and the Nasdaq Small Cap Market. The Nasdaq National Market lists approximately 4,100 actively traded stocks of larger, well-known companies. The Nasdaq Small Cap Market lists approximately 1,400 small, emerging growth companies. More than 500 dealers are involved in the Nasdaq Stock Market with an average of nine market makers per security (*The Nasdaq Stock Market 1997 Fact Book & Company Directory*). The Nasdaq is becoming one of the largest stock markets in the securities industry.

In 1990 when the NASD created the Nasdaq Stock Market, they also set up the OTC Bulletin Board in order to automate the trading of pink sheet stocks. Today, a list of market makers and current bid and ask prices for these over-the-counter, penny stocks can be displayed on a broker's computer screen. The electronic OTC Bulletin Board makes this group of stocks more accessible to investors. No connection exists between the Nasdaq Stock Market and the OTC Bulletin Board.

In 1998, the Nasdaq Stock Market acquired the American Stock Exchange. This gave the Nasdaq access to floor trading and to the AMEX's derivative products. Through the use of cutting-edge technology, increased foreign stock listings, and foreign stock exchange trading agreements, the Nasdaq-Amex is creating a seamless, international securities market. It will be a market where investors can trade at any time from any place in the world using one system called the Market of Markets.

Board of directors

The Nasdaq Stock Market is governed by a board of directors and its president. Half of the directors are elected from the membership and half from outside the securities industry.

Exchange membership

Individuals and brokerage firms do not own seats on the Nasdaq Stock Market. There are no seats. Instead, membership comes through an affiliation with the National Association of Securities Dealers. The NASD is the securities industry's self-regulatory organization that makes and enforces securities rules and regulations (under SEC supervision). By law, all firms and brokers that do business with the public must belong to the NASD. Because the NASD owns, operates, and regulates the Nasdaq Stock Market, it extends Nasdaq membership to all those who belong to the NASD.

Listing requirements

The listing guidelines for the Nasdaq National Market stocks, the larger companies, are as follows: net assets of $4 million with pretax income of $750,000, 500,000 publicly held shares with a minimum of 800 shareholders, each owning at least 100 shares, a minimum share price of $5, and two or more market makers. The company must additionally meet and follow certain corporate governance standards.

The listing requirements for the Nasdaq Small Cap Market, the second tier of stocks, are less rigorous than those for the Nasdaq National Market. They include the following: net assets of $4 million, 100,000 publicly held shares with a minimum of 300 shareholders, each owning at least 100 shares, a minimum price of $3 a share, and two or more market makers. These companies must also meet qualitative standards.

note

Companies that trade on the Nasdaq Stock Market tend to be small, rapid-growth companies in developing industries such as biotechnology and telecommunications. However, not all Nasdaq-listed companies are young companies—some are older, well-established firms such as SAFECO Corporation, incorporated in 1929, McCormick & Company in 1915, and Alexander & Baldwin in 1900. Some of the more mature industries represented on the Nasdaq are banking, financial services, and wholesale and retail trade.

Often, companies that have grown enough to qualify for a NYSE or AMEX listing choose to remain with the Nasdaq Stock Market. Some companies stay with the Nasdaq because of the lower listing fees. A few favor the less stringent financial disclosure and reporting requirements. Others like the stock pricing system of competing dealers rather than the system of floor traders used by the NYSE and the AMEX. Most often, companies feel they receive ample exposure on the Nasdaq Stock Market and do not wish to change their listing. Some of these large companies are household names such as Intel, Microsoft, Cisco Systems, MCI WorldCom, and Costco.

Conclusion

The National Association of Security Dealers created the Nasdaq Stock Market, a full-fledged electronic stock market, from the unlisted over-the-counter stocks that traded on the NASDAQ system. In a few short years, the Nasdaq has become a leader among world stock exchanges. It further strengthened its position with its merger with the American Stock Exchange. Each trading day, as part of its global vision, the Nasdaq begins operating its computer at Trumbull, CT, at 3:30 am (EST) when the London Stock Exchange opens. This allows investors in the United Kingdom to buy and sell stocks listed on the Nasdaq Stock Exchange through branch offices of NASD firms or through their affiliates in the United Kingdom. The Nasdaq Stock Market is open for domestic trading from 9:30 a.m. to 4:00 p.m. (EST) Monday through Friday excluding legal holidays.

Summary of the NYSE, AMEX, and Nasdaq

Category	NYSE[1]	AMEX[2]	Nasdaq[3]
Number of Members	1,366	661	All brokers and firms belonging to NASD
Price for a Seat on the Exchange	High $1,750,000 Low $1,175,000	High $210,000 Low $150,000	Any NASD membership fees
Average Daily Share Volume	526,925,000	22,158,216	543,700,000
Number of Listed Companies	3,047 including 343 foreign	751 including 61 foreign	5,556 including 418 foreign

Listing Requirements

Category	NYSE[1]	AMEX[2]	Nasdaq National Market Issues[3]	Nasdaq Small Cap Issues[3]
Net Assets	$40 M		$4M	$4 M
Pretax Income	$2.5 M	$750,000	$750,000	
Shares Outstanding	1.1 M	500,000	$500,000	100,000
Shareholders (100 shares)	2,000	800	800	300
Minimum Price		$3	$5	$3
Market Value	$40 M	$3 M	$3M	$1M
Market Makers			2	2

[1] *New York Stock Exchange Fact Book 1997 Data*   [2] *1997 AMEX Fact Book*
[3] *The Nasdaq Stock Market 1997 Fact Book & Company Directory*

Regional exchanges

DEFINITION

    Regional exchanges are local exchanges established in metropolitan areas outside New York City. There are five regional stock exchanges—Boston Stock Exchange (BSE), Philadelphia Stock Exchange (PHILX), Cincinnati Stock Exchange (CSE), Chicago Stock Exchange (CHX), and Pacific Stock Exchange (PSE). These exchanges focus their attention on stocks of small, local companies. In addition, they trade dual-listed stocks—stocks listed on the regional exchange and on either the NYSE, the AMEX, or the Nasdaq. Regional exchanges operate trading floors much like the NYSE and the AMEX, and are registered and regulated by the SEC.

History

    Beginning in the late 1800s most major cities had their own stock exchanges. These regional exchanges provided trading facilities for local corporations and investors. The trading floors and auction markets gave small companies, which could not qualify for listing on the NYSE or the AMEX, an opportunity to become publicly traded corporations within their own areas. Likewise, regional exchanges gave investors an opportunity to become shareholders in local firms.

    Regional stock exchanges flourished from the late 1800s until the late 1920s. During this period companies expanded rapidly. Many became publicly owned corporations and listed their stock on the local exchanges. The number of investors grew. More and more people bought stocks—local stocks as well as dual-listed stocks. When dealing in dual-listed stocks, brokers found they could often save time and money by trading on the local exchange. By the late 1920s business on the regional exchanges was growing at a fast pace. Then the stock market crashed.

During the depression of the 1930s and the early 1940s, regional stock exchanges struggled to stay in business. Many of the small, locally listed corporations went broke. Others merged with national firms and withdrew their regional listings. Often local brokerage firms were wiped out, including those that had been members of the exchange. Finally, most people no longer traded stocks—they had no money to invest. As a result, many local exchanges went out of business, or they joined other regional exchanges in order to survive.

Once again, from the early 1960s to the mid-1980s, regional stock exchanges faced a period of declining business. Because of a new nationwide electronic communication network, brokerage offices anywhere in the United States could instantly transmit their orders to a trader on the floor of the NYSE or the AMEX. This split-second, low-cost communications system decreased the need for and the dependence on regional stock exchanges. Trading on a national exchange had become as easy and as convenient as trading on the local exchange. Regional exchanges closed in Detroit, Wheeling, and Pittsburgh. In 1962, 14 regional stock exchanges were actively trading stocks. By 1986 only five SEC-registered regional stock exchanges remained. Those five regional stock exchanges remain active today.

The Chicago Stock Exchange

The Chicago Stock Exchange, the busiest regional exchange, is located in the center of Chicago's financial district. The Chicago Stock Exchange opened in 1882. Much of the trading on this new exchange involved shares of the Pullman Palace Car Company, the First National Bank of Chicago, and the Atchison, Topeka and Santa Fe Railroad.

In 1949 the Cleveland, St. Louis, and Minneapolis-St. Paul stock exchanges joined the Chicago exchange. As a result of this merger the Chicago Stock Exchange became the Midwest Stock Exchange. Ten years later the New Orleans Stock Exchange became part of the organization. In 1993 the Midwest Stock Exchange was renamed the Chicago Stock Exchange.

The Philadelphia Stock Exchange

The Philadelphia Stock Exchange is not only the oldest regional exchange— but also the oldest stock exchange in the United States. It was organized in 1790, two years before the brokers in New York City signed the Buttonwood Agreement.

For a while, due to a merger the Philadelphia Stock Exchange was known as the Philadelphia-Baltimore-Washington Stock Exchange. Later, to identify its location, the Board of Directors renamed it the Philadelphia Stock Exchange.

The Boston Stock Exchange

The Boston Stock Exchange, the third oldest exchange in the United States, opened in 1834. Traders who used this new exchange bought and sold stock in railroads, insurance companies, and New England banks.

The Cincinnati Stock Exchange

The Cincinnati Stock Exchange was founded in 1885. In 1995 it retained its name but moved to Chicago. Currently, it is the smallest regional exchange.

The Pacific Stock Exchange

The Pacific Stock Exchange, the only SEC-registered exchange west of the Mississippi, is the second largest regional exchange. It has two trading floors, one in Los Angeles and one in San Francisco. The Pacific Exchange was formed in 1956 as the result of a merger between the Los Angeles Stock Exchange (1899) and the San Francisco Stock Exchange (1882).

Exchange membership

Seats on a regional stock exchange are significantly less expensive than those on national exchanges. For example, when prices for a seat on the NYSE and AMEX were $2,000,000 and $660,000 respectively, the price for a seat on the Chicago Stock Exchange was $157,000—a more affordable expenditure for small brokerage firms. Membership on a regional exchange allows the brokerage firm to trade dual-listed stocks on the floor of the local exchange without going through a NYSE or AMEX member firm.

Listing requirements

Listing on a local exchange increases the company's visibility with financial analysts and investors in the area. Regional exchanges provide trading facilities for those local companies that want to participate in an auction market but are not large enough to qualify for the NYSE or AMEX. The Chicago Stock Exchange exclusively lists about 20 local corporations.

> *note* Each regional stock exchange has its own listing requirements. They are less stringent than those of the three national markets.

Most of the volume on a regional exchange comes from trading dual-listed stocks. Regional exchanges list the NYSE, AMEX, and Nasdaq stocks that are actively traded in the area. For example, the Chicago Stock Exchange dual-lists approximately 3,000 companies.

All trades of dual-listed stocks are directed through the Intermarket Trading System (ITS), an electronic system that links each regional exchange with the NYSE, the AMEX, and the Nasdaq Stock Market. Any transaction of a dual-listed security made on a regional exchange becomes part of the composite figures for the NYSE, AMEX, or Nasdaq. The hours of operation of the regional exchanges match those of the New York Stock Exchange with the exception of the Pacific Stock Exchange, which stays open an additional 30 minutes.

Foreign exchanges

At any time day or night somewhere in the world people are buying securities on a stock exchange. They may be trading on an exchange in Johannesburg, Warsaw, Bombay, or Sydney. Yet, the busiest exchanges are found in North America, western Europe, and Japan. Japan's leading market is the Tokyo Stock Exchange. The largest exchanges in western Europe are the London Exchange, the Paris Bourse, and the Frankfurt Stock Exchange.

The oldest exchange in the world is the Amsterdam Stock Exchange which began in 1611. The first company to obtain financing by selling its shares through a stock exchange was the United East India Company. It used its new capital to direct Holland's exploration of the East Indies—present-day Indonesia.

The London Exchange, also known as *The Stock Exchange* and the *International Stock Exchange London*, was not officially established until 1773 although it began trading securities sometime in the late 1600s. The London Exchange was the first major stock exchange to replace its trading floor with an electronic trading system.

In the developing countries of Asia, investors and speculators are trading shares on exchanges in Sri Lanka, Thailand, South Korea, Taiwan, the Philippines, Malaysia, and Indonesia. During the mid-1980s the government

HOT spot New and reactivated stock exchanges are appearing throughout the world as countries become more industrialized and move toward capitalism.

of China, in a move toward westernization, reopened the stock exchanges in Beijing and Shanghai and allowed the Chinese people to trade several securities. Before 1949, when the Communists closed the Shanghai Stock Exchange, it was one of the largest exchanges in the world.

Many eastern European countries that emerged from the old Soviet Union have privatized and sold shares of companies previously owned by the government. Stock exchanges have been reactivated in Prague, Warsaw, and Budapest. To begin with, these new exchanges operated only three days a week for two hours a day and listed fewer than two dozen stocks.

Buying foreign stocks

Foreign stocks are shares issued by foreign companies and listed on stock exchanges in the home country. Investors in the United States can participate in this market by purchasing foreign shares through a foreign exchange, through a mutual fund that specializes in foreign securities, or through American Depository Receipts, which are listed on the NYSE, AMEX, or Nasdaq Stock Market.

Stock quotes come from the foreign exchange and are reported in the foreign currency. Investors must deal through a foreign stockbroker. The shares, as well as the broker's commission and other fees, must be paid in the country's currency. It is also complicated to obtain timely and concise information about the company. Foreign exchanges and regulatory bodies do not impose the same high standards of accurate financial reporting that the SEC requires of companies listed on U.S. stock exchanges. If the company publishes an annual report, it will be written in the language of the country and will follow that country's accounting rules. Because foreign accounting procedures differ from those used in the United States, the data may be confusing and difficult to understand. Frequently, the annual reports and other disclosure statements do not contain enough information to give inexperienced investors a clear financial picture of the company.

The most direct but also the most complex way to invest in foreign companies is to purchase shares through a foreign stock exchange.

The fund's money manager deals with all the ins and outs of obtaining accurate financial information, judging the quality of companies, and making informed decisions about a country's economic and political stability. A mutual fund enables investors to indirectly own a diverse group of companies from a number of different countries. However, investors do not have an opportunity to choose specific companies.

If you want to decide whether to own part of Honda, Sony, or British Petroleum without the problems of trading through a foreign exchange, consider American Depository Receipts. ADRs, which are listed on the NYSE, the AMEX, and the Nasdaq Stock Market, are an easy, direct way to invest in shares of specific foreign companies. During the 1920s Morgan Guaranty Trust invented ADRs to overcome some of the obstacles in buying foreign stocks. An ADR represents shares of a foreign company (receipts) deposited in a foreign branch of a U.S. bank (depository). Another term used is American Depository Shares (ADS). Because many countries do not allow nonresident individuals to directly own stocks and remove the stock certificates from the country, ADRs make it possible for U.S. investors to take possession of a "stand-in" for the stock.

An indirect way to participate in foreign markets is to buy mutual funds that invest in foreign companies.

ADRs trade on the NYSE, AMEX, or the Nasdaq Stock Market just like shares of McDonald's. Their quoted prices, converted into dollars, are always very close to the company's share price on the home country exchange. When investors buy

> **note** An ADR is a convenient way for United States residents to buy foreign shares and an effective way for foreign companies to trade on a U.S. exchange.

an ADR, they receive an ADR certificate just like they would receive a domestic stock certificate. The ADR indicates that a stock certificate in their name is deposited in the foreign branch of the U.S. bank. ADR owners have the same rights as share owners in the foreign country—including voting by proxy.

The bank, as the depository, performs a variety of services for the company and for the ADR holders. The bank receives the dividends denominated in foreign currency, converts them to dollars, and sends the dividends to the U.S. holders. The bank also handles stock splits and dividends that are paid in stock. In addition, the bank sends the English translation of the company's annual report to its ADR holders. The annual report that is prepared for ADR holders must adhere to the same stringent guidelines required of all companies listed on a U.S. stock exchange.

More than 750 foreign companies list ADRs on U.S. stock exchanges. Some familiar names are Volvo, Sony, Hitachi, Elan Corporation, and De Beers. Those listed on the Nasdaq Stock Market are identified by the fifth letter of their ticker symbols—a Y (VOLVY). In some NYSE and AMEX stock tables the letters ADR or ADS follow the company name. Each year The Bank of New York publishes an updated, comprehensive list of ADRs titled *The Complete Depository Receipt Directory*. In addition to foreign companies that list ADRs, a few list their stock directly on the NYSE, AMEX, or Nasdaq Stock Market. However, because direct listing is time-consuming and costly, most companies prefer listing ADRs.

Conclusion

A stock exchange, whether in Budapest or New York City, is a marketplace for shares of stock listed on that exchange. Traders on the floor of the exchange, through an auction process, compete for the best buying or selling price for the customers they represent. Dealers on the Nasdaq Stock Market and other electronic markets vie for investors' orders by offering the best bid and ask prices.

> **note** A stock exchange makes it possible for individuals to easily buy and sell shares of any publicly traded company—shares that will further personal financial goals.

Think what it would be like if we each had to place a want ad in order to buy or sell a share of McDonalds—if we had to find our own buyer, bargain over the price, collect the money, and deliver the stock certificate. What an incredible organization a stock exchange is—an organization that automates the entire stock-trading operation for us!

Chapter 5

Story of a stock trade

What you'll find in this chapter:

⮚ Why and how companies go public

⮚ The role of the investment banker

⮚ Types of orders

⮚ Brokers and specialists

⮚ Automated trading systems

"It looks like such chaos on the floor of the New York Stock Exchange. It is amazing to me that traders can handle orders for 700 million shares a day. How do they do it? How can they possibly keep track of my order? In fact, what happens after I tell my broker I want to buy 100 shares of McDonald's?"

In this chapter you will follow an order as it leaves the broker's office, goes to the floor of the exchange, and returns as a confirmed trade. You will learn how computers and modern communication systems allow the NYSE to process orders for hundreds of millions of shares each day. First, however, discover how a company becomes a publicly traded corporation (goes public) so investors such as you and I can buy its stock.

Going public

DEFINITION

Going public is a term used to describe the series of events that occurs when a private company becomes a publicly traded corporation. Although approximately 12,000 companies in the United States are publicly traded, most corporations are privately owned.

A *private corporation* is owned by a small group of investors who hold all the issued shares. The group may be family members (a family-held corporation) or several people who started the firm, or the founder and three or four business associates (a closely held corporation). All owners must retain their shares as an investment and may not resell them to the public.

Decision to go public

When the owners of a private corporation plan a major expansion that requires substantial capital ($10 million or more), they may need to take the company public to raise the necessary funds. Their project—designed to significantly increase company sales and profits—may involve opening a series of new stores, constructing a new manufacturing plant, expanding the business internationally, or buying out the competition or a company that complements the existing business. This requires money for buildings, personnel, inventory, and machinery. Owners of a private corporation have limited access to large amounts of capital. They can use company profits, borrow from financial institutions, or take in additional private investors. If they are unable to obtain the capital from these sources, they must either reduce their growth plans or raise the money by going public.

Although private owners will retain enough stock to hold a controlling interest, they must share their ownership with thousands of public investors. These new investors will impact the way the company is run—the corporation must consider the wishes of its additional owners.

> **HOT** spot Going public creates critical changes in the corporation. Most importantly, private owners must relinquish their full control of the corporation.

note Furthermore, the corporation must comply with all Security Exchange Commission rules and regulations applicable to publicly traded companies. For example, the company must divulge vital data to its shareholders. Each quarter it must publish details about its sales, income, and debt level. Annually, it must disclose information about its operations, financial status, and competitive position within the industry. It must also report certain facts about its officers and directors—their salaries, fringe benefits, the number of shares they own. In a private corporation all such information is closely guarded. Now, competitors as well as shareholders will know what the company is doing and how it is faring.

Finally, analysts will closely examine the company's operations and will advise investors to buy or sell the company's stock. They will scrutinize and pass judgment on management decisions. The world will see the effects of those decisions—the successes and the failures. In brief, the corporation's business will no longer be confidential, and its private owners will no longer have complete control.

Despite the above disadvantages, the corporation will receive significant benefits from becoming a public corporation. First, the company will acquire the capital it needs to expand. (Also, some companies go public to obtain cash for day-to-day operations or money to pay down their long-term debt.) Second, the corporation's owners will be able to sell their shares of stock. They may want to liquidate part of their investment for retirement or diversification purposes. Third, the company will be able to offer stock options to its employees. Options are a way to attract, retain, and reward employees for their part in the growth of the company. It gives them a stake in the success of the business. Fourth, the company will increase its visibility in the corporate world. Its name will be in the business news as it reports its quarterly earnings, issues press releases to keep shareholders informed, and as analysts recommend its stock for purchase. Finally, many of its new individual shareholders will become loyal consumers and faithful long-term owners.

> **HOT spot** It is not surprising that many companies choose to remain private corporations and expand at a rate they can finance through borrowing or from corporate profits.

The process

Going public is a three-step process. First, the investment banker buys all the new shares directly from the corporation (primary market). Second, the investment banker resells those shares in smaller lots to individual and institutional investors (initial public offering). Third, public investors buy and sell the shares on the open market—an exchange—through their brokers (secondary market). Between these major events there are exciting intervening steps. Taking a private corporation public is a high-stakes game.

> **Definition:**
>
> *Going public* means selling shares of a private corporation to the public for the first time.

Investment banker

When a company goes public, the investment banking firm plays a leading role. The firm is neither an investor nor a banker in the familiar sense of the word. As an investor, the firm does not buy shares of stock to hold for the long term. As a banker, it does not accept deposits nor make loans. However, the firm provides the needed capital (a banking activity) by purchasing the stock from the company—underwriting the issue—and immediately reselling the shares to public investors (an investing activity). Three well-known investment banking firms are Goldman Sachs, Lehman Brothers, and Credit Suisse First Boston. Other investment banking firms such as Merrill Lynch, Salomon Smith Barney, and Morgan Stanley Dean Witter also have retail brokerage departments.

> **note** The SEC requires full disclosure of pertinent corporate information so investors can base their decisions on *accurate and complete* data.

Because the success of going public rests heavily with the investment banker, the corporation's owners carefully choose the firm. They interview and hold discussions with several. They look for the firm that will provide the best advice and the most thorough administrative work at the lowest cost. On the other hand, because the investment firm takes all the financial risk, it cautiously examines important aspects of the company's business and operations. After thoughtful consideration by both parties, an agreement is reached and the process is underway.

The investment banker's initial job is to advise. After the firm's research team thoroughly investigates the corporation—everything from financial records to employee turnover rate—the investment banker verifies the amount of capital the company needs, determines how much the company can expect to raise, and ascertains the best way to raise it, e.g., by selling corporate bonds (debt) or common or preferred stock (equity). The amount of capital the company can raise is based on the number of shares the company will put on the market and the initial price per share. The price depends on the corporation's profitability and financial condition, the product's quality and potential for growth, the industry's performance and the company's leadership within the industry, as well as on the current status of the economy and the activity of the stock market. It requires a great deal of expertise for an investment banker to determine the optimum price per share—a price at which the corporation can obtain the maximum capital as it sells its shares to the banking firm and a price at which the firm can immediately resell all shares to individual and institutional investors.

The investment banker's second responsibility is to oversee the administrative tasks involved in going public. For example, the firm's staff assists the corporate directors and attorneys as they collect the necessary data and prepare the documents required for the stock exchange listing and for the SEC registration. The SEC registration statement consists of two parts: Part I, the preliminary prospectus, Part II, additional financial data. Few individual investors know about or realize they can obtain copies of Part II. Institutional investors use it regularly to complete their analysis of a company.

The preliminary prospectus

The preliminary prospectus, Part I of the SEC Registration Statement, is a plain booklet containing the information required by the SEC for the benefit and protection of investors. As such, it is the investor's primary source of company information. It presents a short history of the company, specifies the company's intended use of the proceeds, and expresses the financial data in table form. It also describes the company's products and services, as well as its management, operations, and competitive position in the industry. In addition, a section titled Special Considerations, Investment Considerations, or Special Risks details and warns investors about potential risks the company faces. The final price negotiations between the investment banker and the corporate owners are not concluded until the day before the initial public offering (IPO). The offering date is not given because it cannot be set until the SEC accepts the corporation's registration.

> **note**
> The preliminary prospectus does not list the actual price per share. Instead, it quotes a narrow price range.

DEFINITION

The preliminary prospectus is known as a *red herring*, due to the notice printed in red along the left-hand margin of the cover. It states that the registration has been filed with the SEC but has not yet been accepted. Therefore, the information in the prospectus is subject to change. Furthermore, it declares that the prospectus is not an offer to sell the shares and warns investors that brokers may not take orders nor sell the shares until the registration becomes effective. (It is against the law to sell unregistered securities.)

The cooling-off period

The cooling-off period is the time during which the SEC examines the corporate registration statement. The SEC staff scrutinizes all documents. They determine if the company has met the strict disclosure standards and if the information has been presented fairly and accurately. They may ask the company to add information or to change wording that might be misleading. Later, if investors lose money because their decisions were based on prospectus information that proved to be false or misleading, charges may be filed against the entity providing the information. In jeopardy are corporate officers, investment bankers, independent accounting firms, members of the underwriting groups, or others whose names appear in the prospectus, but not the SEC.

> **note**
> The SEC does not evaluate the company nor judge its merit as an investment. Neither does it attest that the company is free from fraud—only that it has met the disclosure requirements.

The underwriting group

During the cooling-off period, the investment banker forms a purchasing group. Rather than underwriting the entire issue—buying all the millions of shares—the firm may choose to reduce its risk by including other investment bankers. An underwriting firm is at risk during the time it owns the newly issued shares. It may be unable to quickly market them to individual and institutional investors at the preset initial offering price. If the firm misjudges the demand for the new stock and sets the price too high, or if the market declines suddenly, the firm is left holding the overpriced shares and will lose a significant amount of money on the secondary market.

DEFINITION

A *purchasing group*, called an underwriting group or syndicate, spreads this risk among the participating investment bankers. Each syndicate member contracts to purchase a specific number of shares based on its level of involvement—each is responsible for its unsold shares. Because underwriting can be lucrative, smaller investment firms are anxious to join a syndicate. It gives them an opportunity to participate in a significant offering and to prove themselves in the industry. If the offering is particularly large or risky, the underwriting manager may also form a selling group to help move the shares. The selling group, composed of several sizable retail brokerage firms, is not part of the syndicate. The retail firms incur no financial risk and have no responsibility for unsold shares. However, if they want to receive additional invitations, they must successfully place their allocated shares. Participation in a selling group is desirable because it gives the firms an opportunity to sell large blocks of stock for fees that are higher than the standard commission rate.

Despite the risks, underwriting and going public can be financially rewarding for all parties involved—the private corporation, the investment banker, the syndicate member, and the selling group. For example, XYZ Corporation with the help of its investment banker has determined it will issue and sell eight million shares at the negotiated price of $15.50 per share to raise $124 million for its expansion project. As soon as the company and the firm agree on the price per share, the company knows exactly how much capital it will receive—the company is assured of that exact amount. As a unit the syndicate buys the shares from XYZ and immediately pays the company in full.

The investment banker and the syndicate members cover their costs and make their money on the underwriting spread—the difference between the purchase price and the selling price. They buy the shares from XYZ Corporation at $15.50 per share, and they sell them at the initial public offering price of $16.50—a spread of $1.00. (You can find actual underwriting fees and spreads for initial public offerings in the *Investment Dealers Digest*.) The spread may be allocated as follows:

The managing underwriting firm—the principal underwriter—receives:

- $.25 for each of the eight million shares—a manager's fee

- $.75 for each share it underwrites and sells

- $.25 for each share it underwrites, distributes to the selling group, and the group actually sells

Syndicate member firms receive:

- $.75 for each share they underwrite and sell

- $.25 for each share they underwrite, distribute to the selling group, and the group sells.

Selling group firms receive: shares they sell.

- $.50 for each

Marketing the issue

During the latter half of the cooling-off period, members of the syndicate and the selling group begin contacting their clients, individual and institutional, to begin pre-selling the new shares of XYZ Corporation. They go through their customer lists, identify potential purchasers, and begin making calls. Their calls are merely to inform their clients of the offering. They may not solicit or take orders until the SEC has approved the corporation's registration. In fact, at this time they may not send nor give the prospectus to customers unless an investor requests a copy. In addition, there can be no advertising nor mass marketing of any kind and the company may not issue any statements that are not contained in the preliminary prospectus.

 Definition:

Although syndicate members may not visibly market the issue, they may accept a client's indication of interest or intent to purchase a specific number of shares, which is called *pre-selling the issue.*

To further market the issue, the investment banker, two or three corporate officers, and an investment analyst take the company story on the road. This group carefully prepares and rehearses its presentation. For two weeks the team travels from one end of the country to the other courting analysts, mutual fund managers, retirement and pension fund managers, and other institutional investors. This is an intense and grueling time for the presenters. Each day they conduct four to six high-stakes, face-to-face meetings with large investors. These institutional investors listen critically to the presentation, ask pointed, difficult questions, and carefully inspect Parts I and II of the preliminary prospectus. If they determine that the corporation's stock will be an attractive addition to their portfolios, they indicate their intent to purchase a specific number of shares.

Front cover of a preliminary prospectus

Subject to Completion
Preliminary Prospectus dated October 18, 1999

PROSPECTUS

7,700,000 Shares

Finisar

Common Stock

This is Finisar Corporation's initial public offering.

We expect the public offering price to be between $12.00 and $14.00 per share. Currently, no public market exists for the shares. After pricing of this offering, we expect that the common stock will trade on the Nasdaq National Market under the symbol "FNSR."

Investing in the common stock involves risks that are described in the "Risk Factors" section beginning on page 5 of this prospectus.

	Per Share	Total
Public offering price	$	$
Underwriting discount	$	$
Proceeds, before expenses, to Finisar Corporation	$	$

The underwriters may also purchase up to an additional 1,155,000 shares from some of our stockholders at the public offering price, less the underwriting discount, within 30 days from the date of this prospectus to cover over-allotments. We will not receive any of the proceeds from any shares that may be sold by the selling stockholders.

Neither the Securities and Exchange Commission nor any state securities commission has approved or disapproved of these securities or determined if this prospectus is truthful or complete. Any representation to the contrary is a criminal offense.

The shares will be ready for delivery on or about   , 1999.

Merrill Lynch & Co.
J.P. Morgan & Co.
Dain Rauscher Wessels
a division of Dain Rauscher Incorporated

Morgan Keegan & Company, Inc.
SoundView Technology Group

The date of this prospectus is   , 1999.

Front cover of a final prospectus

PROSPECTUS

8,150,000 Shares

F i n i s a r

Common Stock

This is Finisar Corporation's initial public offering.

Prior to the offering, no public market existed for the shares. The common stock has been approved for listing on the Nasdaq National Market under the symbol "FNSR."

Investing in the common stock involves risks that are described in the "Risk Factors" section beginning on page 5 of this prospectus.

	Per Share	Total
Public offering price	$19.00	$154,850,000
Underwriting discount	$1.33	$10,839,500
Proceeds, before expenses, to Finisar Corporation	$17.67	$144,010,500

The underwriters may also purchase up to an additional 1,155,000 shares from Finisar and several of our stockholders at the public offering price, less the underwriting discount, within 30 days from the date of this prospectus to cover over-allotments. We will not receive any of the proceeds from any shares that may be sold by the selling stockholders.

Neither the Securities and Exchange Commission nor any state securities commission has approved or disapproved of these securities or determined if this prospectus is truthful or complete. Any representation to the contrary is a criminal offense.

The shares will be ready for delivery on or about November 17, 1999.

Merrill Lynch & Co.
J.P. Morgan & Co.
Dain Rauscher Wessels
Morgan Keegan & Company, Inc.
SoundView Technology Group

The date of this prospectus is November 11, 1999.

If your broker contacts you about a new issue, you can be sure his or her firm is a member of the underwriting syndicate or a member of the selling group. Remember, the firm has a specific number of shares it must sell. To reduce its financial risk, it would like to pre-sell all its shares before the stock begins trading on the exchange.

HOT spot The stock may or may not be a good investment for you. Request a prospectus, read it carefully, and determine if the stock fits your investment criteria.

- **Effective date:** The effective date or acceptance date—usually 20 days from the date listed on the preliminary prospectus—is the day the SEC formally accepts the company's registration. The shares are legally registered with the SEC and may be officially offered for sale. This marks the end of the cooling-off period.

- **Final meeting:** The evening of the effective date, the lead underwriter and the corporate owners hold their final meeting. For the owners this climaxes the arduous, yet exciting, process of taking their company public. One of the first items on the agenda is to establish the initial public offering date. This decision sets the remainder of the process in motion. The IPO date is usually the following day, the day after the effective date.

- **Initial offering price:** After the lead underwriter and the owners have set the IPO date and reaffirmed the terms of the underwriting agreement, they negotiate the initial offering price. The results of both the road show and the brokers' pre-selling calls to investors play an important role in assessing demand for the stock and determining its price. Millions of dollars are at stake. A difference of $0.50 per share for eight million shares means an

note The company's owners want to set the price as high as possible so they can obtain the maximum amount of capital.

increase or a decrease of $4 million in capital. On the other hand, the underwriters want to set it low enough so they can quickly sell their holdings. If the shares are overpriced, based on investor demand, the price will drop on the open market and the underwriters will have difficulty moving their remaining stock. In fact, they may have to dispose of it at a loss. However, if the price is set too low, the shares may become a hot issue the first day of trading. Demand for them will outpace supply and the price will quickly rise. Consequently, the company could have received additional capital if the public's evaluation of the stock had been accurately judged.

- **Final prospectus:** The lead underwriter and the company's owners review the wording of the prospectus, which is the final version of the preliminary prospectus. They add the share price and the offering date and make any changes required by the SEC. The prospectus is immediately delivered to the printers so it can be completed and ready for investors the next day—the IPO date. Because the final prospectus is a formal offer to sell the new issue, the SEC requires that investors be given a copy before they purchase the shares or receive a copy with the written trade confirmation. However, because the prospectus seldom appears in the mail before the purchase is final, the SEC has established a grace period for IPOs.

> **E-Z TIP** When the final prospectus arrives, if the investor finds a change from the preliminary prospectus that he or she does not like, the investor may renege on the stock purchase.

- **Tombstone:** Next, the underwriter and the owners turn their attention to the advertisement of the IPO—the tombstone announcement. They add the share price and the IPO date, proof the copy, and deliver it to the financial newspapers for publication the following day. Because the SEC forbids IPO advertising and company promotional publicity during the quiet period, which extends from the pre-underwriting decision to 40 or 90 days after the effective date, a tombstone gives limited information about the new issue. Its somber layout is said to have originally reminded people of a gravestone. An investor can recognize a tombstone by its black-lined border. At the top of the tombstone a disclaimer states that the tombstone is merely an announcement and not an offer to sell nor a solicitation of an order to buy the shares—the offering can be made only by the prospectus. The announcement states the number of shares, the offering date, the name of the company, the type of issue, and the price per share. It also lists the members of the syndicate. The name of the managing underwriter is given first followed by the names of syndicate members arranged alphabetically within groups according to the size of their involvement. An investor can obtain a copy of the prospectus from any listed underwriter.

A Tombstone

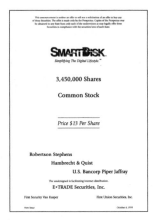

- *Wall Street Journal*

- **Primary market:** The climax of the final meeting is the primary market—an event rather than a location. The primary market is the direct sale of the company's newly issued shares to the lead underwriter at the negotiated price. This is the only time the company receives money from the sale of these shares. The underwriter pays the corporation in full and the corporation transfers the shares. All papers are signed and the transaction is completed. The corporate owners have concluded their part of going public. They have sold a portion of their company ownership for the capital they needed to expand. They will now share their control of the corporation with public shareholders.

Definition:

The *initial public offering (or IPO)* is the purchase of the company's shares by individual and institutional investors directly from the underwriters and members of the selling group at the company-underwriter negotiated price plus the underwriting spread.

- **Initial public offering (IPO):** Although the corporate owners have finished their work, the lead underwriter and members of the syndicate and selling group face another critical day—the public offering day. Early that morning, the sales force calls those clients who have expressed an intent to buy—who have prepurchased shares. Brokers confirm the number of shares and process the orders. As soon as the shares are transferred, sometime midmorning, public trading begins and the initial public offering is concluded.

- **Secondary market:** The initial public offering date is the first day the company's shares trade on the secondary market—on an exchange. The secondary market is the public trading of stock between investors through their brokers on an exchange at the market-determined price. The proceeds from these trades go to the individual and institutional investors who sell their shares.

If public investors are slow to invest in the company's stock during its first days of trading on the secondary market and the price slumps, it is considered a weak issue. The underwriters can legally try to stabilize it to avoid further loss on their unsold shares. The prospectus states how they will do this. Often, the lead underwriter enters a bid to buy shares at or just below the offering price but not above it. Investors who bought their shares at the initial public offering see the buy offer, cease to worry, and decide to keep their stock. In other words, they do not dump or flip their shares and drive the price lower. Brokers and underwriters frown on investors who flip IPO shares, particularly in a weak market for the stock. Those investors may not be included in the next IPO. The shares are to be held as a longer-term investment.

Syndicate members move on to other IPOs as soon as they have finished selling their allotted shares either during the initial public offering or afterward on the secondary market. The lead underwriting firm, however, often remains involved with the company. It continues to make a market in the company's stock and to advise the corporation about public ownership.

In the years to come, if the corporation wants to raise additional funds, its board of directors and shareholders vote to issue (create) several million new shares. To sell these new shares to the public—to do this stock offering—the company goes through much the same process as going public. Often, the company returns to the underwriting firm that managed the first stock issue and asks it to handle the new issue.

To the individual investor

As with any stock, carefully investigate the IPO. It may be a small company that needs to raise capital for growth, a successful privately held corporation whose owners want to liquidate part of their holdings, or a new stock issue from a company that has traded publicly for five years or for 25

HOT spot Going public does not necessarily mean it is a solid company with a quality product or service. It simply means the corporation is sound enough to get its shares on the market.

years. Obtain a copy of the prospectus from any underwriter and read it thoughtfully. Does the company meet your standards?

Sometimes with high-tech offerings the company may not have made a profit yet. Other times the company's product may still be in the development or the testing stage and may or may not work. Learn as much as you can about the company, its product or service, its competitors, and its industry. If you are interested in buying shares, work through your broker. You can buy the stock as an initial public offering if your brokerage account is with one of the underwriters or if your broker has a business relationship with a syndicate member. If the issue is hot, it may be difficult to secure IPO shares. The underwriters and brokers save their allotted shares for their best customers. (However, the SEC forbids underwriters from withholding shares to later sell at the higher price on the secondary market.) If you are unable to obtain shares, you can buy them as soon as the stock begins trading on the exchange the morning of the IPO.

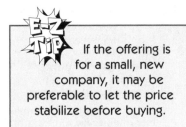

If the offering is for a small, new company, it may be preferable to let the price stabilize before buying.

When buying an IPO from the underwriter, you pay no commission because it is part of the stated price. The commission is the predetermined amount the broker receives from the spread. The price is the same from any underwriter or member of the selling group. This is the only time a stock price is preset or fixed.

IPOs tend to sell at the same or a lower price several weeks after the initial public offering. An effective sales effort can create an inflated interest and demand for the stock. Consequently, the company may not live up to the expectations. Hot IPOs are like other hot tips—very few remain hot for the long term.

Summary of going public

- **Going public:** The first time a privately owned corporation sells its stock to public investors. The process begins when the company chooses an investment banker and ends when the underwriters have sold their shares to individual and institutional investors.

- **Registration date:** The day the company formally files its documents with the SEC seeking approval for the sale of its new shares.

- **Cooling-Off period:** The interlude between the registration date and the effective date. The SEC examines the company's registration papers;

the underwriters create interest in the offering and pre-sell the shares by accepting statements of intent to purchase.

- **Effective date:** The day the SEC approves the corporation's registration papers. The first day the shares may be formally offered for sale.

- **Initial public offering:** The first time the company sells its shares to the public—opens its ownership to public investors.

- **Primary market:** The sale of the shares and the transfer of money between the corporation and the investment banker.

- **Initial public offering date:** The day the underwriters formally sell the new shares to individual and institutional investors at the preset price.

- **Secondary market:** The trading of company shares on the stock exchange between public investors through brokers.

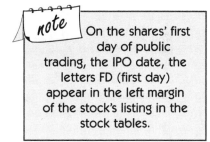

note On the shares' first day of public trading, the IPO date, the letters FD (first day) appear in the left margin of the stock's listing in the stock tables.

A stock trade

You have decided to buy shares of XYZ Corporation, McDonald's Corporation, or one of the other 12,000 publicly traded companies, but you have a concern about the trade. You ask, "How can the New York Stock Exchange possibly keep track of orders for 500, 600 or 700 million shares a day without losing any, particularly mine? In pictures of the floor of the NYSE the trading area is littered with thousands of pieces of paper. How do I know one of them is not my order, lost, forgotten, and unfilled?" To ease your mind and to learn how stocks are bought and sold on an exchange, follow a trade on the floor of the New York Stock Exchange, then, follow the same trade as it moves through the NYSE's automated trading system.

A trade on the floor of the New York Stock Exchange

The New York Stock Exchange, as well as the American, Nasdaq, and five regional exchanges, have organized and perfected trading to make buying and selling shares nearly error-free whether on the automated system or on the floor of the exchange. The exchanges, the SEC, and the National Association of

Securities Dealers have instituted many checks and balances to protect investors. These include the requirement that trading personnel accept responsibility for their own mistakes at no loss to the investor.

When investors think of buying or selling stocks on an exchange, images of the floor of the New York Stock Exchange come to mind. What seems to be total confusion is actually a highly organized, specialized, and closely regulated activity. The chart and explanation below illustrate the traditional method of trading on the floor of the NYSE:

A STOCK TRADE ON THE FLOOR
OF THE NEW YORK STOCK EXCHANGE

Every buy involves a sell.

Every sell involves a buy.

Seller	New York Stock Exchange	Buyer
1) George decides to sell 100 shares of McDonald's. He becomes the **seller**.		1) Mabel decides to buy 100 shares of McDonald's. She becomes the **buyer.**
2) He calls his **broker** at Wedbush to check the price.		2) She calls her **broker** at Merrill Lynch to check the price.
3) George places a **market order** with his broker to sell 100 shares of McDonald's.		3) Mabel places a **market order** with her broker to buy 100 shares of McDonald's.

Seller	New York Stock Exchange	Buyer
4) The broker makes out the sell **order ticket.**		4) The broker makes out the buy **order ticket.**
5) The order is transmitted to the **brokerage firm's central order department** and routed to the floor of the NYSE.		5) The order is transmitted to the **brokerage firm's central order department** and routed to the floor of the NYSE.
	6) The orders arrive at each firm's **booth** on the floor of the New York Stock Exchange.	
	7) Each firm's **floor broker** picks up the orders.	
	8) The floor brokers take the orders to the **trading post** where shares of McDonald's are bought and sold.	
	9) At the post, the **specialist,** who handles McDonald's stock for the exchange, oversees and maintains an orderly market for the shares.	
	10) Through an **auction** process, the floor brokers reach a mutually acceptable price for their firms' clients.	

Seller	New York Stock Exchange	Buyer
	11) The **floor reporter** records the details of the trade. 12) The floor brokers send the **trade confirmations** to their firms' booths. The booth clerks forward the information to their firms' central order rooms.	
13) The central order room at Wedbush Morgan Securities receives the trade confirmation and forwards it to the branch office in Alaska.		13) The central order room at Merrill Lynch receives the trade confirmation and forwards it to the branch office in Florida.
14) The broker in Anchorage calls George to let him know that his 100 shares of McDonald's have been sold at 62 $^{3}/_{16}$.		14) The broker in Tampa Bay calls Mabel to let her know her buy order for 100 shares of McDonald's has been filled at 62 $^{3}/_{16}$.

1) Seller and buyer

Each stock trade requires both a buyer *and* a seller. There cannot be one without the other. If McDonald's volume is listed in the stock tables as 31434, it means that 3,143,400 shares were traded by matching buy and sell orders.

The buyer and the seller may be from anywhere in the United States or the world. For this trade, the seller, George, is a pipeline worker in Alaska, and the buyer, Mabel, is a new retiree enjoying the Florida sun. Unknown to each other, like thousands of other investors, they decide on a particular day at a particular time to buy and sell shares of McDonald's.

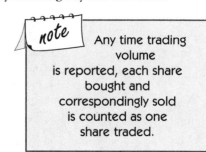

note Any time trading volume is reported, each share bought and correspondingly sold is counted as one share traded.

2) Brokers

Rather than advertising for a buyer or a seller, negotiating a price, and recording the trade, George and Mabel merely call the brokerage offices where they have accounts and place orders with their brokers. George calls his broker at Wedbush Morgan Securities, and Mabel calls hers at Merrill Lynch. Their brokers check the current price for McDonald's. The last trade was at $62\text{-}1/8$ —up $1/8$. Each investor decides the price is right—it is time to trade. George is a relatively new investor. McDonald's was one of his original stocks. He is now involved in the oil industry, is learning about it, and is ready to sell McDonald's to buy an oil stock. Mabel, with a background in a high-tech industry, has invested in a number of rapid-growth stocks over the years and wants to add more long-term growth and stability to her portfolio.

3) Market order

George places a market order with his broker to sell 100 shares of McDonald's, and Mabel asks her broker to buy 100 shares of McDonald's "at the market." Both know that once they place a market order, it is very difficult to cancel. A *market order*, also called "at the market," is by far

DEFINITION

the most widely used type of order. It tells the broker to buy or sell the shares immediately at the best available price. Neither George nor Mabel know what their actual trade price will be. Most likely, it will be close (1/8-1/4 point) to the quote they received from their brokers just before they placed their orders. However,

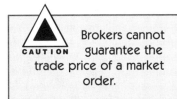

Brokers cannot guarantee the trade price of a market order.

it depends on how the price is moving. If the shares are unavailable at the last price, their orders will be filled at the next available price, either up or down.

Investors use a market order to buy when the stock price is rising, and a market order to sell when the price is declining rapidly. They also use market orders when they want their orders filled immediately. Instead of placing market orders, George and Mabel could have entered either limit or stop orders.

DEFINITION

- **Limit order:** By using a *limit order*, investors can choose the specific price at which they want to buy or sell, a price "away from the market"—a better price than is currently available and one they feel will be reached in a reasonable time. The order states the limit, the maximum the investor is willing to pay if buying and the minimum the investor is willing to accept if selling. Bill, another investor who is interested in buying McDonald's, has noticed the stock has been trading between 59-1/2 and 63-1/8. He believes the price will again drift down at least to 59-3/4 sometime within the next two or three months. Therefore, he enters a buy limit order for 100 shares at 59-3/4 and goes on vacation. When the price hits 59-3/4, his limit order to buy is triggered and filled at 59-3/4 or lower (never at a higher price).

This sounds simple, and it can be, with market knowledge and skill at setting limit prices.

CAUTION

Limit orders, however, do involve risk. First, the price may not be reached. For example, McDonald's drops to 59-7/8, turns around, and continues to rise—Bill misses the rise. Second, the price may be reached, but the order is not filled because the selling demand is satisfied by orders to buy that had been placed before Bill's. Limit orders are filled on a first-in-first-out (FIFO) basis. The unfilled limit orders stay on the books and move forward in line. Perhaps next time when the price dips to 59-3/4, if it does, Bill's buy limit order will be filled. Finally, the price may be reached, Bill's order filled, and the stock continues to fall. In this situation, it might have been better if Bill had tracked the price and entered a market order when the decline ended. These conditions also hold true for limit orders to sell, but the direction is reversed with share owners setting the limit price above the stock's current market price.

Investors may change or cancel a limit order at any time. They can change limit prices by having their broker cancel the current order and enter a new order with the preferred price. If investors decided to trade immediately, they can cancel the limit order and enter a market order. Or, if they determine they do not want to buy or sell at all, they can simply cancel the order.

Attached to limit orders are instructions that state the length of time the orders are to remain in effect—day, or good 'til canceled (GTC). A day order is good for the specific day it is entered. If it is not filled by the end of the day, it is canceled. All limit orders are day orders unless otherwise specified. A good 'til canceled order, also called an open order, is stated as "buy 100 MCD at 59 3/4 GTC." It remains in effect until it is filled or until the investor instructs a broker to cancel it. Most brokerage firms require clients to reconfirm good 'til canceled orders monthly or quarterly. The NYSE requires confirmation semiannually.

Limit orders allow investors who are willing to wait for the market to buy and sell at prices better than the current market. Investors use limit orders to buy at a specific price (or lower) when the price is drifting down and to sell at a specific price (or higher) when the price is slowly rising. They also use limit orders to buy and sell when the price is moving within a trading range.

DEFINITION

- **Stop order:** A *stop order*, also called a stop-loss order, tells the broker to sell at the market price once the specific price, the stop price, has been reached. When the designated price has been activated by another transaction or passed through, the stop order becomes a market order

HOT spot Stop prices should be set 10 to 15 percent below the stock's current market price depending on the stock's volatility. Usually, the 12 to 14 percent range provides adequate protection without triggering premature selling.

and is filled at the next available price. The trade price may be the stop price, one that is better, or one that is worse—in any case, the order will be filled. Stop orders at each price are filled on a FIFO basis. The more volatile the market and the more orders in front of an investor's order, the more the trade price may differ from the stop price.

Investors use stop-loss orders to protect their gains. For example, Carol owns 200 shares of McDonald's that she bought for $45 a share, the price is now $62. She wants to protect at least part of her $3,400 profit from a severe drop. Therefore, she places an order to sell 200 shares of MCD at 53-3/4 stop—a price approximately 13 percent below the current price. If McDonald's drops to 53-3/4, her shares will be sold at the market price, and her profits will be protected from further loss. During the time Carol owns McDonald's, she will periodically move her stop-loss price so that it remains 10 to 15 percent below the current appreciated price.

Many investors also use stop-loss orders to contain losses on newly purchased stock. As soon as they purchase shares, they place a stop-loss order 10 to 15 percent below the purchase price. Over time, as the stock price climbs, they move the stop price up, so it acts as a safety net for the profit.

Stop-loss orders are a way to unemotionally protect profits and cut losses. However, market knowledge is required to set a stop price close enough to substantially protect profits but not so close as to trigger a sell during a normal price fluctuation.

4) Order tickets

George's broker at Wedbush Morgan and Mabel's broker at Merrill Lynch make out order tickets. Each order ticket states whether the trade is a buy or sell, the type of order, the number of shares, the stock's ticker symbol, and the client's name and account number.

Sample order ticket

Each broker hands the ticket to an order clerk who transmits it to the firm's central order room—Wedbush Morgan in Los Angeles and Merrill Lynch in New York.

5) Order department

Each firm's central order room receives the order, checks its accuracy and completeness, and sends it to the NYSE. The order department is responsible for routing all orders. Its decisions are based on customer instructions, the order size and type, and the exchange that displays the best price on the intermarket screen.

If the brokerage firm is not a member of the NYSE, it routes its orders to the member firm with whom it has a trading agreement. The member firm then routes the orders according to the above criteria.

6) Firm's booth at the exchange

A clerk in the firm's communication booth along the perimeter of the exchange floor receives the order via computer. The booth is a small, partitioned work station rented from the stock exchange. It is the firm's office on the floor of the exchange. The clerk makes a copy of the order, checks the information, and stamps the time on it. The clerk then hands the order to the firm's floor broker. If the broker is not at the booth, the clerk contacts him or her on the floor by pager or cellular phone.

Floor of the
New York Stock
Exchange

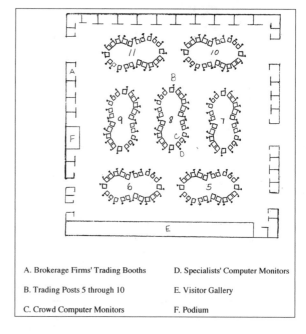

A. Brokerage Firms' Trading Booths   D. Specialists' Computer Monitors

B. Trading Posts 5 through 10   E. Visitor Gallery

C. Crowd Computer Monitors   F. Podium

7) Floor broker

Members of the NYSE are categorized as commission house brokers (floor brokers), two-dollar brokers, registered traders, and specialists. Because seats on the NYSE must be held by individuals, the brokerage firm buys the seat in the individual's name, and the individual, in turn, is an employee of the firm. He or she is a commission house broker and the firm is a member firm. The firm must buy a seat for each of its floor brokers. Because each seat is expensive ($1.7 to $2 million), the firm may own only one or two seats and have only one or two floor brokers. If the brokerage firm receives more orders than its floor brokers can handle, the firm uses an independent member broker called a *two-dollar broker*. Two-dollar brokers own their own seats on the exchange and are self-employed. They make their living executing overflow trades from the brokerage firm members. The name two-dollar broker comes from the original practice of charging $2 per 100-share trade. Their commissions are now based on the dollar value of the trade. Registered floor traders have purchased their seats on the exchange and make their living buying and selling stocks for their own portfolios. Special rules and regulations govern their activities—they may not execute trades for others. Specialists own their seats and are responsible for making a market and overseeing the trading of stocks assigned to them by the exchange.

DEFINITION

8) Trading post

Each stock trades at one specific place on the floor of the exchange called a trading post. Approximately 150 stocks trade at each of the 17 double horseshoe trading posts. Seven posts are located in the main trading room, which is about the size of a football field. It is the room shown in pictures and on television. Two additional trading rooms, one on each side of the main room, the Garage and the Blue Room, contain four and six trading posts, respectively.

9) Specialist

Each trading post has 22 specialists maintaining an orderly market for their designated stocks. The exchange assigns each specialist from one to ten stocks based on the stocks' combined trading volume and the specialist's available capital. Specialists own their seats and rent their small sections of the trading post from the exchange. While the exchange is open, they remain at their stations and perform three important functions for the market of their assigned stocks: They stabilize the price, they handle limit and stop orders, and they act as buyer and seller of last resort. Their services are critical for the liquidity of the market and for an orderly change in stock price.

Specialists lessen price fluctuations by preventing disruptive order imbalances when a majority of investors want to buy or to sell at the same time. Such a one-sided demand would result in serious price swings, up or down. Specialists steady the market for the stock by buying or selling from their inventory in 1/2 or 3/4 point increments until a price is reached that balances the

If there are no matching buy or sell orders at a price within 1/2 or 3/4 of a point ($0.50 or $0.75) of the previous trade, specialists are expected to step in and become the opposing side of the trade. They buy or sell for their accounts at their risk. They or their firm must have enough capital to buy at least five or six thousand shares of each of their stocks.

demand. The NYSE takes pride in the constancy of its stock prices. In 1996, slightly more than 98 percent of all stock transactions on the exchange took place with no price change or with only a 1/8 point difference. During the same year, specialists participated in only 18 percent of all trades (*NYSE Fact Book*).

Specialists make money on the spread between the bid and ask price on the shares they trade from their accounts when stabilizing prices or when buying or selling to fill public orders. (Their trading is thus restricted and closely monitored by the exchange and the SEC.) They sell at the ask price—the higher quote—and buy at the bid price—the lower quote. It is the opposite for investors. In addition, specialists are paid commissions on the limit and stop-loss orders they handle. They do not fill these orders from their inventory. Instead, the orders are electronically entered in their display books. Specialists track the orders until the designated price becomes the current market price. At that time they facilitate the trade through floor brokers.

10) Auction

Trading is conducted around the outer perimeter of the trading posts. Specialists stand with their backs to their stations. Small monitor screens are placed so they can see the price of the last trade and the next bid and ask price for each of their stocks while facing the buyers and sellers congregated around them.

A Trading Post

With orders in hand, two floor brokers, one from Merrill Lynch and the other from Wedbush Morgan Securities, approach Post 10 and the specialist who trades McDonald's. They join the crowd for McDonald's. The crowd includes the specialist and anyone—floor brokers from brokerage firms, either commission house or independent—interested in buying or selling. The brokers check the two vertically stacked computer monitors above the station behind the specialist. The floor brokers representing Mabel and George note that the previous trade for McDonald's was 62 $\frac{1}{8}$—up 1/8. They check the specialist's current bid and ask price of 62 $\frac{1}{8}$ —1/4. To get a feel for the market, one of the brokers asks how McDonald's is doing without indicating whether he is interested in buying or

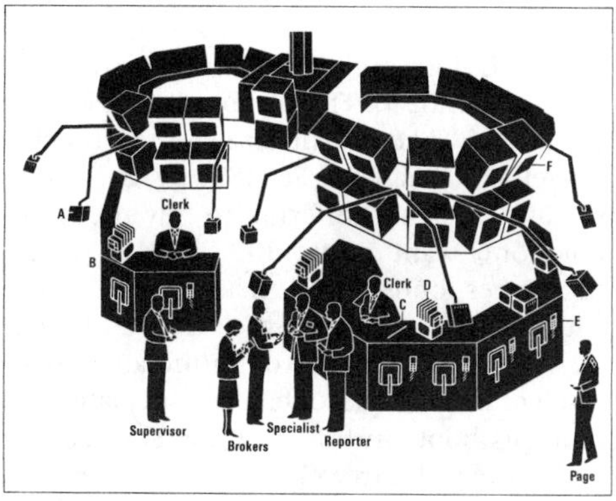

A Free Arm CRTS Display NYSE and regional trades/quotes for specialist.

B Superdot System Allows member firms to route orders directly to specialist post where stock is traded.

C Card Readers Optical mark sense card readers capable of reading all trade related data.

D Display Books Electronic specialist books transmit reports on orders to member firms.

E Electronic Paging Device Enables specialists to contact broker anywhere on floor.

F PDU'S (Post Display Units) Display NYSE trades/quotes and regional quotes.

selling. The specialist replies, "62 and 1/8 to 1/4," which means the best price to sell at is 62 ⅛ (bid price) and the best price to buy at is 62 ¼ (ask price). These are the next buy and sell limit orders in the specialist's display book. Therefore, he knows trades can be immediately executed at these prices. The Wedbush floor broker wants a better price than 62 ⅛ for his firm's client, George, who is selling. He says to the crowd, "100 at 3/16," which means he offers (wants to sell) 100 shares at 62 3/16. The first broker to call out a bid or offer price takes precedence over other brokers and has the right to complete the trade without interference.

Entries in a Specialist's Display Book

	MCD					
	BUY (orders)		PRICE	SELL (orders)		
			62 ⅛			
(floor sells)	Lynch	200	62 ⅛			
	Everan	100				
	AG Edwards	300				
			62 3/16			
			62 ¼	300	Welwood	(floor buys)
				100	Barney	
			62 ⅝	200	Schwab	
				400	STOP Pru	

The Merrill Lynch floor broker who has an order to buy 100 shares (Mabel's) wants to buy for less than 62 $\frac{1}{4}$. The instant the broker representing Mabel hears the 100 at 62 $\frac{3}{16}$ he yells, "Take it." The jargon for selling is "100 at 62 $\frac{3}{16}$." It means I offer (I want to sell) 100 shares at $62.1875 a share. In response to the sell offer a buyer shouts, "Take it." When offering to buy the broker says, "62 $\frac{1}{4}$ for 100," which means I bid for (I want to buy) 100 shares at $62.25 a share. In response to a buy offer, a broker responds, "Sold." As soon as the trade is completed by the response "Take it" or "Sold," all bids are cleared, and the next round begins. The latest price is now 62 $\frac{3}{16}$ up 1/16. Through the auction, George and Mabel were able to buy and sell at a better price than the specialist could have provided from the limit orders in his book. In this case, the specialist was not involved in the trade. He did not fill the order from his book because there was a better price on the floor. He did not trade from his account because there were opposing orders on the floor. Also, he did not need to buy or sell from his own account to maintain an orderly market—the spread between the previous sale and the next limit order in his order book was less than $\frac{3}{4}$ of a point.

To finalize the trade, the buying and selling brokers verify each other's identity from the badges they wear stating name, number, and firm. They record the information in their books. It is the selling broker's responsibility to report the sale to the floor reporter.

11) Floor reporter

The floor reporter, an employee of the stock exchange, records the details of the trade on a wireless hand-held terminal. The new trade price, the amount of decrease or increase from the previous trade, and the number of shares immediately appear at the trading post on the crowd and the specialist monitors. Simultaneously, the information is sent to the computer that supplies trading information to commercial quote providers. The trade price of George and Mabel's buy and sell is displayed around the world on Internet sites, on broker's quote machines, and on television ticker tapes as MCD   62-3/16. Had they traded 200 shares, it would have been listed as MCD 2s62 3/16.

12) Trade confirmation

As soon as each floor broker records the other's identity, runners take the confirmation tickets to the firms' booths. The trade information is routed back through the brokerage firms' central order rooms to the branch offices. As soon as the brokers in their branch offices in Alaska and Florida receive confirmation of the trade, they call their clients, George and Mabel, to verbally confirm the completion of the trade and the trade price. The entire trade takes approximately six or seven minutes.

An automated trade on the New York Stock Exchange

At the New York Stock Exchange automated trading has replaced much of the standard floor trading. In 1996 nearly 85 percent of all orders were processed through the Designated Order Turnaround (DOT) system *(NYSE Fact Book)*. Because DOT completes a trade within one minute or less and simultaneously processes trades for all listed stocks, the exchange can handle high volume days of one billion or more shares. In real life, George and Mabel's trade would have taken place on the DOT system. The chart and commentary below explain an electronic trade. Steps 1 through 5 are the same whether the trade is automated or takes place on the floor of the exchange.

A STOCK TRADE ON THE NEW YORK STOCK EXCHANGE

USING THE AUTOMATED TRADING SYSTEM

Every buy involves a sell.

Every sell involves a buy

Seller	New York Stock Exchange	Buyer
1) George decides to sell 100 shares of McDonald's. He becomes the **seller**.		1) Mabel decides to buy 100 shares of McDonald's. She becomes the **buyer.**
2) He calls his **broker** at Wedbush to check the price.		2) She calls her **broker** at Merrill Lynch to check the price.
3) George places a **market order order** with his broker to sell 100 shares of McDonald's.		3) Mabel places a **market order** with her broker to buy 100 shares of McDonald's.
4) The broker makes out the sell buy **order ticket.**		4) The broker makes out the **order ticket.**

Seller	New York Stock Exchange	Buyer
5) The order is transmitted to the the **brokerage firm's central order department**.		5) The order is transmitted to **brokerage firm's central order department**.
	Takes the Path for Electronic Trades	
6) In the order room the firm's computer system checks the **Intermarket Trading System** for the best price and forwards the order to that exchange—NYSE.		6) In the order room the firm's computer system checks the **Intermarket Trading System** for the best price and forwards the order to that exchange—NYSE.
	7) The orders enter the NYSE **SuperDOT** system, which transmits them to the specialist's book, executes the trade, and reports the trade results.	
	Returns to the Path for Floor Trades	
8) The central order room at Wedbush Morgan Securities receives the trade confirmation and forwards it to the branch office in Alaska.		8) The central order room at Merrill Lynch receives the trade confirmation and forwards it to the branch office in Florida.
9) The broker in Anchorage calls calls George to let him know that his 100 shares of McDonald's have been sold at $62\,^3/_{16}$.		9) The broker in Tampa Bay Mabel to let her know her buy order for 100 shares of McDonald's has been filled at $62\,^3/_{16}$.

6) Intermarket trading system

A stock often trades on more than one exchange. It may trade on the NYSE or AMEX where it has its primary listing, on a regional exchange where it has a secondary listing, and on the Nasdaq where brokerage firms make a market in it. In the central order room of a member firm, a computer system scans the ITS, finds the best price for the stock, and routes the order to that exchange for immediate execution at the stated price. The displayed price is good for at least 100 shares. Likewise, a floor broker at the trading post on the floor of the exchange can check the ITS information on the crowd monitor. If a regional exchange is quoting a better price, the floor broker can electronically transmit the order to that exchange. Bid and ask prices rarely vary more than 1/8 point from exchange to exchange because of the readily available information and the ability to instantly trade on any exchange.

Definition:

The *Intermarket Trading System (ITS)* is an electronic communications system. It provides instant last trade and current bid and ask information to member firms and to floor traders from the specialists and market makers at the eight exchanges.

7) SuperDOT

When the orders from George and Mabel arrive at the NYSE, they are switched to the Super Designated Order Turnaround system (SuperDOT), which is the New York Stock Exchange's automated trading system. DOT routes a member firm's order to the firm's booth or directly to the specialist's station. George's and Mabel's orders are routed to the specialist where they are electronically matched, traded, and recorded. The results of the trade are simultaneously displayed on the specialist and crowd monitors, sent back to the brokerage firms, and forwarded to the system that provides information to commercial quote vendors. If an order cannot be matched electronically, the specialist presents it to the crowd. If there is no opposing order in the crowd and no opposing limit order in the specialist's display book, the specialist buys or sells from his own account. He monitors all trading activity in the stock whether he participates in the trade or not. He must know at all times how the market is moving for each of his stocks.

Orders for fewer than 1,200 shares are automatically sent to the NYSE via SuperDOT (unless otherwise instructed). Market orders from individual investors for 2,099 shares or less are marked with an **I**. This designation signals the order is from an individual investor and as such receives priority delivery through the Individual Investor Express Delivery Service.

Both the American Stock Exchange and the Nasdaq Stock Market have automated transaction systems that work much like SuperDOT. The AMEX calls its setup the Automatic Post Execution and Reporting System (AUTOPER). The Nasdaq's, which may be used only by retail customers, is the Small Order Execution System (SOES). Not to be left out, regional exchanges have developed automated trading so customers can take advantage of any pricing differentials showing on the Intermarket Trading System.

Other automated systems

DEFINITION

Out of the many automated systems involved in stock transactions, two others at the New York Stock Exchange are of interest to individual investors—Crossing Session I and Opening Automated Report Service. *Crossing Session I* (CSI), a component of SuperDOT, is used for trading after the 4:00 p.m. market closing. Market orders are accepted on this system between 4:15 and 5:00 p.m. At 5:00 p.m. orders are electronically matched on a first-in-first-out (FIFO) basis and executed at the closing price. Any unmatched orders are canceled.

DEFINITION

The *Opening Automated Report Service* (OARS), part of SuperDOT, is used in the morning before the market opens. It accepts and matches investors' preopening market orders on a FIFO basis for execution at the stock's opening price.

Specialists use information from OARS each morning to determine the opening price for their assigned stocks. They first note any order imbalances. If the number of shares for buy and sell orders match, the stock's opening price is the same as the previous day's closing. However, if OARS shows an order imbalance for a stock, such as an excess of sell orders, specialists turn to their display books. They determine if there are enough buy limit orders at the previous day's closing price or at 1/8 to 1/4 point lower to balance the number of shares for sale on OARS. If not, they evaluate the situation and decide if they need to buy from their inventory to meet the unfilled selling demand and move the price downward in an orderly manner to trigger the next limit orders to buy. By making these assessments and judgments every morning, specialists establish the opening price for each stock— a price that brings orders into balance, provides for orderly price movements, and corresponds as nearly as possible (3/4 of a point or less) to the previous day's closing.

Conclusion

This dynamic, yet structured, trading on stock exchanges allows individual investors to effortlessly buy and sell shares of any publicly traded corporation. Without stock exchanges, which provide liquidity and orderly price movements, wide-spread public investing would not be possible. However, without the finely tuned process of taking companies public to raise needed capital, there would be few public corporations. Without public corporations there would be no stock exchanges and no public investors.

Chapter 6

Selecting a stockbroker

What you'll find in this chapter:

➠ Full-service vs. discount stock brokers

➠ Assessing your financial resources

➠ Setting your financial goals

➠ Determine your investing style

➠ Evaluating risk

"How can I find a good stockbroker? What questions should I ask? What do I need to know before I meet with a broker? What can I expect a broker to do for me? Should I use a full-service broker or a discount broker?" Do these questions sound familiar? In this chapter, Selecting a Stockbroker, you will find answers to these questions as well as learn how to assess your financial resources, set financial goals, and determine your investing style.

Stockbrokers

Early in history, a broker's business was limited to trading stocks and bonds for wealthy clients. Now, a broker's customers might include institutions, wealthy individuals, people of modest means, those who have been investing for years, those who are buying their first shares of stock, and even children who are investing through a custodial account under the supervision of an adult.

> **note** Today a broker sells stocks, bonds, mutual funds, futures, options, commodities and other products to a wide variety of clients.

Stockbrokers are approved and licensed *(registered)* by the Securities and Exchange Commission. This license allows them to recommend specific securities to clients and to trade securities for customers. In addition, brokers act as *representatives* between their clients and the floor traders who are executing the order. In recent years the securities industry has tried to upgrade the professional image of *stockbrokers* by calling them *registered representatives*. In the industry the term *broker* is used only for individuals who are partners in a firm. However, investors and non-investors still call anyone who sells securities a broker or stockbroker.

To become a registered representative or stockbroker, an individual must fulfill specific requirements. First, the prospective registered representative must be employed by a brokerage firm that belongs to the National Association of Security Dealers. Second, the candidate must submit a detailed application to the NASD stating educational and business background. Third, each applicant must participate in an intensive training program—a minimum of four months—conducted by a brokerage firm. After completing the training course each prospective broker must take a comprehensive six-hour exam—the General Securities Examination (Series 7)—and pass it with a score of 70 percent or better. The New York Stock Exchange creates the questions and the NASD administers the test. The test has a 40 to 50 percent failure rate. In addition to the General Securities Examination, each candidate must pass a state securities test. After the prospective broker has passed the examinations and the District Committee of the NASD has approved the application, the individual is licensed as a registered representative and is legally qualified to give investment advice, express opinions about a particular stock, and take orders for stock trades.

All registered representatives are required to adhere to the rules and regulations of the SEC and the stock exchanges. They must also follow state regulations and the policies and procedures of their firms. A strong code of ethics as well as strict rules and regulations guide a broker's professional conduct. Most registered representatives are honest and reliable.

Whether you call them brokers, account executives, investment executives, or registered representatives, stockbrokers are salespeople who depend on commissions to support themselves and the firms that employ them. The broker and the firm make their money from the commissions you pay when you buy a stock and when you sell it. A brokerage firm needs to sell millions of shares of stock each day to pay its overhead cost. Therefore both the firm and the broker want satisfied customers—customers who bring repeat business and new customers. Stockbrokers have helped many people

> *note*
>
> A registered representative may not provide a customer a guarantee of profit nor a guarantee against loss. A broker can neither share in a customer's profits or losses, nor rebate a client's commissions to acquire additional business.

like you and me become successful investors. If a broker makes a good recommendation for your portfolio, the stock's performance will be worth the commissions many times over.

You will meet all kinds of stockbrokers—men and women who are young, old, speculative, conservative, experienced, inexperienced, aggressive, easygoing.

Brokerage firms

Brokerage firms come in different sizes and shapes to meet customers' demands. Firms may be full service or discount, national or regional, specialized or diversified. Over the years many brokerage firms have specialized and serve only a particular segment of investors. For example, *institutional firms* concentrate on meeting the requirements of large institutional investors such as money managers of mutual funds, pension funds, and

DEFINITION

> Choosing a stockbroker is like choosing a doctor or a dentist. You are selecting someone to help you maintain your investment and financial health. The decision requires careful consideration.

DEFINITION

insurance companies. Because these customers buy stock in huge blocks—tens of thousands of shares at a time—they want to use a brokerage firm that continually deals with that kind of trade. *Investment banking houses* are brokerage firms that specialize in working with private corporations going public and with companies involved in mergers and buyouts. *Research boutiques* serve small select groups of wealthy individuals and private investment funds. Boutiques provide research and investment expertise to meet their clients' specific requests. *Retail firms* cater to the diverse needs of individual investors. On the other hand, some retail firms have diversified by developing an investment banking business and an institutional trading department.

National firms, such as Merrill Lynch and Prudential Securities, have main offices on Wall Street and branch offices throughout the United States and sometimes throughout the world. They are often called *wire houses* because their offices were originally linked together through telegraph and telephone lines. Regional firms are smaller firms whose main offices are located outside New York City. Usually, they have only three or four branch offices in their vicinity. Regional firms specialize in trading local, publicly owned corporations and nationally listed companies that interest the area's investors.

Retail brokerage houses are also divided into full-service firms and discount firms. Full-service and discount firms are similar in many ways. For example, all salespeople who buy and sell securities for customers have had the same training and have passed the same General Securities Examination qualifying test—they are registered representatives. Both types of firms accept a wide variety of accounts including Individual Retirement Accounts. Through the Securities Investor Protection Corporation they insure each customer's account for a maximum of $500,000 against the financial failure of the brokerage firm. Both types of firms send their customers detailed account statements and will either mail dividend checks and the proceeds from the sale of stock, or place the money directly into clients' accounts. Both pay interest on the cash in accounts and provide sweep accounts—sweep the cash from the account into a money market fund, which pays a higher rate of interest than the interest-bearing account. In addition, both full-service and discount firms advertise in financial magazines and newspapers and are listed in the yellow pages of telephone books. Despite these and other similarities, full-service and discount firms are best known for their differences—the commission rates they charge and the personalized service they provide.

Definition:

A *retail brokerage house* may be either a small regional firm or a large national firm.

Full-service brokerage firm

DEFINITION

The words *full service* in the term *full-service brokerage firm* mean that each broker works with his or her clients individually. Brokers help investors choose securities that are appropriate for their investment goals and their resources. Full service also means the firm provides its customers with detailed analyses of industries and companies—those industries and companies the firm's research department tracks.

Full-service brokerage firms, such as Merrill Lynch, Paine-Webber, Dean Witter Reynolds, and Smith-Barney, maintain extensive research departments. These departments are staffed with highly trained professionals. Their full-time job is to gather and analyze information. Some analysts study the economy and others study specific industries and companies. Economic analysts examine current economic conditions and identify national and international economic trends. Industry analysts closely follow two or three industries and the companies within those industries. They read extensively about economic trends and conditions and evaluate how those conditions will affect their particular industries. They study the companies that make up the industries. They sift through company information and find those companies on the rise and those on the decline. They travel around the country and meet with company managers. Through their research, analysts often discover problems that are developing within a company which may lead to a decline in the price of the company's stock. On the other hand, analysts sometimes discover conditions which are likely to increase a company's sales and profits and will soon result in a rise in the company's stock price.

The other important benefit offered by a full-service firm is the development of a long-term working relationship between broker and client. Brokers work closely with clients to help them increase their success in the market. For example, the research department provides stockbrokers with a list of securities that are suitable for different kinds of portfolios. When brokers find an appropriate investment idea, they call their clients. Brokers work with their clients to educate them about the stock market and about the kinds of stocks that will do well in their portfolios. They help investors decide which stocks to buy and which stocks to sell.

note The more brokers understand about their clients' tolerance for risk, their financial resources, and their investment goals and philosophy, the better they can recommend stocks that will increase the value of their clients' portfolios.

For individual investors, the full-service brokerage firm can be a valuable source of information. Each firm subscribes to leading advisory services such as *Value Line Investment Survey, The Outlook, Standard and Poor's Stock Guide*, and *Standard and Poor's Stock Reports*. These resources, as well as copies of the firm's own research reports and advisory letter, are placed in the office reception area so customers can easily use them. Also, many firms have installed a computer-like quote machine in their reception area. By typing in a ticker symbol (MCD for McDonald's), a client can quickly check company data such as the current stock price, the 52-week high and low, the number of shares traded that day, and the current company news. In addition to quote machines, many brokerage firms now have automated phone systems that provide current quotes. Investors can track stock prices from the comfort of their homes, offices, or cars. Of course clients can always call their brokers directly for a price quote and for a company news update.

note To cover the cost of the wide range of services provided by a full-service broker, the firm often charges a commission rate of two percent or more on the total amount of each transaction. For example, if an investor bought 100 shares of XYZ at $25 a share, the commission would be $50 (100 shares x $25 = $2500 x .02 = $50). Income is necessary to support a firm's extensive research department, its office facilities and its services—which clients find helpful and enjoy using. Also, there must be enough income to support the brokers who work with investors one at a time.

In addition to commissions, full-service firms often set other fees to help cover the cost of doing business. For example, they may charge for mailing trade confirmations and for mailing duplicate statements. They may charge for an inactive account or for moving an account to another firm. A client should ask for a list of all miscellaneous costs. These added fees increase the expense of investing.

Discount brokerage firm

DEFINITION

The word *discount* in the term *discount brokerage firm* signifies that the firm charges a lower commission—often 40 to 70 percent lower—than that charged by full-service firms. Most discount firms base their rates on the dollar value of the trade, on the number of shares traded, or a combination of the two. Because of the various methods used to calculate commission rates, each discount firm is likely to be less expensive for one kind of trade and more expensive for another. When choosing a discount broker it is helpful to determine what kinds of trades you will be making. Each year the American Association of Individual Investors (AAII) conducts a discount broker survey and publishes the results in its magazine, *AAII Journal*. It lists the commission charges for three types of trades. In its recent survey, most commissions for 100 shares at $50 a share ranged between $30 and $50 a trade. This survey is a good place to begin when selecting a discount broker. Its chart makes it easy to compare fees, services, account minimums, and commission rates.

In addition to a discount firm's basic commission rate, it may extend other discounts. Several firms such as Schwab and Max Uhle offer additional discounts if their customers use a computer or a touch-tone phone to place their orders. Some firms decrease their commission rate if a client makes a round trip trade (buys and sells the same shares) within a 30-day period. A few charge less if the round trip occurs the same day. Other firms reduce their commissions for trades that involve a large dollar amount or a large number of

> Some brokers set their commissions so they favor investors trading 100 shares of a medium-priced stock ($40 to $70). Others benefit investors buying a thousand or more shares of an inexpensive stock ($8 to $10).

shares. In order to take advantage of a firm's deep discounts, the client must often maintain a substantial account balance and conduct a high volume of trading each year.

In contrast to discounting commissions, many firms charge extra for various services. Some discount firms add fees for trading low-priced shares (less than $5.00). If a trade involves an odd lot—127 shares—the 27 shares may incur additional cost. Others require payment for the delivery of stock certificates and for sending duplicate account statements. Often, firms impose fees for maintaining inactive accounts and for transferring an account to another firm. These costs can diminish the effect of the discount commission rate.

In exchange for low commission rates, discount brokerage firms offer simple, streamlined services. They provide general, non-personalized, efficient service. They employ no commission salespeople, they offer no investment advice, they make no stock recommendations—neither to buy nor to sell—and they maintain no research department. Their number one service goal of the discount firm is the rapid, accurate transaction of trades. To trade, an investor dials an 800 number and places an order with a broker who immediately forwards it to the proper exchange. Often the trade is completed and the price confirmed before the client can hang up the telephone. Many discount brokerage firms offer the option of placing orders by computer and by touch-tone telephone. If an order is entered after the market has closed, it will be filled the following business day. This type of trading is convenient for those individuals who like to do their investing in the evening following their own workday.

In addition to efficiently taking and executing orders, discount firms provide other limited services. Most firms furnish 800-number automated phone services so clients can access quotes and account information at any time. Most discount brokerage firms provide research reports on the economy, on general business conditions, on specific industries, and on individual companies. Generally these reports are from outside sources. Some firms charge extra for research reports while others send them at no cost.

The popularity of a second type of discount broker—on-line brokers—is spreading rapidly. They offer the lowest commission rates—usually a flat rate despite the number of shares traded or the dollar amount involved. Their commissions range between $10 and $20 a trade. Trades are fast and easy to complete via computer. In addition, nearly all offer touch-tone telephone trading and the use of a live broker (for an added fee). On-line brokers offer on-line research materials and a place to track your stock holdings. Many investors like this quick, impersonal way of trading.

Advantages of full-service firms and discount firms

When choosing between a full-service brokerage firm or a discount brokerage firm, consider what you want and the advantages of each.

Full-service brokerage firm:

Choose this if you want:

- recommendations

- advice and guidance

- investment ideas

- feedback on your research

- verification of your stock choices

- easy access to stock data and investment advisory information

- direction, assistance, and confirmation in managing your portfolio

Are the services you will use worth the higher commissions?

Discount brokerage firm:

Choose this if you want to:

- do your own research

- rely on your own investment ideas

- pay lower commissions

- place orders day or night

- trade from your home or office using a computer or a touch-tone telephone

Do you have access to investment information? Do you feel comfortable investing on your own? Do you want your trades to be executed without comment or sales pitch?

Disadvantages of full-service firms and discount firms

Before making a choice between a full-service or a discount brokerage firm, consider the disadvantages of each.

Full-service brokerage firm:

Choose this if you are concerned about:

- high commission rates

- the ability to trade only during business hours

- charges (commission rates) for services not used, such as:

  + reports from the research department

  + investment advisory publications

    ✦   brokers' advice and recommendations

- brokers who may apply pressure:

    ✦   to trade frequently

    ✦   to buy the Stock of the Week—the stock the firm is promoting or selling from its portfolio

Discount brokerage firm

Choose this if you are concerned about:

- the necessity of speaking with a different broker each time

- busy signals when trying to place an order

- the firm's lack of computer and touch-tone phone trading capabilities

- the inability to obtain broker guidance or recommendations

- the limited availability of research reports and investment information

- added fees that diminish the effect of the discount rate

Conclusion

When you are deciding whether to use a full-service or a discount broker, think about the kinds of trades you will make and the types of service you will require. Do you want the low-cost, impersonal trades a discount broker provides, or do you want the advice and guidance of a full-service broker? Many investors use both. They have an active account with a full-service firm to take advantage of their broker's advice and the firm's research materials. They also have an account with a discount firm to trade those stocks that require only a simple, inexpensive trade. You, too, may decide to use both types of firms. Whatever your choice, if your investing needs change, you can change the type of brokerage service you use.

Choosing a full-service broker

When selecting a full-service broker, first become acquainted with yourself as an investor. Are you a long-term investor, a trader, a speculator, or a value investor (buys quality, out-of-favor stocks)? Second, as you interview several stockbrokers, look for a broker who supports your style of investing. Finally, compare and evaluate the information from your interviews, and choose a broker with whom you can work comfortably and effectively.

Know yourself as an investor

The more you know about yourself as an investor, the better prepared you will be to search for a broker who will meet your particular needs. What are your investment goals? Do you want to buy quality stocks and hold them for a long time or do you want to buy and sell stocks frequently? Are you conservative, or do you like to take risks? How much can you afford to invest in stocks? As you answer these and other questions you will begin to develop a clear image of yourself as an investor. Then you will be ready to look for a broker who understands and supports your style of investing—one who is able to recommend the types of stocks that will meet your investing requirements.

Your resources

How much money can you afford to invest in stocks? To answer that question look closely at your total financial picture. For example, how much money do you have coming in and going out each month? What are your present and future cash needs? The following questions will help direct your attention to different aspects of your financial situation and will help you determine how much money you have available to invest in stocks. During the process, you may find additional money to add to your stock fund.

- Do you have cash in a safe, readily accessible place for an emergency? Financial advisors recommend enough cash to cover living expenses for three months.

- Do you have sufficient insurance?

- What is your monthly income?

- What are your monthly expenses?

- How much cash do you need each month?

- What are your future needs?

- How much do you owe?

- What do you own?

- How much can you afford to allot as the total amount for all investments?

- How much do you plan to use for buying stocks?

- Can you do without this money for two or three years? The longer discretionary funds remain invested in stocks, the more the investment grows and the less it is affected by market fluctuations.

- How much loss can you live with?

The Assets & Liabilities Worksheet (in the forms section) will help you review your financial assets and liabilities—your net worth. If you want additional help in any of these areas, your library has a number of good books on financial planning.

Your investment goals

When you have a clear idea of what you want your stock portfolio to accomplish, you put your money to work more productively. Setting goals helps you develop a plan—a road map of where you are going. Ask yourself the following questions: Why am I really investing? Am I investing for conversation appeal? Am I investing because everyone is doing it or because someone said I should? Or do I have a definite purpose for my investments? Specific goals, each with its own time line, keep you moving forward. Precise targets eliminate the many confusing alternatives. Without a definite plan it is easy to jump from one investment strategy to another, from one type of stock to another, from one risk and reward level to another and end up back where you started.

HOT spot Defining investment objectives is critical for successful investing.

If your particular goal is "to make more money," in all probability you will have only limited success. The statement "to make more money" does not have a definite end; it is not a specific destination with a specific schedule and arrival date. It is like saying, "I am driving somewhere." Where is "somewhere"? How do you know what route to take? How will you know when you arrive? What will keep you from driving around in a circle and never going anywhere?

Set exact goals. Are you investing to buy a house, start a business, put children through college, increase your retirement income, go on a trip, or buy a luxury item? What do you want? When do you want it? What does it cost? How much do you have? How much do you need? How long will it take your investments to make the necessary money? Write it down, or fill in the blanks:

"I will have _____ by _____ because my
  description of item   date
investments have earned $_____."
                          dollar amount

Turn your highest priority into a goal. Set exhilarating goals, set down-to-earth goals, set noble goals.

Quantify your goals. Include an end result that can be counted and measured. If your goal is to be "a successful investor," what is success? Quantify success. Write your goal so that even an outsider can tell when you have reached it. For instance, you could say, "I have doubled the value of my current investments, from $_____ to $_____." It is easy to tell when that goal has been reached.

Attach a specific date to each goal. In the above example add "by October 26, 2008." Now your goal reads, "I have doubled the value of my current investments, from $_____ to $_____ by October 26, 2008." Without a specific date it is like saying you will get around to it sometime. "Sometime" never comes. A specific date impacts the mind and sets it to work.

Create a vivid picture of each goal. For instance, if your goal is a new car, see your new car sitting in your driveway. As you walk up to it, admire its bright, shiny paint, and its beautiful sleek lines. When you get into the car, sense its solidness as you close the door, smell the wonderful new-car smell, run your hand over the upholstery and enjoy its texture. Turn the key and hear the engine roar into life. As you back out of your driveway and drive down the street, savor your exhilaration and excitement, feel the car's surge of acceleration, and its ease of handling.

As you build your picture be sure to do the following:

- Visualize in the first person and in the present tense. The mind experiences it as if it were happening and begins its work to turn the goal into reality.

- Use vivid, imaginative language.

- Choose energizing words.

- Use words that create excitement. The mind reacts faster and more forcefully to emotion than it reacts to reason.

In addition to visualizing your goal, make sketches, and cut out pictures that illustrate all aspects of it. Put them where you can easily see them—on your desk where you work on your investments. As you analyze companies, check stock prices, and make investment decisions, stop and look at your pictures or recreate the images in your mind. If your investment goal is to start a business, envision it exactly the way you want it to be. Picture the kind of business it is, where it is located—in which building, on what street. Note all the customers walking through the door and calling on the phone requesting your service or product. Observe your employees making sale after sale and accepting money in exchange for your products. Feel the excitement as you go over your accounts. Enjoy the feeling of exhilaration as you watch your profits increase by the targeted amount each quarter. Have fun! Do the same with whatever goal you have chosen—investing for a new house, retirement, a college education, a trip, a luxury item.

Focus on your goals. Your focus will create energy, inspire you, and reveal hidden possibilities. Take action and do the required work. Do those things that support your goals. Maintain your concentration—avoid scattering your energies. Action is the link between wanting and getting.

Your tolerance for risk

Risk cannot be prevented. Every investment involves risk, including money in a savings account. A savings account, which seems to be risk-free, is subject to inflation risk also known as purchasing power risk. Purchasing power risk is the possibility that the rate of inflation and the taxes on the interest will be greater

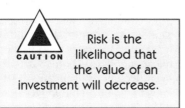

than the interest earned on the account. For example, at this time a savings account pays 3.03 percent interest and the inflation rate is 2.9 percent. If you had $1,000 in a savings account, you would earn $30.30 in interest for the year which would give you a total of $1,030.30. After taxes on the interest, assuming you were in the lowest income tax bracket, you would have $1,025.15. This year inflation takes away 2.9 percent or $29.88 of the purchasing power of your $1,030.30 which would leave you with $995.27 in purchasing power. Thus, after collecting interest on your investment, paying taxes on the interest, and subtracting the loss of purchasing power due to inflation you would have lost $4.73 per $1,000 in savings. Your $1,030.30 would still be in the bank but due to the effects of inflation and taxes, it would be worth only $995.27. Because of purchasing power risk, you must not only protect your capital but also earn more than is lost through taxes and inflation.

Another type of risk, *market risk*, is the chance that the stock market will drop and *all* stock prices will fall. Market risk is related to political and economic factors—recessions, inflation, rising interest rates—that change somewhat unpredictably. Unforeseeable events occur, events we do not expect and are unable to control. These events affect stock prices in general and impact all stock investors, individual investors and institutional investors alike. One way to reduce market risk is to buy quality stocks and to hold them for an extended period of time, through down markets

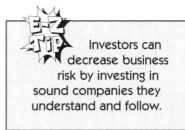

Investors can decrease business risk by investing in sound companies they understand and follow.

as well as up markets. After a market decline, the prices of quality individual stocks return to their initial levels and continue to rise. Over time, the stock market gains more than it loses.

DEFINITION

Industry risk is the threat that specific conditions will negatively affect all companies within an industry. For example, an entire industry may be altered by a change in regulations, political events, foreign competition, or the availability and cost of resources. Investors can minimize industry risk by owning stocks in the industries they understand and follow. Thus, they will be aware of new developments and will be able to sell their stock, if necessary, before the price seriously deteriorates. Another way to lessen industry risk is to own stocks in several different industries—to diversify.

HOT spot The "risk/reward ratio" concept states: "The higher the expected return, the greater the risk." Another way of looking at it: "The less the risk, the less the potential gain."

Business risk is the possibility that a good company will be mismanaged. The quality of its products and services may slip. Its sales performance and marketing strategies may deteriorate. It may become a company that is no longer expanding, no longer developing new products and services, and no longer adjusting to changes within the industry. Under these conditions a company ceases to grow. When a company stops growing, its profits disappear, and its stock price declines. Investors can avoid unpleasant surprises by reading the company's quarterly and annual reports. They can compare the company's current revenues, earnings per share, and management comments to those from previous quarters and years. A drop in earnings for two or three quarters compared to corresponding quarters in the two most recent years is an indication that business conditions are declining within the company or the industry.

E-Z TIP It is important for you to accurately understand your concerns about risk and reward so that you can clearly communicate them to your broker. Then your broker will be able to recommend stocks that not only advance your investment goals but also match your comfort level.

Risk-free investments do not exist. Investors cannot separate risk from reward; they are directly related. A savings account is an example of a low-risk investment—the only risk involved is purchasing power risk. However, the reward is limited to the interest rate paid on the account. An example of a high-risk investment is investing in a start-up company—a company that is developing a new product. Many things can go wrong from the time work begins on a product until its sales make a profit for the company. Investors may make spectacular returns on the investment or may lose all or most of the invested capital. Risk and reward potentials are on a continuum from low risk/low reward to high risk/high reward. The spectrum runs from preserving all capital to maximizing return by risking the loss of a substantial portion of capital.

As an investor, how much risk can you tolerate? How much risk can you comfortably handle? Your investments should not cause sleepless nights or a knot in the pit of your stomach. The potential return on your investments is not worth the anxiety. Because a sense of well-being is important, it is worthwhile for you to explore your feelings about risk. How you *think* you feel about risk and how you actually feel about it may differ considerably. The following questions will help you determine your attitudes toward risk versus reward:

Resources and risk

- How much can you afford to invest without adversely affecting your lifestyle?

- How much money are you willing to risk? How much are you comfortable risking? This is the money that is not needed for living expenses or for insurance or for an emergency savings account. This is your discretionary money.

- How much can you afford to lose without causing a problem for you or your family?

- How would you feel if the stock market dropped 20 percent? Would you panic and sell or would you ride it out and wait for the next upswing?

- How much risk do you want to take?

Portfolio and risk

Aversion to risk:

- Do you want to be able to access all or part of your money quickly?

- Is your primary goal to safeguard your principal? Are you willing to give up growth for the safety of your money?

- Do you want your investment growth to keep pace with inflation but you have a low tolerance for risk?

- Would you prefer a lower return if the capital seemed safer?

Conservative, moderate risk:

- Do you want solid investments with only moderate risk?

- Do you want to invest primarily for growth but want to keep part of your money secure?

Aggressive risk:

- Is your primary goal to maximize the growth of your money?

- Are you willing to risk the loss of part of your capital in return for a potentially top rate of return?

Adventuresome risk:

Do you want to maximize the growth of your money at all costs?

How do you feel about risk? Are you extremely adverse to risk, are you conservative, or are you aggressive and adventuresome? During a one-year period risk-adverse investors are uncomfortable with losing more than 5 percent of the value of their portfolios. On the other hand, conservative investors can tolerate portfolio losses between 5 and 15 percent; aggressive investors can handle losses between 15 and 25 percent.

What is important to you?

Which of the following best describes what you want—your investment objectives?:

- **Liquidity:** You want to have immediate access to your money.

- **Safety of principal:** You are willing to settle for lower growth in exchange for the safety of your capital.

- **Current income:** You are willing to give up growth in exchange for current dividend income.

- **Capital appreciation:** You want to focus on the growth of your principal. You are willing to give up dividend income, and you are willing to take added risk in exchange for added growth potential.

- **A combination of capital appreciation and income:** You are willing to give up some dividend income in exchange for added risk and growth potential. On the other hand, you are willing to trade growth possibilities for additional dividend income and reduced risk.

- **Rapid capital appreciation:** You have a high tolerance for risk. You want your investments to have the chance to grow at the highest possible rate, and you are comfortable with the corresponding degree of risk.

Your portfolio may include different expected rates of return with different risk levels. It does not have to be all one or the other. For example, if you are a conservative investor, try using 10 percent of your capital to buy a stock that has a greater growth potential and a higher risk factor than the stocks you normally buy. On the other hand, if you are an aggressive investor and like high-growth/high-risk stocks, you might want to add a bit of conservatism to your portfolio and buy a low-growth, high-dividend stock that would provide a cushion against any losses that result from the high-risk stocks you prefer.

Experiences may change your tolerance for risk. Success or failure at a risk/reward level may encourage you or prevent you from accepting additional risk. Generally, risk tolerance does not remain static.

Conclusion

As you have worked through this section, Know Yourself As an Investor, you have laid the foundation for years of successful stock investing. You have taken care of your insurance needs and your emergency fund. You know how much money you have available to invest in stocks and you are ready to put it to work. You have chosen your goals and have them vividly in mind, including dates and dollar amounts. You have carefully considered how you react to risk and reward. You realize that you can do specific things to decrease each kind of risk, thereby making the degree of risk more tolerable and manageable. By defining your risk level, setting your goals, and determining the resources you have available for purchasing stocks, you have clarified your style of investing. With this information in mind you are prepared to look for a stockbroker who will support and enhance your stock investments.

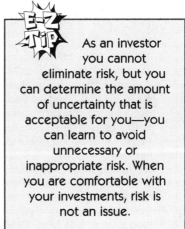

As an investor you cannot eliminate risk, but you can determine the amount of uncertainty that is acceptable for you—you can learn to avoid unnecessary or inappropriate risk. When you are comfortable with your investments, risk is not an issue.

Stockbroker interviews

"I don't know any brokers. I don't know where to start. I don't know what questions to ask. What do I do?" Like doctors and lawyers, brokers have no organization which rates their performance. However, in the absence of a rating service, you can learn about a broker's performance by discussing his or her performance with someone you know who has been a client. Therefore, begin your search by asking friends and relatives for the names of brokers they would recommend. Have they worked with a broker they particularly like? How did their broker help them? Has their broker made good recommendations? If you have acquaintances or business associates who invest, ask them for referrals. Ask your banker, lawyer, or accountant if they know a good stockbroker. When friends and colleagues recommend a broker, ask them what they like about the broker. Because their investing styles may differ from yours, listen for comments and descriptions of brokers that fit your type of investing. Ultimately, their brokers may or may not meet your needs, but their suggestions are an excellent place to begin your search.

> **E-Z Tip**
> Selecting a stockbroker is much like choosing a doctor, a lawyer, or an accountant. You are selecting a professional—in this case a professional to help you work with your stock investments.

Another approach to finding a stockbroker is to call a well-known national brokerage firm or a familiar regional firm located in your area. Ask to speak with the manager. Tell him or her that you are a new investor, and you are seeking an *experienced* broker who works well with conservative (or your type) investors. However, be careful in this situation, you may be given the name of an inexperienced broker or a broker who needs additional clients. When you interview these brokers, listen carefully as they answer your questions concerning how long they have been brokers, how long they have been with the present firm, other firms where they have worked as brokers, and the number of active accounts they currently handle (they may have 150 or more accounts but probably no more than 10 or 15 accounts are extremely active).

> **HOT spot**
> As a potential client, you are looking for an experienced broker who stays with the same firm for a long time, and who already has a solid client base.

Interview questions

While you are collecting the names of brokers to interview, begin making a list of the questions you want to ask. Be direct; don't be hesitant. It is your money. Ask the brokers about their background and experience with stocks, as well as their philosophy of investing. Ask about the firm—the various services it offers, the commissions and fees it charges, the minimum required to open an account. Remember that you are interviewing a potential employee, one you will hire to help you maintain your portfolio and to increase its value. The following questions are some you may want to include in your list:

Training

- What kind of training have you had in addition to studying for the Series 7 exam?

- When and where did you receive your training?

- How extensive were the courses? How long did the courses and training last?

Comment: Look for courses in finance, different types of investments, and portfolio management.

- What other business experience have you had?

Employment

- How long have you been a broker?

Comment: You want your broker to have been in the business for at least five years so he or she will have experienced both a bear and a bull market.

CAUTION

- How long have you been with this firm?

- What other firms have you worked for? How long did you stay with each firm? Why did you leave?

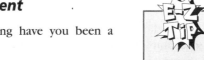

No one can pick all winners. However, the broker's total recommendations should have out-performed the S&P 500 by 2 percent or more—up more than the index in a bull market and down less than the index in a bear market.

Comment: Be wary brokers who appear to frequently change firms. Good brokers usually find a firm they like and stay there. You want your broker to be settled. If he or she moves to another firm, you will be forced to change either brokers or firms.

Performance

- What stocks have you recommended during the past year? How have they performed? Do you have an audited report of their performance?

Comment: Some stocks will have gone up, some will have stayed the same, and some will have gone down. Some brokers are good at picking winning stocks during a bull market. However, those same stocks may go down farther than other stocks in a bear market. On the other hand, some brokers pick stocks that go up less during a bull market but decline less during a bear market.

- Do you have your own investment account? Has that been successful?

Comment: Does the broker follow the advice he gives others?

Philosophy

- How would you describe your philosophy of investing?

- What kinds of stocks do you like?

Comment: Does the broker's philosophy of investing match yours? Does the broker seem to be a conservative investor who likes to buy low-risk stocks that provide safety of principal, current income, and low steady growth and hold them for a long time—five years or longer? Does he or she seem to be moderate and prefer a mixture of income stocks and faster-growth stocks? On the other hand, does the broker appear to be aggressive and adventuresome and choose fast-growing stocks with high risk and high potential return and hold them for a short period of time—three, six, or twelve months? Will the broker's investing style match yours? Will his or her attitudes about stocks support your investment needs?

- What kind of stocks do you tend to avoid?

- How do you feel about risk?

- What is your specialty?

- What are your favorite strategies for picking stocks?

Comment: Does the broker rely on technical analysis—charts showing the movement of stock prices—to determine which stocks to buy and when to buy them? Does he or she focus on discovering new high-growth companies? Does he or she choose quality companies that are out of favor and have low p/e's? Does the broker look for solid-growth companies that are selling for less than they are worth?

- Where do you get your ideas for stocks to recommend?

Comment: Generally, brokers obtain most, if not all, of their ideas from the firm's research department, which is acceptable, particularly if the research department is a good one. However, you will have a broader choice of quality stocks if the broker uses additional sources. You will not be limited to the firm's "stock pick of the week," which every branch office in the United States is trying to sell.

- How do you decide when to sell a stock?

- Do you ever feel that a client should not invest additional money in the market?

- What kinds of mistakes have you made? How do you deal with your mistakes?

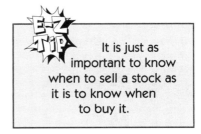

It is just as important to know when to sell a stock as it is to know when to buy it.

Comment: As a potential client, you are looking for a broker who can admit mistakes, learn from them, and move on—you want honesty.

- I have $5,000 (or the amount you choose) I want to use to begin buying individual stocks, what are your suggestions?

Comment: Be leery of the broker who suggests you put all the money into one stock or one industry—diversify, diversify. Even with $5,000 you can buy 100 shares each of two lower-priced stocks. Steer clear of the broker who promises or leads you to believe you can make a quick profit by purchasing a specific stock, stock options, or futures. For new investors like you, the broker should offer several suggestions, explain them, and give you material about the companies to read.

- What do you think about XYZ stock for my portfolio?

Comment: Ask each broker about the same stock. Compare their answers. Their replies will give you an idea of their interest in you as an investor. How did they react to a stock you were interested in? How detailed were their comments? Did they discuss the stock with you or did they brush it off? Given the background you shared with them about your finances and investment goals, what were their recommendations?

- Generally, how do you diversify a portfolio?

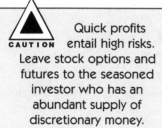

Quick profits entail high risks. Leave stock options and futures to the seasoned investor who has an abundant supply of discretionary money.

Comment: One way to diversify a stock portfolio is to buy stocks in different industries—electronics, building supplies, medical supplies. Another way to diversify is to buy different types of stocks—income stocks, steady-growth stocks, blue chip stocks, cyclical stocks, aggressive-growth stocks.

- How do you feel about small, individual investors (or my investing style)?

- Why do you feel that you would be a good stockbroker for me?

Clients

- Are most of your clients institutional or individual investors?

- How would you describe your typical client?

Comment: The broker's description should include the following information: typical age of clients, whether the majority of clients are men or women, the average portfolio size, the length of time clients have been investing, the length of time they have been with this broker.

- How much guidance do you generally give clients?

Comment: Do clients rely heavily on this broker for advice or do they do most of their own research?

- How much guidance will you be able to give me?

Comment: Will the broker be comfortable with the level of guidance you want—whether a small or a substantial amount?

- Will you help me set up a stock portfolio?

- Under what circumstances can I expect to hear from you? How often should I expect to hear from you?

Comment: Does the broker contact clients regularly or only when a specific need arises? Will the broker call if important news is released that will affect a stock in your portfolio? Will the broker call if he or she feels a stock should be sold? Or will the broker call only when he or she has another stock for you to buy?

- How closely do you monitor your clients' portfolios?

- How closely will you monitor my portfolio? How will you do that?

- Do you advise your clients when to sell?

Comment: Often, a broker finds it difficult to advise clients to sell a stock that is not performing as expected, particularly if the stock was one of the broker's recommendations.

- If you thought a stock I had heard about or had researched and wanted to buy would be detrimental to my portfolio, would you warn me about it?

Comment: Some brokers have a difficult time steering a customer away from something he or she wants.

> *note* Admitting mistakes and cutting losses is often difficult for broker and client alike.

- What percent of your clients make a profit? Why? Why not?

- What do you wish your customers would do?

- How do you feel when clients do not take your advice?

- How do you feel when your advice does not work for a client? What do you do about it?

- Can you give me the names of one or two clients I might call?

Comment: Other clients' comments may give you an idea of how the broker works with his or her clients.

The firm

- Tell me about the firm.

Comment: How long has it been in business? How large is it? What is its specialty?

- What is the firm's strength? What is its weakness?

- What stocks did the firm recommend during the past 12 months? How have they performed? May I have a copy of an audited report of their performance?

Comment: Did the recommended stocks outperform the S&P 500 by 2 percent or more?

- Tell me about your commission policies. Do you discount commissions? If so, under what conditions and how much?

Comment: Ask for a commission rate schedule.

- What additional fees does the firm charge?

Comment: Does the firm charge an additional fee for inactive accounts (if so, what constitutes an inactive account), for odd-lot trades, for orders other than market orders, for the delivery of stock certificates to you? Ask for a list of these additional fees.

- Does the firm require a minimum cash deposit to open and to maintain a cash account?

- If I want to research a stock, what resources does the firm have available for my use?

Comment: Do clients have easy access to copies of *Value Line, Standard & Poor's Stock Guide, Standard & Poor's Stock Reports*, other investment and advisory services, investment newsletters, and the firm's economic, industry, and stock reports? Is there a quote machine available for client use?

- Why do you think this brokerage firm would be a good place for my account?

Conclusion

There are no right or wrong answers to these questions. Use them to become acquainted with each stockbroker. Use the questions to determine if a broker fits your style of investing and to decide if you want to work with a particular broker. Also, use them as a starting point for your own list, include questions that are pertinent to your specific situation.

Interview three or four stockbrokers so you can compare and contrast their different approaches to investing and have several brokers from which to choose. When you call them for an appointment, let them know that you have been referred by one of their clients or by an individual who knows of their expertise such as your banker or lawyer. If possible schedule your meeting for a time when they will be the least distracted by market activity. On the designated day arrive on time with your questions firmly in mind and with your notepad and pen ready for taking notes.

Questions the stockbroker may ask you

As you interview stockbrokers, they, too, will be asking questions. They will be developing a picture of your investment needs. Even during this initial meeting they will be inquiring about your resources and your objectives. By law all financial information you share with a broker is held in strict confidence. Be sure you are honest and candid; you are asking the same of the broker you are interviewing.

The interview

The main office of a major NYSE member firm is often located in a high-rise office building. Its various departments may occupy several floors. A large brokerage firm may have a research department, an investment banking and underwriting department for new issues, an institutional trading department for its institutional clients, a trading department where professional traders buy and sell stocks for the firm's own portfolio, a record-keeping department for account maintenance, and a retail department that serves individual investors.

As a retail client you see only a limited portion of the front office—the public reception area and the broker's office. Usually, the reception room is small, whether it is in the firm's main office or branch office. When you enter, give your name and the broker's name to the receptionist. He or she will inform the broker you have arrived. While waiting, sit down and relax and look through one of their financial magazines. Also, observe the surrounding activity. For example, two or three clients may be waiting to discuss investment ideas with their brokers. Several clients may be using *Value Line* and *Standard & Poor's Stock Guide* to look up information about a stock that interests them while others may be using the computer to retrieve quotes and current news on their stocks.

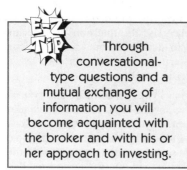

Through conversational-type questions and a mutual exchange of information you will become acquainted with the broker and with his or her approach to investing.

The broker will come to the reception area, greet you, and lead the way to his or her office. Brokers' offices are often small, glassed-in cubicles that contain a set of shelves filled with books, papers, and resource materials, two or three chairs, and a desk with a telephone, the indispensable computer for quotes, and stacks of papers and research reports. From this office you may be able to see other brokers working with their clients.

Think of this meeting as an interview with a broker who is applying for the position of advisor to "My Securities Investments, Inc." However, rather than asking a series of direct questions, try to keep the tone of the meeting relaxed and conversational. The interview should be an even exchange of information; neither individual should monopolize the conversation. Think of it as a working and learning partnership in which both people are getting and giving information. Note the questions the broker asks you. Be honest and direct about your investing experience, your resources and goals, and your tolerance for risk.

Because there are no right or wrong answers to the questions you ask, be sure the broker's answers are clear, direct, and understandable. As the interview proceeds, make notes concerning the broker's answers and any general observations you make.

Does the broker:

- focus attention on you?

- speak directly to you and make good eye contact?

- appear to be thinking about what you are saying?

- show respect for your questions and your ideas and comments?

- seem distracted by telephones, other people, or papers on the desk?

- talk down to you or talk over your head by using Wall Street jargon?

- seem well-organized and able to quickly and easily find information?

- ask the questions that should be asked about your financial and investment goals, your previous experiences with investing, your financial resources, and tolerance for risk?

As the interview progresses consider how you would feel working with this broker.

- Will you have confidence in the advice and suggestions offered?

- Is this broker knowledgeable and interested in the kind of stocks that interest you whether it is aggressive-growth stocks, low-growth high-dividend-paying stocks, or some other kind?

- Is this broker's time frame for holding stocks compatible with yours, whether you want to trade frequently or buy and hold a stock for several years?

- Is this someone with whom you will be comfortable working?

Be wary of brokers who try the hard-sell approach either for working with them or for a particular type of stock or investment. Also be wary if a broker suggests any sure or quick way to make a profit. There are no sure successes in the investing business.

When interviewing brokers, remember that they are salespeople. They not only sell stocks but also sell themselves as brokers. Find a broker whose expertise and philosophy fit your financial goals and investing style.

The choice

When you have finished interviewing the brokers on your list, read through the brochures that tell about their firms. Follow up on the client references they have given you. Also, call or write the National Association of Securities Dealers for a background check on the brokers and firms you are considering (1-800-289-9999 or National Association of Securities Dealers, 1735 K Street N. W., Washington, D. C. 20006-1506). The NASD maintains a data bank, the Central Registration Depository (CRD). It lists information on all registered representatives in the United States concerning any criminal convictions they may have had and any disciplinary actions taken by securities regulators. In addition, the CRD files contain information about any regulatory infractions committed by brokerage firms. The CRD, however, does not contain information on pending actions. Take the time to make this background check.

Look over your interview notes and think about each broker's answers. Compare their replies, comments, suggestions, and your reactions to each.

Look for a broker:

- who is honest and trustworthy

- who is experienced and competent

- who respects you, your investment goals, and your philosophy of investing

- whose philosophy and expertise support your investment objectives and your risk tolerance

- who will be able to recommend stocks that will add value to your portfolio

- who likes dealing with new investors. Some brokers consider small accounts unprofitable

- who will answer your questions in a way you can understand and will help you learn

- who can readily accept no as an answer from you

- who can admit mistakes and move on

Choose a broker you respect, one who will be responsive to you, and one whose advice you will be willing to take. Once you have made a choice, stick with that broker. Listen and evaluate his or her advice and follow it. Do not chase the hot tips from friends, fellow investors, and people at parties.

Selecting a discount broker

Not all discount brokers provide the same kinds of services. When checking commission rates use an example that reflects the type of trades you will be making. Since trading through discount brokers is done by telephone, note whether you are put on hold and have to wait to speak to someone. When you are anxious to trade, particularly in a volatile market, you do not want to wait.

Conclusion

Looking diligently for the right broker, one with integrity in every sense of the word and one who will help you learn to invest, is not difficult. However, it does take time. It requires time to analyze your financial situation, work on your investment goals, assess your tolerance for risk, determine your investing style, draw up your interview questions, talk with several brokers, compare their answers and comments and your reactions to them, and complete a background check on those that interest you. Your reward is finding that one particular broker with whom you will enjoy working as your stocks increase in value and your knowledge of stock investing grows. Use the Selecting a Stockbroker Checklist to guide your search.

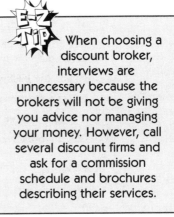

When choosing a discount broker, interviews are unnecessary because the brokers will not be giving you advice nor managing your money. However, call several discount firms and ask for a commission schedule and brochures describing their services.

Checklist for selecting a stockbroker

❏ List my assets and my liabilities and figure my net worth

     • My net worth is $_____.

❏ Determine my financial goal, create a detailed picture of it, calculate the amount of money needed, set the specific date by which I will be enjoying my goal

     • My goal _____

     • Specific dollar amount $_____

     • Specific date _____/_____/_____

❏ Determine the dollar amount I want to invest in stocks

     • At this time I will invest $_____ in stocks.

❏ Determine my tolerance for risk

     • During any 12-month period I can handle a _____ to _____ percent decrease in the value of my portfolio.

❏ Determine the emphasis of my portfolio—liquidity, safety of principal, current income, rapid capital appreciation, etc.

     • My portfolio will focus on _____.

❏ Obtain the names of three brokers to interview

     • 1. _____ 2. _____ 3. _____

❏ List my interview questions

❏ Make an appointment with each broker

     • 1. _____ 2. _____ 3. _____

❏ Meet with each broker

❏ Read through my notes and compare the brokers' comments and their answers to my questions

❏ Check the background of each broker

❏ Select a stockbroker

• My broker is _____.

❏ Call my broker and make an appointment to open an account

Chapter 7
Working with a stockbroker

What you'll find in this chapter:

➟ Opening a brokerage account

➟ Registering account ownership

➟ Record keeping

➟ Working effectively with a broker

➟ Resolving a dispute with a broker

"How do I open an account at a brokerage firm? Is it complicated? How can I build and maintain a good relationship with my broker? What should I do if later on I think my broker has mismanaged my account or has done something unethical?" Have these questions been running through your mind? In this chapter, you will learn how to open a brokerage account and how to keep good records. In addition, you will find tips to help you work effectively with your broker. Furthermore, should you find yourself involved in a serious conflict with your broker, this chapter outlines the steps to take to resolve a broker-client dispute.

Opening your full-service brokerage account

Before you can buy or sell any security, whether you are dealing with a full-service or a discount broker, you must open an account. Brokers may accept orders only from individuals who have accounts with the firm. This is also true if you have a stock certificate and simply want to sell the stock. To protect against fraud the Securities and Exchange Commission has a rule that brokers must know their customers. Through the process of opening an account the broker gains assurance that the client is who he or she purports to be and is indeed the owner of the stock certificate.

Opening an account is a simple process. Once you have selected a stockbroker, make an appointment. Remember your broker will be less distracted if you meet after the market closes. The account costs nothing to open. A broker charges nothing until a stock is bought or sold. However, it is usually necessary to make a deposit before the account becomes active. Ask what the firm requires as a minimum deposit. Your deposit may be a check or a transfer of assets from another brokerage account. If it is the latter, your broker will give you a transfer form to complete, and he or she will handle moving your assets. You need not contact your previous broker.

Opening a brokerage account is much like opening a bank account.

If you give the CAUTION broker misleading information, it may come back to you later through recommendations that do not fit your investment objectives, your investing style, or your financial resources.

However, the broker needs more information about your finances. Brokers are required by law to obtain pertinent financial information about each client to be sure the client is in a position to invest in stocks. Also, Rule 405 of the New York Stock Exchange states that stockbrokers must know their customers' fiscal circumstances so they can make appropriate portfolio recommendations. They are required to develop an investment profile of each client. As with all other professionals, all client information is confidential.

Therefore, you can talk openly and candidly with your broker. At first your broker's questions about money may seem impertinent—that is not his or her intent. Because fiscal information is highly personal, individuals sometimes have difficulty discussing and disclosing the true nature of their finances. However, it is important to do so. Your conversation is the best way your broker has of acquiring a clear, concise picture of your investing requirements. You shared some information during the first interview. Now your broker will be covering the topics in more detail to create your investment profile.

He or she should discuss the following topics either formally, informally, or by working through the customer account form with you:

+ Personal data

   • age, marital status, number of dependents

   • employer

✦ Financial resources

- total income from all sources, income tax bracket

- expenses, loan payments, personal debt, other obligations

- estimated net worth (refer to your completed worksheet in chapter 6 for determining net worth)

✦ Other investments

- savings accounts, mutual funds, retirement accounts

- insurance policies

- real estate

- businesses

✦ Investment objectives

- short-term and long-term goals (those you developed in chapter 6)

- money needed for each goal

✦ Investment funds

- amount available for investments

- additions to the account

✦ Investing style

- frequent trades, intermediate-term buy and hold, long-term buy and hold

✦ Risk tolerance

- conservative, aggressive, adventuresome

✦ Portfolio emphasis

- liquidity, safety of principal, current income, growth and income, capital appreciation, aggressive growth

- a combination

✦ Investment knowledge

- years of investing experience

- types of securities

New account form

Before you officially hold an account, you must complete and sign an account form and receive an account number. The new account form requests the following information:

- full name and address

- telephone number

- date of birth

- social security or tax identification number

- marital status and number of dependents

- citizenship

- name and address of employer, your position, length of time employed

- bank reference—name and address of your bank, account number

- home—rent or own

- approximate annual income

- federal income tax bracket

- estimated liquid assets

- estimated net worth

- investing experience

- previous and existing brokerage accounts

- investment objectives—income, long-term growth, aggressive growth

- risk tolerance—conservative, aggressive

- type of brokerage account—cash, margin

- account registration—individual, joint tenancy, custodial

- stock registration—street name, take possession of stock certificates

- disbursement of dividends and proceeds—deposited in account, mailed

- referring agent

- initial account deposit

Sample New Account Application

The account form is the main and often the only written document that describes your risk tolerance, financial resources, investment strategy, and previous investing experience. It indicates which investments are suitable for you. Be sure the information you give is accurate and complete. Do not overstate anything. If a dispute develops with your broker, your answers on the account form can affect the outcome. Most disagreements occur when a client loses money and feels the broker's recommendations were too risky or the client did not understand the investments. If the case goes to arbitration, the account form may be the first document the brokerage firm references to prove the client had the resources, the experience, and the risk tolerance for the investments.

If you wish, take the Customer Account Application and Agreement home and peruse it. The agreement (the fine print) states, among other things, that the client is subject to the rules and regulations of the exchange. It lists the conditions under which the firm can close an account. It also details the client's rights in a client-broker dispute. By signing this standard document the client agrees that such disputes will be settled by arbitration rather than in a court of law.

Types of accounts

Security transactions are handled through cash accounts or margin accounts. Investors choose one or the other based on how they wish to pay for their stocks. New investors usually prefer a cash account and leave the margin account for more experienced, risk-inclined investors. Both kinds of accounts receive the same standard of service, including monthly statements showing all activity for the period.

Cash account

When buying a stock you have three days after your order is transacted to pay for your shares. The trade date is the date the order is executed. The settlement date (T+3), three business days later, is the date the money and shares change hands. For example, if the trade date is on a Friday, T+3 will be the following Wednesday. The settlement process begins when you pay your brokerage firm for the shares on or before the third day. On the settlement day your brokerage firm pays the seller's firm, the seller's firm credits the seller's account with the proceeds, and the seller's shares are credited to your account.

 Definition:

A *cash account* is the most popular type of account. It is simple and direct to use. You pay for your shares—plus commission—in full by check, cash, or with money previously deposited in the account.

CAUTION

Carefully read everything before you sign. The firm can attach any cash in your account to pay for the loss. If there is no cash, the broker can sell other stock in your account to pay for the shortfall. The brokerage firm then freezes your account for 90 days and you can trade only if there is enough cash in your account to cover the order. This holds true for cash and margin accounts. When selling a stock if you hold the certificate, you must deliver it to your broker properly endorsed on or before the settlement date.

Cash management account

A *cash management account* is a cash account that allows the client to bank and invest at the same institution. This convenient account includes brokerage, money market, and checking accounts and a debit or credit card with ATM access. All activities for each account are reported on a combined monthly statement. Brokerage firms require a minimum of $5,000 to $20,000 to open and maintain a cash management account. In addition, they charge various fees for its use.

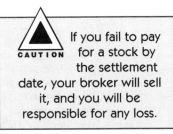

CAUTION If you fail to pay for a stock by the settlement date, your broker will sell it, and you will be responsible for any loss.

Depending on the assessments and requirements it may be less expensive to have separate accounts at your bank and your brokerage firm. Also, because funds are readily accessible, some investors find it too easy to spend their investment dollars for other things.

Margin account

Margin accounts are used by investors who want to finance part of the cost of their stock. By using a margin account they can buy stocks on credit. They pay 50 percent of the cost in cash, borrow 50 percent from the brokerage firm, and use the purchased stock as collateral. They are charged daily interest on the loan—the margined amount—until they sell the stock and repay the loan. When they sell, not all of the proceeds are theirs. They must first pay the loan in full plus any outstanding interest. The remaining proceeds are then credited to their account. The interest rate is from 0.5 percent to 2.5 percent above the *broker call rate*—the rate the bank charges the brokerage firm. It is variable and may change during the life of the loan. The *Wall Street Journal* lists the call rate under Money Rates in the Money & Investing section. Currently it is around 6.50 percent. Even though the interest on the borrowed funds raises the cost of owning the stock, the use of leverage (borrowed money) can increase the return. By borrowing half of the money investors can buy twice the number of shares and make twice the

return on their invested dollars. For example, with $5,000 in cash, by paying $5,000 and borrowing $5,000 they can afford 200 shares rather than 100 shares of McDonald's (MCD) at $50 a share. If the price increases to $55, they will make $1,000 rather than $500. However, it also works the other way—they can lose twice as much when the price declines. If MCD declines $5, they will lose $1,000 instead of $500. The risk and reward both double. A stock's potential

Margin accounts are CAUTION for experienced, speculative investors with substantial means to absorb losses and the ability to handle significant risk.

profit should be large and secure enough to merit the added risk plus the interest costs. Buying on margin turns an ordinary stock purchase into a speculative one.

The Federal Reserve Board requires 50 percent equity to purchase a stock on margin and the industry requires 30 percent equity to maintain the position. When the stock price declines below the purchase price and the position's equity drops below 30 percent, the investor receives a margin call—a call from the broker to add money to return the equity to 30 percent. At that point it is a rule of thumb to sell the stock, take the loss, and pay off the loan. If the investor does not meet the margin call, the broker will sell the stock to repay the loan. To calculate the stock price at which a margin call is imminent, multiply the purchase price by 0.71. To open a margin account, investors must fill out and sign a new account form, a margin agreement, and a lending agreement. They must also supply extensive credit references and make an initial deposit of $2,000.

Account ownership

After you have determined the kind of account you want to open, your next decision is how the account is to be held—who will be the designated owner. For example, accounts can be registered as individual, joint, retirement, or custodial. Many investors have more than one account. They may have an individual account, an IRA account, and be a custodian for a minor's account. Married couples may have separate accounts; spouses often have different investing styles. Select the method of account ownership that fits your circumstances.

Individual account

An individual account is owned in its entirety by one person. The individual owner has total control over the account and its assets. Only his or her name is on the account.

Individual retirement account

Like an individual account, an IRA is owned by one person. The name on the account is that of the individual who earned and contributed the money to the IRA. IRA accounts are cash accounts; government regulations prohibit margined accounts. To open an IRA account, brokerage firms require both a new account form and an Individual Retirement Account form. They charge $25 to $35 to set up an IRA account and a similar amount annually to maintain it.

Joint account

Joint accounts can be opened by two (or more) adults. The adults do not need to be married or related. Both names are listed on the form and appear on the title of the account. Each individual signs the new account form. Each can transact account business. Requests for withdrawals, dividend checks, proxies, and stock certificates must be signed by both owners. A joint account must be further designated as Joint Tenants with Rights of Survivorship or Joint Tenants in Common.

Joint tenancy with rights of survivorship (JTWROS)

Each person owns an undivided equal portion of the account. If one account holder dies, the deceased's portion of the assets passes automatically to the survivor. The assets bypass probate and go directly to the remaining owner. The legacy may or may not incur estate taxes.

Joint tenants in common

Each individual independently owns a clearly defined percentage of the account. The account is treated as a whole, but either owner may dispose of all or part of his or her portion without the consent of the other. Upon the death of one owner the survivor does not automatically inherit the deceased's portion of the assets. Each owner may will his or her portion to anyone. The deceased's assets go to the estate and the survivor opens a new account with his or her portion of the assets.

Uniform gifts to minors account

A Uniform Gifts to Minors Account is for under-aged children—younger than 18 or 21, the age of majority. Children often become interested in owning stocks long before they are 18 or 21. Sometimes grandparents or others give them shares to begin their college funds or to foster their interest in company ownership. The Uniform Gifts to Minors Act (UGMA) makes it possible for children to have brokerage accounts. An adult—a parent or someone else of age— acts as the custodian and manages the account. By law children cannot be held responsible for legal binding contracts which include orders to buy and sell stock. The custodian, the one held responsible, makes the final decisions and places the buy and sell orders. The decisions must be prudent and in the minor's best interest. By law the account may not be a margin account. Often, the child assists with the investment decisions and as a teenager performs the stock analysis and makes specific recommendations to the custodian. When the child comes of age, the account's assets are transferred to his or her new individual account. The securities are reregistered in his or her name rather than in the custodian's name. Any money added to the account as a gift is irrevocable; the donor may not take it back. It is the child's to keep even as an adult.

Other forms of account ownership

Accounts may also be owned by trusts, estates, corporations, partnerships, and investment clubs. These forms of ownership necessitate related account forms in addition to the new account form. Your broker will also request a copy of the document that verifies the trust, estate, etc. Your broker will help you with the forms and proper documentation.

Trading authorization

Sometimes people are too busy to do their own investing, or they want someone else to make all investment decisions for them. In that case, the investor signs a power of attorney or a trading authorization to give a broker, a money manager, or another individual written discretionary permission to trade the account. The designated person may buy and sell any security without the investor's consent or knowledge. If you have given someone discretionary power, carefully check your monthly statements and hold frequent investment conversations with the individual. You can cancel the discretionary permission at any time. If you ever have any doubts, do so immediately.

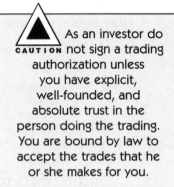
As an investor do CAUTION not sign a trading authorization unless you have explicit, well-founded, and absolute trust in the person doing the trading. You are bound by law to accept the trades that he or she makes for you.

Forms of security registration

Another decision you will need to make as you fill out the new account form is how you want to hold your stocks. Do you want to have them registered in the firm's name (street name), in your name and take possession of the certificates, or in your name and leave the certificates with the firm for safekeeping? Each choice has its advantages.

Transferred and shipped

DEFINITION

Transferred and shipped means the stock is registered in your name and the certificate is mailed to you. The corporation's transfer agent (a bank or trust company) registers the shares in your name on the corporate books and sends you the stock certificate for safekeeping. As soon as you receive the certificate—within two or three weeks—check it carefully. Does it list the correct number of shares? Is the registration (independent, joint) exact? Is your name spelled accurately? If there is a mistake of any kind, immediately return the certificate to the transfer agent so the mistake can be rectified. If your certificate is accurate, record the certificate number in your financial notebook where you entered the details of the stock purchase. Then, because the certificate is negotiable, take it directly to your safe deposit box.

NEVER try to alter CAUTION anything on the certificate.

You may enjoy having the shares registered in your name and the certificates in your possession. Your name and the number of shares you own are listed on the corporate books. You receive dividends, annual and quarterly reports, and proxies directly from the corporation rather than through the brokerage firm. When the stock splits, the additional shares are registered in your name and the certificate for those shares is sent to you. Furthermore, you always have immediate access to your shares. If the brokerage firm suddenly goes out of business, your shares are unaffected. You can sell your stock through any broker where you have or where you open an account. Most importantly, you have physical, negotiable evidence that you own shares of the corporation.

On the other hand, you may find it inconvenient to take possession of the stock certificates. You cannot sell a stock until you have received the certificate.

Certificates are negotiable—therefore, you must keep them in a safe place.

If a certificate is lost or damaged, it is costly and complicated to have it replaced. If you move, it is necessary to send your new address to each transfer agent so you will continue to receive dividends, proxies, annual reports, and certificates for any stock splits. It is also essential to keep a list of the stocks registered in your name and regularly update their value, only those registered in street name appear on your monthly brokerage statement. Finally, when you sell a stock, you must retrieve the certificate from your safe deposit box, have your signature guaranteed by your broker or banker (where your signature is on file) as you endorse the certificate, and hand-deliver or send it by registered mail so your broker receives it by the settlement date.

Transferred and held

DEFINITION

If you have a stock *transferred and held*, it is registered in your name and the certificate is sent to your brokerage firm for safekeeping. Transferred and held is the same as transferred and shipped except the stock certificate is kept in the firm's vault. This arrangement may be more convenient for you. However, brokerage firms dislike being responsible for clients' certificates so they charge substantial fees for the service.

Street name

DEFINITION

Most investors hold their stocks in street name. This means the brokerage firm is listed on the corporate books as the share owner—the *holder of record*. Your name is unknown to the corporation, and no certificates are issued. Your share ownership is recorded electronically in the account records of the brokerage firm. The firm lists you as the *beneficial owner*, you receive the benefits of owning those shares. The firm collects the dividends and immediately credits your account or sends you a check. When the stock splits, the firm adds the new shares to your account. In addition, the firm mails you the corporate proxies and the annual and quarterly reports. You have the same legal rights and protection as you have when the stock is registered in your name.

Holding stocks in street name is convenient and safe. Because your shares are registered in the firm's name, you can sell them by merely calling your broker. You do not have to endorse the stock certificate and deliver it. Therefore, frequent or even infrequent trading is simple and direct. In addition, when you hold shares in street name, you need not worry about the theft, loss, or damage of your stock certificates. The Securities Investor Protection Corporation insures the combined cash and stock value of your brokerage account up to $500,000 ($100,000 for cash) against the bankruptcy of the brokerage firm. If the firm goes bankrupt, which rarely happens, you will be able to recover the full value of your account up to the insured amount. However, you might not have immediate access to your stocks.

Disbursement of income

As you complete the new account form, your final decision is whether to have the interest and dividend income deposited directly into your account or have a check mailed to you each month or quarter. If you are investing for the long term, it is important to leave all interest and dividend income in your account. It can then be used for additional investments. If you are investing for current income, you may want to use the money to supplement your income.

Opening a discount brokerage account

To open an account with a discount brokerage firm, contact the firm and request a new account packet. The packet will contain the necessary forms and information about the firm's services. Because discount brokers do not recommend stocks or give investment advice, most account forms omit the sections about your investment objectives, annual income range, federal income tax bracket, and investment experience. Simply fill out the account application, read the fine print, sign the form, write a check for the initial deposit or fill out an account transfer form, put everything in an envelope, and mail it. You should receive your account number and be ready to trade within two weeks. It may take longer if you are having assets transferred. The firm relinquishing the account sometimes moves slowly.

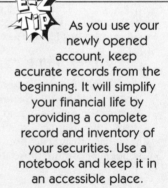

As you use your newly opened account, keep accurate records from the beginning. It will simplify your financial life by providing a complete record and inventory of your securities. Use a notebook and keep it in an accessible place.

Keeping records

Confirmation records

When you are ready to buy a stock, write down the date, company name, ticker symbol, and number of shares. Use this note to place your order whether by telephone, computer, or in person at your broker's office. After your broker has completed the transaction, he or she will verbally confirm the price per share. Add the share price to your purchase note, and place it in your notebook so you can later check the confirmation slip.

You will receive the formal confirmation in four or five days. When it arrives, immediately verify its

> **Definition:**
>
> A *confirmation slip* indicates the type of transaction (buy or sell), the number of shares, corporation name, ticker symbol, CUSIP number (the stock's identification number), exchange where the transaction took place, price per share, commission charge, fees, and total amount of the transaction.

accuracy. Are the name on the account and the account number exact? Refer to your purchase notes. Does the confirmation indicate the correct stock and number of shares at the stated price? Are the fees and commission as you expected? Is there anything you do not clearly understand? If you note a discrepancy or have a question, contact your broker at once.

Sample confirmation slip:

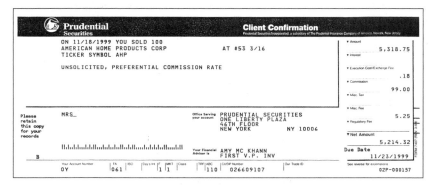

On a new page in your financial notebook record the transaction as a buy. Enter the trade date, stock name, ticker symbol, price per share, fees and commission, and the net amount. Staple the confirmation slip to the back of the page for safekeeping. You will need it for tax documentation when you sell the shares. If you take possession of the stock certificate, copy its number on this page. Each time the stock pays a dividend, post the date and the amount. You can then track the stock's total return. Remember to record any stock splits. When you sell the stock, enter the trade date, price per share, fees and commission, net sales amount, and the amount of gain or loss. To calculate the gain or loss subtract the net purchase amount from the net sales amount. For tax purposes it is necessary to determine the capital gain or loss for each sale. The amount must be disclosed on your tax return. The brokerage firm sends the IRS a form stating the number of shares and the net sales amount. You report the gain or loss. You are also responsible for maintaining the documentation for each stock sale. Staple the buy and sell confirmation slips together, and put them in your income tax folder. Later store them with the year's tax returns.

Brokerage statement

Each month you will receive a statement for your brokerage account. It looks something like a bank statement and gives the status of your account. It documents the beginning and ending account balance, the securities you own, and the month's transactions. At the top of the page you will find your name (the account holder's name) and address, the account number, and the statement's opening and closing dates. The first section of the statement provides a summary of your account. It lists the opening and closing figures for three items: your cash balance, the value of your securities, and the equity or net worth of your account—the cash balance plus the value of the securities. In addition, it lists the total interest and dividend income for the month. The second section, *portfolio positions*, is a detailed register of each security in the account. It contains the stock name, number of shares, current price per share, and total value of the holding. Remember if you have taken possession of a stock certificate, the stock will not be included. The third section, *account activities*, is a log of the transactions that occurred during the month. It reports three types of actions: the sale or purchase of stocks, income or credits to your account—cash deposits, stock splits, dividends, proceeds from the sale of stock, interest on the account cash balance, outgo or debits—personal withdrawals, money used for stock purchases.

When you receive the first statement for a new account, substantiate the account name, address, and social security number. Accuracy is important because this information appears on the end-of-year form the firm sends the IRS—the one that reports the amount of each stock sale and the total interest and dividend income generated by your account. An incorrect account name or social security number could trigger a tax audit.

Each month when your statement arrives in the mail, quickly determine how your investments have performed by reviewing the summary of your account. Note the opening and closing balances. Did the net worth increase? Did the value of your stocks grow? Did your cash balance change?

For further appraisal calculate the rate of growth (new figure minus the old figure, difference divided by the old figure, quotient multiplied by 100 equals percentage change). The growth rate is an evaluation of how effectively your invested dollars are working.

Next, check the account activity. Verify each purchase or sale with the stock's confirmation slip. Be sure you authorized each transaction. Add the interest and dividend amounts. Do their totals match the amounts listed in the summary? If there is a discrepancy of any kind or an entry you do not understand, immediately call your broker.

In your notebook, record each dividend on the appropriate page. Finally, refer to the portfolio positions section of your statement. Compare the current value of each stock with the value listed on last month's statement. If the price of a recommended stock has risen substantially, thank your broker for his or her suggestion. Brokers appreciate the recognition and acknowledgment of their success.

On the other hand, if the stock has declined more than the market, it is cause for concern. Ask your broker why the stock declined. Are the company fundamentals still sound? Should you keep the stock or cut your losses and sell it? When you have finished checking your statement, file it in chronological order in the statement section of your notebook. Your statements provide an official record of your account activity. At the end of the year when you have completed your tax returns, store your statements with the copy of your return. It is a good idea to keep your brokerage statements as long as you keep your tax returns.

Working with your stockbroker

For a long-lasting broker-client relationship start with a foundation of mutual trust, respect, and integrity. Build on that base by holding reasonable expectations, maintaining clear, two-way communication, and letting your broker know how he or she can best help you.

Communication

Your broker's recommendations are based on his or her comprehension of your total financial picture, investment goals, tolerance for risk, and investment knowledge. Have you explicitly advised your broker of the above? Does he or she thoroughly understand? On the first page of your financial notebook record your investment goals, risk tolerance, available resources, time frame for holding a stock, preferred type of stock (slow, intermediate, or rapid growth), and portfolio emphasis (liquidity, current income, capital appreciation). Because of the vast quantity of information and conflicting advice, you may lose sight of your beliefs and objectives. Occasionally reread that first page. Likewise, review it with your broker if you feel his or her recommendations have gone astray. Also, if there has been an actual change in your financial circumstances or if through experience your views on investing have shifted, recognize it, and specifically inform your broker of the changes.

If at any time you disagree with your broker or question his or her advice, judgment, or information, immediately share your feelings and rationally talk about it. This dialogue can build additional trust and understanding. The discussion will be more productive than merely fretting or complaining about the issue over coffee with friends or co-workers. Unless you tell your broker you are displeased, he or she will continue to make the same kinds of recommendations while assuming you are a satisfied client.

Always be considerate when contacting your broker. Call when necessary, but avoid calling to merely chat. If you need to discuss something during market hours, try to keep your conversation short and to the point. It is essential that your broker watch the market and work with all clients. Finally, when possible, schedule your information-gathering sessions after the market closes so your broker will be uninterrupted and able to concentrate on the matters at hand.

Expectations

Determine what you want from your broker. First, insist on pleasant, efficient, and error-free service from the firm. Are your buy and sell orders rapidly and accurately executed? Does the firm promptly move the cash from your account to a money market fund? Are dividends immediately posted? Are monthly statements issued on time? The answer to each of these questions should be yes.

Second, decide how much and what kind of help you will require. For example, do you want your broker to merely execute your trades, or make all investment decisions for you, or guide, advise, furnish research materials, and suggest stocks for you to analyze? Will you make all decisions unassisted? Will you depend solely on your broker's recommendations? Will you and your broker jointly decide on investments? Will you initiate your own analysis and ask your broker to verify your decisions? Thoughtfully answer these questions, then share your conclusions with your broker. The level of help and guidance you desire may vary from time to time

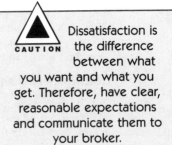

Dissatisfaction is the difference between what you want and what you get. Therefore, have clear, reasonable expectations and communicate them to your broker.

depending on your circumstances. Be aware of any changes and discuss them with your broker so he or she can make the necessary adjustments.

Third, anticipate a reasonable level of personalized service. The attention you receive is usually proportionate to the commissions you pay during a six- or twelve-month period. In all fairness, a client who generates few commissions

HOT spot At a minimum, however, have your broker inform you about any developments that may affect his or her recommended stocks in your portfolio.

should demand a small percentage of the broker's time. Request that your name be added to your broker's client alert list. Ask your broker to tell you when it is time to sell any of the recommended stocks. However, because brokers often find it difficult to advise their clients to sell, do not rely solely on your broker for sell signals. Follow the stock yourself. If it seems to be time to sell, call your broker and ask for his or her opinion and supporting data. If you own a recommended stock in your name rather than street name, your broker has no responsibility for following the stock and advising you. Also, you should not ask your broker to keep you informed about the stocks you initiated. Brokers usually follow only those stocks they recommend—the ones that are familiar to them.

If you have a small account with four or five conservative stocks, you may receive a call every six to eight months. On the other hand, if you have a larger, more aggressive account with ten or twelve stocks, some of which are volatile and require additional supervision, you may hear from your broker every five or six weeks.

note The activity level of your account generally determines how frequently your broker will contact you on routine matters.

Fourth, some investors simply expect too much. They expect miracles. They expect infallible wisdom and judgment—all winners and no losers. They expect maximum profits with little risk. In reality brokers are human, and the market reacts in unpredictable ways. Most brokers are honest and want to do a good job for their clients. They enjoy helping their clients invest profitably. Are you being realistic about what you are asking of your broker?

Broker responsibilities

Your broker's task is to guide and direct your portfolio within the context of your investment goals, resources, and philosophy. This includes making recommendations to buy appropriate stocks, sell under-performing shares, and properly diversify your portfolio. Your broker's goal is to maximize your returns and minimize your risk.

Client duties

Your responsibilities are to ask questions, gather information, make decisions, and monitor your portfolio. Therefore, begin by asking the following questions after each broker recommendation:

- Why should I buy this stock? What makes it attractive? How does it fit my investment strategy?

- What is the stock's estimated total return for the coming year? How much do you expect its price to appreciate? How much will I make from its dividends?

- What is the company's earning-per-share growth rate for the previous five years? How will the company maintain or increase its growth? How does the company compare with others in the industry?

- What are the risks? What percentage of my portfolio does this stock represent?

- How long should I hold it? What developments would be cause for concern or a signal to sell?

- If I have to sell a stock to buy this one, why is the new stock a better investment than the old one? Will the new one appreciate more than the old one after paying the selling commission, capital gains tax, and buying commission?

- Is this your personal recommendation or a recommendation from the firm? Does the firm make a market or carry an inventory in this stock?

- What background material do you have for me to read—annual report, research report, a company page from *S&P Stock Reports* or *Value Line*?

HOT spot Regardless of the temptation, never buy a stock, including a hot tip, until you have carefully checked the figures and agree that it has true potential. Act on fact, not on emotion.

Do not allow yourself to be pressured into feeling that you must buy today before the market closes. Without time to investigate and to consider the purchase, the answer is no. Take two or three days to absorb and think about the information. Evaluate your broker's recommendation and advice. Clearly understand the risks and benefits of the investment.

After you have examined your broker's advice and the available information, it is time to make a decision. Is the stock suitable for you? Does it fit your investment philosophy? Your broker guides and directs, but you make the final decision. It is your money—you have worked for it. If you feel uncomfortable about the stock, do not hesitate to say no. You may sense that it is too conservative or too risky for your portfolio. Sometimes brokers become salespeople first and advisors second. The firm has its own agenda which may compete with quality personalized advice. Your broker may be suggesting a stock the firm wants to sell from its own portfolio—the "stock of the week." This situation raises a conflict because brokers must maximize the return for the firm and for themselves as well as for their clients. Therefore, carefully consider each suggestion. On the other hand, do not turn down all recommendations simply because you are reluctant to act. Ask questions and do your homework. Your money should be working for you. Do not allow it to remain idle while you spend long days at work.

> **HOT** spot Do not feel guilty about refusing to follow the broker's every recommendation.

Each month use your statement to track the performance of your portfolio. You are paying full-service commissions for your broker's expertise. How is he or she doing? Is the growth of your portfolio matching or exceeding the performance of an index such as the S&P 500? (Calculate the percentage change in the S&P 500 the same way you calculated the growth rate of your portfolio.) If your stocks have not kept pace with the index during the previous four or five months, which includes falling less than the index during a down market, talk to your broker. If you are dissatisfied with his or her answers, discuss it with the firm's office manager.

Pay particular attention to your broker's long-term performance. Because brokers are unable to consistently beat short-term market moves, judge your broker by your portfolio's total return over a two- to four-year period. If your portfolio under-performs the S&P 500 index by 10 percent or more in any 12-month period, consider changing brokers. Be an involved caretaker of your money. It in turn will support you.

Broker-client disputes

Serious complaints against brokers are rare considering the total number of broker-client dealings. Because you have carefully chosen your broker and have carried out your responsibilities, you can look forward to a pleasant and successful client-broker relationship for years to come. Yet, there may be a time when things go wrong. You may have just cause to file a complaint against your broker. Fortunately, you can take relatively simple steps to prevent and resolve such conflicts.

Causes

Broker-client disputes involve a loss of money that most often stems from:

1) an unsuitable investment

2) misrepresentation of an investment

3) account churning

4) unauthorized trading

5) missing funds

6) forgery

Because each source of conflict has its own type of warning signals, surveillance is the best prevention.

1) Unsuitable investments

Most disputes result from an unexpected loss on an investment that is later deemed inappropriate. If a security does not fit your financial circumstances, investment goals, and tolerance for risk, it is unsuitable. Likewise, pay attention to the knot in the pit of your stomach or your tossing and turning at night when you think about your portfolio. Acknowledge the validity of your feelings.

Are you worried because you feel the stock is too risky? If so, sell it and invest in something more conservative. Are you disturbed because you have already lost money and are unsure what to do? Check with your broker. If the company is fundamentally sound and the decline is temporary, relax and wait for the price to rise. If the adverse situation seems to be long term, or if the company is not the quality firm you thought it was, sell and reinvest. Do you sense you have too many assets invested in one stock or in a single industry? To decrease the risk, sell some of the shares or one or two of the stocks and reinvest

> **HOT** spot
> Your doubts, uneasiness, and apprehension are important warning signs of an inappropriate investment. Listen to them.

in companies that provide greater diversity. Do you fret about a precipitous market drop? Discuss it with your broker. You can sell several stocks and invest in others that are more defensive. You can also hold additional cash. Finally, has your reaction to risk changed? In reality, is it different from what you thought it would be? Reexamine your feelings. Recognize any differences, and have your broker readjust his or her recommendations.

You have to live with your worries—your broker does not. Make no apologies. Do not continue to hold a stock that worries you. For example, do not allow yourself to be trapped in the cycle of watching the price fall, losing money, worrying about it, and doing nothing. Take action. If at any time you are uncomfortable with your broker's answers, discuss the matter with his or her supervisor or the branch manager.

2) Misrepresentation

As with other professionals, most brokers give sound advice. Some, however, offer unwise suggestions either thoughtlessly or ignorantly. Occasionally, a broker may *deliberately* provide misleading information for his or her own gain. Even though it is unethical and against the law, a broker may *intentionally* omit negative facts, exaggerate positive features, significantly understate the risks, make fraudulent statements, or otherwise misrepresent an investment.

This kind of deliberate distortion is often difficult to recognize until after the fact. Yet, the more thoroughly you question your broker about recommendations, the more critically you listen to what and how he or she answers, and the more carefully you read the company background information, the more expertly you will be able to protect yourself. Listen for warning statements such as "It's a sure thing," "You can't lose," "It's a chance to make a quick profit," "Buy it today or you'll miss out on the opportunity."

Be concerned if you sense you have not received a straight answer to your questions or if your broker puts you down for asking or makes you feel "small" for not knowing or understanding something. He or she may be trying to deflect your attention away from your inquiries. *Always* keep dated notes of conversations with your broker. File them in your financial notebook. Write down what your broker said and what you said. When purchasing a stock, list who recommended it, the reasons you are buying, and any concerns you might

If it sounds too good to be true, it probably is.

have. Include how long you propose to hold it, and under what circumstances you expect to sell. If you are selling, note why you are selling and at whose suggestion. In a broker-client disagreement, these notes provide necessary documentation and eliminate the I said/you said controversy.

3) Account churning

DEFINITION

An investor can lose money through account churning. *Churning* is the *excessive* buying and selling (including mutual funds) at a broker's recommendation for the underlying purpose of generating commissions. To guard against trading too frequently, follow your time frame for holding stocks. Before selling a stock refer to the notes you made when you bought it. How long did you intend to hold it? Under what circumstances did you plan to sell? Why should you sell this stock? What is wrong with it? Will the new stock actually provide a higher return after commissions and taxes than the original one? Has your broker made this type of recommendation before? If so, what was the outcome? If previous trades did not improve your portfolio's performance, do not trade, or proceed with extreme caution.

4) Unauthorized trading

Unauthorized trading occurs when a broker buys or sells a stock without the customer's permission. Be sure you have given permission for each transaction listed in your statement.

5) Missing funds

Money is missing from a client's account. Regularly check your statements. Is the cash balance correct?

6) Forgery

The broker forges a customer's signature on a check or other document. Check your monthly statements to be sure everything is as it should be. If there is anything you do not clearly understand, call your broker.

Broker-client dispute resolution

If you receive a confirmation slip for a stock trade you did not authorize, find an unknown security recorded in your statement, discover a security is missing from the list, or feel the cash balance is incorrect, contact your broker immediately. Probably, it is nothing more than a bookkeeping error that can be quickly and easily corrected. Nevertheless, there are times when fraud, negligence, mismanagement, or misrepresentation take place. In that case, immediately address the situation.

> *note*
> Clients with valid complaints and good documentation have a high rate of success in resolving their broker-client disputes.

1) Approach your broker

If the problem is less tangible or you sense something is not as it should be, such as excessive commission charges, an unsuitable investment, frequent trading that has not improved your portfolio performance, an investment that is producing a major loss or a significantly smaller return than your broker led you to expect, document the problem, then discuss it with your broker. Write down specifically how you feel and why. Make copies of all dated notes of relevant conversations with your broker. For example, include the notes you made when he or she recommended the investment, when you purchased it, during the time you owned it, and when you sold it. Duplicate pertinent brokerage statements and arrange them in chronological order. If applicable, include a copy of your account form that states your investment objectives, approximate annual income, net worth, and previous investing experience. This exercise will help you organize your thoughts and the supporting information. It will allow you to discuss the matter in a quiet, rational, and objective manner. When everything is in order, make an appointment to talk with your broker. He or she may be completely unaware of any problem. It may be a simple misunderstanding that is easily rectified. However, it may not be.

2) Contact the branch manager

If you are displeased with the outcome of the meeting with your broker, write him or her a letter summarizing the meeting and impersonally restating your complaint and your dissatisfaction with its resolution. Next, contact the firm's branch manager. Write a direct and objective letter explaining your problem. Put your emotions aside and focus on the facts. Give the specific details of your complaint. The materials you collected and organized before meeting with your broker are the basis for this letter. Attach copies of all pertinent documentation including notes from the recent meeting with your broker and a copy of your follow-up letter. If you do not receive a reply within two weeks, call the branch manager and arrange a meeting. A firm's success depends on its reputation and the satisfaction of its customers. Therefore, branch managers try to resolve client complaints. If the results of your meeting or the reply to your letter is inadequate, contact the firm's compliance officer and the president of the firm.

3) Notify the compliance officer and the president of the brokerage firm

Write a letter to the firm's compliance officer stating and documenting your complaint. The compliance officer monitors the firm's brokers to ensure they adhere to all rules and regulations applicable to securities trading. These rules include the full and accurate disclosure of information about each recommendation as well as the careful selection of investments to fit the client's risk tolerance and financial circumstances. The compliance department must investigate all customer complaints. If a rule or regulation has been broken, the compliance officer takes appropriate action. Request a written report of the investigation. You should receive a response within three or four weeks. If you have not heard within five weeks, call the compliance officer to check on the status of the investigation.

When you contact the compliance officer, also write a letter to the president of the brokerage firm stating your complaint and the steps you have taken to resolve it. Attach all documentation including copies of letters to your broker and to the branch manager and notes from those meetings. If you have heard nothing within five weeks or have been unable to resolve the conflict in-house, you may wish to pursue the dispute in other arenas. Beyond this point mere disappointment or an even stronger feeling about your loss of money is not enough. Sometimes investors lose money and want to blame someone else for their poor judgment. On the other hand, if you can document the violation of an SEC law or a National Association of Securities Dealers Regulation rule, take the next step. At this point, you can simultaneously follow two separate paths. One path leads toward disciplinary action for the broker and the other toward monetary restitution for you.

4) Pursue disciplinary action

The SEC and NASD Regulation, Inc. are concerned with the enforcement of securities trading laws, rules, and regulations that protect investors. Their role is to investigate the actions of brokers and take disciplinary measures if warranted. They appreciate and often depend on customers' help in bringing possible violations to their attention.

> **HOT spot** If you feel your broker has broken a securities trading rule, call NASD Regulation (212-858-4400), and ask for a brochure that explains how to file a complaint. Also request the address and phone number of the nearest district office—its staff will handle your grievance.

The SEC is a federal regulatory agency that is charged with the enforcement of federal securities laws. It investigates allegations of fraud, insider trading, and unlisted securities. If your complaint entails this type of problem, call the SEC's Office of Investor Education and Assistance (800-SEC-0330) and ask for a copy of the brochure that explains the complaint procedure.

NASD Regulation, supervised by the SEC, is concerned with developing and enforcing industry standards. It investigates each investor's complaint about possible infringements and disciplines firms and brokers who have violated securities rules and regulations. As soon as the district office receives your formal complaint, it begins its investigation. The assigned staff member will contact the brokerage firm and request information. The investigator may ask you for further clarification and documentation. NASD Regulation must establish that a security rule or regulation has been violated. Depending on the complexity of the issue, the investigation may take from one to twelve months. NASD Regulation handles nearly all complaints, but as an alternative investors can file with the exchange that lists the security.

5) Seek restitution

When you file your complaint with the SEC and NASD Regulation to initiate a broker investigation, you can also begin the restitution process by pursuing mediation or arbitration. Both the exchange that lists the security and NASD have mediation and arbitration departments. Most investors choose to work with the latter. NASD Regulation Dispute Resolution carefully selects trained and experienced mediators and arbitrators who are knowledgeable about the securities industry but are outside the industry. They come from diverse cultures, backgrounds, and professions. NASD's mediation and arbitration organization is separate from its broker investigation offices.

6) Mediation

During mediation an impartial third person meets with the opposing parties and guides their discussions. The mediator facilitates negotiations by helping each participant maintain focus, defuse emotions, resolve communication problems, define and clarify the issues, understand the other's position, and in general move the process forward. The mediator may meet with the individuals jointly, separately, or in a combination thereof as he or she assists them to reach their own creative and mutually acceptable solution.

Mediation is less formal and expensive than arbitration. After the entities have agreed to mediation, each pays a fee of $150. Other expenses such as $600 for the initial four-hour session, $150 per hour for additional sessions, and the mediator's travel expenses are shared equally. Mediation has proven to be highly successful because both parties are directly involved in determining the outcome. If you are interested in mediation, contact the NASD Regulation Director of Mediation at (212) 858-4400, or write to the Director of Mediation at NASD Regulation Financial Center, 125 Broad Street, 36th Floor, New York, NY 10004-2193. Ask for the NASD Regulation Dispute Resolution office that serves your area. Also request a booklet that explains the process.

> **note**
> Mediation, which is voluntary and non-binding, has proven to be a useful tool for settling broker-client disputes.

7) Arbitration

Arbitration is a binding alternative to mediation. Because mediation is voluntary, either party may withdraw at any time. If that occurs, the process ends. Should mediation fail, the investor can take the complaint to arbitration. On the other hand, an investor can start with arbitration and bypass mediation. Opening with arbitration does not eliminate the opportunity to mediate. At any time during arbitration the parties can decide to settle the issue or parts of the issue through mediation.

With arbitration the broker-client dispute is settled when an impartial third person or a panel makes a judgment after reviewing the complaint and each party's documentation. Regardless of the size of the claim the arbitrators' decision is final, legal, and binding. Investors agree to arbitration rather than litigation when they open an account with a brokerage firm that trades through the New York Stock Exchange.

note

Although arbitration may be more expensive than mediation, it remains affordable and relatively easy to file. For claims of $10,000 or less the filing fee is $500 and the arbitration fee is $75 without a hearing and $300 per session with a hearing. Claims of this size are handled by one arbitrator. The investor does not need to appear unless he or she chooses to have a hearing. The services of a lawyer are unnecessary. However, an investor may be represented by one if he or she so desires. Cases involving larger claims of $10,000 to $30,000 are heard by a panel of three arbitrators. At this level the filing fee is $500 with an arbitration fee of $600 per session. In these cases it is recommended the investor seek professional advice. The lawyer should be knowledgeable about securities laws and arbitration rather than litigation. Investors can contact the Public Investors Arbitration Bar Association for the names of reliable lawyers nationwide.

A successful filing requires a fully documented and detailed description of the complaint including the NASD rules and regulations the investor feels the broker violated. Disappointment in the outcome of an investment is not enough. When considering arbitration or mediation, an investor should weigh the costs against the size of the claim. If you are interested in arbitration, call NASD at (212) 858-4400 or write the Director of Arbitration, NASD Financial Center, 33 Whitehall Street, New York, NY 10004, for the district office that serves your area. Contact the district office for an arbitration kit. There is a six-year statute of limitations, which may be less if shortened by state limitations. Therefore, do not delay. For information about state limitations contact your state securities office.

> **HOT spot** Investors with legitimate, well-documented complaints, however, have a high rate of success in obtaining restitution. Yet, they seldom, if ever, recover 100 percent of the money they lost.

Conclusion

One does not automatically learn how to be a successful investor. Investing know-how and assets do not come packaged together. What does come is the desire to put your money to work efficiently. An important part of that process is knowing how to work effectively with your stockbroker. Your relationship with your broker can enhance or detract from the success of your portfolio. Therefore, take your responsibilities seriously. Be honest with yourself and your broker about what you have and what you want. Carefully consider your broker's recommendations and ask questions. Remember the only foolish question is the one that should have been asked but was not. Check your statements, keep good records, and track your portfolio's performance. Remain vigilant—it is your money. You are the one who cares most about how you do in the market.

Chapter 8

Picking a stock

What you'll find in this chapter:

⟼ Technical analysis

⟼ Fundamental analysis

⟼ Emerging-growth stocks

⟼ Rapid-growth stocks

⟼ Cyclical-growth stocks

I have a broker. I have opened an account. I am ready to purchase some shares. How can I determine which stock is a good one to buy? How do I research a stock? How can I evaluate my broker's suggestions? In this chapter, Picking a Stock, you will learn how to analyze a company. You will learn what information to use, where to find it, and what it means. You will learn what to look for in a company by using a fundamental analysis approach.

Stock analysis

When investors analyze a company to determine if they want to buy the stock, they use either *technical analysis* or *fundamental analysis*. These two approaches to selecting a stock are based on the assumption that price movements can be predicted.

Technical analysis

note

Technical analysts, also called technicians and chartists, care little about the quality of the company and its business. Instead, they concentrate on the movements and variations of the stock's price and trading volume. Technicians believe that changes in a stock's price create recurring patterns that can be used to predict future price movements. To identify these repeating patterns chartists graph the stock's price over a selected period of time—hours, days, weeks. To forecast the next price trend they look for price formations with names such as *double top, broadening top,* and *falling wedge.*

Variations in a stock's trading volume act as indicators when associated with the corresponding changes in price. For example, when a stock's price and trading volume are both increasing, analysts feel the price will continue to rise. However, if a stock's price is rising but its volume is decreasing, they think the price may be near its top. If its price is falling and its volume is increasing, technicians believe the stock may be starting a major down trend. Finally, a stock may be approaching the end of a long decline when its price is still declining but its trading volume has decreased. In summary:

Price trending up	=	Price rising and volume increasing
Price near the top	=	Price rising and volume decreasing
Price trending down	=	Price falling and volume increasing
Price near the bottom	=	Price falling and volume decreasing

DEFINITION

Technicians also consider a stock's support, breakout, and resistance levels. A *breakout* is a price movement that rises above (breaks) a stock's previous high or drops below its previous low. Often the price continues in that direction. A *support level* is the stock's previous low. When the price approaches a previous low and declines no farther, the support level is said to have held, and the price tends to rally. A resistance level is the stock's previous high. Frequently the price stops rising just before it reaches this level. However, if it climbs above the *resistance level*, the price usually continues to increase.

In addition to tracking individual stocks, technical analysts follow the market as a whole. They plot the number of stocks that are advancing and declining in price as well as the number of stocks that are hitting new highs and

> Technical analysis is used by investors who are interested in short-term trading and short-term capital appreciation.

new lows. Technicians consider it bullish if more stocks are rising than falling and if more stocks are reaching new highs than new lows.

Short-term traders may hold a stock for a few weeks or days or even hours. For example, day traders buy shares of stock when the market opens in the morning and sell some time before the market closes in the afternoon. Traders make money by following the price and volume patterns of 10 to 15 stocks, buying thousands of shares at a time, and selling when the price has risen a quarter or a half point. Some short-term investors find technical analysis reliable enough to make trading profitable over time.

Fundamental analysis

Fundamental analysts are concerned with the quality of the company and with buying the stock at a favorable price. They believe they can predict a stock's broad price movements by determining the company's basic (fundamental) value and comparing their evaluation with the market's evaluation of the shares. Often the market over- or undervalues a stock. Therefore, the stock price will be higher or lower than the company merits. If the market has overvalued a stock, fundamentalists believe there is greater potential for the price to decline than for it to continue to rise at its current rate. At this point buyers will be overpaying for the company's future growth. If the market has undervalued a quality company, investors will be buying the company's potential growth for a bargain price. The broad price trend of the stock will be up as other investors discover the company's value and buy its shares.

To evaluate the quality of a company, fundamental analysts examine the company's past and present sales, earnings, and dividend growth, its level of cash and short- and long-term debt, its dividend payout and price earnings ratios, as well as its competitive position in the industry. They assess the company's financial stability and its ability to increase profits. As a company's profits grow, its stock becomes more valuable to shareholders, and additional investors buy the stock. This demand drives up the price of the stock.

note Fundamental analysis is used by long-term investors—those who buy shares to hold for several years as part owners of the company.

After investors have completed their fundamental analysis and have chosen quality companies with growth potential, they often use technical indicators to time their purchases. They study published price and volume charts and look for trends. Is the price and volume of the stock trending up or down? Is the price approaching a support, resistance, or breakout point? Is it time to buy?

Many fundamental analysts also study the economy and its impact on different industries. They look at economic components such as interest rates, inflation rates, and unemployment figures. These factors alter a company's ability to grow and prosper. The increase or decrease in profits, in turn, affects the company's stock price.

Later in this chapter, as you work through the Smart Stock Analysis Guide, you will learn how to do your own fundamental analysis. You will acquire the knowledge necessary to evaluate a company's profitability and its financial condition. You will understand how to determine whether a stock is overpriced or underpriced. You will be equipped to make an informed decision about buying the stock you are considering.

Types of stocks

Buying shares (part ownership) of a corporation is much like buying a car. You, the purchaser, must first decide what type of company or car you want to own. Do you crave a racy, high-performance car—an aggressive, high-growth stock? Are you longing for a solid, crash-resistant vehicle; a financially strong company that grows slowly but pays a good dividend, a stock that provides protection during market declines? Or do you prefer something in between? Growth stocks can be classified as emerging, rapid, intermediate, slow, and cyclical growth. Each type has its own distinguishing characteristics.

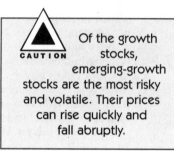

CAUTION Of the growth stocks, emerging-growth stocks are the most risky and volatile. Their prices can rise quickly and fall abruptly.

Emerging-growth stocks

DEFINITION

Emerging-growth companies are those whose earnings have increased an average of 30 to 60 percent a year for the past three years. These unseasoned companies have developed an innovative product or service, and their first attempts have been successful. However, the question is, will the company's earnings continue to increase at the same rate? The high growth rate of these untested companies is difficult to sustain—many things can happen to interfere with it. New investors would be wise to first gain experience with rapid- or intermediate-growth stocks.

Rapid-growth stocks

DEFINITION

Rapid-growth companies are those whose earnings per share have increased an average of 20 to 30 percent a year for the previous five years. They tend to be small, aggressive companies that can maintain the expected growth rate for the next several years. They have learned how to expand profitably. They have learned how to successfully produce and market their innovative products or services. They have learned how to choose favorable locations for new stores and how to operate them successfully. Expansion by itself does not automatically add to a company's earnings. Each additional store and each new customer must mean extra profit for the company. Otherwise, a company can expand its way into bankruptcy.

This proven expansion stage of a company's life spurs demand for its stock which in turn drives up the stock price. When choosing this type, select fairly-priced stocks of financially sound companies. After buying them, track the companies' profits each quarter. Check the earnings growth rate as soon as the company releases the information to the press. The market dislikes any slow-down or perceived slow-down in earnings.

> **HOT spot** Rapid-growth stocks can substantially increase the value of a portfolio. As with any stock, the higher the growth rate, the greater the potential reward.

There is no guarantee the company will continue to grow at its current rate. For any number of reasons a company's earnings may briefly or not so briefly falter. If you own the stock and the growth rate decreases, determine whether the condition will be extended or temporary. If the situation is short term, you may want to ride out any price declines. If the decrease looks as if it will persist, you may decide to sell the stock before the price drops further. In addition, with rapid-growth stocks there is no guarantee a company will be able to always meet investors' and analysts' expectations—sometimes their expectations become unrealistic. A company may be sound and growing 20 to 25 percent per year yet lose favor with analysts. They may downgrade the stock, institutional and individual investors may sell, and the stock price will decline. Prices of rapid-growth stocks can drop more quickly than prices of other types of growth stocks except those of emerging-growth stocks. Be wary of highly popular or fad companies and industries. They are often overrated and overpriced.

Home Depot, Dollar General, and Harley-Davidson are examples of rapid-growth companies whose earnings have increased an average of 20 to 30 percent a year for the past five years. Price and earnings graphs for Home Depot and Dollar General show the overall steep rise in company earnings and stock price.

> **HOT spot** As with any stock, the higher the growth rate, the greater the risk.

Names of rapid-growth stocks are listed in the following sources: *Value Line Investment Survey* in its weekly Summary & Index section publishes a list titled Highest Growth Stocks, *Forbes* magazine reports on the 200 best small companies in America each year in an early November issue, *Standard & Poor's Stock Screens*, which can be obtained from a broker, includes rapid-growth stocks, and *Standard & Poor's Outlook* provides various groupings of stocks with their five-year growth rates. Also, brokers can suggest rapid-growth stocks. Look for companies that have developed innovative products or services. They can be found in slow- as well as fast-growing industries.

Home Depot

Dollar General

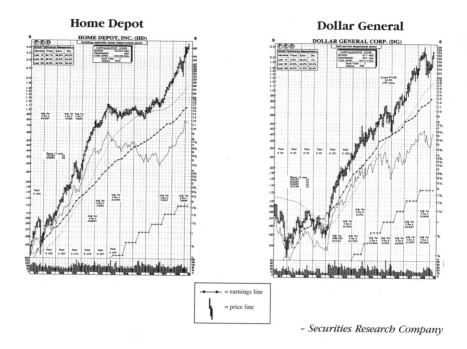

– Securities Research Company

Intermediate-growth stocks

Intermediate-growth companies are large, well-established companies such as Johnson & Johnson and Gillette. These familiar companies have been successful in business for many years and will continue to be an important part of our economy.

The leading characteristic of intermediate-growth companies is their consistent growth of earnings. They have moved from the rapid-growth phase with its ups and downs to the intermediate-growth stage with its more stable and dependable growth. These companies continually develop new products and new markets. Their profits rise year after year.

If a company's earnings increase an average of 15 percent over a five-year period, its stock price tends to double within the five years. There are several advantages to holding these stocks long term—as long as the company remains

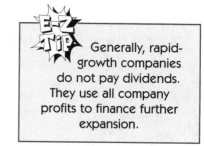

Generally, rapid-growth companies do not pay dividends. They use all company profits to finance further expansion.

Definition:

An *intermediate-growth company* is a corporation whose earnings per share have increased an average of 12 to 20 percent a year for the previous 10 years.

financially sound and growing at the desired rate. First, stockholders gain from the growth in company earnings and the steady increase in stock price despite any temporary declines in price and recessionary decreases in earnings. Second, they profit directly from the dividends the company pays each quarter. Because the company's rapid expansion has come to a close, it now has extra money at the end of each quarter to use for dividends. Although the dividends tend to be small, if reinvested they consistently add to the value of a portfolio. Third, share owners who hold quality stocks for five to ten years benefit from stock splits that occur. When the stock splits the price drops proportionately, but shareholders gain by holding the old and new shares as the price again rises. Fourth, investors are able to improve their portfolio diversification by holding some intermediate-growth stocks. They add stability to a portfolio that contains rapid-growth stocks, and they add growth to a portfolio that contains income or slow-growth stocks.

Walgreen

Schering-Plough

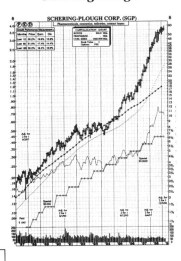

= earnings line

= price line

- Securities Research Company

Walgreen and Schering-Plough are examples of intermediate-growth stocks. Their charts show the steady increase in earnings and stock price. The lines showing the rates of growth are less steep than those of rapid-growth stocks, therefore, the risk level is lower.

For the names of current intermediate-growth stocks refer to the following lists: Conservative Stocks in the weekly Summary & Index section of *Value Line*, Stocks for Long-Term Capital Appreciation in *Standard & Poor's Outlook*, and broker recommendations.

Slow-growth stocks

The earnings of slow-growth companies grow from 6 to 12 percent a year. They are large, mature establishments that have a long history of profitability. Industry and economic downturns impact these financially strong corporations less than other types of companies. These businesses are the dominant firms in their industries. They have saturated the market with their goods and services. They now focus on maintaining their market share.

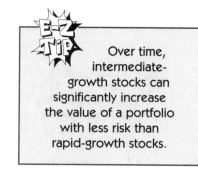

Over time, intermediate-growth stocks can significantly increase the value of a portfolio with less risk than rapid-growth stocks.

DEFINITION

Slow-growth stocks are called *income, blue chip*, and *low-growth, low-risk stocks*. They are the safest type of stocks investors can purchase. Their prices fluctuate less—fall less in a bear market and rise less in a bull market—than the prices of other types of stocks. These firms are low-risk investments because they are very large, financially strong leaders in their industries and because they have a long record of steady earnings and dividend growth. These same features, however, inhibit significant price appreciation. Investors do not buy slow-growth stocks for price appreciation. Instead, they buy them for their relative safety and the generous dividends they pay.

CAUTION

Even though slow-growth stocks are safer than other types of stocks, they are not without risk. Their prices still go down when the market goes down. However, they do not drop as far nor as fast as other stocks. In addition, circumstances can change for any company, including a large, slow-growth company. It is unusual but not impossible for a mature, stable company to fall on hard times. Therefore, investors need to re-evaluate these stocks from time to time.

General Electric and Colgate-Palmolive are examples of slow-growth companies. Their charts show the slow, steady rise of earnings, dividends, and stock prices. The lines illustrating their growth rates appear relatively flat with shallow upward slopes.

For the names of current slow-growth companies refer to the following lists: Conservative Stocks in the weekly Summary & Index section of *Value Line*, Stocks for Superior Long-Term Total Return in *Standard & Poor's Outlook*, general lists of blue chip stocks and income stocks, and broker recommendations.

General Electric   **Colgate-Palmolive**

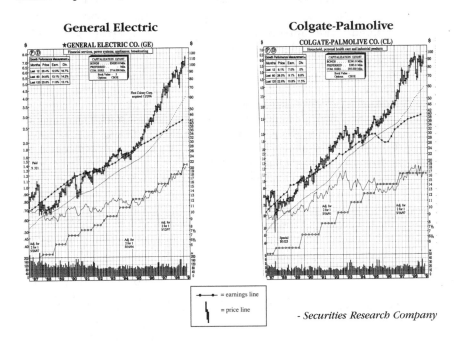

- Securities Research Company

Cyclical-growth stocks

Examples of cyclical industries are steel, machinery, automobiles, home building, and travel and leisure. Companies in these industries produce expensive goods that last for several years—durable goods. When the economy slows and a recession sets in, consumers delay buying these big-ticket items. Instead, they invest in major repairs for their cars, limit expensive trips, and postpone buying new homes. When the economy picks up and people go back to work, they have a pent-up demand for these goods. They are ready to replace their cars, buy new refrigerators and new houses, and go on vacations. As the economy improves and business expands, investors know there will be an increased demand for durable goods.

> **note**
> A cyclical company is one that is involved in an industry whose profits are closely tied to the ups and downs of the economy.

They anticipate the rise of company profits and begin to buy cyclical stocks.

Cyclical stocks are sometimes confused with intermediate-growth stocks. Like intermediate-growth stocks, cyclicals are large well-known companies—Chrysler, Ford, General Motors—that pay dividends. Their earnings over the long term grow by the same 12 to 20 percent. However, cyclicals are less stable than intermediate-growth stocks. Their earnings, dividends, and stock prices vary more than those of intermediate-growth stocks. For example, during economic expansions cyclical companies are able to substantially increase their dividends, but during recessions they may need to reduce them. When the economy is coming out of a recession, the prices of cyclical stocks rise much faster than those of intermediate-growth stocks. On the other hand, when signs of a recession begin to develop, their prices decline farther than those of intermediate-growth stocks.

To successfully invest in cyclical stocks, investors need to understand and follow economic and business cycles. As the economy strengthens, consumer demand grows, business expands, profits increase, and the prices of cyclical stocks rise. On the other hand, as the economy weakens, consumer demand decreases, business conditions worsen, profits fall, and the prices of cyclical stocks decline. Deciding when to buy or sell a cyclical stock is critical. Investors need to be ready to buy at the end of the recession and ready to sell at the height of the economic expansion. However, investors as well as economic forecasters often have difficulty determining when a recession is ending and when an economic boom is drawing to a close.

The charts for Ford and Alaska Airlines show the cyclical rise and fall of each company's earnings and stock price.

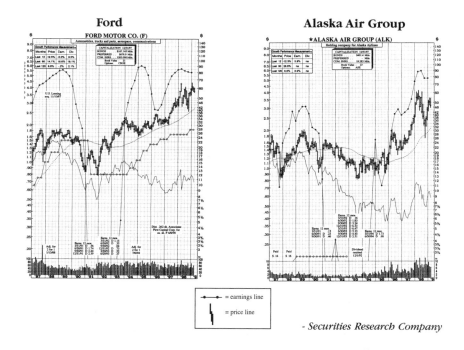

- Securities Research Company

Investors who are interested in cyclical stocks can ask their brokers for suggestions, or they can choose quality companies in cyclical industries. For example, an investor might analyze Nucor and Lukens in the steel industry or Ford, General Motors, and Daimler-Chrysler in the auto and truck industry.

Other types of stocks

In addition to growth stocks, investors often include other kinds of stocks in their portfolios. They may own shares of banks, savings and loans, utilities, and real estate companies. These stocks require a different type of analysis. Also, investors are often attracted to asset plays, takeovers, turnarounds, and special-situation stocks. These call for additional investing and stock analysis expertise. While gaining experience, investors can work with the four kinds of growth stocks. These are the building blocks of any portfolio. They cover a wide range of companies—all of which can be analyzed using a single approach.

Chapter 9

Smart Stock Analysis Guide: Profitability

What you'll find in this chapter:

➠ Learning to use the Smart Stock Analysis Guide

➠ Understanding earnings per share

➠ Evaluating revenue growth

➠ Determining profit margins

➠ Using return on equity

Using the Smart Stock Analysis Guide

For your first experience in using the Smart Stock Analysis Guide (SSAG) you may use the examples in this chapter, McDonald's and Wendy's (all necessary data as well as a sample guide on McDonald's are provided in Appendix A), or you may work with companies of your choice. Perhaps you want to know more about a hot tip, a company a broker suggested, a local publicly owned corporation, or a firm whose product or service you like. When learning to analyze companies, it is helpful to work through two corporations in the same industry. This allows you to note the difference between the firms' profitability and financial conditions as well as the merit of the companies' stock prices. Therefore, if you are studying a stock of your choice, select a second one in the same industry so you can compare the firms. *Value Line* is a good source for names of other corporations in the same industry—it groups the companies it covers by industries.

Before you begin to fill out the Analysis Guide, take time to collect the necessary materials. First, make a copy of the Smart Stock Analysis Guide and the Smart Stock Analysis Summary sheet found in the Forms section. Second, the guide requires information from either the *S&P Stock Reports* or the *Value Line*

page for the company. You can find these at your public library or your stockbroker's office. You can use other sources such as annual reports and investment web sites, but *Value Line* and *S&P Stock Reports* are the easiest to use and the most readily available. When studying a stock, only use **one source** for all company data.

Reporting services often treat statistics differently. For example, when reporting earnings per share, *Value Line* excludes any non-recurring gains and losses and footnotes the amounts. On the other hand, *Standard and Poor's* includes the extraordinary items in its calculations but gives details about the items in its commentary. Also, *Value Line* reports company data based on the calendar year while Standard and Poor's uses the company's fiscal year. Consequently, the S&P and *Value Line* figures do not always agree. The sample guide for McDonald's uses information from *S&P Stock Reports*. In addition, a copy of the *Value Line* page is included and labeled for your reference. Third, purchase a newspaper that lists the stock in the quotation tables. The paper might be a local one, the *Wall Street Journal*, or *Investors Business Daily*. Next, locate a calculator and your favorite pencil. You can use any calculator, but I prefer a Texas Instruments BA-35, the business analyst calculator. It has a built-in formula for calculating the company's compound average annual growth rate. Usually, the BA-35 can be purchased for $20 or less. In summary, you will need the following items:

- a Smart Stock Analysis Guide and a Smart Stock Analysis Summary Sheet

- historical company data

    + an *S&P Stock Reports* or a *Value Line* page for the company

    + the pertinent industry page from *Value Line* which lists the industry's composite figures

- current company data

    + a *Wall Street Journal*, an *Investors Business Daily*, or a local newspaper that contains the stock's current price and p/e

- tools

    + a pencil

    + a calculator

Or use this checklist:

1) Copy of the Smart Stock Analysis Guide and the Smart Stock Analysis Summary Sheet

2) *S&P Stock Reports* or *Value Line* page for the company

3) *Value Line* industry page

4) Newspaper stock quote

5) Calculator

6) Pencil

Now, find a comfortable place to work—desk, favorite chair, dining room table—settle in with a cup of coffee and begin filling in the Analysis Guide.

Basic stock information

On page one of the guide fill in the company name, ticker symbol, exchange where the stock is traded, industry, and current date. From the newspaper list the stock's 52-week high and low, its closing price, p/e, and yield. (If the company has not made a profit in the last four quarters, the p/e column will be blank. If the company does not pay a dividend, the yield column will be blank.) Also, list the closing figure for the S&P 500 Index. As time passes you can measure the stock's price performance against the performance of the S&P 500.

Profitability

DEFINITION

Profit is the amount of money a company makes after all expenses are paid. Profit, also called *net profit, net income,* and *net earnings,* means selling goods and services for more than it costs to produce them. A company reports its net earnings—income after all expenses, bond interest, taxes, and preferred stock dividends have been paid—at the end of each quarter and each fiscal year. These net income figures are listed in news sources and the company's quarterly and annual reports. If the company has not made a profit, it reports the amount it lost. In Category One you will determine the company's profitability for the past five years by finding its earnings-per-share growth rate, revenue growth rate, profit margin, and return on equity. From this information you will be able to make informed judgments about the company's past performance, and informed predictions about its future prospects.

Section A: Earnings-per-share growth

DEFINITION

The terms *earnings per share, EPS, net earnings per share, profit per share, net profit per share, income per share,* and *net income per share* are used interchangeably. A company calculates earnings per share by dividing its net profit by the average number of outstanding shares of common stock. For example, McDonald's 1998 net income of $1,550,000,000 divided by 1,409,000,000 shares equals $1.10 earnings per share. The $1.10 EPS figure is easier to understand and

deal with than the $1,550,000,000 total net income figure. EPS is the standard measure of company growth and profitability. Because it is a gauge of company performance, it is closely monitored by investors, analysts, and the financial media. They compare the figures for the current quarter or the current fiscal year to those of the previous year. In fact, the reporting of quarterly earnings can affect the stock price. If earnings have increased more

Definition:

Earnings per share is the amount of company profit that is designated for each share of common stock.

than analysts expected, the stock price tends to rise. However, if earnings have merely met analysts' predictions or have risen less than expected, or if the company reports a loss, the stock price may decline sharply. Profit per share is the bottom line. Expanding profits are necessary to fund continued company growth and dividends. How much have McDonald's profits grown year to year during the past five years?

Data

The earnings-per-share figures are listed as **Earnings** on the second page of the *S&P Stock Reports* under the heading **Per Share Data ($)**. The ($) means the figures are reported in actual dollar amounts. The earnings for 1998 are listed as 1.10 which means the earnings per share for McDonald's was $1.10. This row is circled and labeled with a **1** because this is the first piece of data you use for the guide.

Filling in the Smart Stock Analysis Guide:

• **Annual earnings-per-share growth rate**

The growth rate—the percentage change—of earnings from year to year gives a more meaningful and revealing picture of company performance than the dollar difference. The following directions lead you step by step through determining the annual earnings-per-share growth rate:

1) On the guide, number the years in pairs as per the McDonald's example. Begin with the most recent year listed in the S&P report. For example, number the years 1998 and 1997, 1997 and 1996, 1996 and 1995 for five pairs of years. The years are arranged in pairs so the percentage change in earnings can be calculated between the two years.

2) List the *earnings* for each pair of years. If needed, refer to the example for McDonald's.

3) To calculate the percentage change in earnings—the growth rate—between each two-year period use the per-share earnings figure for each of the two years and complete the following calculations for McDonald's:

The equation:

EPS amount for [(newer year - older year) ÷ older year] x 100 = % change between these two years.

The calculation:

[(1.10 - 1.15) ÷ 1.15] x 100 = the growth rate between 1997 and 1998.

a) 1.10 - 1.15 = - 0.05

b) - 0.05 ÷ 1.15 = - 0.043

c) - 0.043 x 100 = - 4.34% rounded to - 4.3 percent earnings-per-share growth rate for McDonald's from 1997 to 1998. McDonald's earnings decreased four percent in 1998. Record the results on the guide.

Many calculators automatically compute the percentage change when you enter the figures for each of the two years and press a combination of keys. For the Texas Instruments BA-35:

a) Enter the **EPS figure for the newer year**—1.10

b) Press **2nd** key

c) Press Δ%

d) Enter the **EPS for the older year**—1.15

e) Press =

The result is - 4.34 rounded to - 4.3 percent earnings-per-share growth rate from 1997 to 1998.

Now, calculate and record the percentage change in earnings for each of the remaining two-year periods. If needed, follow the sample guide. When finished, indicate whether McDonald's earnings-per-share growth rate decreased or increased overall. Was the rate of change consistent?

Basic analysis:

Expansion of the company's products or services without a matching rise in profits does not heighten the value of the company. Advancing earnings per share is the result of improved sales, a more efficient operation that results in higher profit, or a decrease in the number of shares outstanding. On the other hand, lower earnings per share comes from a decrease in sales, higher operational costs, or additional shares of stock outstanding. Consider the following points about the company's earnings-per-share growth rate.

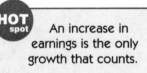

An increase in earnings is the only growth that counts.

Does the company have a stable or an increasing year-to-year earnings-per-share growth rate (percentage change from year to year)? Have the earnings grown more or less consistently or have they grown somewhat erratically over the past five years? Two or more percentage points difference is significant. Because the stock price, thus the value of the investment, follows the EPS pattern, a stable or a regularly increasing growth rate is preferable to one that fluctuates or declines. Past performance predicts future potential.

Make a note of any year in which the earnings per share increased or decreased by an unusual amount. When you read the commentary about the company in the text of the *S&P Report* or the *Value Line* page you will probably find an explanation for the fluctuation. One down year out of five is acceptable. Was it a recessionary year? Check the *Value Line* grid of statistics—the recessionary years are shaded. Generally, five years is long enough to cover a complete business cycle of recession and expansion. Was the company able to reestablish its normal growth rate?

Is the growth rate for the most recent year greater than those of previous years? A difference of two or three percentage points is meaningful—from 12 to

14 percent, from 20 to 23 percent. The company should be maintaining or increasing its growth rate each year. If it has decreased, read the S&P and *Value Line* commentaries to find out what is happening. Is the situation temporary? Is it the beginning of a longer-term decline in profit growth? The company may be having difficulties. Or the company may be changing from a rapid- to an intermediate-growth stock. Whatever the reason, over time the stock price follows the earnings growth rate.

• Five-year compound average earnings-per-share growth rate

To calculate a five-year average, you must have six years of data. However, you use only two figures—the EPS amounts for the most recent year and the oldest year (the sixth year). Both EPS figures must be positive numbers. The average will not calculate if either is negative. If one is a negative number, move to the first positive number and calculate. If your data then covers five years, the result will be a four-year average. If it covers four years, it will be a three-year average. Use one of the two methods below to determine the five-year compound average growth rate.

Method one: Calculate a simple average growth rate and convert it to compound growth rate by using the table.

Step 1: Find the five-year *simple average* growth rate.

The equation:

[(newest year's EPS figure - oldest year's, sixth year's, EPS figure) ÷ oldest EPS figure] ÷ 5 (x 100) = five-year *simple average* growth rate

The calculation:

[(1.10 - 0.73) ÷ 0.73] ÷ 5 (x 100) = 10.1 percent *simple average* growth rate.

Step 2: Use the table to convert the *simple average* to the *compound average*.

Simple Average

TABLE TO CONVERT SIMPLE GROWTH RATE TO COMPOUND GROWTH RATE

Simple Average	2	4	6	8	10	12	14	16	18	20	22	24	26	28	30	32	34	36	38	40
Compound Average	2	3.7	5.4	7	8.4	10	11	12.5	13.7	15	16	17	18.2	19	20	21	22	23	23.7	24.6

Simple Average	42	44	46	48	50	52	54	56	58	60	62	64	66	68	70	72	74	76	78	80
Compound Average	25.4	26.2	27	27.7	28.5	29.2	30	30.6	31.3	32	32.6	33.2	33.8	34.5	35	35.7	36.3	37	37.4	38

Compound Average

simple average of 10.1 percent converts to a compound average of 8.5 percent. Record the company's five-year compound growth rate on the guide.

Method two: Use a Texas Instruments BA-35 Calculator

a. Enter the number of years average—**5**

b. Press **N**

c. Enter the **EPS for the oldest year** (year six)—**0.73**

d. Press **PV**

e. Enter the **EPS for the newest year** (year one)—**1.10**

f. Press **FV**

g. Press **CPT**

h. Press **%i**

The result of 8.5 percent is the five-year compound average annual growth rate.

Basic analysis:

When you calculated the average, was either the newest or the oldest year's EPS unusually high or low? If you used the next EPS figure, what would the four-year average growth rate look like? Would it be more in line with expectations?

Is this an emerging-, rapid-, intermediate-, or slow-growth stock? If the economy has been stable for the past four or five years, either mostly up or mostly down, it may be difficult to tell the difference between an intermediate-growth stock and a cyclical stock. Does the company belong to a cyclical industry?

The five-year compound average earnings-per-share growth rate is considered the company's long-term growth rate. It is a standard for judging the company's current performance and a benchmark for evaluating its future achievements. Therefore, is the most recent year-to-year growth rate equal to or greater than the five-year compound average? If it is less, read the commentary to find out why the EPS growth has decreased.

- **Earnings-per-share growth rate between the most recent quarter and the corresponding quarter a year ago**

Currently, is the earnings growth rate increasing, or is it staying about the same? Or has it decreased? On the first page of the *S&P Report* under the heading **Fiscal Year Ending Dec. 31**, find the subheading **Earnings Per Share ($)** and the row **2Q**. It is circled and labeled with a **2**. (*Value Line* lists the data in the left-hand column.) On the guide, list the 1999 and 1998 second quarter EPS figures. To calculate the percentage of growth, use the same calculations you used to find the earnings growth rate between each of the two years—[(EPS for the newer quarter - EPS for the older quarter) ÷ EPS for the older quarter] x 100 = % change or the growth rate. These calculations work for finding the percentage change and the growth rate between any two amounts. If needed, check the example for McDonald's. Record the results on the guide.

Basic analysis:

By comparing the current quarter with its corresponding quarter a year ago, the effects of seasonal changes are removed that occur when comparing consecutive quarters. Currently, is the earnings growth rate keeping pace or surpassing, first, the most recent year's growth rate and, second, the long-term growth rate? Or has the growth rate declined this quarter? The company should be maintaining or increasing its earnings growth rate even on a quarterly basis.

• Smart Stock Analysis Summary Sheet

Review the earnings-per-share growth rate information by placing a checkmark in the appropriate column—yes, no, neutral—following each topic in Profitability, Section A: Earnings-per-Share (EPS) Growth Rate on the Smart Stock Analysis Summary.

• General Comments

Is this company the type of growth stock that interests you? Perhaps it is growing faster and entails more risk than you want, or perhaps it is growing too slowly for your taste. If this company's growth rate does not meet your criteria, you do not need to continue its analysis. However, if the company looks promising, proceed with its analysis. At this point in the guide you may continue to analyze the company by moving on to Section B, or you may complete Section A for the second company. By working through Section A with the second company you will immediately begin to see the differences between two companies in the same industry. The information needed to analyze Wendy's is included in Appendix A.

Section B: Revenue growth rate

DEFINITION

Revenue is the total amount of money a corporation receives from its various sources of income. Generally, most revenue comes from the sale of products and services; therefore, the terms *sales* and *revenues* are often used interchangeably. Other sources of revenue might include leases, royalties, franchises, and interest income. Revenues tell how much business the company has done during the year or during the quarter. How much have McDonald's revenues or sales increased over the past five years?

Data

The revenue figures are listed as **Revs.** on the second page of the *S&P Report* under the section heading **Income Statement Analysis (Million $)**. The **(Million $)** means that six zeros have been omitted from the figures in the chart. The **Revs.** row is circled and labeled with a 3. The first revenue number, which is for 1998, is listed as 12,421—it actually means $12,421,000,000. For analysis purposes, use the figures as they are listed—12,421, etc.

- **Annual Revenue Growth Rate**

To calculate the year-to-year revenue growth rate for the past five years follow these directions:

1) On the guide number the years (six) in pairs (five) the same as you did when calculating the earnings-per-share growth rate. If needed, refer to the sample guide.

2) List the revenue amounts for each pair of years.

3) Calculate the percentage change in revenues for each two years, by following the same procedure (the equation or the BA-35 calculator) used to calculate the earnings-per-share growth rate. The equation and the calculations for McDonald's are as follows:

The equation:

revenues for [(newer year - older year) ÷ older year] x 100 = % change and the growth rate between the two years.

The calculation:

[(12,421 - 11,409) ÷ 11,409] x 100 = 8.87% rounded to 8.9 percent revenue growth rate for McDonald's between 1997 and 1998.

After recording each percentage change, indicate whether the revenue growth rate decreased or increased overall and whether or not the rate of change was consistent.

Basic analysis:

If the company is in a strong competitive position, it can raise its prices without losing sales. It sells the same number of units at a higher price. However, the time may come when a price war ensues, then the company will have to cut its prices and its revenues will decline. A more dependable way to increase revenues is by selling additional units. A company can sell more goods and services by opening new plants or new stores, by acquiring new companies, or by increasing sales at existing locations. For the long term it is best for a company to have the ability to grow on its own.

Look at the percentage change for each pair of years. Has the revenue growth rate steadily increased? The company must have expanding sales to sustain rising profits. Is the growth rate consistent? Consistent revenue growth tends to produce steady profit growth and stock price increases. Is the most recent year's growth rate equal to or greater than that of the previous year? If not, read the commentary to find out what kinds of problems the company is having with sales.

- **Five-year compound average revenue growth rate**

To calculate the five-year average revenue growth rate use the same method you used to calculate the compound average earnings-per-share growth rate. Record the results in the guide.

Basic analysis:

What is the average rate of revenue growth for the past five years? Is the most recent year's growth rate keeping up with or surpassing the five-year growth rate? The company's previous performance indicates how its revenues may grow during the next five years.

> *note* Growth in revenue comes from either price increases or the sale of additional units—more hamburgers, cars, barrels of oil.

- **Revenue growth rate between the most recent quarter and the corresponding quarter a year ago.**

Is the current revenue growth rate keeping pace with last year's growth rate and the five-year average growth rate? On the first page of the S&P report under the heading Fiscal Year Ending Dec. 31, find Revenues (Million $) and the row 2Q circled and labeled with a 4. On the guide list the revenues for the second quarter of 1999 and 1998, calculate and record the percentage change between the two quarters.

Basic analysis:

Does the current revenue growth rate match or surpass last year's growth rate and the long-term growth rate? Or is the revenue growth rate declining? Slumping sales sooner or later mean weakening profits and falling stock prices.

Compare revenue growth rate with earnings-per-share growth rate

Are the company's revenues and earnings growing at a similar rate? Sales growth means little without expanding profits. On the other hand, earnings growth cannot be sustained for long, more than three or four years, without a matching rise in sales. Long-term company success requires similar growth rates (within three or four percentage points) for both revenues and earnings per share. Similar increases in sales and earnings per share is an indication of quality management. Sound management ensures that sales continue to advance and the company is run efficiently so revenue dollars reach the bottom line.

Compare EPS and revenue year-to-year growth rates, five-year growth rates, and current quarter growth rates. Are revenues growing faster than earnings? Revenues can grow faster than profits for a while, but eventually increased revenues need to add to the company's profits. When revenues

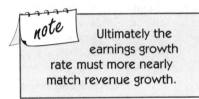

note Ultimately the earnings growth rate must more nearly match revenue growth.

continue to grow faster than earnings per share, it may be a sign of poor management. In that case the additional revenue dollars are used to support an inefficient operation.

Are revenues growing more slowly than earnings? Over the short term (three to four years) revenues can grow more slowly than earnings per share without adversely affecting earnings growth. This is true for rapid-growth companies as well as for companies that are increasing their profits by operating more efficiently and economically. However, over the long term if earnings per share are to continue to grow, they must be supported by growth in revenues (within three or four percentage points) because continuing profits are based on the sale of goods and services. Sooner or later the earnings growth rate drops to match revenue growth, and the stock price declines in response to the disappointing earnings news.

• **Stock Analysis Summary Sheet**

Review the revenue growth rate information by placing a checkmark in the appropriate column—yes, no, neutral—following each topic in section B: Revenue/Sales Growth Rate on the Stock Analysis Summary Sheet.

Section C: Profit margin

DEFINITION

Profit margin, also called *return on sales, return on revenues,* and *percent income of revenues,* measures how efficiently and economically a company makes its money. *Profit margin* (earnings divided by sales) tells what percentage of each sales dollar ends up as profit. It is a way to evaluate its management. Quality managers run productive companies in which time and money are not frittered away. They are able to effectively control costs. Their workforce is highly productive. They follow successful marketing and pricing policies. They are strong competitors. Because of their proficient management, their companies have above-average profit margins. Is McDonald's a low cost producer? Is management effectively controlling costs? Are the employees unusually productive? In other words, does the company have a high profit margin?

Data

To calculate profit margin use the figures for pretax income listed as **Pretax Inc.** and revenues listed as **Revs.** They are found on the second page of the S&P report under the heading **Income Statement Analysis (Million $)**. They are circled and labeled with a 5 and 3, respectively. Because pretax profit margin is free from the effects of taxes, it gives a clearer picture of the company's efficiency than is given by the net profit margin—after-tax profit margin.

HOT **spot** Profit margins are a way to identify companies within an industry that are the low-cost producers of goods and services.

- **Pretax Profit Margin**

On the guide fill in the year and the data. Then, calculate and record the pretax profit margin for each of the previous five years. Follow the example below for McDonald's:

The equation:

(pretax income ÷ revenues) x 100 = pretax profit margin.

The calculation:

$(2,307 ÷ 12,421) = 0.1857$ x 100 = 18.57% rounded to 18.6 percent pretax profit margin for McDonald's in 1998.

Indicate whether the pretax profit margin is increasing or decreasing. Particularly note any increases or decreases within the three most recent years.

If using *Value Line*, note that it lists net profit (after-tax income) rather than pretax income. Therefore, convert the net profit to pretax profit before completing the computation. Follow the example below for McDonald's:

Step 1: Convert net profit to pretax income

The equation:

net profit ÷ (1 - income tax rate as a decimal) = pretax income

The calculation:

$1769.2 ÷ (1 - 0.327) = pretax income

(0.672)

$1769.2 ÷ 0.672 = $2622.7 million pretax income

Step 2: **Calculate pretax profit margin**

The equation:

(pretax income ÷ revenues) x 100 = pretax profit margin

The calculation:

(2632.7 ÷ 12421) x 100 = 21.2 percent pretax profit margin

Basic Analysis:

Over the past five years has the company's profit margin increased or decreased? One percentage point is significant. Was the company able to extract additional profit from each dollar of sales? Is the company becoming more efficient at making a profit? If the pretax profit margin rose, the company either reduced its costs or raised its prices. It is preferable if the company increased its profit margin by reducing costs. Thus, the company improved its internal operations. When a company is able to expand its profit margin, its earnings per share rise. However, be cautious if a company's profit margin has grown suddenly, and it is substantially above its historical and industry average. Try to find out what factors caused the surge in profit margin.

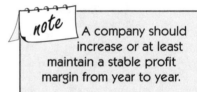

A company should increase or at least maintain a stable profit margin from year to year.

• **Company net profit margin compared with industry net profit margin**

Compare the company's *net profit margin* with the industry's composite net profit margin. Net profit margin is used here because reporting services list industry net profit, not pretax profit margin. When making this comparison, net profit margin gives an adequate picture of the company's efficiency. Is the company's profit margin better than the industry average? Profit margins are industry specific. Each industry has its own typical margin. For example, the net profit margin for grocery stores is about 2.2 percent, and for drug manufacturers it is approximately 16.5 percent.

For company data use **%Net Inc. of Revs.** found on the second page of the S&P report under the heading **Balance Sheet & Other Fin. Data (Million $).** The data for the most recent year are circled and labeled with a **6.** Industry composite figures are found in *Value Line* on the industry page at the beginning of each industry section. For this comparison refer to *Value Line's* **Restaurant Industry** page and use the **Net Profit Margin** figure in the **Composite Statistics: Restaurant Industry** table. The data for the most recent year are circled and labeled with a **6.**

On the guide, fill in the year, the company's net profit margin, and the industry's net profit margin. Indicate whether McDonald's profit margin is above or below the industry profit margin.

If you wish, compare the company's profit margin with those of specific companies in the industry. *Value Line* is a good source for data on competitive companies. Look through *Value Line*'s Restaurant Industry section and find companies similar to McDonald's—fast food rather than family-style restaurants. You will find that Wendy's, Tricon, and CKE Restaurants have operations much like McDonald's. Is McDonald's the most efficient producer in the fast food industry? List the name and the profit margin for each of McDonald's major competitors. Indicate whether McDonald's net profit margin is above or below those of its competitors.

Basic analysis:

How does the company's net profit margin compare with the net profit margin of the industry as a whole? The company should be more efficient at making money than the average company in the industry. The company with a strong profit margin—a low-cost producer—is better able to withstand economic and industry downturns than its competitors with weak profit margins. The company with a low break-even point (high profit margin) will be able to reduce its prices without the adverse effects on profits its weak-margin competitors will experience. A high-profit-margin company has staying power and will ultimately be able to take market share from its less efficient competitors.

How does the company's net profit margin compare with those of similar companies in the industry? Does the company have the highest or one of the highest profit margins in the industry? Generally, one can assume that the company with the higher profit margin is the better run company. For example, it may be better at research or marketing, or it may have a more productive workforce. The higher and the steadier the profit margin, the more profitable the firm.

> **HINT** The company's profit margin should be greater than or at least equal to the industry average.

• **Stock Analysis Summary Sheet**

Review the profit margin information, and place a checkmark in the appropriate column—yes, no, neutral—following each topic in section C: Profit Margin.

Section D: Return on equity (ROE)

DEFINITION

Return on equity (net income divided by common equity—net worth, stockholders' equity) is an additional measure of company profitability. It is also called *profit rate, percent earned on net worth, net income-to-net worth,* and *return on stockholders' equity.* It measures how well management runs the company both operationally and *financially.* It tells investors how effectively their money is being used—how competently management uses their money to make more money. It is the rate of return the company earns on common equity. What percent return on equity has McDonald's been earning? Has it been increasing, decreasing, or remaining about the same? How does the return for the most recent year compare with those of previous years?

Data

The *S&P Report* lists return on equity on the second page as **% Ret. on Equity** under the heading **Balance Sheet & Other Fin. Data (Million$)**. It is circled and labeled with a **7**.

• **Return on equity**

On the guide beginning with the most recent year of data, fill in the year and list the percent return on equity for each of the previous five years. Indicate whether the return is increasing or decreasing. A change of one percentage point is significant. Particularly note the three most recent years.

Basic analysis:

How effectively is management using investors' equity to increase the worth of the company? A standard rate of return on equity is from 13 to 15 percent. If the company is able to maintain a high ROE, it is the dominant company in its industry and controls a major part of the market. However, if a company has strong competition, it will be unable to sustain a high return on equity. If a company already has an outstanding or exceptional ROE, it cannot be expected to increase it from year to year. It is difficult to simply maintain it. In this case, a decline to more normal levels is to be expected.

> **note**
> Analysts usually consider a return of 10 percent or less inadequate, 20 to 25 percent outstanding, and 30 percent exceptional.

On the other hand, if a company's return on equity is low, management should be improving it each year. To raise the return on equity a company must boost its profits from sales (profit margin), manufacture its goods more efficiently, or expand its use of leverage (borrow more money—increase its debt-to-equity). Even though some companies can skillfully use borrowed funds (outside capital that needs to be repaid with interest) to enhance their growth rates, it is preferable for a company to increase its return on equity without additional debt. If the company's debt level remains stable, the heightened return is coming from a more efficient operation and/or expanded sales and profit margin. In the long run it is important for a company to grow internally without borrowing extra funds. An enhanced return on equity requires basic changes in the company's operation and its performance.

In addition, return on equity measures the company's ability to sustain its current rate of growth. Over the long term a company's earnings cannot grow faster than its return on equity—than the company's ability to make money using its equity. If the earnings growth rate is substantially 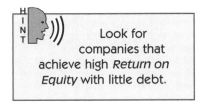 Look for companies that achieve high *Return on Equity* with little debt. higher than the return on equity, eventually the earnings growth tends to decline to more closely match the rate of return on equity.

- **Company return on equity compared with industry return on equity**

How does the company's return on equity compare with the industry average? Return on equity varies with the industry and the current economic conditions. Is McDonald's return higher than the average for the restaurant industry?

The industry composite figure for return on equity is listed on the *Value Line* **Restaurant Industry** page as **Return on Shr. Equity** in the **Composite Statistics: Restaurant Industry** table. It is circled and labeled with a **7**.

On the guide, fill in the year, the company's return on equity, and the industry's ROE. Indicate whether McDonald's return is above or below the industry average.

If you wish, compare the company's ROE with those of specific companies in the industry. Check the ROE for McDonald's competitors by looking at **Return on Shr. Equity** on each of their pages in *Value Line*. On the guide, list the name and the ROE for each major competitor. Indicate whether the company's return is above or below those of its competitors.

Basic analysis:

Because return on equity varies with the industry, evaluate a company's return by comparing it with the industry average or with those of similar companies in the industry. Some industries have a relatively low return on equity because they require high capital expenditures. For example, the heavy equipment industry requires large amounts of capital for plants and machinery. Its return on equity is normally low. Use the industry average as a standard to judge the company's performance. The company's ROE should be equal to or greater than the industry average. Return on equity and profit margin are substitutes for knowing the company's management and being able to accurately assess its effectiveness.

• Stock Analysis Summary Sheet

Review the information about return on equity, and place a checkmark in the appropriate column—yes, no, neutral—following each topic in section D: Return on Equity.

HOT **spot** It is important to know whether a company's low return is due to inefficient management or whether the industry as a whole has a low return.

Chapter 10

Smart Stock Analysis Guide: Financial condition and institutional ownership

What you'll find in this chapter:

⟶ Analyzing short-term finances

⟶ Calculating a current ratio

⟶ Analyzing long-term finances

⟶ The ins and outs of dividends

⟶ Analyzing institutional ownership

If a company is financially strong, it owns more than it owes, and it is able to pay its current bills and debts on time. Fiscally secure companies have a financial cushion that allows them flexibility during any downturn in the company, industry, or economy. Also, they have the resources to expand and to make acquisitions. To assess a company's financial health consider the following: Does the company own more than it owes? Does it have enough cash and other readily available assets to pay its bills this year? What is its debt load? Has its debt increased? What proportion of its earnings does it pay out in dividends? This section of the guide produces a snapshot of the company's financial strength.

Section A: Short-term financial condition

DEFINITION

When discussing a company's finances, *short-term* is defined as one fiscal year—12 months. A financially healthy company has enough cash and cash-like assets (current assets) to pay its bills, debts, and operating expenses during the year. Cash includes not only money in checking and savings accounts but also certificates of deposit (CDs), marketable securities, and other instruments that can be quickly converted into cash with little price change. The idle cash—excess cash, money that is not needed immediately—is invested in low-risk, liquid instruments, the remainder is kept in bank accounts. Often, cash is listed as cash and cash equivalents or cash and cash assets. It is unnecessary to distinguish between cash, cash assets, and cash equivalents because the latter two are easily converted into cash. How much cash does McDonald's have? Has the amount been increasing or decreasing?

Data

The *S&P Report* lists cash (not cash flow) on the second page under the heading **Balance Sheet & Other Fin. Data (Million $)**. It is circled and labeled with an 8.

• Cash

Note the amount of cash the company had on hand at the end of each of the previous five years. On the guide indicate whether the cash generally increased or decreased during that time. In addition, list the amount of cash the company had at the end of the most recent year of data and the previous year; indicate whether it increased or decreased.

Basic analysis:

Often, a growing cash balance is a sign of financial health. Therefore, did the company's balance increase during the past three or four years? Or did it decrease? If it declined, why did it decline? To find out read the *S&P* or *Value Line* commentary about the company. Deteriorating cash balances may indicate declining sales or rising expenses. Either of these situations is cause for concern. However, the corporation may have less cash because it recently funded an expansion or acquisition, paid down long-term debt, bought back shares of stock, or raised its dividend. These uses will enhance the value of the firm. If the company's cash balance has grown substantially for two or three years due to expanded sales or reduced expenses, what does the firm plan to do with the additional funds? Will it let the money sit in the bank or will it put the money to work in ways that add value to the corporation? If the company's current expenses have grown significantly, the company may need the extra funds to pay its bills. At this time in the analysis process, if you are unable to determine the reason for the increase or decrease in cash, it is sufficient to note the changes. The cause of the fluctuations may become apparent later.

• Current Ratio

DEFINITION

Current ratio is the ratio of current assets to current liabilities. It indicates whether a company has enough cash and other current assets to pay its bills, debts, and operating expenses that are due within 12 months. It is calculated by dividing current assets by current liabilities. Current assets are what the company owns and expects to convert into cash during the coming year. Current assets consist of cash, cash equivalents (money market accounts, CDs), marketable securities, accounts receivable (money owed the company for goods or services sold), inventory (value of finished goods, work in progress, and raw materials), and prepaid expenses. Current assets are also called *liquid*, *quick*, and *floating assets*.

DEFINITION

Current liabilities are the debts the company owes and must pay from cash within 12 months. Current liabilities consist of accounts payable (money the company owes others for goods and services), bank loans and notes payable due by the end of the year (including any scheduled long-term debt payments), taxes (payroll, unemployment, state and federal income taxes), salaries and wages, and other costs of doing business.

The *S&P Report* lists the current ratio, **Curr. Ratio**, on the second page under the heading **Balance Sheet & Other Fin. Data (Million $)**. It is circled and labeled with a 9. *Value Line* does not list the current ratio. However, it can be calculated by dividing current assets by current liabilities, they are found in the left hand column in the table titled **Current Position**. On the guide, beginning with the most recent year, fill in the year and list the current ratio for each of the previous five years.

Basic analysis:

The current ratio measures the company's ability to pay its short-term debt and operating expenses from the cash and cash equivalents it has on hand. It measures the company's short-term financial soundness. Does the company have enough cash and cash equivalents to meet its bills and debts that will come due in 12 months? A company's inability to pay its creditors on time damages its credit rating. Also, unpaid creditors may take legal action.

A current ratio of 2:1 ("2 to 1" or simply "2") indicates short-term financial strength. Often, creditors insist on a current ratio of at least 2 before they lend money for expansion. This ratio means the company has twice as many current assets (cash, cash equivalents, inventory) as current liabilities (bills due this year). In other words, the company has $2 of current assets for every $1 of current liabilities. A ratio of 2:1 provides a cushion if a major customer does not pay on time, and it gives the company enough liquid assets to withstand business downturns.

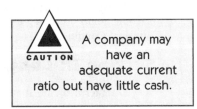

A company may have an adequate current ratio but have little cash.

Even though the preferred current ratio is 2, acceptable ratios vary slightly according to the type of business. For most businesses a standard current ratio ranges between 1.3 and 2. Some businesses that require little inventory and have rapid, dependable cash inflows can operate effectively with a lower current ratio (1 to 0.75). Other companies operate competently with a lower ratio by reducing their inventories through the just-in-time approach. A current ratio of 1.3 is typical for this type of company rather than the 2 that is common for companies that stockpile inventories.

A large part of the company's current assets may be inventories that require time to convert to cash. The company must first sell the goods, then collect the resulting accounts receivables; both tasks may be difficult during a downturn in business. In addition, the goods may sell for less than currently valued. To determine what portion of the company's current assets is composed of actual inventories, check the company's *Value Line* page or its annual report. *Value Line* lists the dollar value of inventories in the left-hand column in the table titled **Current Position**. Annual reports provide this information in the Balance Sheet under Assets.

A ratio of 1:1 means the company has only $1 of current assets for $1 of current debt. Therefore, the company is living hand to mouth without a financial cushion if it has a mishap. A current ratio of 1 or less than 1 indicates a weak short-term financial condition. It suggests the company is short of cash and cash equivalents—working capital (the dollar difference between current assets and current liabilities).

On the other hand, high ratios from 3.5:1 to 5:1 state the company has extra cash resources that are not working. The company needs to employ its resources effectively. Management could use these assets to expand profitably, acquire a quality business, buy back shares of stock, or raise its dividend. Any of these would increase the value of the corporation.

 The current ratio is another piece in the company's financial picture. It is important to know whether the company can pay its current bills, particularly during a recession. Try to buy companies that have a current ratio of 1.3:1 or better.

• **Stock Analysis Summary Sheet**

Place a checkmark in the appropriate column—yes, no, neutral—following Current Ratio in Category Two: Financial Condition, section A: Short-Term Financial Condition.

Section B: Long-term financial condition

 Long-term financial strength is the company's financial soundness beyond the current fiscal year. One sign of financial well-being is a decrease in the company's long-term debt. A second and more important indication of financial strength is how much the company owes compared to the value of what it owns (debt-to-equity ratio). A financially viable company owns substantially more than it owes.

Data

The *S&P Report* lists long-term debt as **LT Debt** on the second page under the heading **Balance Sheet & Other Fin. Data (Million $)**. It is circled and labeled with a **10**.

• Long-Term Debt

Long-term debt includes notes, loans, and bonds that are scheduled for repayment sometime beyond the end of the current fiscal year. Corporations, like individuals, have mortgages and debts that require payments for 10, 20, or 30 years. As a company's debt declines, the business becomes stronger financially. Has McDonald's long-term debt declined over the past five years?

Note the amount of long-term debt the company had at the end of each of the past five years. On the guide indicate whether the amount increased or decreased during that time. Also, list the amount of long-term debt for the most recent year of data and the previous year. Indicate whether it increased or decreased.

Basic analysis:

Any decline in debt is positive, whereas a substantial rise calls for further investigation. Read the *S&P Report* or the *Value Line* commentary to determine possible reasons for the increase. Often, companies need to borrow long-term money to finance expansion. Did the corporation buy

> **HOT** spot The less long-term debt, the more financially secure the company.

another company or new equipment, build a new plant, or open more stores? These and similar uses of long-term debt enhance the value of the company. The growth produces additional profits which are used to pay off the debt—often before it is due. Over a period of years a company's debt level tends to rise and fall. After the debt has risen substantially, it should subside within two or three years as the expansion becomes profitable and the company pays down the debt. If the amount of long-term debt does not decline, perhaps the growth was unsuccessful. The company may not be able to pay off the debt ahead of time, or perhaps it is using the profits for other purposes.

• Debt-to-equity ratio

DEFINITION

The debt-to-equity ratio is the standard measure of company financial strength. It allows investors to compare the financial soundness of any two companies. It states a company's long-term debt as a percentage of its equity—what the company owes as a percentage of what it owns. In the debt-to-equity ratio (long-term debt divided by shareholder equity), *debt* is the dollar amount of the company's long-term debts and *equity* is the dollar value of everything the company owns. Other terms for equity are *total stockholder* or *shareholder equity*, *common equity*, and *net worth*. Equity is the corporation's total assets minus its total liabilities. The lower the percentage of debt the stronger the company. What is McDonald's debt-to-equity ratio?

To calculate the debt-to-equity ratio divide long-term debt by common equity. Use the figures for long-term debt, **LT Debt**, and common equity, **Common Eqty.**, found on the second page of the *S&P Report* under the heading **Balance Sheet & Other Fin. Data (Million $)**. They are circled and labeled with a **10** and **11**, respectively. Follow the example below for McDonald's:

<u>Step 1</u>: **The percentage of debt**

The equation:

(long-term debt ÷ common equity) x 100 = the percentage of debt

The calculation:

($6,189 ÷ $9,464) x 100 = 65.3% rounded to 65 percent debt

<u>Step 2</u>: **The percentage of equity**

The equation:

100 - percent debt = the percentage of equity

The calculation:

100 - 65 = 35 percent equity

McDonald's has 65 percent debt and 35 percent equity

On the guide list the percentage of debt and equity. It is often interesting to calculate the ratio for the two or three preceding years to note any changes.

Basic analysis:

A standard debt-to-equity ratio for financially healthy companies is 25 percent debt to 75 percent equity. Companies that have 50 to 55 percent debt are probably financially sound, but that level of debt begins to raise concerns. Companies that have 80 percent debt to 20 percent equity are considered financially weak. Some companies owe so much they have less than one percent equity. In contrast, other companies have no long-term debt. They have enough cash to pay current expenses and to expand without borrowing.

> ⚠️ **CAUTION** During a business or economic downturn, a high level of debt with its subsequent interest payments may jeopardize the company financially or at least narrow its choices.

For companies that borrow long-term money it is important that management monitor the amount of debt and keep it under control. The more long-term debt a company has the more interest it must pay each year whether or not the company makes a profit. Large interest payments depress the company's earnings and may drain its resources in the years ahead.

The debt-to equity ratio is one way to determine whether a company's long-term debt load is acceptable or whether it is uncomfortably high. As the debt ratio climbs above 60 percent, the risk for shareholders increases. In addition, the stock price tends to become more volatile. The more debt a company has, the less cash, borrowing power, and flexibility it has. Conversely, the less long-term debt a company has, the stronger it is financially, and the more alternatives it has.

- **Stock Analysis Summary Sheet**

DEFINITION

Review the information about the company's long-term financial condition, and place a checkmark in the appropriate column—yes, no, neutral—following each topic in section B: Long-Term Financial Condition.

Section C: Dividends

(If the stock you are analyzing does not pay a dividend, proceed to Category Three: Institutional Ownership.) *Dividends* are the portion of a company's profits it pays directly to its shareholders quarterly, semi-annually, or annually. Common stock dividends are paid from the company's cash balance after all operating expenses, interest on debt, taxes, and dividends on its preferred stock have been paid. The board of directors votes for or against declaring a dividend. Is it the best use of the company's cash? If the vote carries, the board sets the dividend amount, the record date, and the payment date.

Corporations begin paying dividends when they move from their explosive, capital-intensive expansion to a more evenly paced growth period. As the rate of growth and the need for capital decrease, unallocated profits accumulate at the end of each fiscal quarter, these funds can be used for dividends.

In addition to income, dividends provide a floor under the stock price during a falling market. When the market deteriorates, the prices of stocks that pay dividends, particularly large dividends, do not drop as far as those of non-dividend-paying stocks. As the stock price declines, the dividend yield rises and becomes competitive with the yields of CDs, money market accounts, and similar instruments. Investors find the dividend yield attractive and

> *note*
>
> For investors, dividend income from intermediate- and slow-growth stocks replaces the accelerated price appreciation of rapid- and emerging-growth stocks.

purchase the stock. This demand begins to stabilize the stock price. Often, investors buy high-dividend-paying stocks during times of market uncertainty and crisis because the dividend produces additional income, and the dividend provides some protection for the stock price.

Data

The *S&P Report* lists dividends per share on the second page as **Dividends** under the heading **Per Share Data ($)**. It is circled and labeled with a **12**. The figure is the total dividend amount per share for the year.

• Dividend Growth

Because the past is often a predictor of the future, look at the dividend-per-share amount over the past 10 years. Have dividends been paid each year? Has the company consistently raised its dividends? Did the company at any time decrease its dividend? A decrease in dividends means less income for the investor and a drop in the stock price. On the guide indicate whether the dividends have steadily increased from year to year.

Basic analysis:

If you are buying a stock because of the income its dividends generate, be sure the dividend growth has as least kept pace with the effects of taxes plus the rate of inflation. To calculate the dividend growth rate, use the formula for calculating the year-to-year earnings-per-share growth rate, or calculate the five- or ten-year compound average growth rate. As a quick check, if the dividend doubled in 5 years, its compound average growth rate is 15 percent. If it doubled in 10 years, the growth rate is 7 percent. Cyclical stocks may pay dividends that have kept up with inflation or have doubled over the previous 10 years, but they may have had to cut their dividends during the previous recession. Their dividends, as well as their earnings and stock prices,

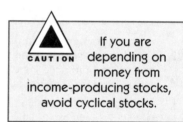

CAUTION If you are depending on money from income-producing stocks, avoid cyclical stocks.

tend to be cyclical, increasing during strong economic periods and decreasing during recessions. When buying a stock for its dividend, look for companies that have paid a dividend each quarter for ten or more years, have continually raised their dividends, have not missed a dividend payment, and have not cut the amount of their dividend at any time. If a company decreases its dividend or does not declare a dividend for a quarter, it indicates the company is having financial problems. Investors react to this news by selling their shares, which drives down the stock price.

• Dividend Payout Ratio

DEFINITION The *dividend payout ratio* is the percentage of company earnings paid out to shareholders as dividends (dividend ÷ earnings per share). It is one way to judge the soundness of the dividend. The lower the payout ratio, the more secure the dividend. What is McDonald's payout ratio?

The *S&P Report* lists **Payout Ratio** on the second page under the heading **Per Share Data ($)**. It is circled and labeled with a 13. On the guide list the dividend payout ratio for the most recent year. The stated figure is the percentage of profits the company paid out in dividends that year.

> *note* Payout ratios tend to be industry specific. Also, they vary according to the type of growth stock.

Basic Analysis:

The dividend payout ratio is a useful gauge for assessing the dependability of future dividends. Will the company be able to continue paying dividends at the current level? Will the company be able to raise its dividends in the coming years? Emerging-growth companies do not pay dividends—they reinvest all profits to finance expansion. Some rapid-growth companies pay small dividends. Their payout ratios generally range between 5 and 10 percent. The payout ratios of intermediate-growth stocks vary between 10 and 30 percent. Often, a ratio above 50 percent raises questions about the reliability of the dividend and the company's ability to continue to grow at its current rate. If the company is a slow-growth company that is no longer expanding and is merely maintaining market share, a dividend ratio of 50 to 60 percent is generally acceptable. However, a high payout ratio may limit the flexibility necessary to maintain a competitive edge. A payout ratio of 100 percent means all company earnings are being used to pay dividends. If the payout ratio is greater than 100 percent, the company is paying more in dividends than it made. A negative ratio indicates the company is paying dividends while it is losing money—it has no profits.

> *note* The company needs to set its dividends at a level it can maintain through good and bad times.

Companies are reluctant to decrease their dividends because it results in bad publicity. A cut in dividends announces the company is in financial trouble—the stock price drops immediately. In fact, some companies raise their dividends after they announce lower earnings. They are telling investors the company's decrease in earnings is only temporary. This may or may not be true. It is important for a company to retain sufficient cash so it has some financial flexibility, adequate monies for research and development, and funds for growth and expansion.

• Stock Analysis Summary Sheet

Review the dividend information, and place a checkmark in the appropriate column—yes, no, neutral—following each topic in section C: Dividends.

Institutional ownership

When institutions such as mutual funds or retirement funds buy and sell a company's stock, their activity can affect the price of the stock. Because institutions deal in large blocks of stock, heavy buying—an increase in the percentage of stock owned by institutions—can drive the price upward. On the other hand, heavy selling—a decrease in the percentage of institutional ownership—can force the price downward. What percentage of McDonald's stock do institutions own? Is it heavily owned by institutions?

Data

The *S&P Report* lists the percentage of company stock owned by institutions as **Inst. holdings** on the first page under the section heading **Key Stock Statistics**. It is circled and labeled with a **14**. *Value Line* does not report the percentage of institutional ownership, but it can be calculated by dividing the number of shares owned by institutions (found in the upper left hand table titled **Institutional Decisions**) by the total number of shares outstanding (listed as Common Stock in the table titled **Capital Structure** in the left hand column in the middle of the page).

> **HOT spot** Institutions like to own these blue chip stocks to add income and stability to their portfolios.

- **Filling in the Stock Analysis Guide**

On the guide record the percentage of institutional ownership.

Basic Analysis:

For rapid and intermediate-growth stocks the lower the percentage of institutional ownership (30 percent or less), the better. As institutions discover valuable companies in these categories and buy into them, the demand creates substantial price increases. If institutions currently own 60 to 65 percent of a company, the stock has already received its price increase from institutional buying. For quality slow-growth stocks that pay strong dividends 60 percent or more institutional ownership is normal. For any type of stock, institutional ownership of 80 percent or more increases the possibility of a price drop due to heavy institutional selling. This selling may be in response to disappointing earnings or perceived changes in the economy.

- **Stock Analysis Summary Sheet**

Place a checkmark in the appropriate column—yes, no, neutral—following Percentage of Institutional Ownership in Category Three: Institutional Ownership.

Chapter 11

Smart Stock Analysis Guide: Stock price evaluation

What you'll find in this chapter:

- The price-earnings ratio
- Proper stock valuations
- How to use the price-earnings ratio
- The price-earnings ratio and growth rate
- How to find price trends

You have analyzed a company and have found that its growth, management, profitability, and financial condition look good, but is the stock overpriced? At the current price would you be overpaying for the company's earnings and dividends? The price-earnings ratio is a way to determine whether the market has overvalued or undervalued a stock. However, p/e by itself has little meaning. It must be compared with something—earnings growth rate, industry p/e.

Section A: Price-earnings ratio

The price-earnings ratio (price divided by earnings per share) shows the relationship between the price of the stock and the company's earnings. (For a review of p/e refer to chapter 2.) To determine whether the market has overvalued a stock, compare the stock's current p/e with its earnings-per-share average growth rate, its 10-year average p/e, and the industry's p/e. Are investors currently paying a premium for McDonald's growth?

Data

Use the company's current p/e that is recorded as **Today's P/E** in the **Basic Stock Information** section of this analysis guide. For the company's earnings growth rate use the calculated figure you recorded as the **Five-Year Compound Average Earnings-per-Share Growth Rate** in **Category One: Profitability, Section A: Earnings-per-Share Growth Rate** in this guide.

• P/E compared with the five-year earnings growth rate

A leading way to judge whether a stock is overpriced is to determine its p/e-to-growth ratio—its PEG. In the guide list McDonald's current p/e and its five-year compound average earnings-per-share growth rate. To calculate the PEG follow the example below.

The equation:

p/e ÷ five-year average earnings growth rate = PEG

The calculation:

33 ÷ 8.5 = 3.88 rounded to 3.9

Record the results in the guide. Indicate whether the stock is underpriced, fairly priced, or overpriced.

Basic analysis:

Use the following PEG ranges as a guideline to evaluate the stock's current price:

PEG of 0.5 to 0.8	Stock is underpriced
PEG of 0.9 to 1.05	Stock is fairly priced
PEG of 1.05 to 1.15	Stock is slightly overpriced
PEG of 1.20 to 2.00	Stock is definitely overpriced
PEG of 2.25 and above	Stock is very overpriced

In other words, if the p/e is more than twice the earnings growth rate, the stock is very overpriced. Investors are paying a large premium for the company's current and future earnings. If the p/e equals the earnings growth rate, the stock is fairly priced. The market has fairly priced the company's potential growth. And if the p/e is half the earnings growth rate, the stock is a bargain. The company's earnings are growing faster than the market has noted. The company's current and prospective performance are yet unrecognized. Each of the above evaluations assumes the corporation is a profitable, well-managed, financially strong company with a bright future. However, if the company is inferior, the stock is overpriced at any PEG.

> **HOT** spot — The more overpriced the stock, the greater the potential price drop.

If a quality stock is overpriced, it does not mean the price will not rise at all. It simply means the price will appreciate less than if the stock were fairly priced or underpriced, the large price increase has already taken place. It also means the risk has increased. Eventually, the stock's p/e and earnings growth rate will come back in line with each other.

The longer a bull market is in effect, the more difficult it is to find fairly priced stocks. However, it remains equally important, if not more important, to do so. Sometimes it is hard to turn your back on the over-hyped, seriously overpriced stocks everyone is talking about.

- **P/E compared with five-year earnings growth rate plus the dividend yield**

Sometimes the dividend yield, if it is high enough, will turn an overpriced stock into a fairly priced one. (To review yield refer to chapter 2.) This evaluation, PEGY, recognizes the contribution the dividend makes. In the guide list the p/e, the five-year earnings growth rate, and the dividend yield (recorded in the **Basic Stock Information** section of this guide). Does McDonald's yield make a difference in its price evaluation? To calculate the PEGY, follow the example below:

The equation:

p/e ÷ (earnings growth rate + yield) = PEGY

The calculation:

33 ÷ (8.5 + 0.5) = PEGY

(9)

33 ÷ 9 = 3.66 rounded to 3.7

Record the PEGY in the guide. Indicate whether the stock is underpriced, fairly priced, or overpriced.

Basic analysis:

Use the PEG guidelines to evaluate the PEGY.

- **P/E compared with the company's ten-year average P/E**

DEFINITION

A company's *standard p/e* is the ten-year average of its average high and low p/e's. Investors use this gauge as another way to determine whether the market has currently over- or undervalued the company's earnings growth. The ten-year average gives a broader picture of the company's p/e than the usual five-year average. Ten years is sure to cover both economic ups and downs and bull and bear markets.

The *S&P Report* lists the average high and low p/e's for each year; use them to determine the 10-year average p/e. You will find the data on the second page as **P/E Ratio -High, -Low** under the heading **Per Share Data ($)**. It is circled and labeled with a **15**. To calculate the company's ten-year average p/e, average the high p/e's, the low p/e's, and the two results. Follow the directions below:

Step 1: Add the 10 years' high p/e figures and divide by 10.

Step 2: Add the 10 years' low p/e figures and divide by 10.

Step 3: Add the two results and divide by two.

The outcome is the company's ten-year average p/e. If using *Value Line*, note that it lists the average p/e for each year. Therefore, simply add the p/e figures for the 10 most recent years and divide by 10.

On the guide, list the company's current p/e and its ten-year average p/e. Indicate whether the current p/e is above or below the company's average p/e.

Basic analysis:

If the current p/e is lower than the ten-year average p/e and the company is financially sound with potential for continued growth, the stock may be undervalued. However, if the company has a low p/e with little growth potential, the p/e indicates the company's earnings and stock price are unlikely to appreciate. If the current p/e approximates the long-term average p/e, the stock may be fairly priced. As the current p/e moves above the historical average, the stock becomes overvalued. The market may or may not recognize the overvaluation. The price may continue to rise. As the p/e moves above the 10-year average, above the average high, and eventually above the previous record high p/e, the risk increases proportionally.

CAUTION

• P/E compared with the Industry P/E

Price-earnings ratios vary from industry to industry. For example, recently the p/e for the airline industry was 13 while the p/e for the semiconductor industry was 41. Industry p/e's change from time to time as the industry gains or loses favor with investors. A company may have a low p/e and look like a bargain only because the industry as a whole has a low p/e. Therefore, because p/e's are industry specific, compare the company's current p/e with that of its industry and/or with those of similar companies in the industry. How does McDonald's current p/e compare with the p/e of the restaurant industry or with the p/e's of similar fast food restaurants?

You will find the industry p/e listed as **Avg Ann'l P/E Ratio** in the **Composite Statistics: Restaurant Industry** table on *Value Line*'s **Restaurant Industry** page. It is circled and labeled with a **15**. Even though the data are from the previous year, it gives investors an idea of the industry's current p/e. Investment web sites and the *Standard & Poor's Industry Reports* are other sources of industry information. Their p/e data are more current than those found in *Value Line*.

> *note* The price-earnings ratio reflects investors' expectations for the growth of the company as well as the premium investors are willing to pay for the company's future earnings.

On the guide, list the stock's current p/e and the industry p/e. Indicate whether the company p/e is above or below the industry p/e.

Basic analysis:

If the stock's current p/e is below the industry average p/e, the company may be a bargain that has been neglected or overlooked by the market, or it may be a company that has growth and financial problems. If the stock's p/e is equal to or slightly greater than the industry p/e, the market has fairly valued the stock. As the p/e climbs above the industry average, investors pay an increasing amount for the company's growth.

Summary

The table below summarizes the use of p/e to evaluate the stock prices of *financially sound companies with growth potential.*

• **Stock Price Evaluation**

Underpriced	Fairly Priced	Slightly Overpriced	Definitely Overpriced	Very Overpriced
p/e less than EPS average growth rate	p/e near the EPS average growth rate		p/e above but less than twice the EPS average growth rate	p/e more than twice the EPS average growth rate
PEG: 0.5 to 0.8	PEG: 0.9 to 1.05	PEG: 1.05 to 1.15	PEG: 1.20 to 2	PEG: above 2
PEGY: 0.5 to 0.8	PEGY: 0.9 to 1.05	PEGY: 1.05 to 1.15	PEGY: 1.20 to 2	PEGY: above 2
p/e less than 10-year average p/e	p/e near the 10-year average p/e		p/e 25 to 30% above 10-year average p/e	
p/e less than industry p/e	p/e near the industry p/e		p/e 25 to 30% above industry p/e	

A low p/e indicates several possible situations. It can mean the stock is an undiscovered bargain, the company is in trouble, the company is mature with little potential for growth, the company belongs to a low p/e industry, or the market overreacted to some kind of news—investors sold, and the price fell. Many successful investors focus on low p/e stocks of financially healthy companies with solid prospects for earnings growth. The shareholders of these quality companies wait for other investors to discover the stocks and begin to buy them. The new demand drives up the price and the p/e.

The higher the p/e moves above the company's average p/e and the industry's p/e, the more growth investors expect from the company. The higher the expectations, the more opportunities there are for the company to stumble. Investors who are less comfortable with risk and volatility become cautious as the p/e moves above 20. Also, they become wary as a stock's p/e rises 20 to 25 percent above its average p/e or the industry p/e. A high p/e indicates the market is bullish on the growth prospects of the company and is willing to pay extra for what it believes is superior growth potential. Sometimes the company is able to deliver that kind of growth for several years and other times not. When it is unable to do so, the market reacts, and the price declines until the p/e is more in line with the company's average EPS growth rate.

Occasionally, companies have unusually high p/e's—those above 45 and 50. An extremely high p/e may mean the company has taken a one-time charge against its earnings which distorts the ratio. On the other hand, the extraordinary p/e may indicate the company has had a recent drop in earnings without a corresponding decline in stock price.

Stock Analysis Summary Sheet

Review the information about evaluating the stock price, and place a checkmark in the appropriate column—yes, no, neutral—following each topic in section A: Price Earnings Ratio (P/E) of Category Four: Stock Price Evaluation.

Section B: Price trend

At this place in the guide, technical analysis briefly crosses the path of fundamental analysis. Over the long term is the stock price trending up or down? Fundamental analysis identifies what to buy, and technical analysis indicates when to buy it.

Data

Use the figures for the **52-Week High** and **Low** and **Today's Price** recorded in the **Basic Stock Information** section of this analysis guide.

• **The 52-week high and low price**

During the year, most stock prices fluctuate 50 percent or more between their 52-week highs and lows. When the price hits a new high or approaches an old high, it generally drifts downward before it continues to rise. Where is McDonald's current price in relation to its 52-week high and low? On the guide record the stock's 52-week high and low

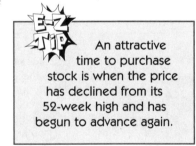

An attractive time to purchase stock is when the price has declined from its 52-week high and has begun to advance again.

prices and today's price. Indicate whether the total cost of the stock—the combined price and estimated commission charge of $0.75 per share—is above or below the 52-week high.

Basic analysis:

It is nice to acquire a stock when its price, including commissions, is 10 to 15 percent below its 52-week high. It gives the investment a boost at the beginning. However, before buying, make sure the price has turned around—the price is starting to climb rather than continuing to slide. (Refer to a price and volume chart.) If the current price has not declined from its 52-week high and you plan to hold the stock for three to five years, it may not be worth missing possible gains while waiting for a price correction.

• A price and volume chart

A price and volume chart adds visual meaning and understanding to the daily, weekly, monthly, and yearly fluctuations in stock price. A chart not only illustrates the direction of the change but also shows its relative magnitude. By looking at a chart you can determine whether the price, overall, has been increasing or decreasing during a particular period. You will find a price and volume chart at the top of the first page of the S&P Report. It covers the weekly price variations for the past three and a half years from the date of the report. You can find current charts—weekly, daily, hourly—on investment web sites. After looking at the most recent 12 months on the price chart, indicate on the guide whether the price seems to be moving up or down or trading in a narrow range.

Basic analysis:

If the price is continuing to decline from its 52-week high, follow it and buy when it begins to rise. Buy when the price is moving up, not down. When the price is declining, there is no way to tell how far it will go. In the meantime, check any recent news about the company. The price may simply be drifting down, or there may be a reason for its decline. Has something happened that is not reflected in the S&P Report or the Value Line commentary? Did the company's most recent earnings or the estimate of next quarter's earnings fail to meet analysts' expectations? Ask your broker or check investment web sites for current news on the stock.

Consider the stock's long-term price movements. Look at the entire chart—three and a half years of price changes. Visually summarize the ups and downs of the stock price, and identify any long-term trends. If the stock is in a general down trend, wait until the price is trending up before you buy.

• The market

Is the market moving up or down, or is it trading in a narrow range? On the guide indicate what the market is doing.

Basic analysis:

Knowing what is happening in the market acts as a reference point rather than as a reason to buy or sell. When the market declines, there are good companies whose stock prices rise. When the market moves upward, not all prices increase. By recording the level of the S&P 500 stock index in the Basic Stock Information section of the guide, you will be able to track the price performance of your stock against the performance of the index. Even though the S&P 500 is a relatively broad index, you may want to use an index or average that more precisely reflects the character of your stock such as the Dow Jones Industrial Average, the Dow Jones Transportation Average, or the Nasdaq Composite Index.

note You are buying shares in a solid company, not shares in the stock market.

• **Stock Analysis Summary Sheet**

Review the information about price and market trends, and place a checkmark in the appropriate column—yes, no, neutral—following each topic in section B: Price Trend. To complete the Analysis Summary sheet, count and record (on the Total line) the number of checkmarks in each of the three columns.

Chapter 12

Smart Stock Analysis Guide: Company background

What you'll find in this chapter:

- ⟼ Evaluating a company's products & services
- ⟼ Evaluating a company's clients
- ⟼ Expansion and a company's future
- ⟼ Concerns and challenges
- ⟼ Choosing the right company for you

This chapter involves learning about the company's products, services, and growth potential. What specific products or services does the company sell? Who are its customers? How will the company continue to grow? Before you make any decisions about a stock, it is important to understand what the company does and how changes in the industry and the economy may affect it. If you decide to become a shareholder in the company, this information will help you follow your investment.

Data

The commentary on pages 1 and 2 of the *S&P Report* provides information on both company background and recent business developments. *Value Line* supplies similar material in the center section of the company page. For information about the industry read the commentary on the *Value Line* industry page.

Filling in the Stock Analysis Guide

As you read about the company, use these questions and comments to direct your thinking about each general topic.

Overview

- Where are the company's headquarters? (This information is at the bottom of page 2 of the *S&P Report*. On the *Value Line* page it is below the statistical table.)

- What is the company's line of business?

- Who are its competitors?

Products and Services

- What are its products or services? (Can you list and describe them to someone who knows nothing about the business?)

- Does the company have a niche in the market? What makes the company's product or service stand out from others? (Why do customers buy from this company? Is it due to name recognition, a specialized product or service, or a high quality product or service?)

- If the company is introducing a new product, how much will the product add to total sales? (If you are interested in the company because of a particular product—new or established—be sure the product contributes significantly to the company's total revenues and earnings. What percentage of sales comes from the product?)

Clients

- Are the company's clients repeat customers or one-time clients? (It is less costly and more dependable to sell the product over and over to the same clients rather than sell to new customers each time.)

CAUTION

- Is the company heavily dependent on one or two clients—corporate or government? (Be cautious about a company if the loss of a large client would significantly impact the company's total sales. Also, large clients are sometimes able to negotiate a more favorable price which will reduce company profit.)

Expansion

- Is there room in the industry for the company to expand, or is the industry already crowded with sellers? Is the company providing a product or service that is different from that of its competitors, or is the company selling more of the same?

> *note* A company needs to be successful where it is, before it undertakes expansion.

- Is the company's current operation successful? Are its present units making a profit? (Expansion without added profit does not count.)

- In what part of the country does the company operate?
- Where is it expanding? Within its current area? Into a new geographical region? Worldwide? (Is the company equipped to expand into that area?)
- How is the company expanding?
  + Opening new units (Are its current units profitable?)
  + Buying other companies (Do the acquisitions complement the current operation, or do they simply provide an opportunity to buy another company? Management does not always make wise decisions.)
  + New products (How much will they impact total sales?)
  + New line of business (Does it fit with the company, or does it require new expertise?)
- Is the rate of expansion increasing or decreasing?
- What are the company's prospects for growth next year and the years thereafter?
- How will the company increase its earnings? Peter Lynch states in *One Up on Wall Street*:

  > *There are five basic ways a company can increase earnings: reduce costs, raise prices, expand into new markets, sell more of its product in the old markets, or revitalize, close, or otherwise dispose of a losing operation.*

Concerns

- How is the company maintaining market share and product vitality?
- What challenges does the company face? What are the concerns?

Basic analysis:

Look for a company that:

- provides innovative goods or services
- produces quality products and services
- sells to repeat customers
- knows how to expand profitably
- belongs to an industry that has room for the company to expand
- demonstrates the ability to prosper for a number of years

Chapter 13

Smart Stock Analysis Guide: The final analysis

What you'll find in this chapter:

➠ Using the Smart Stock Analysis Guide

➠ Find your potential goldmine

➠ Buy, follow or discard?

➠ Making your final analysis

➠ Comparing companies within an industry

Before deciding whether to buy this stock, take a few minutes to review and summarize the information.

Data

To facilitate your review, use the Smart Stock Analysis Guide, the S&P or *Value Line* company commentary, the Smart Stock Analysis summary sheet, and the Smart Stock Comparison sheet (if you are deciding between two or three stocks in the same industry).

Filling in the Stock Analysis Guide

As you re-examine each topic in the Stock Analysis Guide, the Stock Analysis Summary, and the basic analysis information pertaining to each section, note and list the company's strengths and weaknesses in the guide. Also, write down any positive or negative points discussed in the S&P or *Value Line* commentary. If needed, refer to McDonald's sample guide. When reviewing the Stock Analysis Summary, you may want to give extra weight to those criteria that are particularly important to you.

Final analysis

It is rare, indeed, to find a company that has all yesses on the Analysis Summary sheet. Therefore, in the absence of perfect scores, look for a "yes" in the following four areas—each increases the opportunity for success:

- a pretax profit margin that is stable or rising and above the industry average

- a return on equity that is above 15, stable or rising, and above the industry average

- a solid growth in earnings

- a fair or bargain price

note Remember, each person's judgment of company strengths and weaknesses may differ because each individual has unique values and perspectives.

These items address the quality of management, the growth of earnings, and the stock price in relation to earnings. Is there a "yes" in most of these areas? In a bull market it may be difficult to find a stock that is not overpriced. In addition to the above items, does the stock have a positive rating in other areas that are important to you? For example, some investors feel that a low debt-to-equity ratio is particularly important; therefore they weight it heavily. Others place a high value on low institutional ownership.

After the final tally, does the yes column have a large majority of the checkmarks? Weigh specific yesses and nos against your criteria for the stock. Finally, check current news about the company by calling your broker or using an investment web site. Look for anything negative that might adversely affect the firm.

When you have finished surveying and evaluating the data, summarize your findings by giving a short description of the company. Include definite information about its profitability, financial condition, share ownership, products or services, price evaluation, and its suitability for your portfolio. Be specific. Think of it as a sales pitch for the stock or as a warning to your best friend—why he or she should not buy it. Often, it requires analyzing four to six stocks to find one that merits purchase.

If you have decided to purchase the stock, indicate the number of shares you will buy. Consider the type of stock, your investment goals, your tolerance for risk, your financial resources, and the percentage of your portfolio it represents. Then list the conditions under which you will sell the stock. (Refer to chapter 9 for tips on selling.) This establishes a goal for the stock and helps you follow it to keep your portfolio on track.

On the other hand, if you feel this is not quite the time to buy the stock and you want to follow it, record the specific changes that need to occur. If your analysis has uncovered more nos than yesses or if a specific criterion is so negative you do not want to own the stock, place a checkmark in the blank following **Do Not Buy**. This may have just saved your portfolio from serious damage.

Conclusion

The Smart Stock Analysis Guide gives you a way to systematically gather, analyze, and evaluate company information. However, the guide does not conclude with a formula that gives you an automatic yes—a magic number of yesses that guarantees success. Instead, this approach allows you to tailor the evaluation to reflect those criteria you consider most important. You do not have to squeeze your investment goals and philosophy into a specific formula that does not fit your circumstances.

> **note** Every investor values each piece of data and information a bit differently because of his or her objectives, resources, and risk tolerance.

Whatever your final decision regarding the stock, whether to buy it, follow it, or discard it, you have based your decision on solid information. You have made a knowledgeable decision. No longer do you need to buy someone's hot tip that later turns into a nightmare and find yourself saying, "If I had only known!"

Initially, the Smart Stock Analysis Guide may seem confusing, indefinite, and time consuming. (If you wish, use the Smart Stock Quick Preview to screen a company to determine if it merits full analysis.) Your learning will accelerate if you analyze two or three companies in the same industry, one right after the other. You will immediately see the differences between the companies. (If you have not already done so, look at the Smart Stock Comparison sheet in the Appendix. It shows the analysis for McDonald's, Wendy's, and Papa John's Pizza.) After you have completed the full analysis of three or four pairs of stocks, you will become familiar with the data and the guide. The process will become faster and easier. Recording and evaluating the data and making a decision will take less than two hours.

E-Z TIP Invest in the types of businesses you currently know or study the new businesses and industries that interest you.

Taking judicious action, by itself, is success.

How exciting it will be to find that "high-scoring" company—that potential gold mine!

When you invest, buy what you understand. Also, understand what you buy so you can competently follow what is happening in the economy and the industry and will be able to recognize how it may affect the company.

Success in anything, including investing in stocks, requires hard work and learning. It requires discerning where you are going, committing to your goal, doing the work to get there, and having the patience and determination to stay on track. Also, it requires overcoming indecision and inertia. The Smart Stock Analysis Guide provides a way to collect and evaluate data. Because it helps you make a rational decision, you will find it easier to overcome the natural hesitancies you might have about buying or selling a stock. Finally, follow your decision with action.

Chapter 14

Following a stock

After having completed the analysis of several stocks, you have found a stock that meets your investment criteria and have purchased it. Now you want to track its progress. You may ask the following questions: How often should I check it? What information do I need? Where can I find the information? How do I decide whether to keep it or sell it? In this chapter, Following a Stock, you will learn how to update your analysis at the end of each quarter and each fiscal year. In addition, you will find suggestions that will help you decide when to sell.

Monitoring a company

Because companies, industries, and the economy change, it is necessary to recheck your stock's fundamentals (i.e. debt, earnings, revenues) on a regular schedule. Is the company still on track? Is it meeting your expectations? Even though you have purchased shares of a high-quality, fairly priced company, it is unwise to simply add those shares to your portfolio and forget them. Even quality companies develop problems. Of the growth stocks, emerging and rapid-growth stocks are the most dramatically affected by developments and fluctuations in the economy, the company, and the industry. The fundamentals of intermediate-growth and slow-growth or income stocks tend to change more slowly and subtly, but the results still influence the stock's performance. Watching the companies in which you own stock does not need to be difficult nor time consuming. It involves only three tasks: following current business news, checking quarterly earnings, and updating the stock analysis at the end of each fiscal year.

> **E-Z TIP**
> By checking the company's performance at the end of each fiscal quarter you can monitor the company's progress.

Company news

The first part of the tracking process is an easy one—simply become aware of the company's name in the news. Now that you own shares in the company, its name seems to appear frequently. You may see it as you read or browse through magazines such as *Money Magazine, Smart Money, Individual Investor, Forbes,* and *Worth,* and as you read the business section of daily newspapers. You may hear its name when you listen to "Marketplace" on public radio or watch the "Nightly Business Report" on public television or watch the business news programs on cable television. It is a pleasure to hear and read positive reports about the company's growth, acquisitions, and new products. It is reassuring to note that the company is doing well. On the other hand, it is disturbing to hear news that will adversely affect the company, such as a major lawsuit, a catastrophe of some kind, a significant increase in competition, a cut in the price of its goods or services, or a rise in the price of its resources (a rise in the cost of production). Any one of these can depress the company's earnings and its stock price. Will the consequences be long term or short term? Ask your broker for his or her interpretation of the news and how it may affect the stock. Will it damage the company's ability to grow at the desired rate? If so, it may be time to sell the stock. However, if the difficulty will impact the company only in the short term (one, two, or three quarters), it may be an opportunity to buy additional shares at a lower price.

> **note**
> Magazines and radio and television programs will keep you informed about current company, industry, and economic changes.

Quarterly stock checkup

note

The second part of the monitoring process involves quickly rechecking the company's revenue and earnings-per-share growth rate at the end of each quarter. Are earnings on track? The company releases its quarterly figures two to six weeks after the end of the fiscal quarter. The delay is due to the time required to collect the data and complete the accounting reports. This is also the time to check the stock's price performance compared with that of the *S&P 500 Index.*

Data

New quarterly earnings figures can be found in *Barron's* and the *Wall Street Journal*, on the Internet, from updated company pages in the S&P Stock Reports or *Value Line*, and in the company's quarterly report. *Barron's* is a convenient and timely source if you are using just the EPS figures; it does not report revenue data. As soon as the company releases its quarterly information, the next week *Barron's* publishes the EPS. In the stock tables the new earnings per share figure is listed in the **Earnings** column under the heading **Latest Qtr**. The figure for the previous year's corresponding quarter is listed under the column heading **Year Ago**. Three or four weeks after the end of the quarter, begin checking *Barron's* stock tables for the company's new earnings.

To save money, many companies do not routinely send quarterly reports to their shareholders.

New earning and revenue reports can be found first on Internet investment web sites—minutes after the company releases them. The next day the *Wall Street Journal* publishes the figures in its Digest of Earnings Reports. It prints earnings per share, sales, net income figures, and the average number of shares outstanding for both the current and the previous year's quarter. When it is time for the company to release its quarterly figures, check the *Wall Street Journal* each day.

If timeliness is not crucial, and it may not be, you can obtain the figures from *Standard & Poor's Stock Reports* or *Value Line* when the company's page is routinely updated. The *S&P Stock Reports* lists quarterly earnings per share and revenues on the first page of the company report. *Value Line* lists them in the tables dealing with quarterly data in the left column of the page.

New earnings figures are also available from the company's quarterly report. It is an additional two or three weeks after the release of the earnings before the quarterly report arrives in the mail. If the stock is registered in your name, it is sent directly to you. On the other hand, if the stock is registered in the name of your brokerage firm, the quarterly report is mailed to the brokerage firm, and the firm forwards it to you. If you do not receive one, call the company's investor relations department. The

Definition:

The *quarterly report* is a shortened form of an annual report.

quarterly report may be confusing at first, but you will quickly become familiar with its format and terminology. To find the revenue and the earnings-per-share figures, look on the page titled Condensed Consolidated Statement of Earnings, Condensed Consolidated Statements of Income, or Consolidated Statements of Operations. Revenue is usually the first entry on the page. It may be listed as

Revenues, Net Revenues, Net Operating Revenues, Total Operating Revenues, Net Sales, or Sales to Customers. The earnings-per-share figure can be found near the bottom of the same table. It will be listed as Net Earnings Per Share or Net Income Per Share.

Using the Smart Stock Quarterly Checkup

First, on a copy of the Smart Stock Quarterly Checkup form found in the Forms section, enter the name of the stock and its purchase price. From the Analysis Guide list the five-year compound average growth rate and the most recent year-to-year growth rate for both the earnings per share and the revenues. On the EPS table record the date of the current quarter, use either the end-of-quarter date, the earnings release date, or today's date. It will be the date of the current stock price, p/e, and *S&P 500* Index figures. Next, record the EPS figures for the current quarter and for the same quarter last year. Calculate the earnings-per-share growth rate—the rate of change—between this quarter and the previous year's corresponding quarter. (If needed, refer to chapter 9 to review calculating rate of change.) Record the results—the percentage of growth—in the growth rate column. Then, list the figures for the p/e, price, and *S&P 500*. Using the revenue data, complete the revenue table in the same manner as the earnings per share.

Basic Analysis

- **Earnings and Revenues**

Is the company maintaining the earnings growth rate expected for its type of stock, its five-year average growth rate, and its last year's growth rate? Has the rate increased? Has it declined? If there has been a decrease in earnings or if they have failed to increase by the anticipated amount, what has happened? Has revenue growth slipped? Has the company had to cut prices because of oversupply or increased competition? Or has it been unable to raise its prices to match the increased costs of natural resources? Has the company become less efficient? On the other hand, have earnings temporarily decreased for a positive reason such as an acquisition or expansion? Check the S&P report or the *Value Line* commentary. Also, ask your broker. Is it a company issue? Is the industry depressed? Is there an economic recession? Will the problem be short term (two or three quarters) or long term (one or two years)? Your broker can help you determine this. If the difficulty is short term, your broker will probably advise you to hold the stock. In fact, you may decide to buy additional shares at

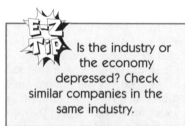

Is the industry or the economy depressed? Check similar companies in the same industry.

the lower price. However, if it is a longer-term situation, you may want to sell your shares and invest in another company.

- **P/E**

To monitor the stock's price evaluation, compare the p/e with the earnings-per-share growth rate. If the p/e is more than two and a half times the EPS growth rate (overvalued), decide whether you want to hold the stock for additional growth, sell it, or sell part of your shares to take some of the profit. Your decision depends in part on your tolerance for risk and your investment timeline.

- **Price**

Has the price risen since you bought the stock? How did it perform last quarter? Did it increase by the same percentage as the S&P 500 Index? Did it outperform the index? Figure the rate of change for each and compare. If the stock is down, what has happened? Have there been a decrease in earnings, bad news, and industry problems? Is the market down? Or is the stock simply trading near its 52-week low? If the price has stagnated, be patient. A stock often trades in a narrow range for several months or even a year or so before it moves upward.

The Comment Lines

On the comment line for the current quarter, record your thoughts and conclusions about the company's earnings, revenues, p/e, stock price, and the market in general. Include pertinent information from your broker, the commentary section of the S&P report or *Value Line* page, and the president's letter in the quarterly report.

Conclusion

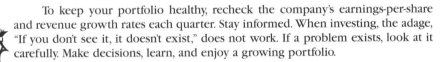

To keep your portfolio healthy, recheck the company's earnings-per-share and revenue growth rates each quarter. Stay informed. When investing, the adage, "If you don't see it, it doesn't exist," does not work. If a problem exists, look at it carefully. Make decisions, learn, and enjoy a growing portfolio.

Annual stock checkup

When the company has released its annual figures (as long as two months after the end of the fiscal year), update your original analysis by using a copy of the Smart Start Annual Stock Checkup. Obtain a current copy of the data resource—S&P, *Value Line*—you used for the Analysis Guide. Be sure it includes all the new year-end data. Sometimes there is a delay in reporting the entire array. From the stock's Analysis Guide, enter last year's data in the initial **Year** column of the Stock Checkup. Using the figures from the current data source, complete any necessary calculations and record the figures for the year just completed in the second **Year** column. Then compare the stock's current performance with its performance the previous year. Also compare this year's profit margin, ROE, and p/e with the industry average. For each section of the Annual Stock Checkup, review the analysis information given in chapters 8 through 13. Is the company losing market share? Has it had to cut its prices because of product oversupply or increased competition? Has the company experienced a rise in the cost of labor and natural resources and been unable to raise the price of its product?

Be concerned about any decline in the earnings-per-share growth rate, pretax profit margin, and return on equity.

Has it become less efficient? In addition, has there been a significant change in the debt-to-equity ratio? Has the firm borrowed extra money to expand? On the other hand, has it paid down its long-term debt? Is there continued dividend growth? Has the stock price kept pace with the appropriate index? Read the commentary about the company in the S&P report and *Value Line* page. If the company is no longer meeting your expectations, check with your broker. Is the economy depressed? Is the industry in a recession? Does the company have a problem? Is it a temporary or a long-term situation? Has the company fundamentally changed? If it has, then it may be time to sell and look for a replacement.

Company life cycles

As you follow a stock from year to year, watch for changes in the life cycle of the company—moving from emerging-growth to slow-growth. The changes will be subtle, just like the maturing process of individuals. A rapid-growth company is characterized by a swift expansion of sales and profits. As its goods and services are proven to be highly successful, demand quickly builds. At this stage there is little competition. The corporation experiences soaring sales and earnings growth with lofty profit margins. However, because of the firm's success, competition develops and the corporation's profit margins begin to decline to more normal levels. Over time the initial pent-up demand for the company's goods and services is satisfied. The firm's rapid growth rate decreases, eventually, it

note When a company no longer needs to build new stores or factories, it uses its cash to pay generous dividends.

becomes an intermediate-growth company. Its earnings increase 12 to 20 percent annually instead of the previous 20 to 30 percent. The corporation now begins to pay dividends with the cash it previously used for accelerating expansion. As the years pass and the company saturates the market with its goods and services,

it moves into the slow-growth stage. Its earnings grow from 6 to 12 percent a year. The company now concentrates on maintaining market share. Profit margins are slim because of competition. Profits vary with the firm's ability to control costs and to effectively market its goods and services. Successful slow-growth companies are large, profitable leaders in their industries. They remain in the slow-growth category for a very long time—decades—before they deteriorate or disappear.

Sometimes a company declines before it has a chance to mature naturally. Premature aging occurs when the board of directors falters. Its actions and policies result in the loss of the company's innovative and competitive edge. The board may spend less on research and development and introduce fewer new products. It may lose its focus and try to take the company in a direction it is not equipped to go. However, with positive changes the aging process can be reversed. New, refocused, or reenergized leadership can turn the company around and put it back on track.

When to sell a stock

Deciding whether to sell a stock is often more difficult than deciding whether to buy it. There are no unconditional yes or no rules for selling just as there are none for buying. There are no guarantees. In fact, the stock price will undoubtedly go up after you sell your shares and go down if you keep them. Selling a stock at its high or buying at its low is mere luck. It is a great feeling, but it rarely happens. You can consistently make more money by leaving the top 15 percent and the bottom 15 percent for others and take the 70 percent in between. Generally, when thinking about selling, let your successes run and cut your losses. For additional guidelines, consider the **Reasons to Sell** and the **Reasons to Hold** that follow.

For protection against market drops buy financially sound, high-quality companies.

Reasons to sell

The three major reasons for selling a stock are to correct a mistake, to eliminate a deteriorating company, and to take a profit.

1) Sell all mistakes

Admitting and selling a mistake is often the most difficult kind of selling to do. The company, for various reasons, is not behaving as you expected. Remember, you analyzed it with past and current data, not with a crystal ball. No one can foresee the future. Acknowledge the misstep—yours, the company's—and quickly sell your shares. Don't wait for the flaw to fix itself. The price may increase, but it may never return to its previous high. On the other hand, the stock may sink further while you try to avoid calling it an error. When emotions and egos get in the way, little slips turn into huge ones. Get rid of the losers so they don't eat the winners. Take losses while they are small. A 15 percent loss will not ruin your portfolio, but a 50 or 75 percent reduction can seriously damage it. Understand the reality of percentage decrease versus percentage increase. Because of the way percentages are calculated, a 25 percent decline requires a 33 percent gain to break even. For example, if a $20 stock drops to $15, it is a 25 percent drop. However, it is a 33 percent gain from $15 back to $20. If a stock drops 50 percent, it has to gain 100 percent to get back where it started. Prosperity is taking losses while they are small. You are a

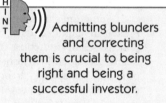

Admitting blunders and correcting them is crucial to being right and being a successful investor.

more accomplished investor after you have taken your loss and reinvested the remaining funds. Think of selling a loser as weeding your garden.

2) Sell a deteriorating company

Even though the business has done well for a long time, you see signs of company weakness despite a healthy economy. For example, the firm's earnings, revenue, and dividend growth rates have decreased. Its profit margin and return on equity have declined. Its debt-to-equity ratio has increased significantly. It is not the strong company you bought due to either the natural aging process, poor management, or industry problems. If these conditions appear to be long term, sell your shares and invest in another company.

3) Take a profit

Selling a stock to convert your paper profit to actual dollars is an exciting event. However, the question remains: How can I determine when to sell? And should I sell? If the stock has done very well, it can be an agonizing decision whether to hold it for additional profits or to take those you have. If you are a long-term investor and the company is fundamentally sound, you will undoubtedly hold the stock for years through all its price ups and downs. Otherwise, consider the following suggestions. Sell the stock when its price reaches the target you set at the time of purchase. That helps to eliminate emotion and indecision. Realize your profits if the price has doubled within a short time. Dispose of your shares when the stock becomes grossly overpriced, e.g., its p/e is three to four times its EPS growth rate. If you have 200 or more shares, sell half of them or sell enough to recover your cost and let the rest increase. Be aware that at some point every overpriced stock declines—usually when you least expect it. Remember these are guidelines, not rules for selling.

Finally, do not miss taking a profit because you are reluctant to pay commissions or taxes. The taxes can be offset by selling a loser. On the other hand, if the company continues to be a sound investment and you are a long-term investor, the total of the tax you pay on the gain and the buy and sell commissions are often nearly the same percentage as the average price decline.

Reasons to hold

Sometimes investors should keep their stock—not sell it. For example, retain your shares if the company is still a good investment at the current price. Hold a quality stock if the bad news is temporary and the reasons for the decline are short term. In fact, it might be a good time to buy additional shares. Hang on to your shares if the entire market is going down and your company is a solid one. Don't try to time the market. That requires two decisions—when to sell and when to buy again. If you sell, you will more than likely miss the benefits of the recovering market. Finally, if a stock has made a small profit, let it grow. As the price continues to grow, consider using a stop-loss order to protect your gains.

Summary

Knowing when to sell is as important as knowing what to buy. These suggestions for selling will help you keep your portfolio on track year after year.

Sell when:

- You have made a mistake.

- The company has reduced or canceled its dividend.

- A serious lawsuit has been filed against the company.

- The company and the industry are both declining.

- The company is deteriorating despite a strong industry and economy.

- The company's fundamentals have fallen below the industry average or below those of similar companies in the industry.

- The company no longer meets your objectives for earnings growth, dividend growth, profit margin, and debt.

- You have found a substantially better stock for the money.

- Another company will provide a higher return or a more secure place for your money.

- The price has reached your preset target.

- The price has doubled or tripled on the upside or declined 15 to 20 percent on the downside.

- The stock is significantly overpriced.

Do not sell when:

- You have the urge to sell a winner to avoid selling a loser.

- You are merely looking for something to do.

- You are unsure or uninformed and just want to follow the crowd.

- You are bored with the lack of price appreciation.

Hold the stock when:

- The company is fundamentally sound.

- It still meets your criteria for purchase.

- The effects of the bad news are temporary.

- All stocks are going down and the market is correcting.

Do not hold the stock when:

- You are waiting for the price to recover so you can break even.

- You are emotionally attached to the company or to your analysis of it.

- You don't want to pay tax on your profits.

Conclusion

> *note* Following your stocks and selling for the right reasons are among the final steps to becoming a successful investor.

Monitor company and industry news throughout the year. Reevaluate company performance at the end of each quarter and each fiscal year. Is the company on track? Is it meeting your expectations? Review the reasons to sell and the reasons to hold a stock. Make any necessary decisions and take action. You are on your way to creating a productive portfolio.

Chapter 15
Successful investing

What you'll find in this chapter:

- ⟶ Planning your portfolio
- ⟶ Stock diversity
- ⟶ Risk level
- ⟶ Types of portfolios
- ⟶ How many and which stocks to include

You have purchased a stock and are tracking it. You now want to analyze and acquire others. But you ask, "How many stocks should I own? How do I put together a portfolio? What about diversification?" In this chapter, Successful Investing, you will learn about portfolio size, type, diversification, and risk level. This information will help you plan your portfolio. The chapter concludes with Rules for Successful Investors.

Portfolios

A complete investment portfolio may consist of cash, savings accounts, CDs, life insurance, real estate, mutual funds, common stocks, bonds, options, gold, and collectibles. Your stock portfolio is an important component of your total investment picture. Carefully tailor it to fit your particular needs and your investing style.

Size

The size of your portfolio will be determined by the funds you have available to invest in stocks. Discount brokers with commissions of $15 to $20 have made buying individual stocks affordable for the small investor. Now it is feasible to begin investing with $1,000 rather than the commonly suggested $10,000. Your account, large or small, will grow as you regularly add cash and as you reinvest the money from dividends and stock sales. With your

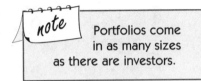

Portfolios come in as many sizes as there are investors.

emergency fund in place your portfolio can grow without interruption. What was $1,000 will become $2,000, then $3,000.

Number of stocks

If you are beginning with a small amount of capital, from $1,000 to $3,000, you will be able to buy only one or two stocks. Choose financially strong companies whose earnings show solid, consistent growth. The firms should be among the top corporations in their industries. Buy only underpriced or fairly priced shares.

Investors with larger portfolios often ask how many stocks they should own. The optimum number of stocks for the average portfolio is between 10 and 12. This allows investors to diversify among industries and types of growth stocks. However, a standard portfolio may contain as few as 5 or as many as 15. Tracking

To reduce the risk of putting all your eggs in one basket, watch the basket closely and be more conservative than usual.

more than 15 often becomes difficult and time consuming. Investors tend to lose interest, neglect their portfolios, and lose money. If you find this happening to you, reduce the number of stocks in your portfolio and increase the number of shares per company.

Emerging and rapid-growth stocks necessitate close monitoring. Following five volatile, rapid-growth stocks may require more attention than you can

easily provide. In that case replace one or two with steadier intermediate-growth stocks. Regardless of the number of stocks you hold, do not overcommit your time—the time you can comfortably devote to portfolio management.

CAUTION

Goals

Set specific goals for your portfolio. Set short-term (one-year), intermediate (three-year), and long-term (five-to-ten-year) targets—those you developed in chapter 6. With your aims clearly in mind you will be less tempted to jump on the latest bandwagon or to pursue the newest get-rich-quick scheme. The true reward for investing comes as you use your investment profits to turn each goal into reality. It is the excitement you feel as you take the cruise, move into your dream house, or open your new business. It is knowing that your investments have made it possible. From time to time review your goals. If your family or financial circumstances have changed, make the necessary adjustments.

Portfolio types

Portfolios are classified according to their overall functions. They are constructed to preserve capital, produce current income, promote capital growth, expedite rapid appreciation, or to facilitate speculation. The type of stock portfolio you develop depends on your major investment goal, your time horizon, and your tolerance for risk. The latter has the greatest impact. Therefore, while reading about the kinds of portfolios, review the questions concerning risk in Chapter 6 under the headings **Resources and Risk**, **Portfolio and Risk**, and **What is Important to You**.

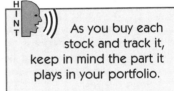

As you buy each stock and track it, keep in mind the part it plays in your portfolio.

Preservation of capital

The most conservative of all portfolios is the capital preservation portfolio. Its purposes are to protect and preserve the initial principal, to yield a higher return than a CD or savings account, and to ensure a return (after taxes) that exceeds the inflation rate. Safety of principal is important to all investors but for some it is paramount. These individuals are willing to sacrifice the possibility of making substantial gains for the certainty of retaining their original investment. The capital preservation portfolio offers the lowest level of risk but the least potential for growth. The typical portfolio contains high-dividend, slow-growth stocks of long-established, profitable companies. These financially strong companies produce goods or services that will be in demand for decades to come. As investors become more comfortable with investing in individual stocks, they might include one or two high-quality intermediate-growth stocks in their portfolios. These stocks will produce additional capital appreciation with little added risk.

Current income

The current-income portfolio provides a stream of revenue monthly, quarterly, or annually. It is for investors who live on fixed incomes. They may be retirees who need additional proceeds to supplement their retirement incomes. Or they may be individuals depending on the yield from an inheritance or from a once-in-a-lifetime settlement. The current-income portfolio is also for investors who dislike risk but want a higher return than that provided by a capital preservation portfolio. These individuals continually reinvest the proceeds. A portfolio structured to create current earnings contains high-dividend stocks of quality, slow-growth companies. These corporations are the dominant firms in their industries and have a long history of increasing their dividends. Some portfolios include other revenue-producing instruments such as bonds, utility stocks, and real estate trusts. In each case the dividend or interest must be secure.

Capital growth

A capital growth portfolio is for those who want growth over time for retirement, or perhaps for a college education, a house, or a new business. The increase in value comes through total return—income and appreciation. A capital growth portfolio contains stocks of solid, intermediate-growth companies. The companies have a

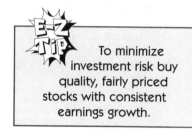

To minimize investment risk buy quality, fairly priced stocks with consistent earnings growth.

history of steady growth and stock splits. A capital growth portfolio provides average capital appreciation with average risk. It is for those who are comfortable with money and can easily sell to take a profit. If investors are more conservative, they can lower their risk by adding one or two high-quality slow-growth stocks. On the other hand, if they are more adventuresome and their risk tolerance permits, they can add a rapid-growth stock for faster capital appreciation.

Rapid appreciation

A rapid-appreciation portfolio provides higher than average returns in exchange for higher than average risks. These investors are comfortable taking the added risk for the potentially greater rewards. They are prepared to accept large successes and to cut their losses quickly and unemotionally. A rapid-appreciation portfolio contains carefully researched rapid-growth stocks. Investors closely monitor their portfolios because they know these stocks respond quickly to economic, industry, and corporate changes. To decrease risk without significantly reducing returns, they can purchase one or two intermediate-growth stocks for their portfolios.

Speculative

The speculative portfolio is for seasoned investors who have substantial net worth and steadily rising incomes. They aggressively pursue capital gains with extreme degrees of risk. They invest in emerging-growth stocks with high risk/reward ratios. Some try to outwit the market by speculating on potential buyouts, takeovers, and turn-around situations. Others buy options and trade commodity futures. They often make and lose money rapidly. Speculators should use only the funds they can afford to lose. These investments are inappropriate for new investors.

Diversification

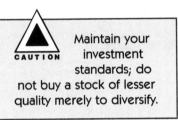

DEFINITION

Diversification is putting your eggs in different baskets or spreading the risk over a number of stocks in unrelated industries. The goal is to prevent a simultaneous decline of all stocks in a portfolio. It is a way to reduce risk without significantly diminishing the average rate of return over time. Experienced investors use three basic techniques to accomplish this. You can use the same approach as you develop your portfolio.

First, increase the number of stocks you own. By holding four stocks instead of two or eight instead of four you reduce the probability that all shares will drop at the same time. Initially, you may be able to afford only 50 or 100 shares of two companies.

> ⚠ **CAUTION**
> Maintain your investment standards; do not buy a stock of lesser quality merely to diversify.

Second, buy stocks in unrelated industries. Even your second company should be in a different industry—an industry that responds to dissimilar economic and political factors. Often industries seem unalike, yet they respond to comparable conditions. The semi-conductor and the computer industries are different industries but they respond to the same business conditions. In another example, the auto and airline industries are two distinct industries, but they are both cyclical stocks. They respond to the same economic shifts. Therefore, be sure the industries are indeed unrelated.

Third, invest in different types of growth stocks. Build your portfolio around the kind of stock that best meets your needs. Then add several stocks from one or two of the remaining categories. This group of slow-, intermediate-, and rapid-growth stocks will also provide diversity by company size. This adds further balance to your portfolio because the stock prices of large and small companies tend to move at varying times.

Risk

For a new investor it is better to be too conservative than too speculative. By carefully protecting your investment at first, you will be able to remain in the market for the long haul. When weighing the risk of a particular stock consider the stock itself and its relationship to your portfolio. Does it represent 2 percent, 10 percent, or 30

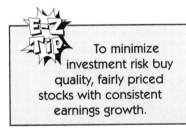

E-Z TIP

To minimize investment risk buy quality, fairly priced stocks with consistent earnings growth.

percent of the total value of your portfolio? How conservative or aggressive is the stock within the context of your total portfolio?

Risk is part of living and investing. Carefully research the companies, invest in businesses you understand, and diversify among unrelated industries and different types of stocks. Track your stocks and sell for the right reasons. Finally, hold stocks for the long term.

Conclusion

Because people's backgrounds, resources, and objectives differ, they look at stocks and the stock market in distinct ways. They prefer different kinds of stock. They expect diverse rates of return. They tolerate dissimilar levels of risk. They diversify to varying degrees. As a consequence, probably no two portfolios will be the same size nor contain the same mix of stocks.

Rules for successful investing

As you analyze companies and buy and sell shares to build your portfolio, follow the principles used by successful investors. Let these rules be your guide. Use them to enhance your investing experience.

Rule one: Avoid the five foes of successful investors

1) failure to stick to a plan

2) excessive risk

3) indecision

4) inertia

5) inability to recognize and learn from mistakes

These common mistakes can seriously damage your portfolio. As you invest, turn them into positives. First, give your portfolio the opportunity to prosper over time by developing and adhering to a specific investment strategy that meets your needs. Second, maintain a risk level that allows you to sleep peacefully. Undue risk clouds your judgment. You become apprehensive about every market move; investing ceases to be fun and rewarding. Third, as soon as you have finished your analysis, make a decision and take action. Vacillation and procrastination are costly. Finally, when a stock fails to appreciate as expected, face it squarely, determine the problem, learn from the experience, move on, and invest again.

Rule two: Cultivate the five qualities of successful investors

1) patience and persistence

2) consistency

3) objectivity

4) discipline

5) responsibility

These qualities lead to prosperity. During bear markets be patient and persistent as you seek strong companies on the rise. Likewise, during bull markets be tenacious when looking for quality, undervalued growth companies. Regardless of the type of market, retain your composure as you wait for the value of companies to grow and their prices to increase. Hold steadfastly to your principles and goals of investing. At all times preserve your objectivity. If you fall in love with a company, its management, or its products, you will be unable to accurately evaluate it. Remain unmerciful, uncompromising, and unemotional in your evaluations. Lastly, be disciplined and responsible. Accept the responsibility and have the discipline to follow your approach and to do those things that need to be done. Children, flowers, and stock portfolios require attention for healthy growth.

Rule three: Develop competency in the five practices of successful investors

1) seek knowledge

2) think and reason

3) accept reality

4) set your ego aside

5) believe in yourself

Mastery of these practices is crucial for effective investing. Continually seek information by reading about companies, products, industries, and the economy. Analyze each stock before buying whether the suggestion comes from a friend, a hot tip, a stockbroker, a magazine, or an investment newsletter. Reason and think things through before acting. Weigh the pros and cons. Buy and sell rationally. Refrain from reacting emotionally like the masses. Accept the reality that not all stocks in your portfolio will be winners. One or two will fail to appreciate as expected. You are not trying to prove anything—you are simply adding to your original investment. You are supervising your money and ensuring that it works productively. Most importantly, think for yourself, believe in yourself, and maintain the strength of your convictions.

Conclusion

Stock Market Investing Made E-Z has given you a systematic, definable way—a process, an approach—for choosing individual common stocks. Investing is a craft. It is a disciplined art, not a precise science. Believe in your stock analysis. Invest in quality companies, not the market. Be patient and persistent. Celebrate your successes. And enjoy the fruits of your labor.

HOT spot Remember the value of your portfolio is a measure of your net worth; it is not a measure of you as a person.

The forms in this guide

Smart Stock Analysis Summary...257

Smart Stock Analysis Guide...258

Smart Stock Analysis Comparison.......................................264

Smart Stock Quarterly Analysis Checkup...........................265

Smart Stock Annual Checkup 266

Smart Stock Quick Analysis Preview...................................267

NOTE: The forms in this publication have been reduced in size. To restore them to their correct size on a photocopier, increase the size to 122% .

Enlarging Forms Included in this Guide

1. Align center of form with mid-point on the glass plate guide—FACE DOWN.

2. Set the copy machine to print in the same format as the form is set on the glass—portrait or landscape.

3. Set the copy machine for enlargement to 122% of the original form.

4. Press the copy button.

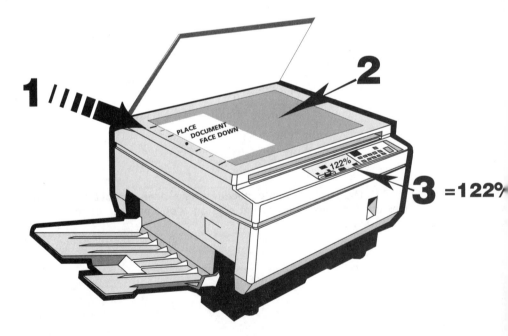

Smart Stock Analysis Summary

Company Name	Yes	No	Neutral
Category One: Profitability	/ / /	/ / /	/ / /
A. Earnings-per-Share (EPS) Growth Rate			
Year-to-Year Growth Rate Increasing			
Year-to-Year Growth Rate Consistent			
Most Recent Year's Growth Rate ≥ 5-Year Average			
Most Recent Quarter's Growth Rate ≥ 5-Year Average			
5-Year Average Growth Rate = Your Type of Growth Stock			
B. Revenue/Sales Growth Rate			
Year-to-Year Growth Rate Increasing			
Year-to-Year Growth Rate Consistent			
Most Recent Year's Growth Rate ≥ 5-Year Average			
Most Recent Quarter's Growth Rate ≥ 5-Year Average			
5-Year Average Growth Rate Supports EPS Average Growth			
C. Pretax Profit Margin			
Pretax Profit Margin Steady or Increasing			
Net Profit Margin ≥ Industry Average			
D. Return on Equity			
Most Recent Year's Return on Equity ≥ 15 %			
Return on Equity Increasing			
Return on Equity ≥ Industry Average			
Category Two: Financial Condition	/ / /	/ / /	/ / /
A. Short-Term Financial Condition			
Current Ratio ≥ 0.75			
B. Long-Term Financial Condition			
Long-Term Debt Decreased Last Year			
Debt-to-Equity Ratio ≤ 50% Debt			
C. Dividends			
Dividends Increased over Previous Ten Years			
Payout Ratio ≤ 40%			
Category Three: Institutional Ownership	/ / /	/ / /	/ / /
Percentage of Institutional Ownership ≤ 50%			
Category 4: Stock Price Evaluation	/ / /	/ / /	/ / /
A. Price-Earnings Ratio (P/E)			
Current P/E ≤ 5-year EPS Growth Rate			
Current P/E ≤ 10-Year Average P/E			
Current P/E ≤ Industry P/E			
B. Price Trend			
Current Price ≤ 52-Week High			
Price Trending Up			
TOTAL			

Smart Stock Analysis Guide

Basic Stock Information

Company_____ Symbol_____ Exchange_____ Industry_____

Date_____ 52-Week High_____ Low_____ Today's Price_____ Today's P/E_____

Today's Yield_____ S&P 500_____

Category One: Profitability

Section A: Earnings-per-Share Growth Rate

1) Annual Earnings-per-Share Growth Rate Calculate the percentage change in earnings per share for each two-year period using the EPS figure for each year beginning with the most recent year listed for the company in the S&P Stock Reports or the Value Line page. Follow the equation below:

EPS amount for [(new year - old year) ÷ old year] x 100 = % change between these two years

Year	EPS	% Change	(Growth Rate)
199___	_____	_____	
199___	_____		
199___	_____	_____	
199___	_____		
199___	_____	_____	
199___	_____		
199___	_____	_____	
199___	_____		
199___	_____	_____	
199___	_____		
200___	_____	_____	
200___	_____		

2) Five-Year Compound Average Earnings-per-Share Growth Rate
Calculate the five-year compound average growth rate (long-term growth rate): _____
Emerging-growth stocks grow from 30 to 60 percent; rapid-growth, 20 to 30 percent; intermediate-growth, 12 to 20 percent; slow-growth, 6 to 12 percent.

3) Earnings-per-Share Growth Rate between the Most Recent Quarter and the Corresponding Quarter a Year Ago The data are found on the first page of the company's S&P Stock Reports or in the left-hand column of the Value Line page.

Current Quarter _____ Same Quarter a Year Ago _____

The percentage of growth _____
Is it equal to or greater than last year's growth rate? Is it equal to or greater than the average growth rate?

Smart Stock Analysis Guide

Section B: Revenue/Sales Growth Rate

1) Annual Revenue/Sales Growth Rate Calculate the percentage change in revenues for each two-year period using the revenue figures for each year beginning with the most recent year listed in the S&P report or the Value Line page. Follow the same steps used to calculate the earnings-per-share growth rate.

Year	Revs	% Change	(Growth Rate)
199___	_____	_____	
199___	_____		
199___	_____	_____	
199___	_____		
199___	_____	_____	
199___	_____		
199___	_____	_____	
199___	_____		
199___	_____	_____	
199___	_____		
200___	_____	_____	
200___	_____		

Revenue/Sales Growth Rate: Decreased _____ Increased _____ Mixed _____
Revenue/Sales Growth Rate Consistent: Yes _____ No _____

2) Five-Year Compound Average Revenue/Sales Growth Rate Calculate the five-year compound average revenue growth rate: _____
Does the revenue growth match the earnings growth?

3) Revenue Growth Rate between the Most Recent Quarter and the Corresponding Quarter a Year Ago The data are found on the first page of the S&P report or in the left-hand column of the Value Line page.

Current Quarter _____ Same Quarter a Year Ago _____

The percentage of growth _____
Is it equal to or greater than last year's growth rate? Is it equal to or greater than the average growth rate?

Section C: Profit Margin

1) Pretax Profit Margin Calculate the pretax profit margin for each of the previous five years beginning with the most recent year of data listed in the S&P report or the Value Line page.

S&P Stock Reports: (pretax income ÷ revenues) x 100 = pretax profit margin
Value Line: Step #1 net profit ÷ (1 - income tax rate as a decimal) = pretax income
Step #2 (pretax income ÷ revenues) x 100 = pretax profit margin

199___	_____ ÷ _____ x 100 = _____
199___	_____ ÷ _____ x 100 = _____
199___	_____ ÷ _____ x 100 = _____
199___	_____ ÷ _____ x 100 = _____
199___	_____ ÷ _____ x 100 = _____
200___	_____ ÷ _____ x 100 = _____

Pretax Profit Margin: Increasing _____ Decreasing _____ Steady _____

2) Company Net Profit Margin Compared with Industry Net Profit Margin Industry net profit is found on the Value Line Industry page.

Company Net Profit Margin (after taxes): (199) _____

(200) _____

Industry Net Profit Margin _____

Company Net Profit Margin: above ___ below ___ industry net profit margin

And/Or

Similar companies in the same industry (ENTER SYMBOLS): 1._____ 2._____ 3._____

Company Return on Equity: above ___ below ___ those of similar companies

Section D: Return on Equity (ROE)

1) Return on Equity List the Return on Equity (S&P, % Ret. on Equity; Value Line, Return on Shr. Equity) for each of the previous five years beginning with the most recent year of data listed in the S&P report or the Value Line page.

199___ _____

199___ _____

199___ _____

199___ _____

199___ _____

200___ _____

Return on Equity: Increasing _____ Decreasing _____ Steady _____

ROE of less than 10 percent is poor.

2) Company Return on Equity Compared with Industry Return on Equity The industry ROE is found on the Value Line Industry page as Return on Shr. Equity.

Company ROE: (199) _____ Industry ROE _____

Company ROE: (200) _____ Industry ROE _____

Company Return on Equity: above ___ below ___ industry return on equity

And/Or

Similar companies in the same industry (ENTER SYMBOLS): 1._____ 2._____ 3._____

Company Return on Equity: above ___ below ___ those of similar companies

Category Two: Financial Condition

Section A: Short-Term Financial Condition

1) Cash Note the amount of cash (not cash flow) for each of the past five years.

a) The amount of cash has: Increased _____ Decreased _____ Mixed _____

b) The amount of cash: (199___) This Year _____ Last Year _____
The amount of cash: Increased _____ Decreased _____

c) The amount of cash: (200___) This Year _____ Last Year _____
The amount of cash: Increased _____ Decreased _____

2) Current Ratio List the current ratio for each of the previous five years.

199__ ____ 199__ ____ 199__ ____ 199__ ____ 199__ ____ 200__ ____

2 is good; 1.3 is adequate.

Smart Stock Analysis Guide

Section B: Long-Term Financial Condition

1) **Long-Term Debt** Note the amount of long-term debt for each of the past five years.

    a) Long-term debt has: Increased _____ Decreased _____ Mixed _____

    b) The amount of long-term debt: (199__) This Year _____ Last Year _____
    The amount of long-term debt has: Increased _____ Decreased _____

    c) The amount of long-term debt: (200__) This Year _____ Last Year _____
    The amount of long-term debt has: Increased _____ Decreased _____

2) **Debt-to-Equity Ratio for the Most Recent Listed Year**
Calculate: (long-term debt ÷ common equity or net worth) x 100 = % debt

Debt-to-Equity Ratio: Debt _____% Equity _____%
Is the debt 50 percent or less?

Section C: Dividends

1) **Dividend Growth** Note the dividend amounts for the past ten years.
Dividends have steadily increased: Yes _____ No _____

2) **Dividend Payout Ratio for the Most Recent Listed Year**
Calculate: (dividend ÷ earnings per share) x 100 = dividend payout ratio

Dividend Payout Ratio: _____% of company's profits are paid to shareholders
Is the payout ratio 50 percent or less?

Category Three: Institutional Ownership

Institutional Ownership

_____percent of stock is owned by institutions
The lower the better. Less than 60 percent is preferable; 30 percent is very good.

Category Four: Stock Price Evaluation

Section A: Price-Earnings Ratio (P/E)

1) **Price-Earnings Ratio Compared with Earnings Growth Rate (PEG)**
Calculate: P/E ÷ five-year compound average EPS growth rate = PEG

Current P/E _____ Five-Year Average Earnings-per-Share Growth Rate _____

PEG _____
_____ Underpriced if between 0.5 and 0.9
_____ Fairly priced if between 0.9 and 1.05
_____ Slightly overpriced if between 1.05 and 1.30
_____ Overpriced if between 1.30 and 2.00
_____ Very overpriced if 2.25 and above

2) **P/E Compared with Earnings Growth Rate Plus Yield (PEGY)**
Calculate: P/E ÷ (five-year average EPS growth rate + dividend yield) = PEGY

P/E _____ Five-Year Earnings Growth Rate _____ Dividend Yield _____

PEGY _____
_____ Underpriced if between 0.5 and 0.9
_____ Fairly priced if between 0.9 and 1.05
_____ Slightly overpriced if between 1.05 and 1.30
_____ Overpriced if between 1.30 and 2.00
_____ Very overpriced if 2.25 and above

Smart Stock Analysis Guide

3) P/E Compared with the Company's Ten-Year Average P/E

Current P/E _____ Ten-Year Average P/E _____
Current P/E: above _____ below _____ ten-year average P/E

4) P/E Compared with the Industry Average P/E

Company P/E _____ Industry P/E _____
Company P/E: above _____ below _____ industry P/E

And/Or

Similar companies in the same industry: 1._____ 2._____ 3._____
Company P/E: above _____ below _____ those of similar companies

Section B: Price Trend

1) The 52-Week High and Low Price
52-Week High _____ 52-Week Low _____ Today's Price _____

After you have paid for the stock and the commissions (add $0.75 to the per-share price), is there room for the price to increase before it hits the 52-week high? Yes _____ No _____

2) Price Chart Check a price chart.
The price is moving generally: Up _____ Down _____ Mixed _____

3) Market
The market is moving generally: Up _____ Down _____ Mixed_____

Category Five: Company Background

Overview
1. Where are the company headquarters?

2. What does the company do?

3. Who are its competitors?

Products and Services
1. List the company's products and services.

2. Does the company have a niche in the market?

3. How are its products/services different from those of its competitors?

4. If a new product/service is involved, how much will it add to earnings?

Smart Stock Analysis Guide

Clients

1. Are the company's clients repeat customers?

2. Is the company heavily dependent on one or two large customers?

Expansion

1. Is there room for the company to expand in the industry?

2. Are existing units making a profit? Has the company proven it can expand profitably?

3. Where is it currently expanding—regionally, nationally, internationally?

4. How is it expanding? The **4 ways to expand** are to add new units, buy other companies, develop new products, and start a new line of business.

5. Is its rate of expansion increasing or decreasing?

6. What are its prospects for continued growth?

7. How will the company continue to increase its earnings per share? The **6 ways to increase EPS** are to cut costs, raise prices, increase sales in existing markets, develop new products, expand regionally, nationally, or internationally, and correct, close or sell losing operations.

Concerns

1. What challenges does the company face?

2. What are your concerns?

Category Six: The Decision

1. The Stock's Strengths—reasons to buy

2. The Stock's Weaknesses—reasons to question buying

3 . Neutral Considerations

4. Check Current News about the Company

5. Buy _____ Number of Shares _____ Sell if _____

6. Follow It _____ Buy If _____

7. Do Not Buy _____

SMART STOCK ANALYSIS COMPARISON

Company Names				
Category One: Profitability				
Most Recent Year's Earnings-per-Share Amount				
Most Recent Year's Earnings-per-Share Growth Rate				
Five-Year Compound Average Growth Rate				
Most Recent Quarterly Growth Rate				
Most Recent Year's Revenue/Sales Amount				
Most Recent Year's Revenue/Sales Growth Rate				
Five-Year Compound Average Growth Rate				
Most Recent Quarterly Growth Rate				
Pretax Profit Margin (Pretax Profit ÷ Sales x 100)				
Net Profit Margin (Net Profit ÷ Sales x 100)				
Industry Net Profit Margin				
Return on Equity (Net Profit ÷ Stockholder Equity x 100)				
Industry Return on Equity				
Category Two: Financial Condition				
Cash Increased/Decreased over Previous Year				
Current Ratio (Current Assets ÷ Current Liabilities)				
Long-Term Debt Increased/Decreased over Previous Year				
Debt-to-Equity Ratio (LT Debt ÷ Stockholder Equity x 100)				
Dividend Increasing				
Payout Ratio (Dividend per Share ÷ Earnings per Share x 100)				
Current Dividend Yield				
Category Three: Institutional Ownership				
Percentage of Stock Owned by Institutions				
Category Four: Stock Price				
52-Week High and Low				
Today's Price				
Today's P/E				
Five-Year EPS Growth Rate				
Company's 10-Year Average P/E				
Industry P/E				

SMART STOCK QUARTERLY ANALYSIS CHECKUP

Stock Name _____

Purchase Price _____

Earnings Per Share
P/E, Price, S&P 500

Earnings-per-Share Five-Year Growth Rate _____

Earnings-per-Share Most Recent Year's Growth Rate _____

Quarter	Date	Current Quarter	Same Quarter Previous Year	Growth Rate	P/E	Price	S&P 500
1st							
2nd							
3rd							
4th							
Year							

Revenues

Revenue Five-Year Growth Rate _____

Revenue Most Recent Year's Growth Rate _____

Quarter	Date	Current Quarter	Same Quarter Previous Year	Growth Rate
1st				
2nd				
3rd				
4th				
Year				

Comments

1st Quarter

2nd Quarter

3rd Quarter

4th Quarter

SMART STOCK ANNUAL CHECKUP

Company Name	Yr	Yr	Yr	Yr
Category One: Profitability				
Most Recent Year's Earnings-per-Share Amount				
Most Recent Year's Earnings-per-Share Growth Rate				
Five-Year Compound Average Growth Rate				
Most Recent Year's Revenue/Sales Amount				
Most Recent Year's Revenue/Sales Growth Rate				
Five-Year Average Growth Rate				
Pretax Profit Margin (Pretax Profit ÷ Sales x 100)				
Net Profit Margin (Net Profit ÷ Sales x 100)				
Industry Net Profit Margin				
Return on Equity (Net Profit ÷ Stockholder Equity x 100)				
Industry Return on Equity				
Category Two: Financial Condition				
Amount of Cash				
Increased/Decreased				
Current Ratio (Current Assets ÷ Current Liabilities)				
Amount of Long-Term Debt				
Increased/Decreased				
Debt-to-Equity Ratio (LT Debt ÷ Stockholder Equity x 100)				
Dividend Amount				
Payout Ratio (Dividend Per Share ÷ Earnings Per Share x 100)				
Current Dividend Yield				
Category Three: Institutional Ownership				
Percentage of Stock Owned by Institutions				
Category Four: Stock Price				
S&P 500 Index				
52-Week High and Low				
Today's Price				
Today's P/E				
Five-Year EPS Growth Rate				
Company's 10-Year Average High P/E				
Industry P/E				

SMART STOCK QUICK ANALYSIS PREVIEW

Does the Stock Merit Full Analysis?

QUESTIONS	YES	NO
Have **Earnings per Share** increased each of the past five years?		
Have **Earnings per Share** doubled in the past five years? (a 15 percent compound average growth rate)		
Have **Sales** (revenues) increased each of the past five years?		
Have **Sales** (revenues) doubled in the past five to seven years?		
Has the **Profit Margin** increased or remained stable over the past three years?		
Is the **Return on Equity** ≥ 15 percent?		
Has the **Return on Equity** increased or remained stable over the past three years?		
Is **Long-Term Debt** ≤ 1/2 of **Common Equity**?		
Is the current **P/E** similar to the company's average P/E during the past five years?		
Conclusion: Does the stock merit full analysis?		

Glossary of useful terms

A

Acceptance date
See Effective date

Account executives
See Registered representatives

American depository receipt (ADR)
Shares of foreign companies (receipts) deposited in a foreign branch of a U.S. bank (depository), traded on U.S. stock exchanges like other securities; stand-ins for foreign stocks from countries in which nonresidents are not allowed to directly own stocks and remove stock certificates from the country

American Stock Exchange (AMEX)
A national stock exchange in New York City that specializes in listing midsize companies and in trading derivative products such as warrants and options, owned by the Nasdaq Stock Market

AMEX
See the American Stock Exchange

AMEX composite index
A Market-value-weighted index that measures the performance of the stocks traded on the American Stock Exchange

Annual meeting
A yearly corporate meeting to inform shareholders about the financial status of the company

Annual report
A booklet sent to each shareholder at the end of every business year, detailing the company's financial condition and describing the company's business activities during the year

Arbitration
A final, legal, and binding conflict resolution option provided by NASD regulation dispute resolution to investors seeking restitution of money lost due to alleged broker violation of NASD rules or regulations

Ask price
The dealer's selling price and the investor's buying price

At the market
See Market order

Automatic post execution and reporting
The American Stock Exchange's automated transaction system

AUTOPER
> See Automatic post execution and reporting

Average annual P/E
> A p/e calculated using the stock's average closing price for the year divided by the earnings per share for the year

Away from the market
> A stock price that is better than is currently available

B

Bear market
> A period of generally falling stock prices

Beneficial owner
> The investor who receives all benefits of owning the shares even though the stock is held in street name

Bid price
> The dealer's buying price and the investor's selling price

Big board
> See New York Stock Exchange

Black Tuesday
> October 29, 1929. The date of the 1929 stock market crash

Blue chip stock
> Stocks of large, mature, reliable, high-quality firms with long histories of earnings and dividend growth

Board of directors
> A board elected by the shareholders, which establishes the basic policies of the corporation and hires top management personnel

Bond
> A corporate or government entity debt instrument that pays interest to the owner of the security

Breakout
> A technical analysis term for a stock price movement that rises above (breaks) the stock's previous high or drops below its previous low

Broad-based index or average
> An index or average that contains stocks from a wide range of industries, representing the overall market

Broker
> 1) An individual who is a partner in a securities firm
> 2) A term used by the investing public to mean a registered representative

Broker call rate
> The interest rate banks charge brokerage firms to borrow money

Brokerage statement
> A monthly status report of an investor's account, documenting the beginning and ending account balance, the securities owned, and the month's transactions

Bull market
> A period of generally rising stock prices

Business risk.
> The possibility that a good company will be mismanaged and its stock price will fall

Buttonwood Agreement

A pact signed in 1792 by 24 brokers who agreed to trade only among themselves, to forgo trading at other stock auctions, and to charge a commission on all sales of securities; the predecessors of the New York Stock Exchange

C

Cash

The money corporations have in checking and savings accounts, certificates of deposit, marketable securities and other instruments that can be quickly converted to cash with little price change; sometimes called cash and cash assets or cash and cash equivalents

Cash account

A brokerage account in which the investor must pay in full for the shares purchased

Cash management account

A brokerage cash account that allows the client to bank and invest at the same institution, which may include a money market account, a checking account, and a debit or credit card

Central registration depository (CRD)

A data bank maintained by the NASD that lists information on all registered representatives in the United States concerning any criminal convictions they may have had or any disciplinary actions taken by securities regulators. Also contains information about any regulatory infractions committed by brokerage firms

Churning

The excessive buying and selling at a broker's recommendation for the broker's purpose of generating commissions

Close

The stock's price at its last trade for the day

Commission

A fee charged by stockbrokers on each buy or sell order executed for a customer

Commission house brokers

See Floor Brokers

Committee on uniform securities identification (CUSIP)

An identification number assigned to each publicly traded security, used when recording stock purchases and sales

Common equity

See Equity

Composite transactions

A stock's total volume of trading from either the NYSE, AMEX, or Nasdaq, where it has its primary listing and the regional exchanges where it has secondary listings

Confirmation slip

A document the brokerage firm sends the investor after a buy or sell order has been executed, giving the details of the order such as the date of the execution, the name of the stock, the number of shares, the price per share, the commission fee, and the total dollar amount

Cooling-off period

The period of time during which the SEC examines the corporate registration statement of a company that is going public, and during which the corporation may not issue any statements not contained in the preliminary prospectus

Corporation

A company owned by its shareholders, who elect the board of directors which makes the policies and hires the company's top management; a separate legal entity, thereby protecting its shareholders from liability

Crossing session I (CSI)

A component of the NYSE's SuperDot system used to trade from 4:15 to 5:00 P.M. after the market closes, matching orders electronically and executing at the closing price

CSI

See Crossing session I

Cumulative voting rights

Voting rights determined by the shareholder's number of shares multiplied by the number of directors to be elected. A shareholder may cast all votes for one director and none for the other directors or proportion the votes any way desired. Cumulative voting rights require only a plurality to elect

Current assets

What the company owns and expects to convert into cash during the following year; also called liquid, quick, and floating assets

Current liabilities

Debts the company owes and must pay from cash within 12 months, consisting of taxes, salaries, accounts payable, interest on long-term loans, bank loans and notes payable due by the end of the year, and other costs of doing business that must be paid during the year

Current P/E

A p/e calculated using the stock's closing price divided by the earnings per share for the past six months and an estimate of the earnings for the next six months

Current ratio

The ratio of current assets to current liabilities (current assets divided by current liabilities), indicating whether a company has enough cash and other current assets to pay its bills and operating expenses due within the Fiscal Year

Current yield

See Dividend yield

CUSIP

See Committee on Uniform Securities Identification Procedures

Cyclical-growth stock

The stock of companies whose earnings-per-share growth rate is closely tied to the ups and downs of the economy

D

Day order

An instruction attached to a Limit Order that states the order is to remain in effect for that day only

Dealer

A security firm, large or small, that is willing to make a market for a stock by buying and selling from its inventory of shares at its own risk; also called market maker

Debt-to-equity ratio

A standard measure of company financial strength (long-term debt divided by shareholder equity) stating a company's long-term debt as a percentage of its common equity

Declaration date
> The date the board of directors announces it will pay a dividend

Designed order turnaround (DOT)
> The New York Stock Exchange's automated trading system

Direct investors
> Persons who participate directly in the stock market by placing orders to buy or sell individual stocks and bonds

Discount brokerage firm
> A brokerage firm that charges low commission rates but does not offer investment advice, stock recommendations, or personalized service

Dividend pay-out ratio
> The percentage of company earnings paid to shareholders as Dividends (dividend divided by earnings per share)

Dividends
> The portion of company profits the board of directors vote to pay stockholders

Dividend yield
> The percentage of profit an investor earns on a stock investment through dividend payments (dividend per share per year divided by purchase price per share); also called yield, current yield, and rate of return

DJIA
> See the Dow Jones Industrial Average

DJUA
> See the Dow Jones Utilities Average

DOT
> See Designated Order Turnaround

The Dow
> See the Dow Jones Industrial Average

Dow Jones composite average
> A Price-Weighted Average composed of the 30 industrial companies in the DJIA, the 20 transportation companies in the DJTA, and the 15 utilities in the DJUA; also called the 65 Stocks Composite Average, the 65 Stock Average, and the 65 Stocks

Dow Jones global stock index
> A measurement of worldwide stock performance, composed of approximately 2,800 companies from 29 countries

Dow Jones industrial average (DJIA)
> The oldest, best known, and most often quoted measure of stock market performance, a Price-Weighted Average composed of the 30 leading companies in the leading industries; also called the Dow, the 30 Industrials, the Industrial Average, and the DJIA

Dow Jones transportation average (DJTA)
> A Price-Weighted Average that measures the stock performance of the transportation industry; also called the 20 Transportation

Dow Jones utility average (DJUA)
> A Price-Weighted Average that measures the performance of the utility industry; also called the 15 Utilities and the Utility Average

Downtrend
> The price of a stock or the market as a whole is moving lower

Dual-listed stock
> A stock listed on either the NYSE, AMEX, or Nasdaq and also listed on a regional exchange

E

Earnings

The company's net profit; the money remaining after all expenses, including taxes, have been paid

Earnings per share (EPS)

A standard measure of company growth and profitability, calculated by dividing a company's net profit figure by the number of shares of common stock outstanding; also called net earnings per share, profit per share, net profit per share, income per share, and net income per share

Effective date

The day the SEC formally accepts the company's registration—a step in the company's going-public process; the first day the corporation's shares may be formally offered for sale

Emerging-growth stock

The stock of companies whose earnings per share have increased an average of 30 to 60 percent a year for the past three years

EPS

See Earnings per share

Equity

The dollar value of everything the company owns (total assets minus total liabilities); also called total stockholder or shareholder equity, common equity, and net worth

Ex-dividend date

The first day the stock trades without the immediate dividend being paid, two working days before the record date; necessary for record-keeping purposes

F

15 Utilities

See the Dow Jones Utilities Average

52 (Fifty-two) week high and low

The highest and lowest price paid per share for the stock during the past year

Final prospectus

The final version of the preliminary prospectus, containing the share price, the offering date, and any SEC-required changes in the preliminary prospectus information

Fiscal year

The 12-month business year which may or may not coincide with the calendar year

Floating assets

See Current assets

Floor brokers

The brokers who execute trades on the floor of an exchange for their firms' clients

Floor reporters

The employees of the stock exchange who record the details of each stock trade

Foreign stocks

The shares issued by foreign companies and listed on stock exchanges in the home country

Forward P/E

The p/e calculated using the stock's closing price divided by an estimate of the earnings per share for the next 12 months

401(K) Plan

A tax-deferred retirement plan

Full-service brokerage firm
> A firm whose brokers work with their clients individually, providing in-depth stock analysis reports, making specific stock recommendations to fit their clients' needs, and helping their clients manage their portfolios

Fundamental analysis
> An approach to selecting stocks based on identifying quality companies by looking at the company's profitability, financial strength, and future growth potential

Futures contract
> An agreement to buy or sell a commodity in a certain quantity at a particular price on a specific future date

G

Going public
> A term used to describe a series of events that occurs when a private corporation becomes a publicly traded corporation and sells its shares to public investors for the first time

Good 'til cancelled (GTC)
> An instruction attached to a limit order that states the order is to remain in effect until the investor cancels it; also called an open order

Growth rate
> The percentage change in earnings, revenues, or dividends from year to year, which gives a more meaningful and revealing picture of company performance than the dollar difference provides; calculated as follows: [(newer year - older year) ÷ older year] x 100 = percent change between the two years

GTC
> See Good 'til canceled

H

Holder of record
> The share owner's name listed on the corporate books

Hot issue
> An IPO for which there is strong demand, which significantly drives up the price when the shares begin trading on an exchange

I

Income per share
> See Earnings per share

Indirect investors
> Individuals who own stock through a mutual, pension, or retirement fund and have no control over the particular stocks that are bought and sold

Individual account
> A brokerage account owned by one person

Individual investors
> Individuals who decide what stocks to buy and when to buy and sell them

Individual investor express delivery service
> A priority delivery service for individual investors trading 2,099 shares or less on the New York Stock Exchange's SuperDot automated trading system

Individual retirement account (IRA)
A personal tax-deferred retirement account

Industrial average
See the Dow Jones Industrial Average

Industry risk
The possibility that specific conditions will negatively affect all companies within an industry and that the price of the stocks in the industry will decline

Inflation risk
The possibility that the rate of inflation will be greater than the amount earned on an investment

Initial public offering (IPO)
1) The first time a Private Corporation sells its shares to the public. 2) The direct selling by the Investment Banker to individual and institutional investors at the preset price those shares the investment banker bought from the private corporation at the primary market

Initial public offering date
The day the investment banker sells (transfers) its shares to those individual and institutional investors who prepurchased the shares directly from the investment banker at the preset price, after which later that morning the shares begin trading on the open market—the exchange where they are listed

Initial public offering price
The preset price investors pay for a new stock that is purchased directly from the Investment Banker; the price negotiated between the corporation and the investment banker—the price the investment banker paid the corporation for all new shares—plus the investment banker's fees

Institutional brokerage firm
A brokerage firm that specializes in meeting the needs of large Institutional Investors

Institutional investors
Money managers employed by institutions such as banks, insurance companies, mutual funds, pension funds, and retirement funds to choose, buy, and sell stocks and bonds for the institutions' portfolios

Institutional ownership
The percentage of a company's stock that is owned by institutions such as mutual, pension, and retirement funds

Intermarket trading system (ITS)
An electronic system that links regional stock exchanges with the NYSE, AMEX and Nasdaq. It displays instant last trade prices and current bid and ask information for dual-listed stocks

Intermediate-growth stock
The stock of companies whose earnings per share have increased an average of 12 to 20 percent a year for the previous 10 years

Investment executive
See Registered Representative

Investment banker
A firm that specializes in working with private corporations going public and with companies involved in mergers and buyouts by advising, overseeing the administrative work, and underwriting the new shares

IRA
See Individual retirement account

ITS
See Intermarket trading system

J

Joint account
A brokerage account owned by two or more adults which requires that proxies and requests for withdrawals be signed by all owners

Joint tenants in common
A brokerage joint account in which each individual independently owns a clearly defined percentage of the account

Joint tenancy with rights of survivorship (JTWROS)
A brokerage joint account in which each person owns an undivided equal portion of the account

K

Keogh
A tax-deferred retirement account for those who are self-employed and for employees of unincorporated businesses

L

Large cap stocks
The stocks of companies that have a market value of $5 billion or more, calculated by multiplying the number of shares outstanding by the price per share

Limited liability
Limitation of corporate debt liability to corporate assets, with shareholders free from financial responsibility

Limit order
An order to buy or sell a stock at a specific price (or better) that is superior to the price currently available

Listing
Acceptance of a company for trading on a particular stock exchange after requirements have been met

Liquid assets
Resources that can be quickly and easily converted to cash. Also see current assets

Long-term debt
Notes, loans, and bonds that are scheduled for repayment sometime beyond the end of the current business year

Long-term financial condition
The company's financial strength beyond the current business year

Long-term investors
Those who buy and hold their stocks for three to five years or longer

M

Margin account

A brokerage account in which investors may finance part of the cost of their stock

Margin call

A telephone call from the broker that instructs the investor to deposit additional funds in his or her account because the price of the stocks the investor has financed has declined and the account's equity has fallen below the minimum required in a margin account (30 percent)

Market average

See Stock market index

Market capitalization

See Market value

Market index

See Stock market index

Market maker

See Dealers

Market order

Instructions that tell the broker to buy or sell the shares immediately at the best available price; also called "at the market."

Market risk

The possibility that the stock market will drop and all stock prices will decline

Market trend

Long-term (two to three years), repetitive patterns of stock price movements

Market value

A measure of company size calculated by multiplying the number of shares outstanding by the price per share

Market-value weighted index

Indexes based on the market value of the component stocks, calculated by adding the market value of the component stocks, dividing the total by a current baseline market-value figure, and multiplying the quotient by a baseline-value figure

Mediation

A voluntary, non-binding conflict resolution option provided by NASD Regulation Dispute Resolution for investors seeking restitution of money lost due to alleged broker violation of NASD rules or regulations

Mid-cap stocks

Stocks of those companies which have a market value between $1.5 and $5 billion, calculated by multiplying the total number of shares outstanding by the price per share

Money managers

See Institutional investors

Multiple

See Price-earnings ratio

N

Narrow-based index or average

A representation of the stock price movements of a particular segment of the market or of a specific industry

NASD

See National Association of Securities Dealers

NASDAQ composite index

A market-value-weighted index that measures the performance of the Nasdaq stock market, composed of the nearly 5,500 stocks listed on the Nasdaq stock market

NASDAQ

See Nasdaq stock market

NASDAQ national market issues

The larger, more actively traded stocks listed on the Nasdaq stock market

NASDAQ small-cap issues

The smaller, less actively traded stocks listed on the Nasdaq stock market

NASDAQ stock market

Pronounced "naz-dak." A full-fledged, national electronic marketplace for trading stocks where stocks are bought and sold by brokers for their clients via computer screens rather than face to face on the floor on an exchange; prices being determined by competition between the market makers and the broker rather than by auction between several buyers and sellers on the floor of an exchange

NASD regulation dispute resolution

A division of NASD Regulation that provides mediation and arbitration services to help investors recover funds lost due to broker violations of NASD rules and regulations

NASD Regulation, Inc.

A division of NASD that investigates complaints of alleged broker infringements of NASD rules and regulations, and disciplines brokers and firms if a violation has occurred

National Association of Security Dealers (NASD)

The securities industry's self-regulatory organization that, under SEC supervision, makes and enforces securities rules and regulations

National Association of Security Dealers Automated Quotation System (NASDAQ)

The computerized trading system introduced by the National Association of Security Dealers that became the Nasdaq Stock Market, a full-fledged electronic stock market.

Net earnings

See Profit

Net earnings per share

See Earnings per Share

Net change

The difference between the previous day's closing price and today's closing price

Net income

See Profit

Net income per share

See Earnings per share

Net income-to-net worth

See Return on equity

Net profit

See Profit

Net profit margin

The percentage of each after-tax dollar that is profit, calculated by dividing revenues by after-tax income; also see profit margin

Net profit per share
See Earnings per share

Net worth
The value of everything owned minus everything owed; total assets minus total liabilities; also see equity

New issue
Shares offered to the public for the first time

New York Stock Exchange (NYSE)
A national exchange located in New York City at 11 Wall Street; the largest exchange in the United States; also called the Big Board and The Exchange

New York Stock Exchange composite index
A market-value-weighted index that contains all stocks listed on the NYSE

NYSE
See New York Stock Exchange

O

OARS
See Opening automated report service

Odd lot
Less than 100 shares

Opening automated report service (OARS)
A component of the NYSE's SuperDOT system that is used in the morning before the market opens for accepting and matching market orders for execution at the opening price

Open order
See Good 'til canceled

Option
The right to buy or sell a stock at a specified price within a stated period; traded like stocks

OTC bulletin board
An electronic quotation system that displays quotes for stocks that are not listed on an exchange; a marketplace for very small companies which have filed annual and quarterly financial information with the SEC

Over-the-counter
A market that trades those stocks not listed and traded on an exchange

P

Partnership
A company owned by two or more people

Payment date
The day a dividend is paid

Payout ratio
See Dividend payout ratio

PEG
See P/E-to-growth ratio

PEGY

A measurement for judging whether a stock is underpriced, fairly priced, or overpriced (p/e divided by the company's five-year average earnings-per-share growth rate plus the dividend yield), taking into consideration the contribution made by the dividend

P/E-to-growth ratio (PEG)

A measurement for judging whether a stock is underpriced, fairly priced, or overpriced (p/e divided by the company's five-year average earnings-per-share growth rate)

Percent earned on net worth

See Return on equity

Percent income of revenues

See Profit margin

Percentage change

The difference between two amounts of money measured as a percent, which gives a clearer picture than the simple dollar difference; calculated as follows: [(new price - old price) ÷ old price] x 100 = percent change

PFD

See Preferred stock

Pink sheets

1. The thin, pink paper on which were printed the names of dealers and their prices for each over-the-counter stock and which were mailed to brokers by the National Quotation Bureau, a reporting service. 2. The equivalent information displayed on computer screens by the National Quotation Bureau for pink sheet companies, those companies whose stocks are the bottom tier of publicly traded securities and who are waiting for SEC registration

Points

1. Stock quotes: equivalent of a dollar 2. Index and average quotes: a unit of measure

Preferred stock

A class of stock that pays a fixed annual dividend and provides a higher yield than the company's common stock, whose owners' claims in case of company failure take precedence over those of common

Preliminary prospectus

A booklet containing pertinent information, required by the SEC, about a company that is going public; also called a "red herring"

Price-earnings ratio (P/E)

The relationship between the price of the stock and the company's earnings (price divided by earnings per share), reflecting investors' expectations for the growth of the company—the higher the p/e, the more growth expected; an industry-specific evaluation tool used to determine whether a stock is fairly priced; also called price-earnings multiple and multiple

Price-earnings multiple

See Price-earnings ratio

Price-weighted average

A market average giving equal consideration to each company, large or small, with high-priced stocks affecting the average more than low-priced stocks

Primary listing

The company's listing on either the NYSE, AMEX, or Nasdaq Stock Market

Primary market

An event when a company goes public or puts a new issue of shares on the market; the moment at which the corporation sells all newly issued shares to the investment banker and the investment banker transfers the money for the shares to the corporation

Private corporation

A corporation whose shares are owned by a small group of people—family, close business associates

Profit

The money a company makes after all expenses are paid (income minus all expenses including taxes); also called net profit, net income, and net earnings

Profit margin

The percentage of each sales dollar that is profit (earnings before taxes divided by sales), a way to evaluate the effectiveness of management; also called return on sales, return on revenues, and percent income of revenues

Profit per share

See Earnings per share

Profit rate

See Return on equity

Proportional ownership

The percentage of the whole company a stockholder's shares represent

Proprietorship

A company owned by one person

Proxy

A written authorization from the shareholder to someone else to vote the shares as directed at the annual meeting

Public corporation

A corporation whose shares may be purchased by anyone

Purchasing power risk

See Inflation risk

Q

Quarterly report

A brief account of the company's business during the previous four months, listing income and expense figures for the quarter just completed and the corresponding quarter the year before

Quick assets

See Current assets

R

Rapid-growth stock

The stock of companies whose earnings per share have increased an average of 20 to 30 percent a year for the previous five years

Rate of return

The percentage of profit earned on a stock investment through its dividend payments. It is the percentage of the cost of the stock that is returned each year through its dividends. Also called yield, current yield, and dividend yield

Record date

The date by which a shareholder's ownership must be recorded on the corporation's books for the shareholder to receive the dividend

Red herring

A preliminary prospectus, called a "red herring" because a notice is printed in red along the left-hand margin of the cover, stating that the SEC registration has been filed but not yet accepted and the information contained within is subject to change

Regional exchange

A local exchange established in a metropolitan area outside New York City, listing stocks of local or regional companies that are not listed on a national exchange (NYSE, AMEX, Nasdaq), also trading a limited number of stocks listed on the national exchanges that are of particular interest to local investors

Registered floor traders

Brokers who have purchased seats on the exchange and make their living buying and selling stocks for their own portfolios

Registered representative

An individual licensed by the SEC to recommend specific securities and to trade securities for customers; also called brokers, stockbrokers, account executives, and investment executives

Registrar

An entity outside the company hired to maintain a list of current stockholders and to make sure the number of shares bought equals the number of shares sold; which also makes certain the total number of shares owned by investors does not exceed the number of shares issued by the company; often a commercial bank

Registration date

The date the company formally files its documents with the SEC seeking approval for the sale of its new shares when going public or when offering a new block of shares to the public

Research boutique

A brokerage firm that specializes in serving small select groups of wealthy individuals and private investment funds

Residual rights

The rights whereby shareholders may file a claim on the company's assets after all creditors have been satisfied a company fails and is dissolved

Resistance level

A technical analysis term; the stock's previous high

Retail brokerage firms

Brokerage firms that cater to the diverse needs of individual investors

Return on equity

The rate of return a company earns on shareholder common equity (net income divided by common equity), which quantitatively measures how well management runs the company both operationally and financially; also called profit rate, percent earned on net worth, net income-to-net worth, and return on stockholders' equity

Return on revenues

See Profit margin

Return on sales

See Profit margin

Return on stockholders' equity

See Return on equity

Revenue
> The total amount of money a corporation receives from its various sources of income; often used interchangeably with sales

Right
> A type of security that allows a stockholder to buy newly issued shares directly from the company at a lower price before the company offers the shares to the public, usually valid for two to four weeks and traded like a stock until it expires

Risk
> The possibility that the value of an investment will decrease

Risk-reward ratio
> The correlation between risk and reward; the higher the expected return, the greater the risk

Round lot
> One hundred shares of stock

Round trip trade
> A buy and sell trade involving the same shares

Russell 2000 index
> A Market-value-weighted index that measures the performance of small-company stocks

S

S&P 500
> See Standard & Poor's 500 composite stock index

Seat on the exchange
> A purchased membership on an exchange giving the member the right to buy and sell stocks directly on the exchange

SEC
> See Securities Exchange Commission

Secondary listing
> The stock's listing on a regional exchange in addition to its NYSE, AMEX, or Nasdaq listing

Secondary market
> The public trading of stock between investors through their brokers on an exchange at the market-determined price

Securities
> Stocks, bonds, options, rights, warrants

Securities Exchange Commission (SEC)
> A federal regulatory agency that is charged with enforcing federal securities laws, rules, and regulations that ensure that securities markets are free of price manipulations and unfair practices, and which investigates allegations of fraud, insider trading, and the trading of unlisted securities

Securities Investor Protection Corporation (SIPC)
> A nonprofit corporation that insures each investor's cash and securities deposited with a brokerage firm against loss in case the brokerage firm goes bankrupt

Settlement date
> Three days after a buy or sell order is executed; the day the money and shares change hands; also called T + 3

Share of stock
> A unit of company ownership

Shareholder
> Part owner of the company through ownership of shares of the company's stock; also called stockholder

Short-term financial condition
> The company's financial strength for the fiscal year—the 12-month business year

SIPC
> See Securities Investor Protection Corporation

65 Stock average
> See Dow Jones Composite Stock Index

65 Stocks
> See Dow Jones Composite Stock Index

65 Stocks Composite Average
> See Dow Jones Composite Stock Index

Slow-growth stock
> The stock of companies whose earnings per share have grown from 6 to 12 percent a year for many years, including income, blue chip, and low-growth, low-risk stocks

Small-cap stocks
> Stocks of companies that have a market value of $1.5 billion or less, calculated by multiplying the number of shares outstanding by the price per share

Small Order Execution System (SOES)
> The Nasdaq's automated trading system which may be used only by retail customers

SOES
> See Small Order Execution System

Specialists
> Individuals or members of specialist firms who own seats on an exchange, oversee the trading of the stocks the exchange assigns them, and make an orderly market in those stocks by buying and selling shares from their inventory at their risk

Speculators
> Individuals who assume a high degree of risk when making an investment

Standard & Poor's 500 Composite Stock Index (S&P 500)
> A broad-based measure of stock performance composed of 500 widely held and actively traded stocks of leading companies in leading industries that trade on the NYSE, AMEX, and Nasdaq

Statutory voting rights
> Voting rights determined by the number of shares owned, with one share equaling one vote for each director, and requiring a majority vote to elect a director

Stock certificate
> A document that proves the investor owns a specific number of shares in a particular company

Stock exchange
> A marketplace where members buy and sell for their customers shares of stock that are listed on the exchange

Stockholder
> See Shareholder

Stock market average
> See Stock market index

Stock market index

A measurement of the general movement of stock prices

Stock quotation

A statement that gives the stock's price per share for the most recent trade, and may include the stock's high and low prices during the past 52 weeks, the dividend per share, the dividend yield, the price-earnings ratio, the number of shares traded during the day, and the high and low prices during the day

Stock split

An increase, by a specific proportion, in the number of company shares outstanding, which decreases the price and the dividend by the same proportion

Stock symbol

An official one-to-five letter representation for a particular stock in electronic quotations and buy or sell orders

Stop-loss order

See Stop order

Stop order

Order instructions that tell the broker to sell the shares at the market price once a specific price has been reached

Street name

A way to record stock ownership in which the brokerage firm is listed on the corporate books as the share owner and the investor's ownership is electronically recorded in the brokerage firm's account records

Super Designated Order Turnaround (SuperDot)

The NYSE's automated trading system that routes incoming orders to the member firm's floor booth or directly to the specialist's station

SuperDOT

See Super Designated Order Turnaround

Support level

A technical analysis term; the stock's previous low price

Syndicate

Several investment banking firms working together as the purchasing or underwriting group when a company goes public, spreading the financial risk for buying and reselling the corporate shares

T

T + 3

See Settlement date

Technical analysis

An approach to selecting stocks based on using charts and graphs of the movements of a stock's price and trading volume

30 Industrials

See Dow Jones Industrial Average

Tombstone

A discreet announcement—advertisement—in financial publications that informs investors about a new stock offering

Total stockholder equity

See Equity

Trade date

The date the buy or sell order is executed

Traders

Investors who buy and hold their stocks for a short time—hours or days—without thought of company ownership

Trading authorization

A power of attorney that gives the investor's broker, money manager, or another individual written discretionary permission to trade the account without the investor's consent or knowledge of specific trades

Trading post

A specific place on the floor of an exchange where a particular stock is traded

Trailing P/E

A p/e calculated using the current closing price divided by the earnings per share for the past four quarters

Transfer agent

An entity that records the stock trades in the company's books, cancels the certificates for the sold shares, and issues new certificates for the purchased shares; usually the company itself

Transferred and held

A way to record stock ownership by registering the stock in the investor's name and sending the certificate to the brokerage firm for safekeeping

Transferred and shipped

A way to record stock ownership by registering the stock in the investor's name and mailing the certificate to the investor for safekeeping

Trend

Overall price movements in any direction of a stock or of the market as a whole over a period of one, two, three or five years

20 Transportations

See Dow Jones Transportation Average

Two-dollar brokers

Self-employed brokers who own their own seats on an exchange and make their living executing overflow orders from brokerage firms

U

Underwriter

The investment banker hired by a corporation to take the company's stock public, who buys all the new shares directly from the corporation at a negotiated price, thereby providing the company with the capital needed

UGMA

See Uniform Gifts to Minors Account

Uniform Gifts to Minors Account (UGMA)

A brokerage account for underaged children, with an adult acting as the custodian and managing the account

Uptrend

Upward moving prices of a stock or of the market as a whole

Utility average

See Dow Jones Utilities Average

V

Value investors

Individuals and money managers who buy quality, out-of-favor stocks

Value Line composite index
A measurement of the price performance of approximately 1,700 stocks reviewed by the *Value Line Investment Survey* reporting service; an unweighted index with high-priced stocks having the same impact as low-priced stocks

Volatility
Frequent and substantial percentage increases and decreases in a stock's price

Volume
The number of shares traded

W

Warrant
The right to buy a limited number of shares directly from the company for a certain price during a specific time, usually from two to five years, traded like stocks

Weak issue
An IPO for which there is faltering demand resulting in a price slump when the shares begin trading on the exchange

Working capital
The dollar difference between current assets and current liabilities

Y

Yield
The percentage of profit earned on a stock investment through its dividend payments; also called dividend yield, current yield, and rate of return

Resources

Where you'll find these Resources:

⟫ Online resources 289

⟫ Related sites 292

⟫ Legal search engines............293

••• Online Resources •••

◆ **About.com-Finance & Investing**
http://home.about.com/finance/index.htm?PM=59_206_T

◆ **AfterHourTrades**
http://www.afterhourtrades.com

◆ **AllPennyStocks.com**
http://www.allpennystocks.com

◆ **AltaVista Personal Finance-Investing**
http://money.av.com

◆ **American Association of Individual Investors (AAII)**
http://www.aaii.org

◆ **America Online-Investing**
http://search.aol.com/cat.adp?id=68

◆ **American Stock Exchange (AMEX)**
http://www.amex.com

◆ **BigCharts**
   http://www.bigcharts.com

◆ **Bureau of the Public Debt Online-U.S. Savings Bonds Online**
   http://www.publicdebt.treas.gov/sav/sav.htm

◆ **CBS MarketWatch.com**
   http://cbs.marketwatch.com/news/newsroom.htx

◆ **ClearStation**
   http://www.clearstation.com

◆ **CNET Investor**
   http://investor.cnet.com

◆ **CNN America**
   http://www.cnnfn.com

◆ **DailyStocks.com**
   http://www.dailystocks.com

◆ **Dividend Reinvestment Plans (DRP) Authority**
   http://www.moneypaper.com/publications/drpauthority/
   index.html

◆ **Dow Jones & Company, Inc.**
   http://www.dowjones.com/corp/index.html

◆ **Easy Stock**
   http://www.easystock.com

◆ **EquityTrader**
   http://www.equitytrader.com

◆ **Excite Money & Investing**
   http://quicken.excite.com

◆ **FannieMae**
   http://www.fanniemae.com

◆ **FinanceWise**
   http://www.financewise.com

◆ **Frank Russell Co.-Russell 3000 Stock Index Forecast**
   http://www.russell.com/toc/toc.htm

◆ **Government National Mortgage Association (Ginnie Mae)**
http://www.ginniemae.gov

◆ **Investor's Business Daily**
http://www.investors.com

◆ **Labpuppy.com**
http://www.labpuppy.com

◆ **Looksmart Money**
http://money.looksmart.com/indices.asp

◆ **Lycos Investing**
http://investing.lycos.com/lycos/home.asp

◆ **Market Guide, Inc.**
http://yahoo.marketguide.com/mgi

◆ **Money & Investing by Quicken**
http://quicken.webcrawler.com

◆ **Moody's Investors Service**
http://www.moodys.com

◆ **Morningstar.com**
http://www.morningstar.net

◆ **Motley Fool, the**
http://www.fool.com

◆ **National Association of Investors Corporation (NAIC)**
http://www.better-investing.org

◆ **NASDAQ (National Association of Security Dealers Automatic Quotation System)**
http://www.nasdaq.com

◆ **National Association of Real Estate Investment Trusts (NAREIT)**
http://www.nareit.com

◆ **Pacific Exchange**
http://www.pacificex.com

- **Prophet Charts**
  http://www.prophetfinance.com/charts/pc.asp

- **Quote.com, Inc.**
  http://www.quote.com/index.html

- **Standard & Poor's**
  http://www.stockinfo.standardpoor.com

- **Starting Point Investing & Finance**
  http://www.stpt.com/channel.asp?id=5

- **Stock Market Update**
  http://nw3.nai.net/~virtual/sot/update.htm

- **Stock Splits**
  http://www.stocksplits.net

- **TechWeb**
  http://www.techweb.com/wire/finance

- **U.S. Treasury Department**
  http://www.ustreas.gov

- **VectorVest**
  http://www.vectorvest.com

- **Wall Street Directory**
  http://wallstreetdirectory.com

- **Yahoo! Finance**
  http://finance.yahoo.com/?u

••• Related Sites •••

- **Barrons-Dow Jones & Company, Inc.**
  http://www.barrons.com

- **Bloomberg Personal Finance**
  http://www.bloomberg.com/personal/index.html?sidenav=front

- **Business Week**
  http://www.businessweek.com

- **The Economist**
  http://www.economist.com

◆ **Financial Times, The**
  http://www.ft.com

◆ **Forbes**
  http://www.forbes.com

◆ **Fortune**
  http://www.pathfinder.com/fortune

◆ **Go Network**
  http://money.go.com/Portfolio.html

◆ **Grant's Interest Rate Observer**
  http://www.grantspub.com

◆ **Kiplinger's Personal Finance Magazine**
  http://www.kiplinger.com/magazine/maghome.html

◆ **Money**
  http://www.pathfinder.com/money

◆ **Morningstar**
  http://www.morningstar.com

◆ **Smart Money**
  http://www.smartmoney.com

◆ **Value Line**
  http://www.valueline.com

◆ **The Wall Street Journal Interactive Edition**
  http://interactive.wsj.com

◆ **Worth**
  http://www.worth.com/frame.html

••• Legal Search Engines •••

◆ **All Law**
  http://www.alllaw.com

◆ **American Law Sources On Line**
  http://www.lawsource.com/also/searchfm.htm

- **Catalaw**
  http://www.catalaw.com

- **FindLaw**
  http://www.findlaw.com

- **Hieros Gamos**
  http://www.hg.org/hg.html

- **InternetOracle**
  http://www.internetoracle.com/legal.htm

- **LawAid**
  http://www.lawaid.com/search.html

- **LawCrawler**
  http://www.lawcrawler.com

- **LawEngine, The**
  http://www.fastsearch.com/law

- **LawRunner**
  http://www.lawrunner.com

- **'Lectric Law Library**™
  http://www.lectlaw.com

- **Legal Search Engines**
  http://www.dreamscape.com/frankvad/search.legal.html

- **LEXIS/NEXIS Communications Center**
  http://www.lexis-nexis.com/lncc/general/search.html

- **Meta-Index for U.S. Legal Research**
  http://gsulaw.gsu.edu/metaindex

- **Seamless Website, The**
  http://seamless.com

- **USALaw**
  http://www.usalaw.com/linksrch.cfm

- **WestLaw**
  http://westdoc.com (Registered users only. Fee paid service.)

Appendix A

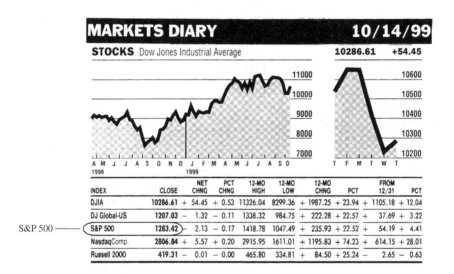

MARKETS DIARY   10/14/99

STOCKS Dow Jones Industrial Average   10286.61   +54.45

INDEX	CLOSE	NET CHNG	PCT CHNG	12-MO HIGH	12-MO LOW	12-MO CHNG	PCT	FROM 12/31	PCT
DJIA	10286.61	+ 54.45	+ 0.53	11326.04	8299.36	+ 1987.25	+ 23.94	+ 1105.18	+ 12.04
DJ Global-US	1207.03	− 1.32	− 0.11	1338.32	984.75	+ 222.28	+ 22.57	+ 37.69	+ 3.22
S&P 500	1283.42	− 2.13	− 0.17	1418.78	1047.49	+ 235.93	+ 22.52	+ 54.19	+ 4.41
NasdaqComp.	2806.84	+ 5.57	+ 0.20	2915.95	1611.01	+ 1195.83	+ 74.23	+ 614.15	+ 28.01
Russell 2000	419.31	− 0.01	− 0.00	465.80	334.81	+ 84.50	+ 25.24	− 2.65	− 0.63

S&P 500 ——

	55½	40 15/16	HarcourtGen	H	.84f	2.0	19	672	43⅝	42⅞	42⅞	– 5/16
	60	45⅝	HarcourtGen pfA		.98f	2.1	...	6	47 9/16	47 9/16	47 9/16	– 11/16
	21¼	12¼	Harland	JH	.30	1.5	dd	93	19 9/16	19 5/16	19 7/16	...
	64 1/16	29¼	HarleyDav	HDI	.18	.3	36	6744	58⅝	56¾	58⅛	+ 11/16
	47½	31½	HarmanInt	HAR	.20	.5	67	535	41	40⅝	40⅞	+ ⅜
	11⅜	11/16	vjHarnisch	HPH	j	...	...	1540	1¼	1 3/16	1 3/16	...
	29 15/16	12	HarrahEntn	HET		...	22	3656	28⅛	27½	27¾	– 5/16
	40⅝	23⅝	Harris	HRS	.96	3.8	17	2759	26 3/16	24¾	25 5/16	– ¾
▼	26 9/16	22	HarrisPfCap pfA		1.84	8.4	...	212	22 5/16	21 15/16	21 253/256	– 35/256
	35	23 1/16	Harsco	HSC	.90	3.4	13	454	27⅛	26 7/32	26 9/16	– 5/16
	29¼	19¾	HarteHanks	HHS	.08	.4	23	1138	23⅝	21⅞	22 1/16	– 1 3/16
	25⅛	23 5/16	HrtfrdCap pfA		1.93	8.3	...	145	23¾	23⅝	23⅝	– ½
	26 11/16	24½	HrtfrdCap pfB		2.09	8.5	...	168	24 11/16	24½	24½	– 27/256
▼	66 7/16	37½	HrtfrdFnl	HIG	.92	2.4	9	9689	38⅝	36½	37 15/16	+ 1/16
	26¼	21 5/16	HrtfrdLf pfA		1.80	8.2	...	182	22	21⅝	21⅞	– ⅛
	60 9/16	37¼	HrtfrdLf A	HLI	.36	.9	14	1251	42½	41	41 5/16	– 15/16
	6 13/16	3⅝	♣ Hartmarx	HMX		...	36	287	4 7/16	4⅜	4⅜	...
s▼	37	19	Hasbro	HAS	.24	1.2	16	46612	21	18¼	19¼	– 1 11/16
	15¼	12½	HatterasSec	HAT	1.02a	8.2	...	28	12⅝	12½	12½	– 1/16
s	19 9/16	8 11/16	♣ HavrtyFurn	HVT	.20	1.3	15	112	15 5/16	15 1/16	15¼	+ 1/16
	42 9/16	34⅝	HI EleclInd	HE	2.48	7.1	13	274	34 15/16	34 13/16	34⅞	– 1/16
	26¾	24¼	HA EleclInd TOPrS		2.09	8.5	...	53	24 11/16	24½	24 9/16	– 21/256
	12½	4⅝	Hawk A	HWK		...	4	5	4⅞	4 11/16	4⅞	+ 3/16
	35⅝	20⅛	♣ HayesLemmrz	HAZ		...	13	134	24 5/16	23⅝	23⅝	– ⅝
	35⅞	24 1/16	♣ HlthCrProp	HCP	2.84f	10.8	11	1778	26⅜	25 13/16	26⅜	+ 3/16
▼	25 9/16	19⅜	♣ HlthCrProp pfA		1.97	10.1	...	25	19½	19¼	19½	...
	25⅝	19 9/16	♣ HlthCrProp pfB		2.18	10.6	...	196	20⅝	19 7/16	20½	+ ⅞
	26⅝	19⅛	♣ HlthCrRE	HCN	2.28f	11.6	9	458	19¾	19¼	19⅝	+ ¼
▼	25	16⅞	♣ HlthCrRE pfB		2.22	13.4	...	65	17	16½	16⅝	– 5/16
	23½	7	HlthMgt A	HMA		...	14	22569	8 1/16	7 5/16	8	+ 11/16
	25¼	18	♣ HlthcrRlty	HR	2.16f	11.9	11	945	18⅝	18⅛	18 3/16	+ 1/16
	22 13/16	17 9/16	♣ HlthcrRlty pfA		2.22	12.5	...	42	18	17 11/16	17¾	– 3/16
	11½	5 11/16	HlthplnSvc	HPS	.55	8.8	5	1745	6½	5 15/16	6¼	+ ¼
	17¾	4 9/16	Hlthsouth	HRC		...	60	45495	5 9/16	5¼	5 7/16	– 1/16
	35⅛	20	♣ HearstArgyl	HTV		...	31	338	25¼	24 7/16	24 13/16	– 5/16
	4 15/16	1 15/16	HeclaMin	HL		...	dd	5410	2 15/16	2½	2½	– ⅜
	42⅛	27	HeclaMin pfB		3.50	10.3	...	34	34	33 9/16	34	+ ¼
	26 5/16	23¼	HecoCapTr QUIPS		2.01	8.6	...	37	23⅝	23 5/16	23½	+ 3/16
n▼	25¾	21¼	Heco QUIPS	HE+T	1.83	8.6	...	51	21½	21 3/16	21¼	...
	32¾	16⅞	Heico	HEI	.05	.3	20	42	17 15/16	17⅝	17⅞	– ⅛
	24⅝	13⅝	Heico A	HEIA	.05e	.3	...	1	17 7/16	17 7/16	17 7/16	– 1/16
	8 15/16	4⅜	HeiligMyrs	HMY	.28	6.3	dd	1046	4 9/16	4 7/16	4 7/16	– ⅛
	61¾	41⅞	Heinz	HNZ	1.47f	3.2	35	13492	45¾	42⅞	45 5/16	+ 2 5/16
n	16½	9¾	HellenicTelcm	OTE	.32p	...	...	1544	12	11⅝	11 15/16	– 1/16
	31 15/16	18⅝	HellerFnl A	HF	.36	1.7	10	2208	22 5/16	21 5/16	21 7/16	– 5/16
	27⅛	25 5/16	HellerFnl pfA		2.03	7.8	...	4	25 15/16	25 15/16	25 15/16	...
	30⅝	16	HelmPayne	HP	.28	1.2	23	975	24⅛	23½	23½	– 13/16
	40 11/16	24	Hercules	HPC	1.08	4.3	cc	3378	25 7/16	24⅞	25⅛	+ ⅛
n	26½	23 13/16	HrculsTrl TOPrS		2.36	9.8	...	166	24 1/16	23 15/16	24	– ⅛
	24	20 13/16	HertgPropn	HPG	2.25	10.2	31	44	22¼	22	22⅛	+ ¼
	75 13/16	47⅝	Hershey	HSY	1.04f	2.1	15	2794	50 5/16	48	49⅝	+ 1⅛
	64⅜	31½	♣ Hertz	HRZ	.20	.5	14	1101	41¾	41 1/16	41⅛	– 7/16
	118⅞	49⅝	HewlettPk	HWP	.64	.8	25	40240	84¼	81½	82	– 1¼
	14½	5 9/16	Hexcel	HXL		...	9	1886	5 15/16	5 9/16	5 11/16	– ⅛
	17 15/16	11⅛	Hibernia	HIB	.42	3.5	11	6226	12¼	11¾	11 15/16	– 5/16
▼	11½	8 13/16	♣ HiIncoFd	HIO	1.01	11.5	...	2065	8⅞	8¾	8 13/16	– 1/16
	7½	6¼	HighYldFd	HYI	.72	11.3	...	15	6⅜	6⅜	6⅜	– 1/16
	8 11/16	6 15/16	HighYldPlsFd	HYP	.87a	12.5	...	200	7 1/16	6 15/16	6 15/16	– 1/16
	14 15/16	7⅝	HighlndsIns	HIC		...	12	24	7¾	7 11/16	7 11/16	– 1/16
	29⅛	22⅛	♣ HighwdProp	HIW	2.22f	9.1	14	1591	25⅛	24 7/16	24 7/16	– ⅝
	24¾	17 9/16	♣ HighwdProp pfB		2.00	11.1	...	35	18	17½	18	+ ¼
▼	24 [illegible]	17⅜	♣ HighwdProp pfD		2.00	11.6	...	217	18¼	16⅞	17¼	– ¾
	25⅛	15 9/16	♣ HilbRogl	HRH	.66	2.7	21	28	24¾	24 7/16	24⅝	+ 1/16
	62⅜	26⅛	Hillenbrnd	HB	.78	2.8	12	1399	28 5/16	27⅝	28 5/16	+ 11/16
s▼	17⅛	9 5/16	Hilton	HLT	.08	.8	11	10063	9⅝	9½	9½	– 1/16
	114⅞	45⅛	Hitachi	HIT	.74e	.7	...	463	110	108¼	109 5/16	– ⅝
	49½	35 5/16	Hoechst	HOE	.82e	1.8	...	2079	45 13/16	44 15/16	45	– ⅜
	16 13/16	9 13/16	HollngrInt A	HLR	.55	5.3	10	2593	10 7/16	10 5/16	10 5/16	+ ⅛
	14⅝	8¾	Hollngr PRIDES		.95	10.4	...	5	9⅛	9⅛	9⅛	+ ⅛
	19	8	HollywdPk	HPK		...	22	419	17½	16 15/16	17 7/16	+ 7/16
	75 1/16	37 1/16	HomeDepot	HD	.16	.2	55	30507	71 1/16	69⅝	71	– ¼
	29⅛	22¼	♣ HomePropNY	HME	1.92	7.2	19	139	26⅝	26 9/16	26 9/16	...
	7⅝	3 9/16	HomeBase	HBI		...	9	1094	3¾	3 9/16	3 11/16	+ 1/16
	13⅝	7 3/16	Homestake	HM	.05m	.5	dd	19497	10⅛	9½	9½	– ½
	7¼	1⅞	HmstdVlg	HSD		...	...	197	2 13/16	2 11/16	2 11/16	– 1/16
	29⅞	19 1/16	HonInd	HNI	.38	1.8	14	670	21 11/16	20 15/16	21⅝	+ ⅛
	94	53⅝	♣ HondaMotor	HMC	.37e	.5	...	232	78 15/16	78 5/16	78⅝	+ 1/16
	126 5/16	62	♣ Honeywell	HON	1.16	1.1	24	7268	111¾	107¾	110 5/16	+ 1 9/16
	33	20¼	♣ HoraceMn	HMN	.37	1.4	15	1725	25 15/16	25½	25 11/16	– 3/16
▲	44¾	29⅜	HormelFood	HRL	.66	1.5	22	1450	45⅝	43 1/16	45 1/16	+ 1 11/16
	29⅞	21⅝	HsptlyProp	HPT	2.76	12.4	11	1093	22⅝	22	22 1/16	– 1/16
n	26	20 5/16	HsptlyProp pfA		2.38	11.6	...	28	20½	20⅜	20 7/16	+ 1/16
n	25½	24⅝	HostMar pfA		.50p	...	...	58	25 9/16	25	25 1/16	– 69/256
s	14 13/16	8⅞	HostMar REIT	HMT	.84	9.0	11	4816	9 7/16	9 1/16	9⅜	– 1/16
	52½	31¾	♣ HougtnMif	HTN	.52f	1.3	27	768	40⅜	39⅝	40	...
	26 5/16	24⅛	HshldCapI TOPrS		2.06	8.5	...	29	24 9/16	24 5/16	24 5/16	– 3/16
	26 11/16	24	HshldCapII TOPrS		2.18	8.8	...	23	24⅞	24 11/16	24 11/16	...
	25 221/256	20 11/16	HshldCapIV TOPrS		1.81	8.4	...	100	21 11/16	21 3/16	21½	– ⅛
	52 9/16	30¾	HshldInt	HI	.68	1.7	15	9066	39⅝	38⅛	38 15/16	– 13/16
	29½	26¼	HshldInt pfZ		2.06	7.8	...	19	26⅝	25 7/16	26 7/16	+ 1/16
	23⅝	12	HoustonExplr	THX		...	dd	303	21	20⅝	21	+ ⅜
	131 15/16	71	HoustnInd ACES		3.22	3.1	...	10	104	102⅛	102¾	– 1¼
	7½	1 11/16	HowellCp	HWL	.16	2.5	dd	13	6½	6 7/16	6 7/16	...
	20⅝	11 9/16	HowmetInt	HWM		...	10	199	12 7/16	12 5/16	12⅜	– 1/16
	17½	8⅞	HuanengPwr	HNP	.39p	...	...	317	11 13/16	11½	11 13/16	+ ⅜
	45¾	28	HubbellA	HUBA	1.28	4.4	12	65	29⅝	29	29	+ 5/16
	49 9/16	26⅞	HubbellB	HUBB	1.28	4.4	12	1180	29 9/16	28⅞	29 1/16	...
	36⅜	21½	HudsnUtdBcp	HU	1.00	3.4	22	1237	29 7/16	28 11/16	29⅜	+ ⅜
	26¼	20 7/16	♣ JDN Rlty pfA		2.34	11.1	...	20	21⅛	21⅛	21⅛	+ ⅛
	22	11½	♣ JLG Ind	JLG	.02	.1	10	499	14 3/16	13⅞	13 15/16	– 3/16
	13½	7	JLK Direct A	JLK		...	10	111	8⅝	8	8 1/16	– 7/16
▼	22½	17	♣ JP Realty	JPR	1.86	11.0	11	354	17⅛	16 11/16	16 15/16	– ⅛
	59 11/16	47⅜	JSB Fnl	JSB	1.80	3.2	16	48	58	57	57	– 1 1/16
s	56 13/16	19 7/16	JabilCircuit	JBL		...	45	4271	52 5/16	50⅝	50 11/16	– 1/16
	29 7/16	13 5/16	JackInTheBx	JBX		...	15	1387	26¼	25⅝	26 1/16	+ 3/16
	11½	7 1/16	Jackpot	J		...	18	456	9 7/16	9 5/16	9 5/16	– ⅛
	42¾	27 9/16	JacobEngrg	JEC		...	15	560	34⅝	34 5/16	34⅜	– ⅛
	4⅛	1⅞	JakartaGrFd	JGF		...	...	6	3	3	3	...
	11 3/16	6 5/16	♣ JapanEquity	JEQ		...	...	228	9 13/16	9 11/16	9¾	...
	14 15/16	4⅜	JapanOTC	JOF	.01e	.1	...	1244	13⅜	12⅞	13	– 1/16
	8¾	4⅞	♣ JF China	JFC		...	...	190	6½	6 7/16	6 7/16	+ 1/16
	9⅞	4⅞	♣ JF India	JFI		...	...	133	9⅝	9¼	9 5/16	+ 1/16
n▼	30⅜	19 11/16	JeffriesGp	JEF	.20	1.0	7	947	19⅞	19 9/32	19 13/16	+ ⅛
	78¾	57 1/16	JeffPilot	JP	1.32	2.1	15	2092	64 7/16	63	64 5/16	+ 1⅜
	31¼	15 5/16	JSmurfit	JS	.66e	2.3	...	227	28 7/16	28	28⅜	+ 1⅛
	127¼	80⅜	JeffPilot ACES		5.26	6.2	...	925	86¼	85	85⅛	– 1⅜
	6 15/16	2⅛	♣ JennyCraig	JC		...	dd	20	2¼	2⅛	2 3/16	...
	14	4 1/16	JilinChem	JCC	.12e	1.2	...	123	10¼	10⅛	10¼	+ 1 1/16
	19⅜	12 5/16	JoAnnStrs A	JASA		...	13	45	14½	14⅜	14⅜	+ 1/16
	16½	10⅝	JoAnnStrs B	JASB		...	...	86	12 5/16	12 1/16	12 1/16	– 3/16
	43 11/16	32	JohnNuveen	JNC	1.15	3.2	17	53	37⅜	36 13/16	36 13/16	– 7/16
	5½	3⅛	JQHamons A	JQH		...	16	1	3⅞	3⅞	3⅞	...
	19½	10 15/16	♣ JohnsManvil	JM	.24	2.0	9	456	12½	11⅞	11⅞	– 5/16
	105⅞	76 3/16	JohnsJohns	JNJ	1.12	1.2	39	22968	96⅝	94	94⅝	– 11/16
	76 11/16	45¼	JohnsCtrl	JCI	1.00	1.5	15	2011	67 13/16	66⅝	66¾	– ¾
	4	1 7/16	JohnstnInd	JII		...	dd	36	2 5/16	2¼	2¼	...
	35⅞	15⅞	JonesApparel	JNY		...	18	8214	30⅛	29 9/16	29¾	+ 7/16
	36½	12⅝	JonsLngLaSal	JLL		...	dd	632	15	14¾	14 13/16	+ 5/16
	27⅛	18¾	Jostens	JOS	.88	4.6	16	348	19 7/16	19	19 5/16	+ 1/16
	23	11⅝	JrnlRgstr	JRC		...	14	316	13⅝	13 1/16	13⅜	+ 5/16

-K-K-K-

	26¾	24¼	KCPL TOPrS		2.08	8.4	...	28	24¾	24 9/16	24¾	+ 1/16
	6 5/16	5/16	KCS Engy	KCS	j	...	dd	310	1	⅞	15/16	– 1/16
	34⅛	24 5/16	KLM	KLM	.71e	2.5	...	258	28 7/16	27 13/16	28 1/16	– 1/16
n	44½	23⅜	KN Engy PEPS un		1.82p	...	...	133	36 13/16	36 5/16	36 5/16	– ⅛
	64	32⅞	KPN	KPN	1.12e	2.3	...	69	48 3/16	48	48 3/16	– 3/16
	23⅝	12¾	♣ KV Pharm A	KVA		...	14	152	16½	15⅝	16⅜	+ 1¼
	23 7/16	13	♣ KV Pharm B	KVB		...	21	63	16 5/16	15 11/16	16¼	+ 7/16
	12⅝	7⅞	K2	KTO		...	29	529	8⅝	8⅜	8½	– 3/16
	10⅛	4⅝	KaiserAlum	KLU		...	dd	169	7 5/16	7 1/16	7⅛	– 1/16
	34 7/16	28 1/16	KanPipLP	KPP	2.80	9.7	...	76	29 1/16	28 13/16	28⅞	– 1/16
	5⅛	3 13/16	KanebSvc	KAB		...	11	455	4 13/16	4⅝	4 13/16	+ 1/16
	11	9¾	KanebSvc pf		.99e	9.7	...	5	10¼	10¼	10¼	...
	31 13/16	22 3/16	♣ KanCityP&L	KLT	1.66	6.9	13	960	24¼	24 1/16	24⅛	– 1/16
	66 7/16	27½	KanCitySo	KSU	.16	.4	21	5517	42 7/16	41 1/16	41⅝	– ½
	21 7/16	10⅞	KatyInd	KT	.30	2.7	9	72	11 3/16	10⅞	11	– ⅛
	31¼	18	KaufBrdHm	KBH	.30	1.4	8	2921	21⅝	21¼	21½	...
	10	6½	KaufBrdInc PRIDES		.83	11.4	...	1640	7½	7¼	7 5/16	– 1/16
	41 1/16	23	Kaydon	KDN	.40	1.6	12	534	24¾	24 3/16	24 5/16	+ 1/16
	40½	25 7/16	KeeblerFood	KBL		...	37	538	31 5/16	30½	31⅛	+ ⅝
	16 15/16	4⅛	KeithlyInstr	KEI	.15f	1.0	9	98	15¾	15⅝	15⅝	– 1/16
	42¼	31⅜	Kellogg	K	.98f	2.5	35	13924	40⅝	38	39 11/16	+ 2 3/16
	30¾	20¼	Kellwood	KWD	.64	3.0	cc	173	21½	21⅜	21 5/16	+ ⅛
	10⅛	8 5/16	♣ KemperHigh	KHI	.97	11.4	...	467	8 9/16	8 7/16	8½	– 1/16
	8	6 3/16	♣ KemperGvt	KGT	.54	8.2	...	82	6 9/16	6 9/16	6 9/16	+ ⅛
	9 11/16	8 3/16	♣ KemperMulti	KMM	.93	10.7	...	205	8 11/16	8 9/16	8 11/16	...
	14 15/16	10⅜	♣ KemperMuni	KTF	.82	7.7	...	431	10 15/16	10⅝	10 11/16	– ⅛
	17¾	14 9/16	♣ KempStratIn	KST	1.80	12.2	...	113	15 1/16	14 9/16	14¾	– 5/16
▼	13	10⅝	♣ KemperStrat	KSM	.75a	7.2	...	268	10¾	10⅝	10 5/16	– 5/16
	31 5/16	16⅝	Kennmetl	KMT	.68	2.5	12	738	27	26 7/16	27	+ 1/16
	39⅞	14¾	KenCole A	KCP		...	28	151	36 15/16	36 11/16	36⅞	+ ⅛
	20 5/16	8⅛	KentElec	KNT		...	dd	808	16 15/16	15¾	16⅜	– 7/16
	26 7/16	24½	KY Pwr jrA	KPC	2.18	8.8	...	1	24¾	24¾	24¾	+ ⅛
	60 1/16	28½	KerrMcGee	KMG	1.80	3.2	dd	3034	56 15/16	55 15/16	56⅛	– 7/16
n	43¼	33 9/16	KerrMcGee DECS		.45p	...	...	34	38¾	38½	38½	+ ½
	11⅜	2 15/16	KeyEngy	KEG		...	dd	5700	4⅝	4 5/16	4½	...
	11	5	KeyPdtn	KP		...	37	24	9 5/16	9	9 5/16	+ ¼
	38⅛	24⅝	KeyCorp	KEY	1.04	4.1	10	9145	25⅜	24 7/16	25¼	+ ⅝
	31 5/16	24⅝	♣ KeySpan	KSE	1.78	6.2	...	1348	28⅞	28¼	28¾	+ 5/16
	27⅛	25 7/16	♣ KeySpan pfA		1.99	7.8	...	1	25⅝	25⅝	25⅝	...
	9¾	4 3/16	♣ KeystnCon	KES		...	dd	2	5	5	5	...
	26½	19 1/16	♣ KilroyRlty	KRC	1.68	8.6	13	588	19 13/16	19½	19½	– ¼
	64 1/16	44 9/16	KimbClark	KMB	1.04	2.0	21	17885	53 7/16	51¾	53¼	– 5/16
	40¾	34⅛	KimcoRlty	KIM	2.40	6.9	16	388	34 11/16	34 5/16	34⅝	...
	25⅝	20 3/16	KimcoRlty pfA		1.94	9.5	...	23	20½	20 5/16	20½	– ⅛
	26	21⅝	KimcoRlty pfB		2.13	9.4	...	4	22 15/16	22¾	22¾	– 1/16

McDonald's ——

	41 9/16	24 1/16	KingWorld	KWP		...	17	2602	36 7/16	35 9/16	35⅝	– ⅝
	3¾	1½	♣ KinrossGld	KGC		...	dd	4294	2¾	2⅝	2⅝	– ⅛
	22⅜	16¾	KirbyCp	KEX		...	42	18	19¼	19 1/16	19 3/16	+ ⅛
	7 7/16	6 3/16	♣ KleinBenAus	KBA	.48a	7.7	...	208	6 5/16	6 3/16	6¼	...
	18⅝	10⅛	Kmart	KM		...	15	34520	10¾	10 5/16	10½	+ ¼
	65⅝	44 5/16	Kmart pfT		3.88	6.5	...	1279	45¾	44 7/16	45½	+ 1 5/16
	60 5/16	41⅜	KnghtRidder	KRI	.92	1.6	20	3662	58⅞	57½	58¼	+ 11/16
	30⅝	15¼	Knoll	KNL		...	13	707	27¼	27 3/16	27¼	...
	81¼	38	KohlsCp	KSS		...	52	4596	70 15/16	68 5/16	70¼	+ 15/16
▼	19 5/16	10 9/16	Kollmrgn	KOL	.08	.8	17	417	11¼	9 13/16	9 13/16	– 1 7/16
	110¾	51½	KonPhilips	PHG	1.10e	1.1	...	4858	98 1/16	96½	97 9/16	– 11/16
	9 5/16	4¾	♣ Konover	KPT	.50	7.8	24	86	6⅜	6⅜	6⅜	– 1/16
	25⅝	12½	KoorInd	KOR	.42e	2.4	dd	210	17 15/16	17⅝	17 13/16	+ 5/16
	22¼	10⅜	KoreaElecPwr	KEP	.15e	.9	...	4229	16¾	15⅞	16⅝	+ 1
	27⅝	24 11/16	♣ MBNA Cp pfA		1.88	7.4	...	10	25⅝	25⅝	25⅝	...
	24¾	15 13/16	MCN Engy	MCN	1.02	4.2	dd	6256	24⅝	24 1/16	24 9/16	+ ¼
	42⅝	30 1/16	MCN EngyFel PRIDES		4.00	9.5	...	339	42	41¼	42	+ 9/16
	26¾	23¾	MCN Fin TOPrS		2.16	8.7	...	15	24 11/16	24 7/16	24 11/16	+ ⅛
n	26⅞	23½	MCN Fin TruPS		2.16	8.9	...	49	24¼	24 1/16	24 3/16	– 5/16
	26	24⅝	MCN MI pfA		2.34	9.4	...	13	25 1/16	24 15/16	25	...
	22	13⅝	MDC Hldg	MDC	.20	1.3	5	148	15½	15⅛	15⅛	– 5/16
	27⅝	20 5/16	♣ MDU Res	MDU	.84f	3.5	24	174	23⅞	23 11/16	23¾	– 1/16
	21⅝	4¼	MEMC Elec	WFR		...	dd	1653	12	11 9/16	11 11/16	– ¼
	27¼	24⅝	MEPC pfA		2.28	9.0	...	57	25¼	25⅛	25¼	+ 1/16
	10 1/16	8 1/16	MFS Charter	MCR	.71	8.7	...	1242	8¼	8 3/16	8 3/16	...
	6⅝	6	MFS GvMkTr	MGF	.47	7.8	...	684	6 1/16	6	6	...
	7⅛	6¼	MFS Intermd	MIN	.52	8.3	...	1622	6 5/16	6¼	6¼	...
	7	5 15/16	MFS MulInco	MMT	.54	9.0	...	1143	6	5 15/16	6	+ 1/16
▼	9 7/16	7	MFS MuniTr	MFM	.53	7.6	...	848	7 1/16	6⅞	6 15/16	– ⅛
	18 15/16	14⅞	MFS SpcVal	MFV	1.65	10.1	...	24	16⅝	16 1/16	16⅝	+ 5/16
	56¾	28⅞	MGIC Inv	MTG	.10	.2	13	5165	53⅛	51 11/16	52⅝	+ ¾
s	10⅝	8⅝	MGI Prop	MGI	19.9c	...	...	379	9 7/16	9¼	9¼	– 1/16
	52⅝	22⅞	MGM Grand	MGG		...	35	10656	51½	49¼	49⅝	+ ⅛
n	18 5/16	14 5/16	MIIX Grp	MHU	.05p	...	...	893	15⅞	15⅝	15⅝	– ¼
	24 11/16	16 5/16	MI SchottHm	MHO	.20	1.2	4	68	16 15/16	16⅝	16 13/16	+ ½
	3 13/16	3	ML Macdmia	NUT	.40	11.2	32	21	3⅝	3 9/16	3 9/16	– ⅛
▼	19 5/16	8¼	MMI Cos	MMI	.36	4.4	55	200	8⅜	7⅞	8¼	...
n	33 13/16	23¼	MONY Gp	MNY	.30e	1.1	...	897	26¾	26	26 7/16	+ ⅝
	26¼	23 15/16	MP&L QUIPS		2.01	8.2	...	21	24 7/16	24⅜	24 7/16	+ 1/16
	27 5/16	8	MSC IndDir A	MSM		...	11	1406	8⅜	8 3/16	8¼	– 1/16
	7⅝	4⅞	MSC Sftwr	MNS		...	dd	59	6½	6½	6½	...
	22½	10 1/16	MYR Gp	MYR	.15	.8	13	206	19⅜	19	19	– 5/16
▼	13	5 9/16	MacGray	TUC		...	11	276	5 9/16	5¼	5⅜	– 3/16
	46¾	28⅞	MacDermd	MRD	.08	.3	21	279	32¼	31 11/16	32	– 13/16
	28 7/16	20⅜	♣ Macerich	MAC	1.94	9.4	17	746	20 15/16	20⅝	20 11/16	+ 3/16
	33⅝	25 9/16	♣ MackCaliRlty	CLI	2.32f	9.1	13	483	25 11/16	25⅝	25⅝	– 1/16
	12¼	5⅜	Madeco ADR	MAD	.48e	4.8	...	60	10¼	10	10	– ⅜
	11⅛	3 9/16	MagellnHlth	MGL		...	6	721	5½	5 5/16	5 5/16	– 3/16
▼	68 15/16	48 7/16	♣ MagnaInt	MGA	1.00	2.1	...	1641	48 15/16	47 9/16	47¼	– 1 11/16
n	24¾	24	♣ MagnaInt QUIPS			...	...	202	24 7/16	24⅛	24⅛	– 5/16
	13⅞	8¼	MagneTek	MAG		...	7	5146	8⅞	8¾	8¾	– ⅛
	17 13/16	7¼	♣ MailWell	MWL		...	20	307	13 9/16	12⅞	13 1/16	– ¼
	16⅛	12⅝	MalanRlty	MAL	1.70	12.8	13	41	13 5/16	13⅛	13 5/16	+ 1/16
	8 5/16	3⅜	MalaysaFd	MF		...	...	278	6	5 15/16	6	...
	37 9/16	21 1/16	Mallinckrodt	MKG	.66	2.1	12	1557	31 15/16	31 5/16	31 13/16	+ 5/16
▼	10 15/16	8⅝	♣ MngdHghInc	MHY	.97	11.6	...	1521	8 7/16	8 5/16	8⅜	...
▼	12 13/16	10⅛	MgdHiYld	PHT	1.26	12.4	...	88	10⅛	9⅞	10⅛	...
	13 1/16	10⅞	MngdHiYldPl	HYF	1.50	13.6	...	944	11⅛	10 15/16	11	...
	11 13/16	9 5/16	♣ MgdMuni	MMU	.60a	6.2	...	829	9 11/16	9⅝	9 11/16	...
	11⅞	9½	MgdMuni II	MTU	.60a	6.2	...	571	9¾	9⅝	9⅝	– 1/16
	26 9/16	7⅞	Mandalay	MBG		...	22	8917	19 1/16	18 5/16	18 11/16	+ 7/16
s	43¾	17	♣ Manitowc	MTW	.30	1.0	13	926	31¼	30⅝	30¾	– 1/16
	31 5/16	20¼	♣ Manpower	MAN	.20f	.7	29	3006	29½	28½	29⅜	– ⅜
	27	21 13/16	MfrHome	MHC	1.55	6.8	21	112	22 13/16	22 11/16	22¾	...
n	12 5/16	10 5/16	Manulife	MFC		...	...	4141	11 11/16	11½	11⅝	...
	16 9/16	10½	♣ MarcusCp	MCS	.22	1.6	18	99	13¾	13⅝	13⅝	– ⅛
	18 11/16	5 15/16	MarineDrill	MRL		...	13	2155	14⅞	13⅞	14½	+ 3/16
	13	7 5/16	Marinemax	HZO		...	6	134	9	8 13/16	8⅞	– 3/16
	7⅛	5/64	MarinNtwk	MPN		...	dd	5459	5/32	5/64	⅛	+ 1/32
	7¾	4 13/16	♣ Maritrans	TUG	.40	7.5	16	148	5⅜	5 5/16	5 5/16	+ 1/16
	21⅞	12⅛	MarkIV	IV	.22	1.1	20	1772	19 15/16	19⅝	19⅞	+ 1/16
	193	137¾	♣ MarkelCp	MKL		...	17	77	172½	171	172½	+ 1
	44½	22⅝	MarriottInt A	MAR	.22	.7	21	5275	33⅝	32⅞	33 5/16	+ ⅜
	81½	50⅜	MarshMcL	MMC	1.80	2.7	22	8056	67¼	64⅜	67	– ¼
	38 9/16	12⅝	Marshl Ind	MI		...	26	400	35⅝	35	35⅛	– 1/16
	68⅛	35¼	MartnMarMat	MLM	.52	1.3	15	8533	40 7/16	39 15/16	40⅛	– 1/16
	9¾	4 9/16	MarvEnterp	MVL		...	dd	277	5	4⅞	4 15/16	– 1/16
	33 11/16	21⅝	Masco	MAS	.48f	1.6	19	12901	29 5/16	28⅝	29⅜	+ 1/16
	18¾	14	♣ Mascotech	MSX	.32	2.1	9	600	15⅝	15⅜	15⅜	– ⅜
	11⅛	4⅝	Masisa ADS	MYS	.38e	3.8	...	102	10	9⅞	9⅞	– ⅜
	26	20⅝	MassMuInv	MCI	1.72f	8.2	...	31	21	20¾	20⅞	+ 1/16
	12⅝	9¾	MassMuPrt	MPV	.96a	9.3	...	32	10 5/16	10 5/16	10 5/16	+ 1/16
	37¼	14	MasTec	MTZ		...	cc	886	33½	32 13/16	33½	+ 11/16
	34⅛	21 13/16	Matav	MTA	.17e	.5	...	537	27 9/16	27¼	27¼	– ¾
	16	6⅜	MaterlSci	MSC		...	14	62	13 11/16	13⅝	13⅝	– 1/16
	239	136	MatsuElec	MC	.69e	.3	...	77	202¾	198	199¾	– 5¼
	40½	11 11/16	Mattel	MAT	.36	2.8	45	41311	13 3/16	12⅝	12 11/16	...
	5	2¼	Mavesa ADR	MAV	.08e	2.5	14	942	3 5/16	3⅛	3 3/16	+ 1/16
	25⅝	4	MaximGrp	MXG		...	dd	591	6 5/16	5¾	6	...
	30⅝	14⅞	MaxximMed	MAM		...	13	5111	22¾	19 11/16	19¾	– 2 15/16
s	45⅝	35⅞	MayDeptStrs	MAY	.89	2.4	15	6596	37¾	36⅝	37 1/16	+ 11/16
	74 13/16	31¼	Maytag	MYG	.72	2.0	11	41261	37¼	33¼	36⅞	+ 3⅞

	52 Weeks Hi	Lo	Stock	Sym	Div	Yld %	PE	Vol 100s	Hi	Lo	Close	Net Chg
s	47⅜	31⅝	McDonalds	MCD	.20	.5	33	32571	42 7/16	41½	41⅝	– 13/16
	26¾	24¼	McDonalds 2037		1.88	7.7	...	36	24 9/16	24⅜	24⅜	– ⅛
	26⅛	24⅛	McDonalds sbdb		1.88	7.7	...	96	24 9/16	24 7/16	24½	...
s	60¾	36⅛	McGrawH	MHP	.86	1.6	30	4847	53¾	50 13/16	53 9/16	+ 2 1/16
▼	89¾	24 15/16	McKessnHBOC	MCK	.24	1.0	46	63681	25	22¾	22 15/16	– 2
n	23	12	McMoRanExpl	MMR		...	...	107	21 3/16	20¾	21 1/16	+ ⅜
	23 13/16	12 5/16	McWhorter	MWT		...	14	14	14¼	14	14	– ¼
	46 5/16	27 11/16	Mead	MEA	.64	1.8	27	3396	36½	35 13/16	36⅜	+ ¾
	24⅞	10	♣ MdwbrkInsGp	MIG	.12	1.2	dd	40	10⅛	10	10	...
	27¼	17½	♣ MedcoRsrch	MRE		...	18	191	22½	22	22 5/16	– ⅜
	11 7/16	5⅜	Medeva	MDV	.41e	4.8	...	78	8 13/16	8 7/16	8⅝	– ⅛
	16	3⅞	MediaArts	MDA		...	4	409	4⅜	4 1/16	4⅛	– 3/16
	26⅞	25	MediaOne pfA		2.33	9.2	...	34	25 7/16	25 5/16	25 5/16	– 1/16
	27 3/16	25¼	MediaOne pfB		2.38	9.4	...	13	25⅜	25⅜	25⅜	...
n	27⅝	25	MediaOne pfC		2.26	8.9	...	107	25½	25 5/16	25 5/16	– ⅛
	26	23¼	MediaOne X TOPrS		1.99	8.2	...	2	24⅜	24¼	24⅜	⅜
	26⅜	23¾	MediaOne Y TOPrS		2.06	8.3	...	5	24¾	24 11/16	24¾	+ ¼

STANDARD &POOR'S
STOCK REPORTS

McDonald's Corp.

NYSE Symbol **MCD**

In S&P 500

09-OCT-99

Industry:
Restaurants

Summary: MCD is the largest fast-food restaurant company in the U.S. and the world. Nearly half of its more than 24,000 restaurants are outside the U.S.

S&P Opinion: Hold (★ ★ ★)		
Recent Price • 43¼	Yield • 0.5%	
52 Wk Range • 47⅞-31	12-Mo. P/E • 34.9	

Quantitative Evaluations

Outlook
(1 Lowest — 5 Highest)
• 1

Fair Value
• 40

Risk
• Low

Earn./Div. Rank
• A+

Technical Eval.
• Bullish since 9/99

Rel. Strength Rank
(1 Lowest — 99 Highest)
• 73

Insider Activity
• Unfavorable

Earnings vs. Previous Year
▲=Up ▼=Down ▶=No Change

10 Week Mov. Avg. ----
30 Week Mov. Avg. ·····
Relative Strength —

OPTIONS: CBOE

Overview - 28-JUL-99

In 1999 and beyond, we expect this well managed company to post further double digit earnings growth from international operations, excluding currency fluctuations. Additional benefits from economies of scale are likely in foreign markets, as MCD's presence continues to grow. Earnings from outside the U.S. recently accounted for over 60% of operating profit. In the U.S., MCD has re-examined its domestic operations, changed management, and is focusing on boosting productivity and lowering the overall cost structure. MCD has overhauled its food preparation procedures to provide fresher, hotter food, and reduce labor costs; it recorded a related pretax charge of $350 million ($0.33 a share) in the 1998 second quarter. Domestically, the company continually tests new product offerings. We expect continued moderate profit increase in domestic operating earnings in 1999. For the longer term, MCD faces the challenge of an aging U.S. population that is increasingly shifting to casual dining restaurants that offer more amenities and a fuller menu.

Valuation - 28-JUL-99

The shares were recently trading about 10% below their record high. Earnings in the second quarter were in line with expectations. U.S. operating income advanced 13%, and international operating income increased 7.6%, before adjusting for currency fluctuations. We expect operating earnings overall to grow about 14% annually. The company's strong cash flow generation (its free cash flow tripled in 1998, to $887 million) is reflected in the stock's premium valuation. MCD's core EPS growth rate is 12% to 13%. Excess cash is earmarked for the repurchase stock under a $3.5 billion buyback program; about $1.2 billion of stock was purchased in 1998. The shares offer both growth and defensive characteristics.

Key Stock Statistics

S&P EPS Est. 1999	1.40	Tang. Bk. Value/Share	6.69
P/E on S&P Est. 1999	30.9	Beta	0.95
S&P EPS Est. 2000	1.60	Shareholders	925,000
Dividend Rate/Share	0.20	Market cap. (B)	$ 58.6
Shs. outstg. (M)	1354.7	Inst. holdings	64%
Avg. daily vol. (M)	2.523		

Value of $10,000 invested 5 years ago: $ 31,427

Fiscal Year Ending Dec. 31

	1999	1998	1997	1996	1995	1994
Revenues (Million $)						
1Q	3,035	2,805	2,618	2,426	2,161	1,796
2Q	3,407	3,181	2,833	2,665	2,468	2,029
3Q	—	3,215	3,006	2,774	2,580	2,225
4Q	—	3,221	2,953	2,822	2,586	2,270
Yr.	—	12,421	11,409	10,688	9,795	8,321
Earnings Per Share ($)						
1Q	0.29	0.26	0.24	0.20	0.20	0.16
2Q	0.37	0.25	0.30	0.29	0.26	0.22
3Q	E0.40	0.34	0.32	0.30	0.28	0.24
4Q	E0.34	0.25	0.29	0.28	0.26	0.21
Yr.	E1.40	1.10	1.14	1.10	0.96	0.61

Next earnings report expected: mid October

Dividend Data (Dividends have been paid since 1976.)

Amount ($)	Date Decl.	Ex-Div. Date	Stock of Record	Payment Date
2-for-1	Jan. 26	Mar. 08	Feb. 12	Mar. 05 '99
0.049	Jan. 26	Mar. 11	Mar. 15	Mar. 31 '99
0.049	May. 21	May. 27	Jun. 01	Jun. 15 '99
0.049	Jul. 13	Aug. 30	Sep. 01	Sep. 15 '99

A Division of The McGraw-Hill Companies

STANDARD
&POOR'S
STOCK REPORTS

McDonald's Corporation

09-OCT-99

Business Summary - 28-JUL-99

One of the most widely known brand names in the world, McDonald's serves 35 million customers every day. The company operates and licenses more than 25,000 restaurants in 115 countries. At December 31, 1998, there were 12,472 restaurants in the U.S. and 10,752 elsewhere.

Contributions by geographic area in 1998 were: U.S. (50% of revenues); Europe (25%); Asia/Pacific (16%); Latin America (5%); and other (4%). International business contributed 57% of operating income in 1998.

Restaurants offer a substantially uniform menu, including hamburgers, french fries, chicken, fish, specialty sandwiches, beverages and desserts. Most units also serve breakfast.

The company's long-term strategy is to identify and evaluate profitable growth opportunities. The company believes its greatest expansion opportunities are outside the U.S. While in the U.S. there are 22,000 people per McDonald's, in the rest of the world there is only one McDonald's for every 605,000 people. At the end of 1998, 85% of systemwide restaurants were located in 11 markets: Australia, Brazil, Canada, England, France, Germany, Hong Kong, Japan, the Netherlands, Taiwan, and the U.S. Some 65% of restaurant additions in 1998 were in these markets, and a similar percentage is expected in 1999. However, new and emerging markets, such as Central Europe, the Philippines, China and Africa/ Middle East, should account for a growing percentage of restaurants. Rapid expansion is expected to continue in Latin America.

The company owns or leases a substantial amount of the real estate used by franchisees in their operations. Fees from franchisees to McDonald's typically include rents and service fees, often totaling at least 11.5% of sales.

Average annual sales at U.S. restaurants in operation at least 13 months increased slightly, to $1.58 million in 1998. Average sales are affected by comparable-sales, the size of new restaurants, and the expansion rate. New restaurants have historically taken about four years to reach long-term volume. Average annual sales at international restaurants in operation at least 13 months decreased 8%, to $1.80 million in 1998. Nearly half of the decrease was due to foreign currency translation. Average sales per new restaurant rose 7.6% in the U.S., to $1.33 million, while new international restaurants average per unit fell 5%, to $1.36 million.

U.S. company unit margins rose to 17.3% of sales in 1998, from 16.5% in 1997. Margins in the international division declined in 1998, to 18.8% of sales, from 19.1% in 1997. Increased occupancy and other costs were the primary factors in the decline.

Per Share Data ($) (Year Ended Dec. 31)	1998	1997	1996	1995	1994	1993	1992	1991	1990	1989	
Tangible Bk. Val.	6.26	5.86	5.49	4.99	4.30	3.66	3.31	3.11	2.65	2.08	
Cash Flow	1.73	1.71	1.64	1.52	1.28	1.07	0.99	0.91	0.86	0.75	
(1) Earnings	1.10	1.15	1.10	0.98	0.84	0.73	0.65	0.59	0.55	0.49	
(12) Dividends	0.18	0.16	0.15	0.13	0.12	0.11	0.10	0.09	0.08	0.08	
(13) Payout Ratio	16%	14%	13%	13%	14%	15%	15%	15%	15%	15%	
Prices - High	39¾	27½	27⅛	24	15¾	14¾	12⅝	10	9⅝	8¾	
- Low	22⅝	21⅛	20½	14⅜	12¾	11⅝	9⅝	6½	6¼	5¾	Average High PE 22
(15) P/E Ratio High	36	24	25	24	19	20	19	17	18	18	Average Low PE 15.2
- Low	20	18	19	15	15	16	15	11	11	12	Average PE 18.6
Income Statement Analysis (Million $)											
(3) Revs.	12,421	11,409	10,687	9,795	8,321	7,408	7,133	6,695	6,640	6,065	
Oper. Inc.	3,903	3,488	3,331	3,204	2,801	2,415	2,290	2,022	1,944	1,772	
Depr.	881	794	743	709	629	493	493	457	444	390	
Int. Exp.	414	363	365	363	326	336	393	418	417	332	
(5) Pretax Inc.	2,307	2,408	2,251	2,169	1,887	1,676	1,448	1,299	1,246	1,157	
Eff. Tax Rate	33%	32%	30%	34%	35%	35%	34%	34%	36%	37%	
Net Inc.	1,550	1,643	1,573	1,427	1,224	1,083	959	860	802	727	
Balance Sheet & Other Fin. Data (Million $)											
(8) Cash	299	341	330	335	180	186	437	220	143	137	
Curr. Assets	1,309	1,142	1,103	956	741	663	865	646	549	495	
Total Assets	19,784	18,242	17,386	15,415	13,592	12,035	11,681	11,349	10,668	9,175	
Curr. Liab.	2,497	2,985	2,135	1,795	2,451	1,102	1,545	1,288	1,199	1,017	
(10) LT Debt	6,189	4,834	4,803	4,258	2,935	3,489	3,176	4,267	4,429	3,901	
(11) Common Eqty.	9,464	8,851	8,360	7,503	6,446	6,350	5,984	4,537	3,984	3,349	
Total Cap.	17,228	15,178	15,251	12,784	10,930	10,744	9,911	9,837	9,306	8,064	
Cap. Exp.	1,879	2,111	2,375	2,064	1,539	1,354	1,171	1,129	1,613	1,556	
Cash Flow	2,431	2,412	2,288	2,136	1,806	1,528	1,437	1,297	1,232	1,113	
(9) Curr. Ratio	0.5	0.4	0.5	0.5	0.3	0.6	0.6	0.5	0.5	0.5	
% LT Debt of Cap.	35.9	31.8	31.5	33.3	26.9	32.5	32.0	43.4	47.6	48.4	
(6) % Net Inc.of Revs.	12.5	14.4	14.8	14.6	14.7	14.6	13.4	12.8	12.1	12.0	
% Ret. on Assets	8.2	9.2	9.6	9.9	9.6	9.3	8.3	7.8	8.1	8.5	
(7) % Ret. on Equity	16.9	18.8	19.5	20.5	19.3	17.0	17.4	19.7	21.6	21.8	

Data as orig reptd.; bef. results of disc opers/spec. items. Per share data adj. for stk. divs. Bold denotes diluted EPS (FASB 128)-prior periods restated. E-Estimated. NA-Not Available. NM-Not Meaningful. NR-Not Ranked.

Office—McDonald's Plaza, Oak Brook, IL 60521. **Tel**—(630) 623-3000. **Chrmn & CEO**—M. R. Quinlan. **SVP & Treas**—C. D. Pearl. **Investor Contact (Broker Inquiries)**—Barbara Ven Horst (630-623-5137). **Investor Contact (Shareholder Services)**—Lynn Irwin Camp (630-623-8432). **Dirs**—H. Adams, Jr., R. M. Beavers Jr., J. R. Cantalupo, G. C. Gray, J. M. Greenberg, E. Hernandez, Jr., D. R. Keough, D. G. Lubin, W. Massey, A. J. McKenna, M. R. Quinlan, T. Savage, R. W. Stone, R. N. Thurston, F. L. Turner, B. B. Vedder Jr. **Transfer Agent & Registrar**—First Chicago Trust Co., Jersey City, NJ. **Incorporated**—in Delaware in 1965. **Empl**— 212,000. **S&P Analyst:** Karen J. Sack, CFA

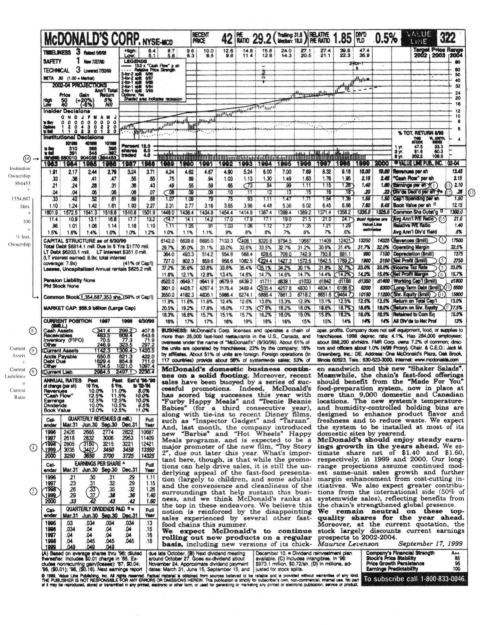

Value Line — McDONALD'S CORP. NYSE-MCD — RECENT PRICE 42 — P/E RATIO 29.2 (Trailing: 31.8, Median: 18.0) — RELATIVE P/E RATIO 1.85 — DIV'D YLD 0.5% — VALUE LINE 322

September 17, 1999   **RESTAURANT INDUSTRY**   **308**

The stocks of many of the companies included in our coverage of the Restaurant Industry have moved lower in price in recent months, likely due to a more cautious attitude on the part of some investors toward the economy. Also, fast food and casual dining chains have been reporting mixed sales results recently, some of which can be attributed to poor promotional responses.

Overall, the Restaurant Industry's Timeliness rank has slipped 13 notches in the last three months, and now resides among those industry groups expected to mirror the overall market averages over the next six to 12 months. Nevertheless, we think opportunities exist for those investors willing to take a selective approach toward the group.

The Economic Viewpoint

The Restaurant Industry has benefited from the nation's long-running economic expansion. Low interest rates have enabled more chains to expand relatively cheaply, while consumers were demonstrating a willingness to dine out more often. Moreover, modest inflation has helped keep a lid on operating costs. Value Line's view of the economy remains generally positive. And, although revised second-quarter GDP showed a less-ebullient 1.8% rise, current data still suggests stronger growth for the back half of 1999, possibly reaching or exceeding 3% in each quarter.

The latest consumer confidence readings from The Conference Board and the University of Michigan indicate some signs of wavering, although overall sentiment remains near historic highs. Meanwhile, wage gains have accelerated, in part due to a tight labor market, and some key commodity prices have been on the upswing, including oil and dairy products. As a result, the Federal Reserve Board has twice boosted interest rates in recent months, clearly demonstrating its commitment to fight against any possibility of an overheating economy or signs of inflation that might derail the economy's uptrend. If the Fed remains concerned, then interest rates will likely move higher in the months ahead. And further rate increases would raise the costs of expansion, and increase the risks for some financially troubled operators. One positive for investors from this development, however, would be the curtailment of the rampant expansion that has characterized this over-stored industry in the last few years.

The Beanie Babies Crush The Jedi

The summer months often feature major promotional tie-ins between fast-food chains and the movies or a popular toy line. This year, the long-awaited Star Wars prequel was TRICON Global's key promotional event. But, surprisingly, the costly promotion didn't catch fire with customers, resulting in disappointing sales at Pizza Hut, Taco Bell, and KFC. Meantime, McDonald's resorted to an old standby, Teenie Beanie Babies (for the third straight year), and the clear-cut victor was the fast-food behemoth. The failure of "The Force" may have had more to do with overexposure of the product and, perhaps, too much reliance on the toy aspect of the promotion, rather than the underlying appeal of the chains' food offerings to the designated target audience. Chalk one up for the hamburger people.

What Grown-Ups Prefer

Adults like to take advantage of restaurant promotions as well, although they are as likely to be turned on by consistent values, attractive, and convenient surroundings, responsive service, and menu differentiation. For example, in the casual-dining sector, Darden's Red Lobster and The Olive Garden chains have lifted their performance by updating their facilities and menus, and combining that with regular, attention-grabbing promotions. The Cheesecake Factory's broad menu and appealing restaurants have helped it win converts wherever they're built. And, Ruby Tuesday has improved menus and service by giving its managers an opportunity to own a piece of their location. Meantime, the ubiquitous McDonald's has more than 25,000 fast-food outlets that attract fans with their speedy service, convenience and clean surroundings.

Investment Considerations

The Restaurant Industry's Timeliness rank suggests that the group will move in line with the overall market in the year ahead. But a handful of stocks here may interest those subscribers looking for timely selections. Longer-term investors might gravitate to a number of interesting situations with above-average 3- to 5-year price-appreciation prospects. As always, investors would be well advised to review the individual Value Line reports before making their investment decisions.

Maurice Levenson, CFA

Composite Statistics: Restaurant Industry

1995	1996	1997	1998	1999	2000		02-04
24653.9	28258.9	41205.0	43794.7	47200	50750	Sales ($mill)	62500
21.4%	20.6%	18.0%	18.5%	18.0%	18.0%	Operating Margin	19.5%
1381.9	1553.9	2275.3	2277.5	2375	2600	Depreciation ($mill)	3350
2240.4	2557.9	3023.9	3368.1	3725	4150	Net Profit ($mill)	5375
35.0%	33.1%	34.1%	35.4%	35.0%	35.0%	Income Tax Rate	35.0%
9.1%	9.1%	7.3%	7.7%	8.0%	8.2%	Net Profit Margin	8.8%
d1052.1	d966.7	d2261.2	d2186.1	d2000	d1950	Working Cap'l ($mill)	d1750
5950.2	6965.6	12236.9	12285.8	12500	12800	Long-Term Debt ($mill)	14500
14134.7	16676.0	16244.1	17934.3	20000	22500	Shr. Equity ($mill)	31000
12.3%	11.8%	12.0%	12.6%	12.5%	12.5%	Return on Total Cap'l	13.0%
15.9%	15.3%	18.8%	18.8%	18.0%	18.5%	Return on Shr. Equity	17.5%
14.0%	13.6%	16.5%	17.0%	17.0%	16.5%	Retained to Com Equity	18.0%
14%	13%	12%	10%	10%	10%	All Div'ds to Net Prof	8%
19.4	20.9	19.4	20.9			Avg Ann'l P/E Ratio	18.5
1.30	1.31	1.12	1.09			Relative P/E Ratio	1.10
8%	6%	8%	5%			Avg Ann'l Div'd Yield	.5%

Bold figures are Value Line estimates

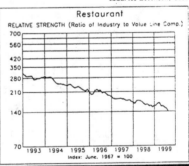

Restaurant

RELATIVE STRENGTH (Ratio of Industry to Value Line Comp.)

Index: June, 1967 = 100

To subscribe call 1-800-833-0046.

Smart Stock Analysis Guide

Basic Stock Information

Company _McDonald's_____ Symbol _MCD___ Exchange _NYSE__ Industry _Restaurant_

Date _10/14/99___ 52-Week High _47 ⅜_ Low _31 ⅝_ Today's Price _41 ⅝_ Today's P/E _33___

Today's Yield _0.5_ S&P 500 _1283.42_

Category One: Profitability

Section A: Earnings-per-Share Growth Rate

1) Annual Earnings-per-Share Growth Rate Calculate the percentage change in earnings per share for each two-year period using the EPS figure for each year beginning with the most recent year listed for the company in the S&P Stock Reports or the Value Line page. Follow the equation below:

EPS amount for [(new year - old year) ÷ old year] x 100 = % change between these two years

Year	EPS	% Change	(Growth Rate)
① 199 _8_	_1.10_	_−4.3 %_	
199 _7_	_1.15_		
199 _7_	_1.15_	_4.6 %_	
199 _6_	_1.10_		
199 _6_	_1.10_	_12.2 %_	
199 _5_	_0.98_		
199 _5_	_0.98_	_16.7 %_	
199 _4_	_0.84_		
199 _4_	_0.84_	_15.1 %_	
199 _3_	_0.73_		

Earnings-per-Share Growth Rate: Decreased _X_ Increased ____ Mixed ___
Earnings-per-Share Growth Rate Consistent: Yes _X_ No _____
(consistently down)

2) Five-Year Compound Average Earnings-per-Share Growth Rate
Calculate the five-year compound average growth rate (long-term growth rate): _8.5 %_
Emerging-growth stocks grow from 30 to 60 percent; rapid-growth, 20 to 30 percent; intermediate-growth, 12 to 20 percent; slow-growth, 6 to 12 percent.

3) Earnings-per-Share Growth Rate between the Most Recent Quarter and the Corresponding Quarter a Year Ago The data are found on the first page of the company's S&P Stock Reports or in the left-hand column of the Value Line page.

② Current Quarter _0.37_ Same Quarter a Year Ago _0.25_

The percentage of growth _48 %_____
Is it equal to or greater than last year's growth rate? Is it equal to or greater than the average growth rate?   yes
        yes

Page 1 of 6

301

Smart Stock Analysis Guide

Section B: Revenue/Sales Growth Rate
    1) Annual Revenue/Sales Growth Rate Calculate the percentage change in revenues for each two-year period using the revenue figures for each year beginning with the most recent year listed in the S&P report or the Value Line page. Follow the same steps used to calculate the earnings-per-share growth rate.

Year	Revs	% Change	(Growth Rate)
③ 199 8	12,421	8.9 %	
199 7	11,409		
199 7	11,409	6.8 %	
199 6	10,687		
199 6	10,687	9.1 %	
199 5	9,795		
199 5	9,795	17.7 %	
199 4	8,321		
199 4	8,321	12.3 %	
199 3	7,408		

Revenue/Sales Growth Rate: Decreased _____ Increased _____ Mixed _X_
Revenue/Sales Growth Rate Consistent: Yes _____ No _X_

    2) Five-Year Compound Average Revenue/Sales Growth Rate Calculate the five-year compound average revenue growth rate: _10.9 %_
        Does the revenue growth match the earnings growth? _rev. above EPS growth rate_

    3) Revenue Growth Rate between the Most Recent Quarter and the Corresponding Quarter a Year Ago The data are found on the first page of the S&P report or in the left-hand column of the Value Line page.

    ④ Current Quarter _3,407_ Same Quarter a Year Ago _3,181_

    The percentage of growth _7.1 %_
        Is it equal to or greater than last year's growth rate? no Is it equal to or greater than the average growth rate? no

Section C: Profit Margin
    1) Pretax Profit Margin Calculate the pretax profit margin for each of the previous five years beginning with the most recent year of data listed in the S&P report or the Value Line page.

⑤③ S&P Stock Reports: (pretax income ÷ revenues) x 100 = pretax profit margin
    Value Line: Step #1 net profit ÷ (1 - income tax rate as a decimal) = pretax income
        Step #2 (pretax income ÷ revenues) x 100 = pretax profit margin

199 8	2,307 ÷ 12,421 x 100 =	18.6 %
199 7	2,408 ÷ 11,409 x 100 =	21.1%
199 6	2,251 ÷ 10,687 x 100 =	21.1%
199 5	2,169 ÷ 9,795 x 100 =	22.1%
199 4	1,887 ÷ 8,321 x 100 =	22.7%

Smart Stock Analysis Guide

Pretax Profit Margin: Increasing _____ Decreasing _X_ Steady _____

2) Company <u>Net Profit</u> Margin Compared with Industry Net Profit Margin Industry net profit is found on the Value Line Industry page.

ⓑ Company Net Profit Margin (after taxes): (199**8**) _12.5_ %
ⓒ Industry Net Profit Margin _7.7_ %
Industry page Company Net Profit Margin: above _X_ below ___ industry net profit margin

And/Or

Similar companies in the same industry: 1._____ 2._____ 3._____
Company Net Profit Margin: above ___ below ___ those of similar companies

Section D: Return on Equity (ROE)
1) Return on Equity List the Return on Equity (S&P, % Ret. on Equity; Value Line, Return on Shr. Equity) for each of the previous five years beginning with the most recent year of data listed in the S&P report or the Value Line page.

⑦ 199 **8**   _16.9%_
199 **7**   _18.8%_
199 **6**   _19.5%_
199 **5**   _20.5%_
199 **4**   _19.3%_

Return on Equity: Increasing _____ Decreasing _X_ Steady _____
ROE of less than 10 percent is poor.

2) Company Return on Equity Compared with Industry Return on Equity The industry ROE is found on the Value Line Industry page as Return on Shr. Equity.
⑦ **Industry Page**
Company ROE: (199**8**) _16.9%_ Industry ROE _18.8%_
Company Return on Equity: above ___ below _X_ industry return on equity

And/Or

Similar companies in the same industry: 1._____ 2._____ 3._____
Company Return on Equity: above ___ below ___ those of similar companies

Category Two: Financial Condition

Section A: Short-Term Financial Condition
1) Cash Note the amount of cash (not cash flow) for each of the past five years.

⑧ a) The amount of cash has: Increased _____ Decreased _____ Mixed _X_
b) The amount of cash: (199 **8**) This Year _299_ Last Year _341_
The amount of cash: Increased _____ Decreased _X_

2) Current Ratio List the current ratio for each of the previous five years.

⑨ 199 **8** _0.5_ 1997 _0.4_ 199 **6** _0.5_ 1995 _0.5_ 199 **4** _0.3_
2 is good; 1.3 is adequate.

Smart Stock Analysis Guide

Section B: Long-Term Financial Condition

1) **Long-Term Debt** Note the amount of long-term debt for each of the past five years.

(10) a) Long-term debt has: Increased __X__ Decreased _____ Mixed ____

b) The amount of long-term debt: (199_8_) This Year _6,189_ Last Year _4,834_
The amount of long-term debt has: Increased _X__ Decreased _____

2) **Debt-to-Equity Ratio for the Most Recent Listed Year**
(10) (11) Calculate: (long-term debt ÷ common equity or net worth) x 100 = % debt

Debt-to-Equity Ratio: Debt _65.4_% Equity _34.6_%
Is the debt 50 percent or less? _no_

Section C: Dividends

(12) 1) **Dividend Growth** Note the dividend amounts for the past ten years.
Dividends have steadily increased: Yes _X__ No _____

2) **Dividend Payout Ratio for the Most Recent Listed Year**
Calculate: (dividend ÷ earnings per share) x 100 = dividend payout ratio

(13) Dividend Payout Ratio: _16_% of company's profits are paid to shareholders
Is the payout ratio 50 percent or less? _yes_

Category Three: Institutional Ownership

Institutional Ownership

(14) _64_ percent of stock is owned by institutions
The lower the better. Less than 60 percent is preferable; 30 percent is very good.

Category Four: Stock Price Evaluation

Section A: Price-Earnings Ratio (P/E)

1) **Price-Earnings Ratio Compared with Earnings Growth Rate (PEG)**
Calculate: P/E ÷ five-year compound average EPS growth rate = PEG

Current P/E _33_ Five-Year Average Earnings-per-Share Growth Rate _8.5_

PEG _3.9_
_____ Underpriced if between 0.5 and 0.9
_____ Fairly priced if between 0.9 and 1.05
_____ Slightly overpriced if between 1.05 and 1.30
_____ Overpriced if between 1.30 and 2.00
__X__ Very overpriced if 2.25 and above

2) **P/E Compared with Earnings Growth Rate Plus Yield (PEGY)**
Calculate: P/E ÷ (five-year average EPS growth rate + dividend yield) = PEGY

P/E _33_ Five-Year Earnings Growth Rate _8.5_ Dividend Yield _0.5_

PEGY _3.6_
_____ Underpriced if between 0.5 and 0.9
_____ Fairly priced if between 0.9 and 1.05
_____ Slightly overpriced if between 1.05 and 1.30
_____ Overpriced if between 1.30 and 2.00
__X__ Very overpriced if 2.25 and above

Smart Stock Analysis Guide

3) P/E Compared with the Company's Ten-Year Average P/E

Current P/E _33_ ⑮ Ten-Year Average P/E _18.6_

Current P/E: above _X_ below _____ ten-year average P/E

4) P/E Compared with the Industry Average P/E

⑮ Industry Page

Company P/E _33_ Industry P/E _20.9_

Company P/E: above _X_ below _____ industry P/E

And/Or

Similar companies in the same industry: 1._____ 2._____ 3._____

Company P/E: above ____ below ____ those of similar companies

Section B: Price Trend

1) The 52-Week High and Low Price

52-Week High _47 3/8_ 52-Week Low _31 5/8_ Today's Price _41 5/8_

After you have paid for the stock and the commissions (add $0.75 to the per-share price), is there room for the price to increase before it hits the 52-week high? Yes _X_ No _____

2) Price Chart Check a price chart.

The price is moving generally: Up _X_ Down _____ Mixed _____

3) Market

The market is moving generally: Up _X_ Down _____ Mixed _____

Category Five: Company Background

Overview

1. Where are the company headquarters? Oak Brook, Illinois

2. What does the company do? World's largest fast food chain — licenses and operates a chain of fast food restaurants

3. Who are its competitors? Wendy's, Burger King, Taco Bell

Products and Services

1. List the company's products and services. hamburgers, chicken + fish sandwiches, salads, french fries, soft drinks, desserts — serves breakfast

2. Does the company have a niche in the market? yes — convenience, cleanliness, appeal to children, name recognition

3. How are its products/services different from those of its competitors? name recognition, the promotional items for children

4. If a new product/service is involved, how much will it add to earnings? not applicable

Smart Stock Analysis Guide

Clients

1. Are the company's clients repeat customers? *yes*

2. Is the company heavily dependent on one or two large customers? *no*

Expansion

1. Is there room for the company to expand in the industry? *yes, internationally — international units provide 60% of the operating profit*

2. Are existing units making a profit? Has the company proven it can expand profitably? *existing units are expected to continue modest sales growth*

3. Where is it currently expanding—regionally, nationally (internationally)

4. How is it expanding? The **4 ways to expand** are to (add new units,) buy other companies, (develop new products,) and start a new line of business.

5. Is its rate of expansion increasing or decreasing? *decreasing in the U.S., continues to increase internationally*

6. What are its prospects for continued growth? *modest nationally, good internationally*

7. How will the company continue to increase its earnings per share? The **6 ways to increase EPS** are to (cut costs,) raise prices, increase sales in existing markets, develop (new products,) expand regionally, nationally, or (internationally,) and correct, close or sell losing operations.
new food-preparation system

Concerns

1. What challenges does the company face?

2. What are your concerns?

Category Six: The Decision

also depends on each person's perspective

1. **The Stock's Strengths—reasons to buy**
   - *corner stone in fast food industry*
   - *international growth — becoming an international company*
   - *net profit above industry average*
   - *dividend growth with low payout ratio*

2. **The Stock's Weaknesses—reasons to question buying** *with this quarter*
   - *decline in EPS growth rate — perhaps beginning to improve*
   - *pretax profit margin drifting down*
   - *ROE declining and less than industry average*
   - *debt in the debt-to-equity ratio is high*
   - *very overpriced*

3. **Neutral Considerations**

4. **Check Current News about the Company**

5. **Buy** _____ **Number of Shares** _____ **Sell if** _____

6. **Follow It** _____ **Buy If** _____

7. **Do Not Buy** _____

depends on each individual's resources investment goals, and tolerance for risk

Page 6 of 6

Smart Stock Analysis Summary

Company Name McDonald's	Yes	No	Neutral	
Category One: Profitability	/ / / /	/ / / /	/ / / /	
A. Earnings-per-Share (EPS) Growth Rate				
Year-to-Year Growth Rate Increasing		X		
Year-to-Year Growth Rate Consistent		X		consistently down
Most Recent Year's Growth Rate ≥ 5-Year Average		X		
Most Recent Quarter's Growth Rate ≥ 5-Year Average	X			
5-Year Average Growth Rate = Your Type of Growth Stock				
B. Revenue/Sales Growth Rate				
Year-to-Year Growth Rate Increasing		X		up the most recent year
Year-to-Year Growth Rate Consistent		X		
Most Recent Year's Growth Rate ≥ 5-Year Average		X		
Most Recent Quarter's Growth Rate ≥ 5-Year Average		X		
5-Year Average Growth Rate Supports EPS Average Growth	X			
C. Pretax Profit Margin				
Pretax Profit Margin Steady or Increasing		X		
Net Profit Margin ≥ Industry Average	X			
D. Return on Equity				
Most Recent Year's Return on Equity ≥ 15 %	X			
Return on Equity Increasing		X		
Return on Equity ≥ Industry Average		X		
Category Two: Financial Condition	/ / / /	/ / / /	/ / / /	
A. Short-Term Financial Condition				
Current Ratio ≥ 0.75		X		
B. Long-Term Financial Condition				
Long-Term Debt Decreased Last Year		X		
Debt-to-Equity Ratio ≤ 50% Debt		X		
C. Dividends				
Dividends Increased over Previous Ten Years	X			
Payout Ratio ≤ 40%	X			
Category Three: Institutional Ownership	/ / / /	/ / / /	/ / / /	higher than 50% but not particularly high (75%) for a major company like McDonald's
Percentage of Institutional Ownership ≤ 50%			X	
Category 4: Stock Price Evaluation	/ / / /	/ / / /	/ / / /	
A. Price-Earnings Ratio (P/E)				
Current P/E ≤ 5-year EPS Growth Rate		X		
Current P/E ≤ 10-Year Average P/E		X		
Current P/E ≤ Industry P/E		X		
B. Price Trend				
Current Price ≤ 52-Week High	X			
Price Trending Up			X	
TOTAL	7	16	2	

Appendix B

NEW YORK STOCK EXCHANGE COMPOSITE TRANSACTIONS

Continued From Page C6

-U-U-U-

-V-V-V-

Wendy's

-W-W-W-

-X-Y-Z-

STANDARD &POOR'S
STOCK REPORTS

Wendy's International

NYSE Symbol **WEN**

In S&P 500

09-OCT-99

Industry: Restaurants

Summary: This company operates or fra[nch]ises more than 5,400 Wendy's restaurants, and also operates th[e] [b]reakfast-oriented Tim Hortons food-service chain.

S&P Opinion: Hold (★★★)	Recent Price • 26	Yield • 0.9%
	52 Wk Range • 31⅜-18½	12-Mo. P/E • 24.3

Quantitative Evaluations

Outlook (1 Lowest—5 Highest)
• **3+**

Fair Value
• **31⅛**

Risk
• **Average**

Earn./Div. Rank
• **A-**

Technical Eval.
• **Bearish** since 9/99

Rel. Strength Rank (1 Lowest—99 Highest)
• **42**

Insider Activity
• **Unfavorable**

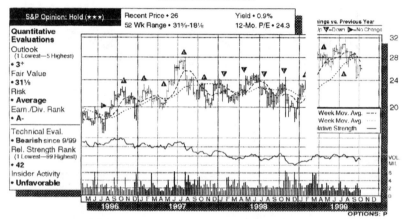

Earnings vs. Previous Year
Up ▼=Down ▶=No Change

Week Mov. Avg. ---
Week Mov. Avg
Relative Strength —

OPTIONS: P

Overview - 03-AUG-99

Sales growth in 1999 should be fueled by 560 to 590 new units; same-unit sales should rise moderately. In the Wendy's chain, we look for the company to continue its successful strategy of offering a diversified menu, including both relatively low-cost items and special premium sandwiches. The closure of unprofitable stores and writedown of others, in addition to cost reduction initiatives, should offset continued higher labor costs. Food price inflation will remain tame. Although WEN is opening units overseas, growth is being slowed by economic problems in certain countries, such as Indonesia. WEN is focusing its international expansion primarily on Latin America and the Caribbean region. The company recorded a charge of $25 million in the 1998 fourth quarter, for a writedown of assets in the U.K. and Argentina, and other items. Gains from asset sales were $6 million, versus $25 million a year earlier. As consolidation in the restaurant industry continues, we expect WEN to make additional strategic acquisitions of units.

Valuation - 03-AUG-99

We continue to recommend holding the shares of this well-managed fast-food chain. Second quarter earnings exceeded expectations, rising 21%, to $0.35 a share, before a $0.04 gain from an asset sale. Wendy's domestic operating margin widened to 17.7%, from 16.6%, due to strong sales gains, reflecting a solid 8.3% gain in same-unit sales, and productivity initiatives to reduce store labor hours. WEN's overall goal for 1999 EPS growth has been raised to a range of 18% to 21%, from 16% to 18%. An additional $0.06 to $0.07 a share may be generated from gains in real estate, franchising and fees. A $350 million share purchase program adds support to the shares.

Key Stock Statistics

S&P EPS Est. 1999	1.30	Tang. Bk. Value/Share	9.37
P/E on S&P Est. 1999	20.0	Beta	0.56
S&P EPS Est. 2000	1.50	Shareholders	93,000
Dividend Rate/Share	0.24	Market cap. (B)	$ 3.2
Shs. outstg. (M)	121.4	Inst. holdings	63%
Avg. daily vol. (M)	0.467		

Value of $10,000 invested 5 years ago: $ 16,004

Fiscal Year Ending Dec. 31

	1999	1998	1997	1996	1995	1994
Revenues (Million $)						
1Q	476.5	455.6	458.9	409.9	398.0	319.8
2Q	526.5	530.0	540.2	491.9	437.4	367.2
3Q	—	485.2	525.5	506.6	451.5	359.4
4Q	—	477.5	512.7	488.8	459.4	351.5
Yr.	—	1,948	2,037	1,897	1,746	1,398
Earnings Per Share ($)						
1Q	0.25	0.18	0.19	0.16	0.15	0.12
2Q	0.39	0.34	0.42	0.38	0.38	0.32
3Q	E0.38	0.33	0.39	0.36	0.34	0.29
4Q	E0.28	0.09	-0.03	0.30	0.15	0.21
Yr.	E1.30	0.95	0.97	1.19	0.88	0.93

Next earnings report expected: late October

Dividend Data (Dividends have been paid since 1976.)

Amount ($)	Date Decl.	Ex-Div. Date	Stock of Record	Payment Date
0.060	Oct. 29	Nov. 05	Nov. 09	Nov. 23 '98
0.060	Feb. 11	Feb. 18	Feb. 22	Mar. 08 '99
0.060	May. 04	May. 12	May. 14	May. 28 '99
0.060	Jul. 28	Aug. 05	Aug. 09	Aug. 23 '99

Wendy's International, Inc.

09-OCT-99

Business Summary - 03-AUG-99

Wendy's International, Inc. is the third largest quick-service restaurant chain in the world. It was founded in 1969 by Dave Thomas, the company's ubiquitous spokesperson, as Wendy's Old Fashioned Hamburgers. At the end of 1998, the company operated 5,333 Wendy's units and 1,667 Tim Hortons. Annual 1998 systemwide sales of the Wendy's and Tim Hortons (the second largest quick-service chain in Canada) totaled $6.5 billion. Wendy's share of the quick-service hamburger market grew to a record 12.9% in 1998, while Tim Hortons' share of the coffee and donut market in Canada reached 53%, also a record high.

In 1998, average net sales at domestic company operated restaurants in the Wendy's chain were $1.17 million, up 5.7% from the 1997 level. Average net sales per domestic Wendy's franchise totaled $1.03 million. Average sales per Canadian Tim Hortons were $1.09 million (in Canadian dollars).

In December 1995, Wendy's purchased Tim Hortons, Canada's largest chain featuring coffee and freshly baked goods. The company plans to expand the number of Tim Hortons in Canada to 2,000 and to develop and expand the number of Wendy's-Tim Hortons combination units in the U.S.

International expansion represents a long-term growth opportunity for the company. It operated only 657 units outside of the U.S. in 1998. Canada is the largest international market with 267 Wendy's at the end of 1998. Since Tim Hortons is widely known in Canada, there are strong opportunities for expansion there, as outlined above. In early 1999, the company acquired restaurant sites from its former joint venture partner in Argentina. The company planned to open 40 to 45 new Wendy's in international markets outside North American in 1999, with a primary focus on Latin America. International operations in Canada are profitable, but operations outside of Canada, particularly in the U.K., are not yet profitable.

New unit development in the U.S. and Canada was cut to 460 in 1998, from an expected 575; the company is accelerating its unit development in 1999 to 560 to 590 units. This includes 290 to 300 Wendy's U.S., 40 to 45 Wendy's Canada, 40 to 45 Wendy's international, 170 to 175 Tim Hortons Canada and 20 to 25 Tim Hortons U.S. The company's capital expenditure program in 1999 was projected at $300 million, up from $241.5 million in 1998.

In an effort to improve its return on invested capital (ROIC), the company planned to close or franchise 77 underperforming units, repurchase shares, improve store level productivity and refranchise some portion of the 660 restaurants leased to franchisees. About 145 leased properties were sold to franchisees in 1998. Pretax gains from the sale of restaurants and other asset sales totaled $21.4 million in 1998.

Per Share Data ($)

(Year Ended Dec. 31)	1998	1997	1996	1995	1994	1993	1992	1991	1990	1989	
Tangible Bk. Val.	9.37	9.78	8.89	7.47	6.37	5.70	5.07	4.61	4.31	4.16	
Cash Flow	1.63	1.68	1.91	1.56	1.59	1.41	1.25	1.08	0.97	0.83	
Earnings	0.95	0.97	1.20	0.90	0.93	0.77	0.64	0.52	0.40	0.25	
Dividends	0.24	0.24	0.24	0.24	0.24	0.24	0.24	0.24	0.24	0.24	
Payout Ratio	25%	25%	20%	27%	26%	31%	37%	45%	60%	96%	
Prices - High	25¹/₃	27⁷/₈	23	22³/₄	18¹/₂	17³/₄	14¹/₄	11	7¹/₂	7	Average High PE 23.3
- Low	18¹/₈	19⁴/₈	16³/₄	14¹/₄	13¹/₄	12³/₈	9⁵/₈	5⁷/₈	3⁷/₈	4¹/₂	Average Low PE 15.3
P/E Ratio - High	27	29	19	25	20	23	22	21	19	28	Average PE 19.3
- Low	19	20	14	16	14	16	15	11	10	18	

Income Statement Analysis (Million $)

	1998	1997	1996	1995	1994	1993	1992	1991	1990	1989
Revs.	1,948	2,037	1,897	1,746	1,370	1,303	1,220	1,048	1,002	1,051
Oper. Inc.	346	335	356	306	199	176	157	135	120	89.0
Depr.	100	105	95.0	84.4	68.1	65.7	61.7	56.1	55.1	56.4
Int. Exp.	19.8	18.9	20.3	20.4	18.7	21.6	22.5	23.3	21.4	22.3
Pretax Inc.	208	219	255	165	149	116	101	78.0	61.0	37.0
Eff. Tax Rate	41%	41%	39%	33%	35%	31%	36%	34%	37%	36%
Net Inc.	123	131	156	110	97.2	79.3	64.7	51.7	38.6	23.7

Balance Sheet & Other Fin. Data (Million $)

	1998	1997	1996	1995	1994	1993	1992	1991	1990	1989
Cash	161	234	224	214	135	112	112	135	55.0	74.0
Curr. Assets	314	382	337	321	203	179	162	176	98.0	122
Total Assets	1,838	1,942	1,781	1,509	1,086	996	920	880	758	780
Curr. Liab.	249	213	208	296	207	143	128	133	109	129
LT Debt	446	250	242	337	145	201	234	240	168	179
Common Eqty.	1,068	1,184	1,057	822	681	601	529	478	447	429
Total Cap.	1,575	1,715	1,501	1,207	866	842	786	742	646	647
Cap. Exp.	242	242	307	218	142	117	120	69.0	42.0	39.0
Cash Flow	224	236	251	191	165	145	126	108	94.0	80.0
Curr. Ratio	1.3	1.8	1.6	1.1	1.0	1.2	1.3	1.3	0.9	0.9
% LT Debt of Cap.	28.3	14.6	15.5	27.9	16.7	23.8	29.7	32.3	26.0	27.7
% Net Inc. of Revs.	6.3	6.4	8.2	6.3	7.1	6.1	5.3	4.9	3.9	2.3
% Ret. on Assets	6.5	7.0	9.5	8.1	9.3	8.2	7.1	6.3	5.0	3.0
% Ret. on Equity	11.0	11.7	16.6	14.4	15.1	13.9	12.8	11.2	8.8	5.6

Data as ong. reptd.; bef. results of disc opers/spec. items. Per share data adj. for stk. divs. Bold denotes diluted EPS (FASB 128) prior periods restated. E-Estimated. NA-Not Available. NM-Not Meaningful. NR-Not Ranked.

Office—1288 West Dublin-Granville Rd., P.O. Box 256, Dublin, OH 43017-0256. **Tel**—(614) 764-3100. **Website**—www.wendys.com **Chrmn, Pres & CEO**—G. F. Teter. **Treas**—J. Brownley. **Investor Contacts**—John D. Barker (614-764 3044) for analysts and portfolio managers; Marsha Gordon (614-764-3019) for general inquiries. **Dirs**—W. C. Hamner, E. S. Hayeck, J. Hill, P. D. House, R. V. Joyce, F. Keller, T. H. Knowles, A. G. McCaughey, R. E. Musick, F. B. Nutter Sr., J. V. Pickett, F. R. Reed, T. R. Shackelford, G. F. Teter, R. D. Thomas. **Transfer Agent & Registrar**—American Stock Transfer & Trust Co., NYC. **Incorporated**—in Ohio in 1969. **Empl**—39,000. **S&P Analyst**: Karen J.Sack, CFA

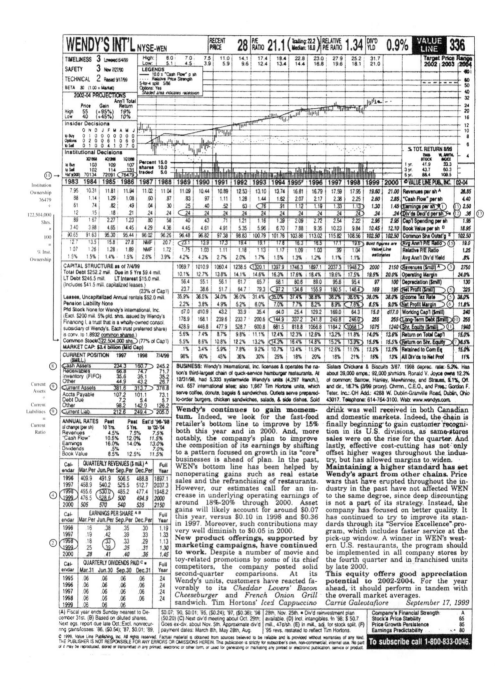

The stocks of many of the companies included in our coverage of the Restaurant Industry have moved lower in price in recent months, likely due to a more cautious attitude on the part of some investors toward the economy. Also, fast food and casual dining chains have been reporting mixed sales results recently, some of which can be attributed to poor promotional responses.

Overall, the Restaurant Industry's Timeliness rank has slipped 13 notches in the last three months, and now resides among those industry groups expected to mirror the overall market averages over the next six to 12 months. Nevertheless, we think opportunities exist for those investors willing to take a selective approach toward the group.

The Economic Viewpoint

The Restaurant Industry has benefited from the nation's long-running economic expansion. Low interest rates have enabled more chains to expand relatively cheaply, while consumers were demonstrating a willingness to dine out more often. Moreover, modest inflation has helped keep a lid on operating costs. *Value Line's* view of the economy remains generally positive. And, although revised second-quarter GDP showed a less-ebullient 1.8% rise, current data still suggests stronger growth for the back half of 1999, possibly reaching or exceeding 3% in each quarter.

The latest consumer confidence readings from The Conference Board and the University of Michigan indicate some signs of wavering, although overall sentiment remains near historic highs. Meanwhile, wage gains have accelerated, in part due to a tight labor market, and some key commodity prices have been on the upswing, including oil and dairy products. As a result, the Federal Reserve Board has twice boosted interest rates in recent months, clearly demonstrating its commitment to fight against any possibility of an overheating economy or signs of inflation that might derail the economy's uptrend. If the Fed remains concerned, then interest rates will likely move higher in the months ahead. And further rate increases would raise the costs of expansion, and increase the risks for some financially troubled operators. One positive for investors from this development, however, would be the curtailment of the rampant expansion that has characterized this over-stored industry in the last few years.

INDUSTRY TIMELINESS: 42 (of 92)

The Beanie Babies Crush The Jedi

The summer months often feature major promotional tie-ins between fast-food chains and the movies or a popular toy line. This year, the long-awaited *Star Wars* prequel was *TRICON Global's* key promotional event. But, surprisingly, the costly promotion didn't catch fire with customers, resulting in disappointing sales at *Pizza Hut*, *Taco Bell*, and *KFC*. Meantime, *McDonald's* resorted to an old standby, *Teenie Beanie Babies* (for the third straight year), and the clear-cut victor was the fast-food behemoth. The failure of "The Force" may have had more to do with overexposure of the product and, perhaps, too much reliance on the toy aspect of the promotion, rather than the underlying appeal of the chains' food offerings to the designated target audience. Chalk one up for the hamburger people.

What Grown-Ups Prefer

Adults like to take advantage of restaurant promotions as well, although they are as likely to be turned on by consistent values, attractive, and convenient surroundings, responsive service, and menu differentiation. For example, in the casual-dining sector, *Darden's Red Lobster* and *The Olive Garden* chains have lifted their performance by updating their facilities and menus, and combining that with regular, attention-grabbing promotions. *The Cheesecake Factory's* broad menu and appealing restaurants have helped it win converts wherever they're built. And, *Ruby Tuesday* has improved menus and service by giving its managers an opportunity to own a piece of their location. Meantime, the ubiquitous *McDonald's* has more than 25,000 fast-food outlets that attract fans with their speedy service, convenience and clean surroundings.

Investment Considerations

The Restaurant Industry's Timeliness rank suggests that the group will move in line with the overall market in the year ahead. But a handful of stocks here may interest those subscribers looking for timely selections. Longer-term investors might gravitate to a number of interesting situations with above-average 3- to 5-year price-appreciation prospects. As always, investors would be well advised to review the individual *Value Line* reports before making their investment decisions.

Maurice Levenson, CFA

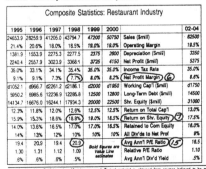

Composite Statistics: Restaurant Industry

1995	1996	1997	1998	1999	2000		02-04
24653.9	28259.9	41205.0	43794.7	47200	50750	Sales ($mill)	62500
21.4%	20.6%	18.0%	18.5%	18.0%	18.0%	Operating Margin	18.5%
1381.9	1553.9	2275.3	2277.5	2375	2600	Depreciation ($mill)	3350
2240.4	2557.9	3023.9	3368.1	3725	4150	Net Profit ($mill)	5375
35.0%	33.1%	34.1%	35.4%	35.0%	35.0%	Income Tax Rate	35.0%
9.1%	9.1%	7.3%	7.7%	8.0%	8.2%	Net Profit Margin	8.6%
d1052.1	d966.7	d2261.2	d2186.1	d2000	d1850	Working Cap'l ($mill)	d1750
5950.2	6985.6	12236.9	12285.8	12500	12800	Long-Term Debt ($mill)	14500
14134.7	16676.0	16244.1	17934.3	20000	22500	Shr. Equity ($mill)	31000
12.3%	11.8%	12.0%	12.6%	12.5%	12.5%	Return on Total Cap'l	13.0%
15.9%	15.3%	18.6%	18.8%	18.0%	18.5%	Return on Shr. Equity	17.5%
14.0%	13.6%	16.5%	17.0%	17.0%	16.5%	Retained to Com Equity	16.0%
14%	13%	12%	10%	10%	10%	All Div'ds to Net Prof	9%
19.4	20.9	19.4	20.9	*Bold figures are Value Line estimates*		Avg Ann'l P/E Ratio	18.5
1.30	1.31	1.12	1.09			Relative P/E Ratio	1.10
.6%	.6%	.6%	.5%			Avg Ann'l Div'd Yield	.5%

Restaurant

RELATIVE STRENGTH (Ratio of Industry to Value Line Comp.)

Index: June, 1967 = 100

313

Smart Stock Analysis Guide

Basic Stock Information

Company _Wendy's_ Symbol _WEN_ Exchange _NYSE_ Industry _Restaurant_

Date _10/14/99_ 52-Week High_31 1/16_ Low _18 1/8_ Today's Price_25 1/16_ Today's P/E _24_

Today's Yield _1.0_ S&P 500 _1283.42_

Category One: Profitability

Section A: Earnings-per-Share Growth Rate

1) Annual Earnings-per-Share Growth Rate Calculate the percentage change in earnings per share for each two-year period using the EPS figure for each year beginning with the most recent year listed for the company in the S&P Stock Reports or the Value Line page. Follow the equation below:

EPS amount for [(new year - old year) ÷ old year] x 100 = % change between these two years

Year	EPS	% Change	(Growth Rate)
① 199_8_	_0.95_	_-2.1 %_	
199_7_	_0.97_		
199_7_	_0.97_	_-19.2 %_	
199_6_	_1.20_		
199_6_	_1.20_	_33.3 %_	
199_5_	_0.90_		
199_5_	_0.90_	_-3.2 %_	
199_4_	_0.93_		
199_4_	_0.93_	_20.8 %_	
199_3_	_0.77_		

Earnings-per-Share Growth Rate: Decreased _X_ Increased ____ Mixed ___
Earnings-per-Share Growth Rate Consistent: Yes ____ No _X_

2) Five-Year Compound Average Earnings-per-Share Growth Rate
Calculate the five-year compound average growth rate (long-term growth rate): _4.3 %_
Emerging-growth stocks grow from 30 to 60 percent; rapid-growth, 20 to 30 percent; intermediate-growth, 12 to 20 percent; slow-growth, 6 to 12 percent.

3) Earnings-per-Share Growth Rate between the Most Recent Quarter and the Corresponding Quarter a Year Ago The data are found on the first page of the company's S&P Stock Reports or in the left-hand column of the Value Line page.

② Current Quarter _0.39_ Same Quarter a Year Ago _0.34_

The percentage of growth _14.7 %_
Is it equal to or greater than last year's growth rate? Is it equal to or greater than the average growth rate?   _yes_
yes

Page 1 of 6

Smart Stock Analysis Guide

Section B: Revenue/Sales Growth Rate

1) Annual Revenue/Sales Growth Rate Calculate the percentage change in revenues for each two-year period using the revenue figures for each year beginning with the most recent year listed in the S&P report or the Value Line page. Follow the same steps used to calculate the earnings-per-share growth rate.

	Year	Revs	% Change (Growth Rate)
③	199 _8_	_1948_	_-4.4%_
	199 _7_	_2037_	
	199 _7_	_2037_	_7.4%_
	199 _6_	_1897_	
	199 _6_	_1897_	_8.7%_
	199 _5_	_1746_	
	199 _5_	_1746_	_27.5%_
	199 _4_	_1370_	
	199 _4_	_1370_	_5.1%_
	199 _3_	_1303_	

Revenue/Sales Growth Rate: Decreased __X__ Increased _____ Mixed _____
Revenue/Sales Growth Rate Consistent: Yes _____ No _X_

2) Five-Year Compound Average Revenue/Sales Growth Rate Calculate the five-year compound average revenue growth rate: _8.4%_
Does the revenue growth match the earnings growth? rev. above EPS growth rate

3) Revenue Growth Rate between the Most Recent Quarter and the Corresponding Quarter a Year Ago The data are found on the first page of the S&P report or in the left-hand column of the Value Line page.

④ Current Quarter _528.5_ Same Quarter a Year Ago _530.0_

The percentage of growth _-0.3_
Is it equal to or greater than last year's growth rate? Is it equal to or greater than the average growth rate? yes
no

Section C: Profit Margin

1) Pretax Profit Margin Calculate the pretax profit margin for each of the previous five years beginning with the most recent year of data listed in the S&P report or the Value Line page.

⑤ ③ S&P Stock Reports: (pretax income ÷ revenues) x 100 = pretax profit margin
Value Line: Step #1 net profit ÷ (1 - income tax rate as a decimal) = pretax income
⑤
Step #2 (pretax income ÷ revenues) x 100 = pretax profit margin
③

199 _8_	_208_ ÷ _1948_ x 100 =	_10.7%_
199 _7_	_219_ ÷ _2037_ x 100 =	_10.8%_
199 _6_	_255_ ÷ _1897_ x 100 =	_13.4%_
199 _5_	_165_ ÷ _1746_ x 100 =	_9.5%_
199 _4_	_149_ ÷ _1370_ x 100 =	_10.9%_

Smart Stock Analysis Guide

Pretax Profit Margin: Increasing _____ Decreasing _X_ Steady _____

2) Company Net Profit Margin Compared with Industry Net Profit Margin Industry net profit is found on the Value Line Industry page.

⑥ Company Net Profit Margin (after taxes): (199⑧) _6.3 %_

Industry Page ⑥ Industry Net Profit Margin __7.7%__

Company Net Profit Margin: above ___ below _X_ industry net profit margin

And/Or

Similar companies in the same industry: 1._____ 2._____ 3._____
Company Net Profit Margin: above ___ below ___ those of similar companies

Section D: Return on Equity (ROE)

1) Return on Equity List the Return on Equity (S&P, % Ret. on Equity; Value Line, Return on Shr. Equity) for each of the previous five years beginning with the most recent year of data listed in the S&P report or the Value Line page.

⑦ 199_8_ ___11%___

199_7_ ___11.7%___

199_6_ ___16.6 %___

199_5_ ___14.4 %___

199_4_ ___15.1%___

Return on Equity: Increasing _____ Decreasing _X_ Steady _____
· ROE of less than 10 percent is poor.

2) Company Return on Equity Compared with Industry Return on Equity The industry ROE is found on the Value Line Industry page as Return on Shr. Equity.

⑦ **Industry Page**

Company ROE: (199⑧) _11 %_ Industry ROE _18.8%_
Company Return on Equity: above ___ below _x_ industry return on equity

And/Or

Similar companies in the same industry: 1._____ 2._____ 3._____
Company Return on Equity: above ___ below ___ those of similar companies

Category Two: Financial Condition

Section A: Short-Term Financial Condition

1) Cash Note the amount of cash (not cash flow) for each of the past five years.

except for most recent year

⑧ a) The amount of cash has: Increased _X_ Decreased _____ Mixed _____

b) The amount of cash: (199_8_) This Year _161_ Last Year _234_
The amount of cash: Increased _____ Decreased _X_

2) Current Ratio List the current ratio for each of the previous five years.

⑨ 199_8_ _1.3_ 199_7_ _1.8_ 199_6_ _1.6_ 199_5_ _1.1_ 199_4_ _1.0_
2 is good; 1.3 is adequate.

Smart Stock Analysis Guide

Section B: Long-Term Financial Condition

1) **Long-Term Debt** Note the amount of long-term debt for each of the past five years.

⑩ a) Long-term debt has: Increased __X__ Decreased _____ Mixed _____

b) The amount of long-term debt: (199_8_) This Year _446_ Last Year _250_
The amount of long-term debt has: Increased __x__ Decreased _____

2) **Debt-to-Equity Ratio for the Most Recent Listed Year**

⑪ ⑪ Calculate: (long-term debt ÷ common equity or net worth) x 100 = % debt

Debt-to-Equity Ratio: Debt _41.7_ % Equity _58.3_ %
Is the debt 50 percent or less? **yes**

Section C: Dividends

⑫ 1) **Dividend Growth** Note the dividend amounts for the past ten years.
Dividends have steadily increased: Yes _____ No _X_____

2) **Dividend Payout Ratio for the Most Recent Listed Year**
Calculate: (dividend ÷ earnings per share) x 100 = dividend payout ratio

⑬ Dividend Payout Ratio: _25_ % of company's profits are paid to shareholders
Is the payout ratio 50 percent or less? **yes**

Category Three: Institutional Ownership

Institutional Ownership

⑭ _63_ percent of stock is owned by institutions
The lower the better. Less than 60 percent is preferable; 30 percent is very good.

Category Four: Stock Price Evaluation

Section A: Price-Earnings Ratio (P/E)

1) **Price-Earnings Ratio Compared with Earnings Growth Rate (PEG)**
Calculate: P/E ÷ five-year compound average EPS growth rate = PEG

Current P/E _24_ Five-Year Average Earnings-per-Share Growth Rate _4.3_

PEG _5.6_
_____ Underpriced if between 0.5 and 0.9
_____ Fairly priced if between 0.9 and 1.05
_____ Slightly overpriced if between 1.05 and 1.30
_____ Overpriced if between 1.30 and 2.00
__x__ Very overpriced if 2.25 and above

2) **P/E Compared with Earnings Growth Rate Plus Yield (PEGY)**
Calculate: P/E ÷ (five-year average EPS growth rate + dividend yield) = PEGY

P/E _24_ Five-Year Earnings Growth Rate _4.3_ Dividend Yield _1.0_

PEGY _4.5_
_____ Underpriced if between 0.5 and 0.9
_____ Fairly priced if between 0.9 and 1.05
_____ Slightly overpriced if between 1.05 and 1.30
_____ Overpriced if between 1.30 and 2.00
__X__ Very overpriced if 2.25 and above

Smart Stock Analysis Guide

3) P/E Compared with the Company's Ten-Year Average P/E

Current P/E _24_ Ten-Year Average P/E _19.3_ ⑮

Current P/E: above _x_ below ____ ten-year average P/E

4) P/E Compared with the Industry Average P/E ⑮ _Industry Page_

Company P/E _24_ Industry P/E _20.9_

Company P/E: above _x_ below ____ industry P/E

And/Or

Similar companies in the same industry: 1._____ 2._____ 3._____

Company P/E: above ___ below ___ those of similar companies

Section B: Price Trend

1) The 52-Week High and Low Price

52-Week High _31 ¹¹/₁₆_ 52-Week Low _18 ⅞_ Today's Price _25 ¹/₁₆_

After you have paid for the stock and the commissions (add $0.75 to the per-share price), is there room for the price to increase before it hits the 52-week high? Yes _x_ No _____

2) Price Chart Check a price chart.

The price is moving generally: Up _____ Down _x_ Mixed _____

3) Market

The market is moving generally: Up _x_ Down _____ Mixed_____

Category Five: Company Background

Overview

1. Where are the company headquarters?

2. What does the company do?

3. Who are its competitors?

Products and Services

1. List the company's products and services.

2. Does the company have a niche in the market?

3. How are its products/services different from those of its competitors?

4. If a new product/service is involved, how much will it add to earnings?

Smart Stock Analysis Guide

Clients
1. Are the company's clients repeat customers?

2. Is the company heavily dependent on one or two large customers?

Expansion
1. Is there room for the company to expand in the industry?

2. Are existing units making a profit? Has the company proven it can expand profitably?

3. Where is it currently expanding—regionally, nationally, internationally?

4. How is it expanding? The **4 ways to expand** are to add new units, buy other companies, develop new products, and start a new line of business.

5. Is its rate of expansion increasing or decreasing?

6. What are its prospects for continued growth?

7. How will the company continue to increase its earnings per share? The **6 ways to increase EPS** are to cut costs, raise prices, increase sales in existing markets, develop new products, expand regionally, nationally, or internationally, and correct, close or sell losing operations.

Concerns
1. What challenges does the company face?

2. What are your concerns?

Category Six: The Decision
1. The Stock's Strengths—reasons to buy

2. The Stock's Weaknesses—reasons to question buying

3. Neutral Considerations

4. Check Current News about the Company

5. Buy _____ Number of Shares _____ Sell if _____
6. Follow It _____ Buy If _____
7. Do Not Buy _____

Page 6 of 6

319

Save On Legal Fees

Whatever you need to know, we've made it E-Z!

Informative text and forms you can fill out on-screen.* From personal to business, legal to leisure—we've made it E-Z!

Get Out Of Debt

Credit Repair

Vital Records

Personal & Family

For all your family's needs, we have titles that will help keep you organized and guide you through most every aspect of your personal life.

Living Wills
Includes Power of Attorney for Healthcare

Asset Protection

Buying/Selling Your Home

Business

Whether you're starting from scratch with a home business or you just want to keep your corporate records in shape, we've got the programs for you.

Incorporation

Corporate Records

Accounting

Your Profitable Home Business

Selling on the Web (E-Commerce)

Advertising Your Business

	ITEM #	QTY.	PRICE‡	EXTENSION
MADE E-Z SOFTWARE				
E-Z Construction Estimator	SS4300		$29.95	
E-Z Contractors' Forms	SS4301		$24.95	
Contractors' Business Builder Bundle	CD325		$59.95	
Asset Protection	SS4304		$24.95	
Corporate Records	SS4305		$24.95	
Vital Records	SS4306		$24.95	
Personnel Forms	HR453		$24.95	
Accounting	SS4308		$24.95	
Limited Liability Companies (LLC)	SS4309		$24.95	
Partnerships	SS4310		$24.95	
Solving IRS Problems	SS4311		$24.95	
Winning In Small Claims Court	SS4312		$24.95	
Collecting Unpaid Bills	SS4313		$24.95	
Selling On The Web (E-Commerce)	SS4314		$24.95	
Your Profitable Home Business	SS4315		$24.95	
E-Z Business Lawyer Library	SS4318		$49.95	
E-Z Estate Planner	SS4319		$49.95	
E-Z Personal Lawyer Library	SS4320		$49.95	
Payroll	SS4321		$24.95	
Personal Legal Forms and Agreements	SS4322		$24.95	
Business Legal Forms and Agreements	SS4323		$24.95	
Employee Policies and Manuals	SS4324		$24.95	
Incorporation	SS4333		$24.95	
Last Wills	SS4327		$24.95	
Business Startups	SS4332		$24.95	
Credit Repair	SW2211		$24.95	
Business Forms	SW2223		$24.95	
Buying and Selling A Business	SW2242		$24.95	
Marketing Your Small Business	SW2245		$24.95	
Get Out Of Debt	SW2246		$24.95	
Winning Business Plans	SW2247		$24.95	
Successful Resumes	SW2248		$24.95	
Solving Business Problems	SW2249		$24.95	
Profitable Mail Order	SW2250		$24.95	
Deluxe Business Forms	SW2251		$49.95	
E-Z Small Business Library	SW2252		$49.95	
Paint & Construction Estimator	SW2253		$19.95	
MADE E-Z BOOKS				
Bankruptcy	G300		$24.95	
Incorporation	G301		$24.95	
Divorce	G302		$24.95	
Credit Repair	G303		$14.95	
Living Trusts	G305		$24.95	
Living Wills	G306		$24.95	
Last Will & Testament	G307		$24.95	
Buying/Selling Your Home	G311		$14.95	
Employment Law	G312		$14.95	
Collecting Child Support	G315		$14.95	
Limited Liability Companies	G316		$24.95	
Partnerships	G318		$24.95	
Solving IRS Problems	G319		$14.95	
Asset Protection	G320		$14.95	
Buying/Selling A Business	G321		$14.95	
Financing Your Business	G322		$14.95	
Profitable Mail Order	G323		$14.95	
Selling On The Web (E-Commerce)	G324		$14.95	
SBA Loans	G325		$14.95	
Solving Business Problems	G326		$14.95	
Advertising Your Business	G327		$14.95	
Rapid Reading	G328		$14.95	
Everyday Math	G329		$14.95	
Shoestring Investing	G330		$14.95	
Stock Market Investing	G331		$14.95	
Fund Raising	G332		$14.95	
Money For College	G334		$14.95	
Marketing Your Small Business	G335		$14.95	
Owning A No-Cash-Down Business	G336		$14.95	

‡ *Prices are for a single item, and are subject to change without notice.*

TO PLACE AN ORDER:

1. Duplicate this order form.

2. Complete your order and mail or fax to:

Made E-Z Products

384 S. Military Trail

Deerfield Beach, FL 33442

www.MadeE-Z.com

Tel: 954-480-8933

Toll Free: 800-822-4566

Fax: 954-480-8906

continued on next page

	ITEM #	QTY.	PRICE†	EXTENSION
Offshore Investing	G337		$14.95	
Multi-level Marketing	G338		$14.95	
Free Legal Help	G339		$14.95	
Get Out Of Debt	G340		$14.95	
Winning Business Plans	G342		$14.95	
Mutual Fund Investing	G343		$14.95	
Business Startups	G344		$14.95	
Successful Resumes	G346		$14.95	
Free Stuff For Everyone	G347		$14.95	
On-Line Business Resources	G348		$14.95	
Life Insurance	G349		$14.95	
Health Insurance	G350		$14.95	
Successful Selling	G351		$14.95	
Everyday Legal Forms & Agreements	BK407		$24.95	
Personnel Forms	BK408		$24.95	
Collecting Unpaid Bills	BK409		$24.95	
Corporate Records	BK410		$24.95	
Everyday Law	BK411		$24.95	
Vital Records	BK412		$24.95	
Business Forms	BK414		$24.95	

MADE E-Z KITS

	ITEM #	QTY.	PRICE†	EXTENSION
Bankruptcy Kit	K300		$24.95	
Incorporation Kit	K301		$24.95	
Divorce Kit	K302		$24.95	
Credit Repair Kit	K303		$24.95	
Living Trust Kit	K305		$24.95	
Living Will Kit	K306		$24.95	
Last Will & Testament Kit	K307		$19.95	
Buying and Selling Your Home Kit	K311		$24.95	
Business Startups Kit	K320		$24.95	
Small Business/Home Business Kit	K321		$24.95	

MISC. PRODUCTS

	ITEM #	QTY.	PRICE†	EXTENSION
☆ Federal Labor Law Poster	LP001		$5.99	
☆ State Specific Labor Law Poster (see state listings below)			$29.95	
E-Z Legal Will Pac	WP250		$9.95	

State	Item#	QTY	State	Item#	QTY	State	Item#	QTY
AL	83801		KY	83817		ND	83834	
AK	83802		LA	83818		OH	83835	
AZ	83803		ME	83819		OK	83836	
AR	83804		MD	83820		OR	83837	
CA	83805		MA	83821		PA	83838	
CO	83806		MI	83822		RI	83839	
CT	83807		MN	83823		SC	83840	
DE	83808		MS	83824		S. Dakota not available		
DC	83848		MO	83825		TN	83842	
FL	83809		MT	83826		TX	83843	
GA	83810		NE	83827		UT	83844	
HI	83811		NV	83828		VT	83845	
ID	83812		NH	83829		VA	83846	
IL	83813		NJ	83830		WA	83847	
IN	83814		NM	83831		WV	83849	
IO	83815		NY	83832		WI	83850	

ORDER TOTAL ☆ Required by Federal & State Laws $

SHIPPING & HANDLING
$4.95 for first item, $1.50 for each additional item $
All orders shipped Ground unless otherwise specified.

SUBTOTAL $

Florida Residents add 6% sales tax $

TOTAL $

† Prices are for a single item, and are subject to change without notice.

MADE E-Z PRODUCTS

Name

Company

Address

City

State Zip

Phone
(   )

PAYMENT METHOD:

☐ Charge my credit card:
  ☐ MasterCard
  ☐ VISA
  ☐ American Express

☐ Check enclosed, payable to:
  Made E-Z Products
  384 S. Military Trail
  Deerfield Beach, FL 33442

ACCOUNT NO. EXP DATE

Signature:

(required for credit card purchases)

Company Purchase Orders Are Welcome With Approved Credit

Comments & Suggestions

Thank you

Index

A-Di•••••

Account ownership, types of160-161
Accounts
    Cash 158
    Cash management................158
    Margin 159
American Stock Exchange..........78
American Stock Exchange
    Composite Index 63
Arbitration 178
Auction....................................116
Automated systems 122
Automated trade........................119
Bear markets...............................65
Broker-client disputes 171
Brokerage firms 125
Brokerage statement..................166
Brokers 111
Bull markets 64
Buying and selling......................24
Churning 173
Client duties 169
Close...41
Company ownership 13
Confirmation records 165
Cooling-off period......................97
Cumulative voting rights............17
Cyclical-growth stocks 189
Disbursement of income..........164
Discount brokerage account 164
Discount brokerage firm 128
Diversification..........................251

Do-I•••••

Dividends 18, 29, 217
Dow Jones Composite Average ...59
Dow Jones Global Stock Index ...59
Dow Jones Industrial Average 48
Dow Jones Transportation
    Average 55
Dow Jones Utility Average 58
Earnings-per-share growth 196
Emerging-growth stocks............184
Exchange membership..........76, 89
Final prospectus 103
Floor, NY Stock Exchange.........114
Floor broker 115
Floor reporter...........................118
Footnote letters & symbols22, 27, 32
Foreign exchanges......................90
Forgery.....................................174
Full-service brokerage firm........126
Fundamental analysis................183
Going public 93
High and low 21, 41
History.......................................71
Indirect investor 11
Individual investor 11
Initial offering price 102
Initial public offering (IPO) 104
Institutional ownership 220
Intermarket trading system 121
Intermediate-growth stocks.......186
Interview 140
Investment goals 133

L-Re••••••

Limit order 111
Listing requirements 76
Long-term financial condition....214
Market order 111
Marketing the issue 99
Mediation.................................... 177
Misrepresentation 173
Nasdaq Stock Market 82
Nasdaq Composite Index 62
Net change 41
NY Stock Exchange 70
NY Stock Exchange Index........... 62
Order tickets 113
PE 37
    Calculation............................ 36
    Meaning 37
    Increases 37
    High....................................... 38
    Decreases............................... 38
    Low 39
    Comparisons.......................... 39
Points.. 21
Portfolios 247
Preliminary prospectus............... 96
Price-earnings ratio 35, 221
Price trend 24, 226
Price volatility 24
Primary market........................... 104
Profit margin 204
Profitability............................... 195
Proportional ownership 13
Proxy 17
Purchasing group....................... 98
Quarterly report 239
Rapid-growth stocks 184
Rate of return 35
Regional exchanges................... 87
Return on equity 207
Revenue growth rate 201

Ri-Y••••••

Rights of ownership................... 16
Risk 135, 251
Russell 2000 Index..................... 63
Secondary market...................... 105
Security registration 162
Share ownership......................... 12
Shareholder 12
Short-term financial condition ...211
Slow-growth stocks 188
Smart Stock Analysis Guide....... 193
Specialist 115
Standard & Poor's 500
    Composite Index.................. 60
Statutory voting rights............... 17
Stock certificate......................... 15
Stock delistings 77
Stock name................................. 25
Stock symbol.............................. 28
Stock table 19
Stock trade................................. 107
Stockbroker............................... 123
    Selecting............................... 123
    Working with 153
Stop order 112
Street name................................ 163
Successful investing rules.......... 252
SuperDOT 121
Technical analysis 181
Tombstone 103
Trade confirmation.................... 118
Trading authorization 162
Trading post 115
Transferred and held 163
Transferred and shipped........... 162
Underwriting group................... 97
Value Line Composite Index....... 64
Variations................................... 23
Volume 40
Yield 33